I'm always glad to get letters from my readers. Recently a junior high school girl sent me a picture of herself and her friends on a school trip. They looked like they were having the time of their lives. It really made me feel good. They had such wonderful smiles!
　—**Katsura Hoshino**

Shiga Prefecture native Katsura Hoshino's hit manga series *D.Gray-man* has been serialized in *Weekly Shonen Jump* since 2004. Katsura's debut manga, "Continue," appeared for the first time in *Weekly Shonen Jump* in 2003.

Katsura adores cats.

 D1017995

GRAPH
HOSHINO
v.14

# D.GRAY-MAN
## VOL. 14
### SHONEN JUMP ADVANCED
Manga Edition

STORY AND ART BY
## KATSURA HOSHINO

English Adaptation/Lance Caselman
Translation/John Werry
Touch-up Art & Lettering/HudsonYards
Design/Matt Hinrichs
Editor/Gary Leach

D.GRAY-MAN © 2004 by Katsura Hoshino. All rights reserved.
First published in Japan in 2004 by SHUEISHA Inc., Tokyo. English translation rights arranged by
SHUEISHA Inc.

The rights of the author(s) of the work(s) in this publication to be so identified have been asserted
in accordance with the Copyright, Designs and Patents Act 1988. A CIP catalogue record for this
book is available from the British Library.

The stories, characters and incidents mentioned in this publication are entirely fictional.

Printed in the U.S.A.

Published by VIZ Media, LLC
P.O. Box 77010
San Francisco, CA 94107

10 9 8 7 6 5 4
First printing, August 2009
Fourth printing, November 2011

THE WORLD'S MOST
CUTTING-EDGE MANGA
SHONEN JUMP
ADVANCED
www.shonenjump.com

www.viz.com

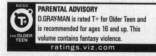

RATED
T+
FOR OLDER
TEEN

**PARENTAL ADVISORY**
D.GRAY-MAN is rated T+ for Older Teen and
is recommended for ages 16 and up. This
volume contains fantasy violence.
ratings.viz.com

SHONEN JUMP ADVANCED MANGA EDITION

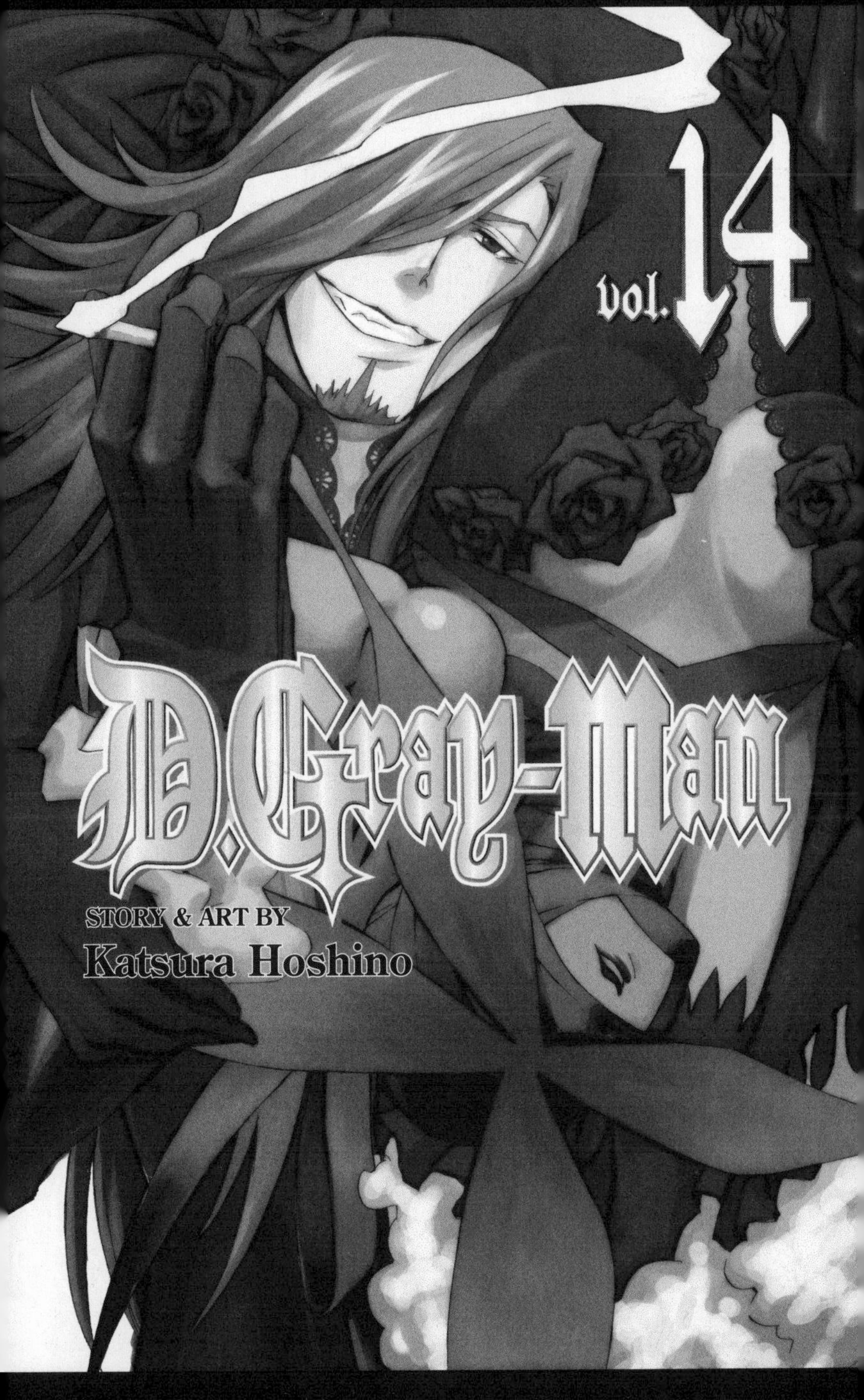
vol. 14
D.Gray-man
STORY & ART BY
Katsura Hoshino

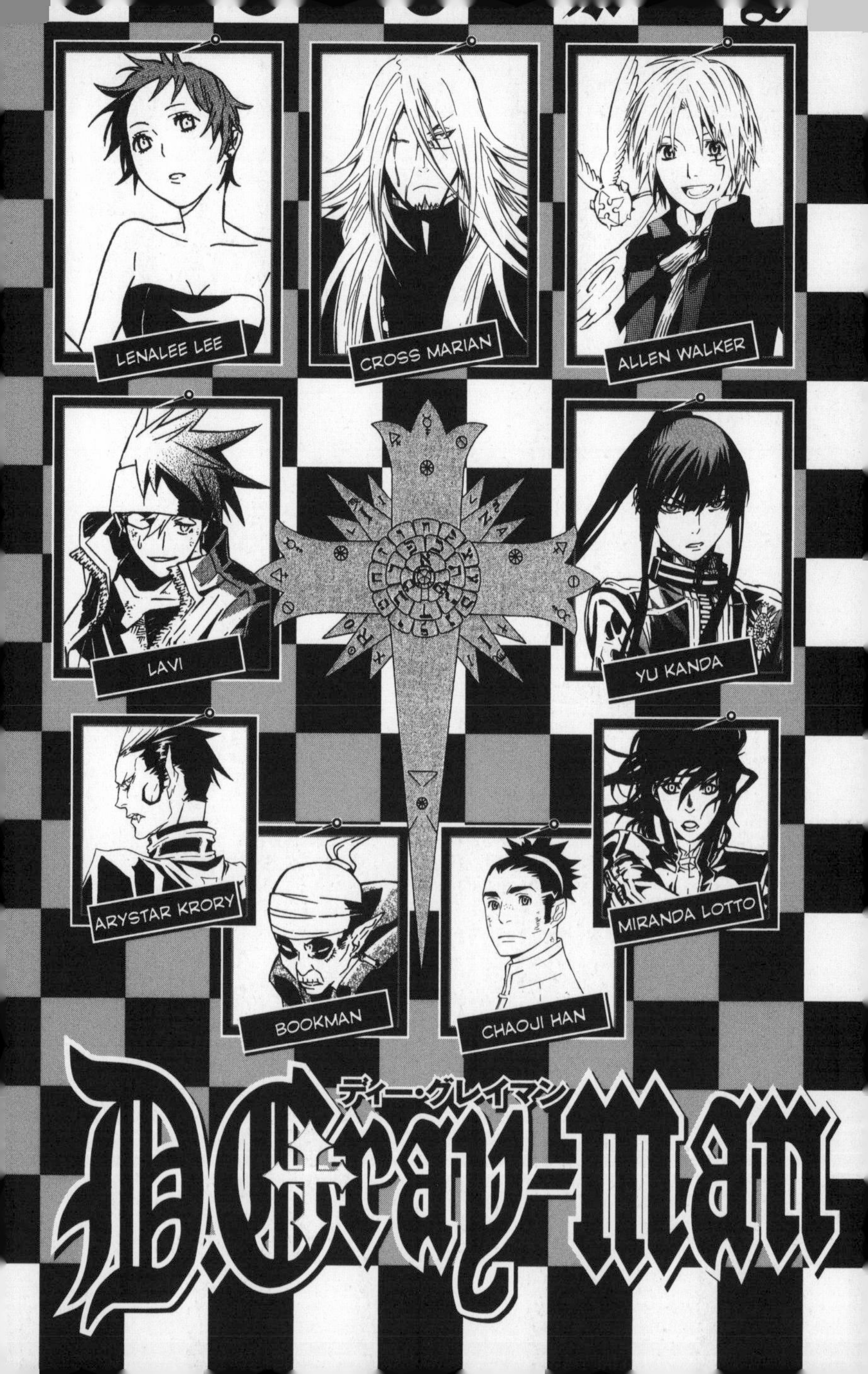
ALLEN WALKER
CROSS MARIAN
LENALEE LEE
YU KANDA
LAVI
MIRANDA LOTTO
ARYSTAR KRORY
CHAOJI HAN
BOOKMAN
ディー・グレイマン
D.Gray-man

JOHNNY GILL

BAK CHAN

KOMUI LEE

ROUVERLIER

REEVER WENHAM

MILLENNIUM EARL

TYKI MIKK

HOWARD

## STORY

IT ALL BEGAN CENTURIES AGO WITH THE DISCOVERY OF A CUBE CONTAINING AN APOCALYPTIC PROPHECY FROM AN ANCIENT CIVILIZATION AND INSTRUCTIONS IN THE USE OF INNOCENCE, A CRYSTALLINE SUBSTANCE OF WONDROUS SUPERNATURAL POWER. THE CREATORS OF THE CUBE CLAIMED TO HAVE DEFEATED AN EVIL KNOWN AS THE MILLENNIUM EARL BY USING THE INNOCENCE. NEVERTHELESS, THE WORLD WAS DESTROYED BY THE GREAT FLOOD OF THE OLD TESTAMENT. NOW, TO AVERT A SECOND END OF THE WORLD, A GROUP OF EXORCISTS WIELDING WEAPONS MADE OF INNOCENCE MUST BATTLE THE MILLENNIUM EARL AND HIS TERRIBLE MINIONS, THE AKUMA.

ALLEN AND THE OTHER EXORCISTS FIND THEMSELVES FIGHTING FOR THEIR LIVES ON A RAPIDLY DISINTEGRATING ARK. BUT EVEN AS THE ARK COLLAPSES AROUND THEM, ALLEN DESTROYS TYKI MIKK'S INNER NOAH, TRIGGERING A RAMPAGE OF DESTRUCTION. AND IF MATTERS WEREN'T COMPLICATED ENOUGH, ALLEN'S LONG-LOST MASTER, CROSS MARIAN, SUDDENLY SHOWS UP!!

# D.GRAY-MAN
## Vol. 14

# CONTENTS

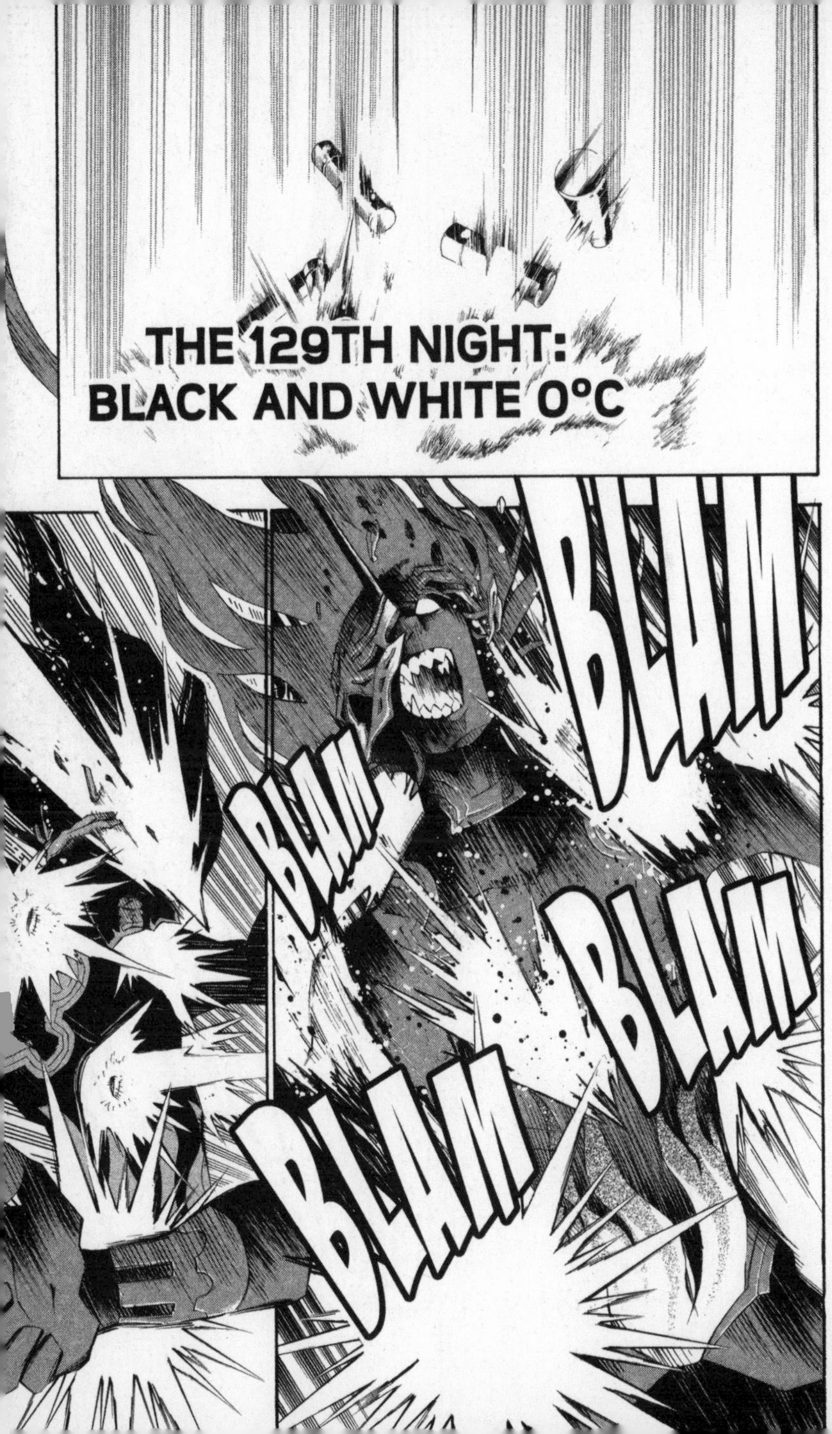
THE 129TH NIGHT:
BLACK AND WHITE 0°C
BLAM
BLAM
BLAM
BLAM

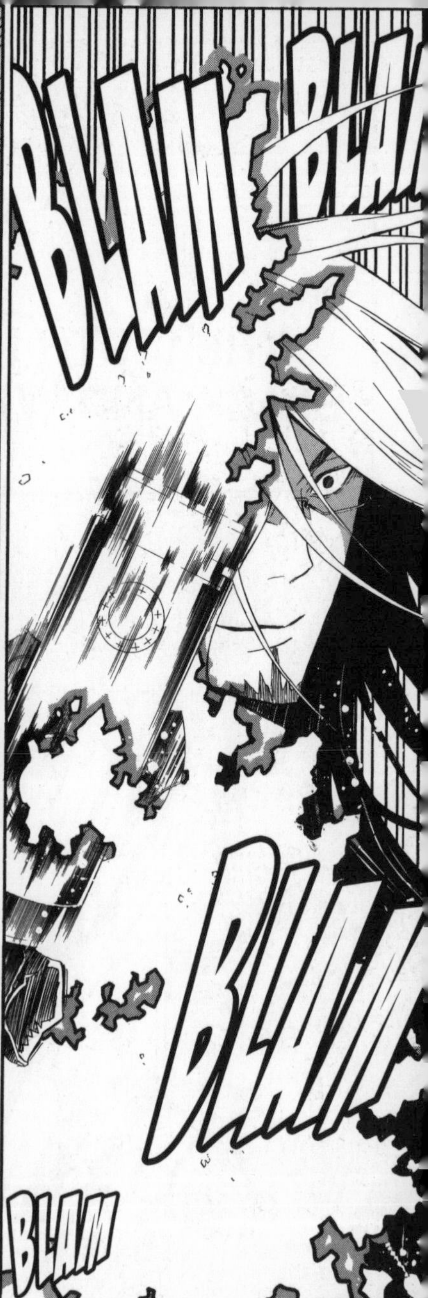
BLAM
BLA
BLA
BLAM
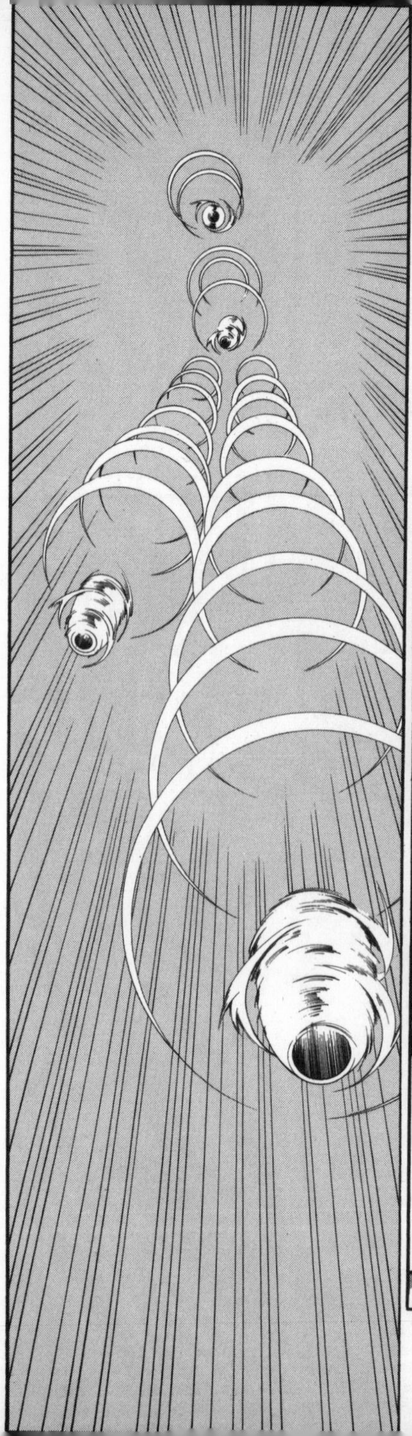

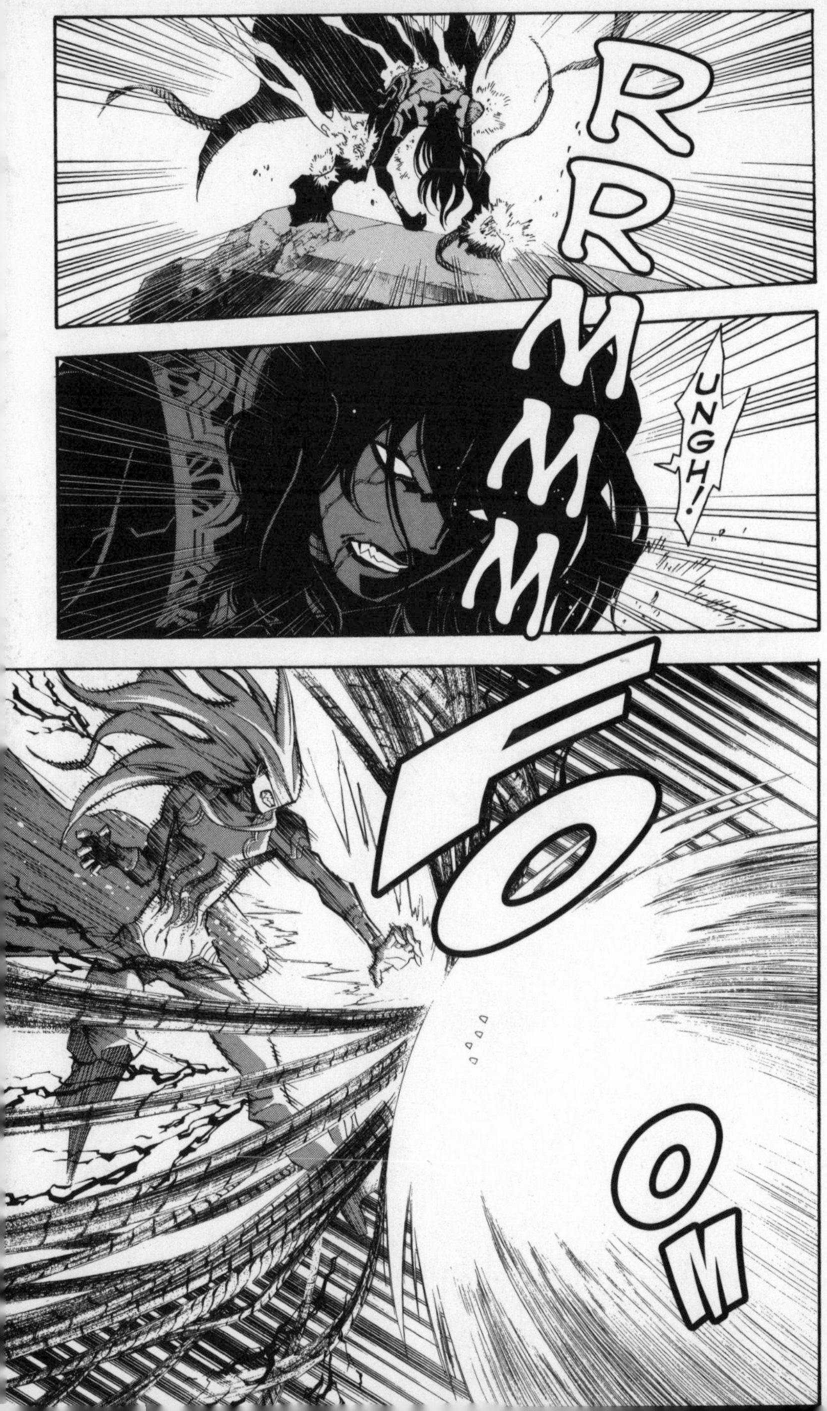
RRMMM
UNGH!
BOOM

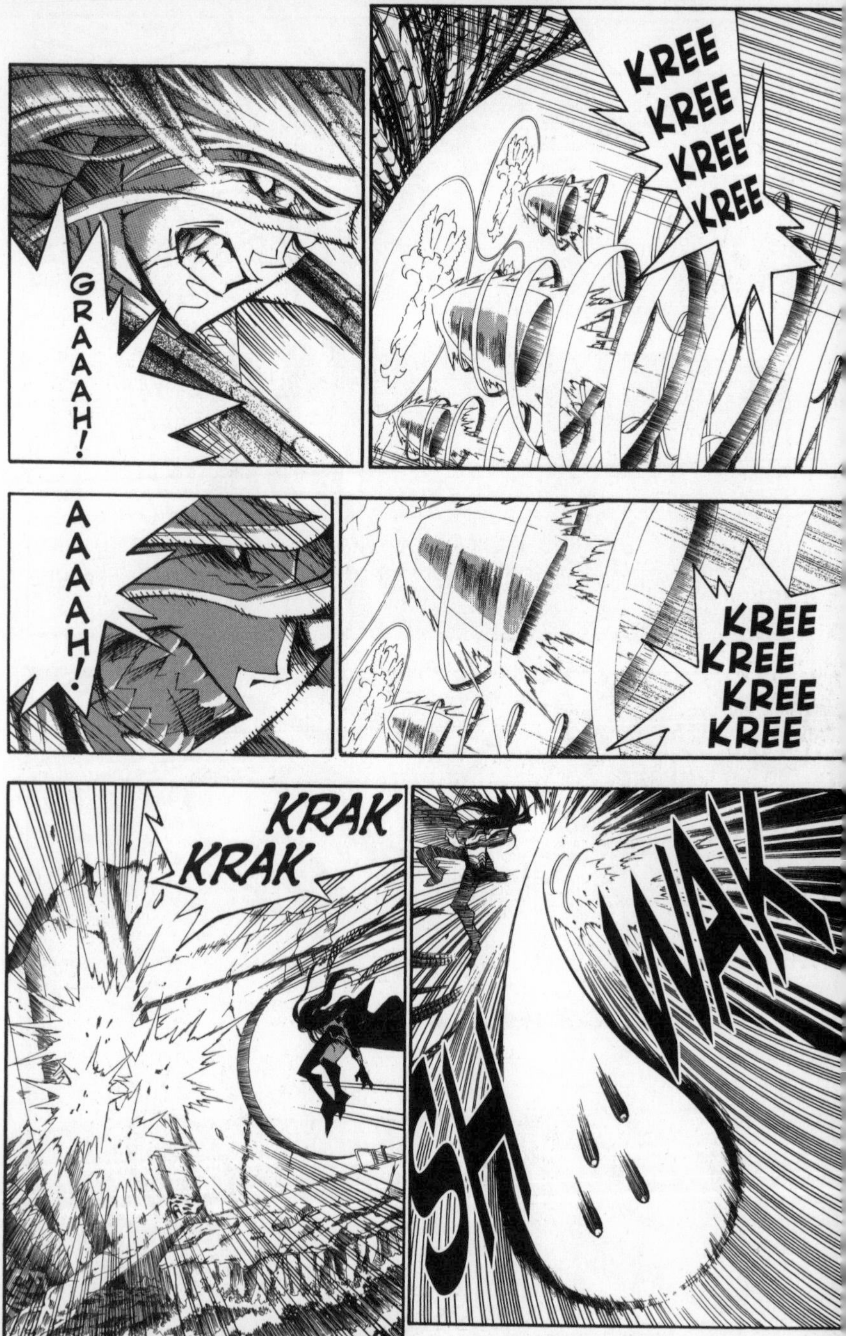
KREE
KREE
KREE
KREE
GRAAAH!
KREE
KREE
KREE
KREE
AAAAH!
SHWAK
KRAK
KRAK

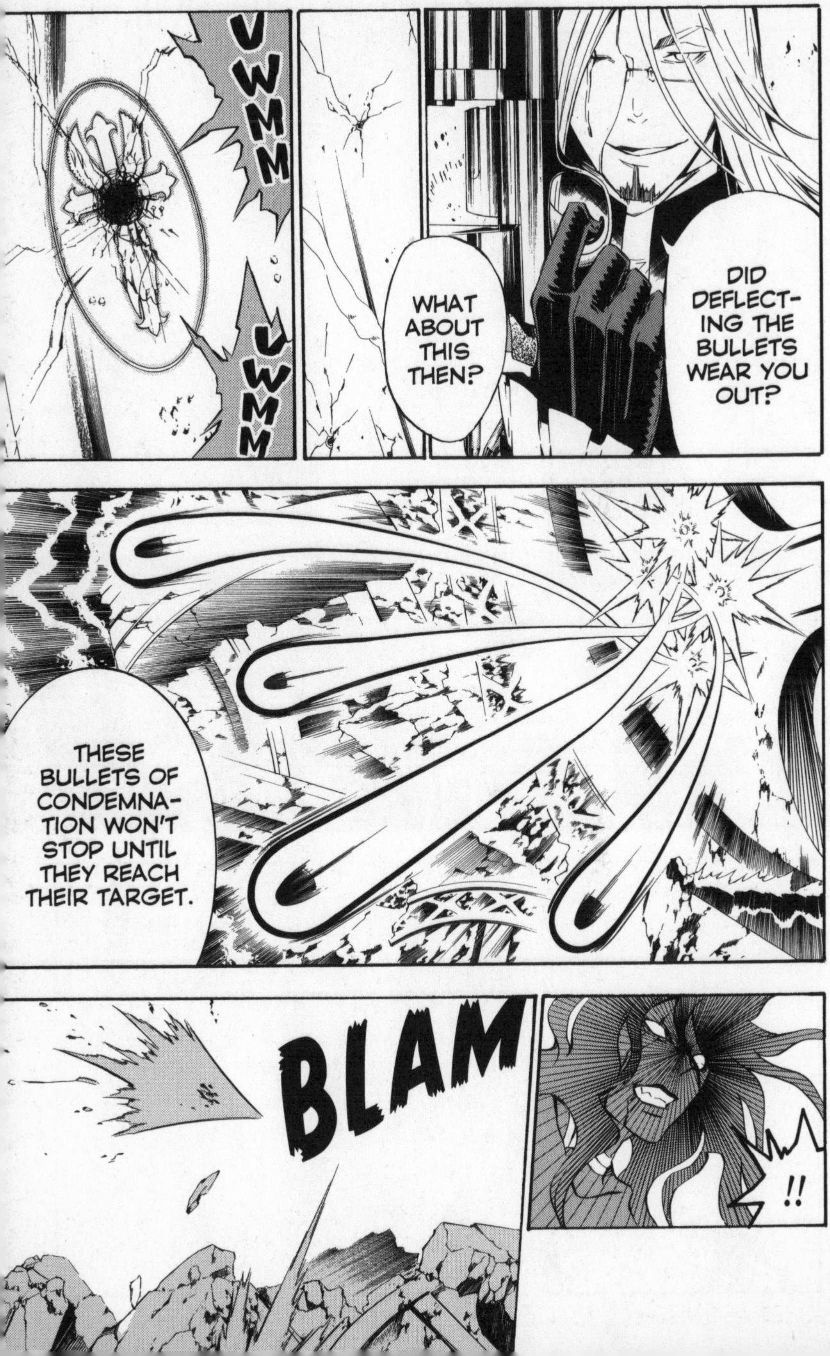
DID DEFLECTING THE BULLETS WEAR YOU OUT?
WHAT ABOUT THIS THEN?
VWMM
VWMM
THESE BULLETS OF CONDEMNATION WON'T STOP UNTIL THEY REACH THEIR TARGET.
!!
BLAM

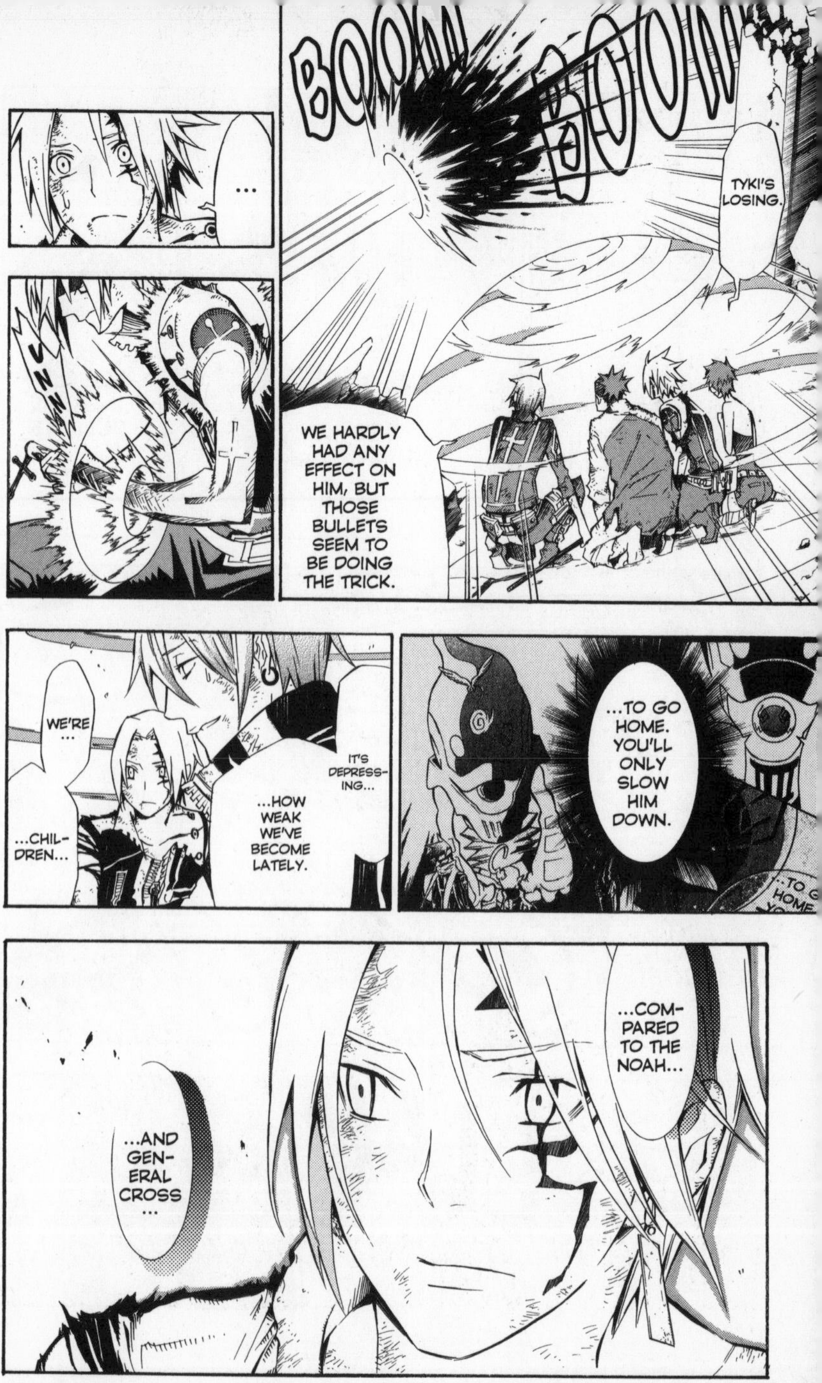
BOOM
BOOOM
TYKI'S LOSING.
WE HARDLY HAD ANY EFFECT ON HIM, BUT THOSE BULLETS SEEM TO BE DOING THE TRICK.
...
UNN
...TO GO HOME. YOU'LL ONLY SLOW HIM DOWN.
IT'S DEPRESSING...
...HOW WEAK WE'VE BECOME LATELY.
WE'RE ...
...CHILDREN...
...COMPARED TO THE NOAH...
...AND GENERAL CROSS ...

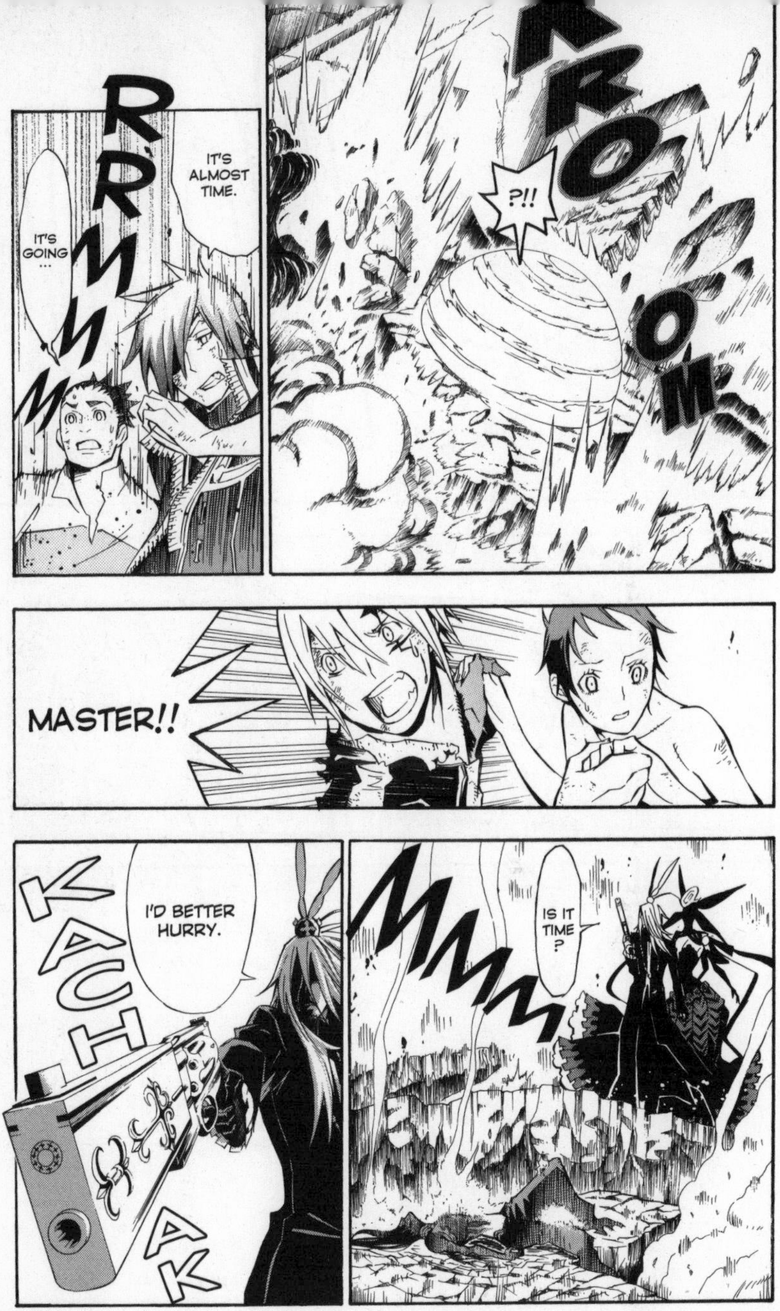
KROOOM
?!!
IT'S ALMOST TIME.
IT'S GOING ...
RRMMMM
MASTER!!
IS IT TIME?
MMMM
I'D BETTER HURRY.
KACHAK

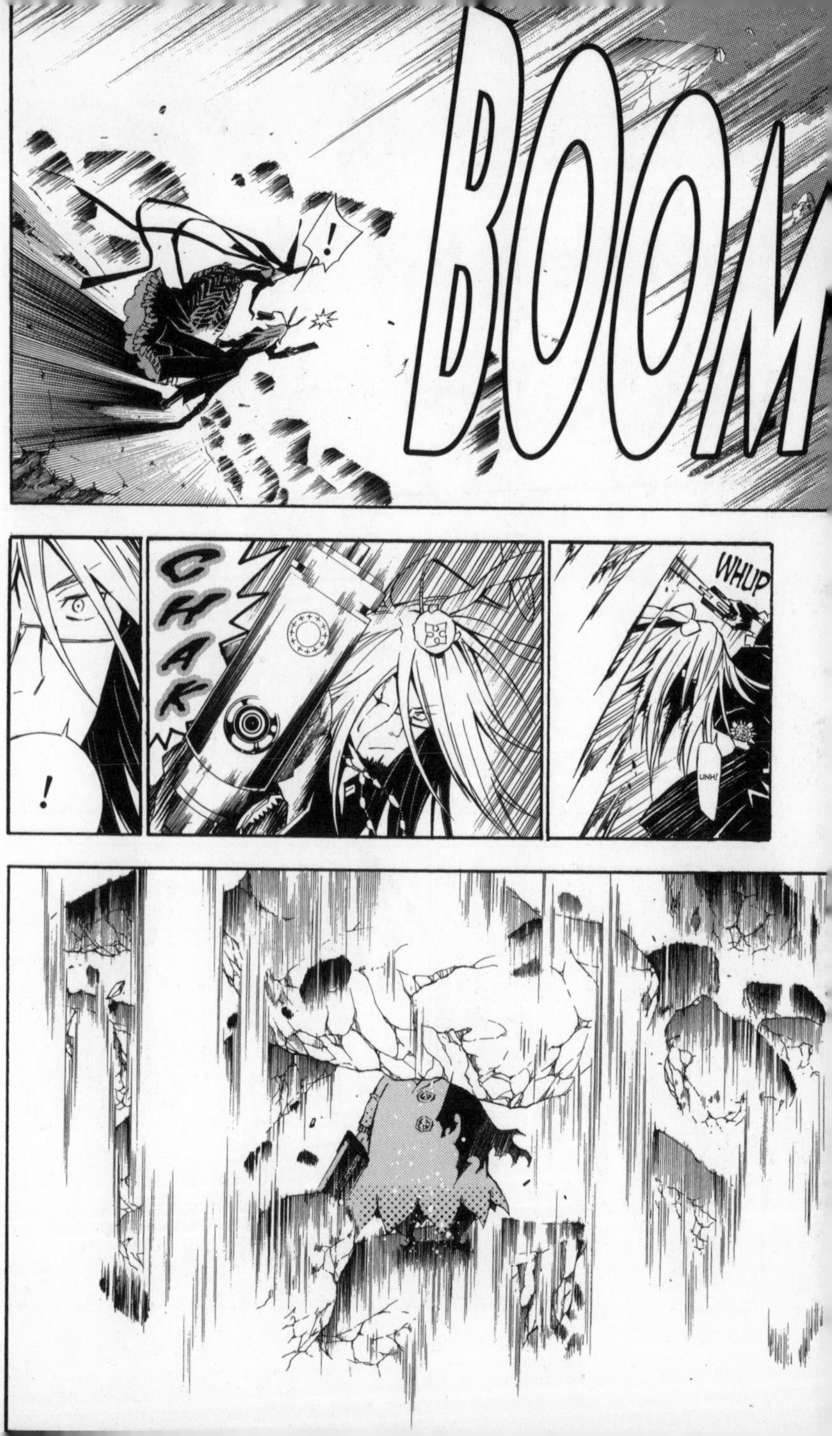
BOOM
!
WHUP
UNH!
CHAK
!

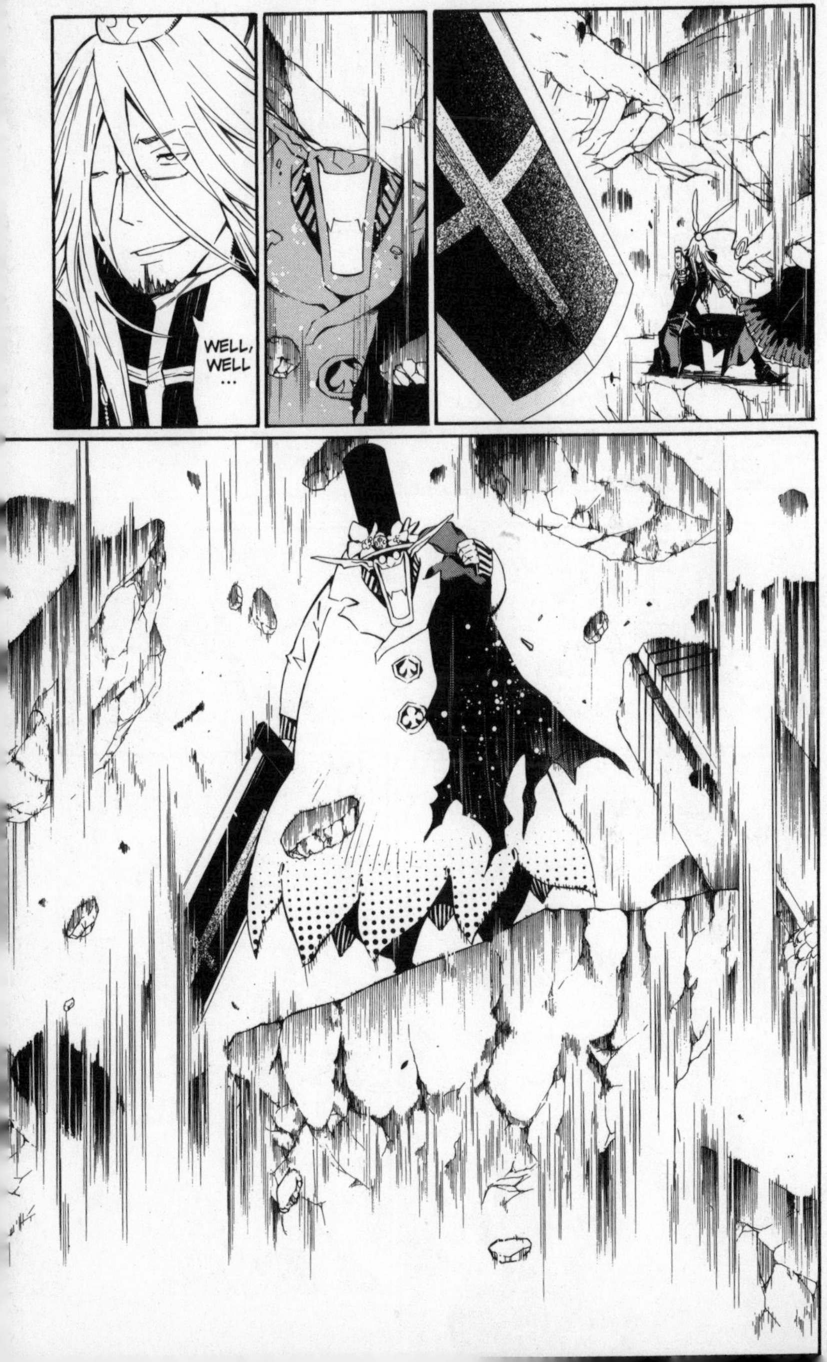

WELL, WELL ...

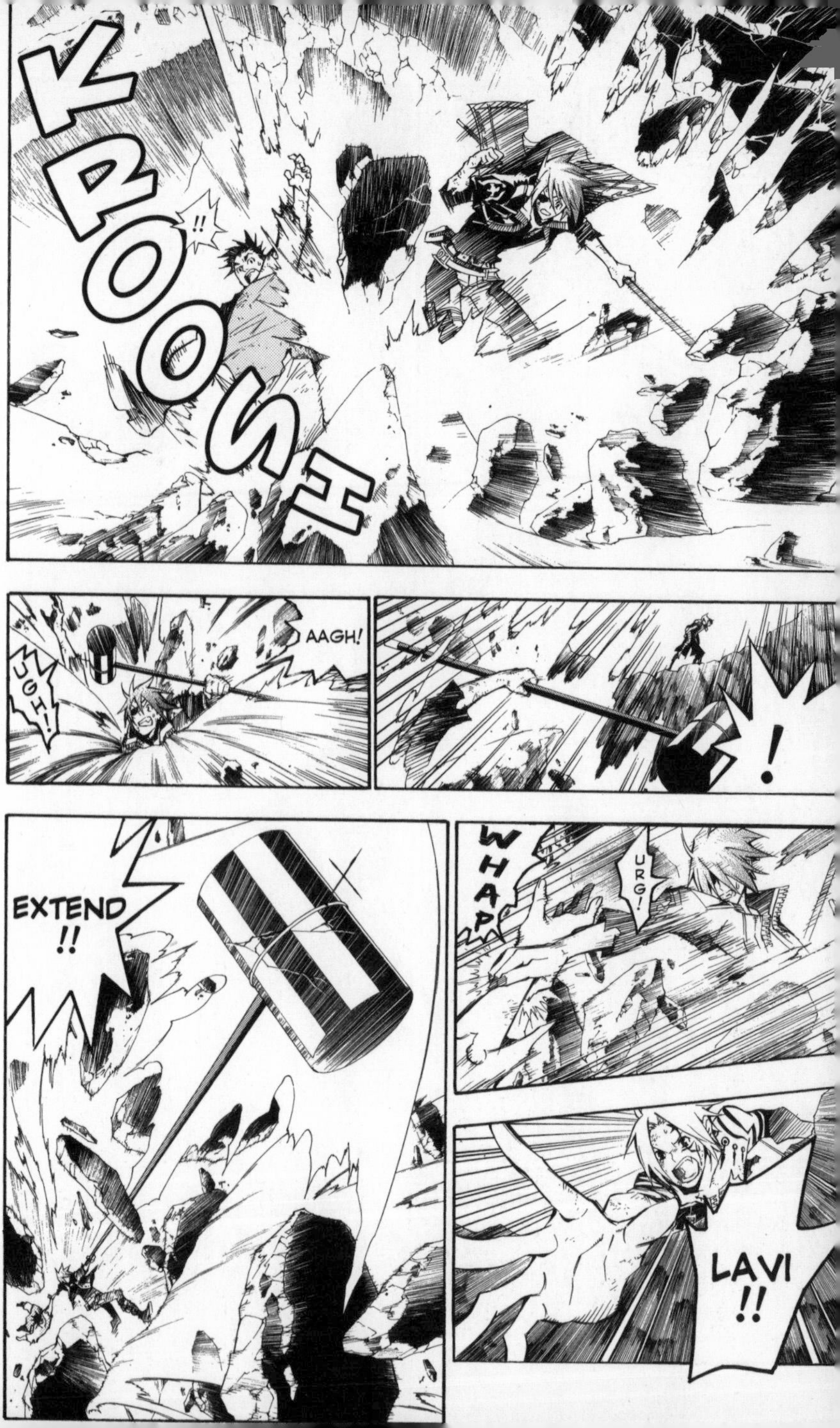

KROOSH
!!
!
AAGH!
UGH!
WHAP
URG!
LAVI!!
EXTEND!!

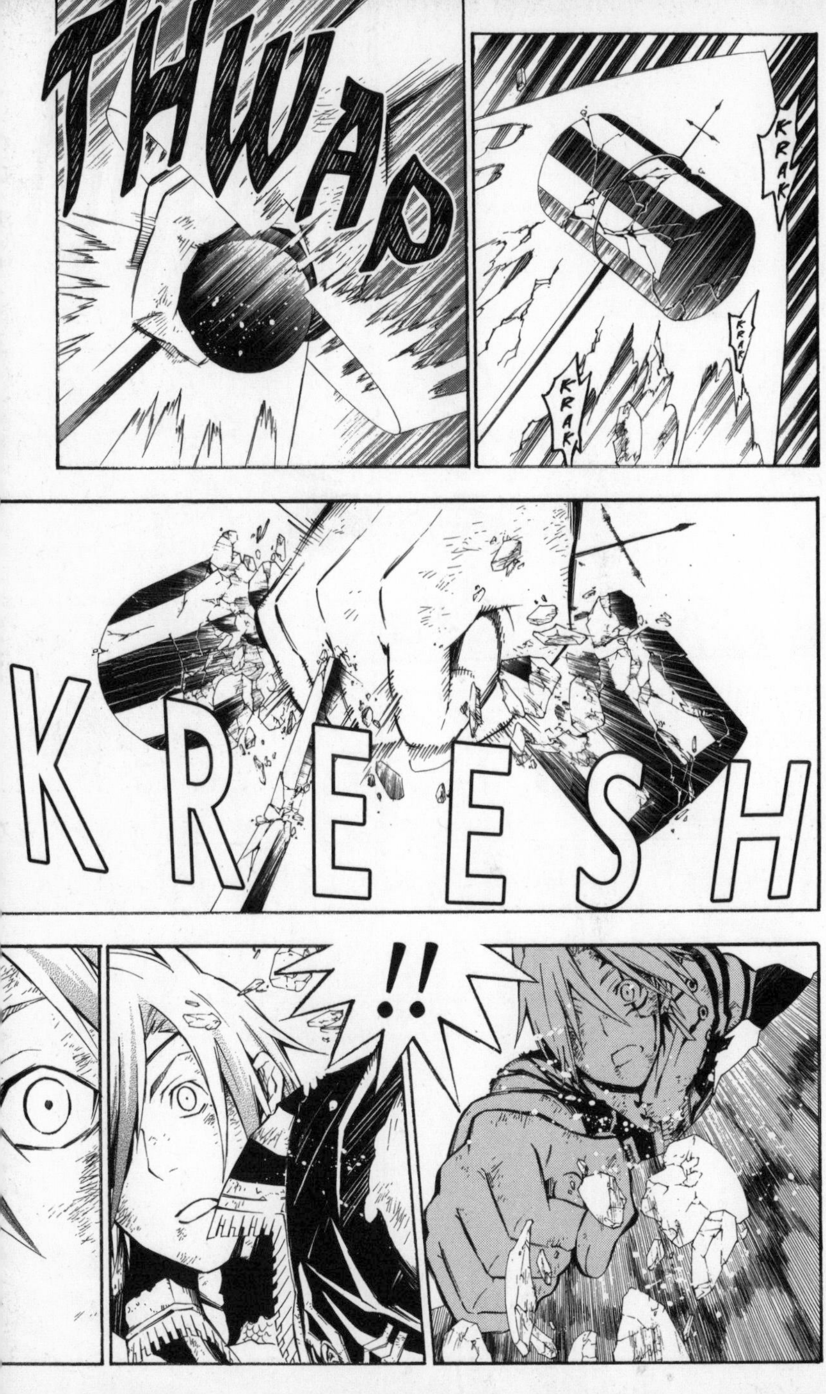
KRAK
KRAK
KRAK
THWAP
KREESH
!!

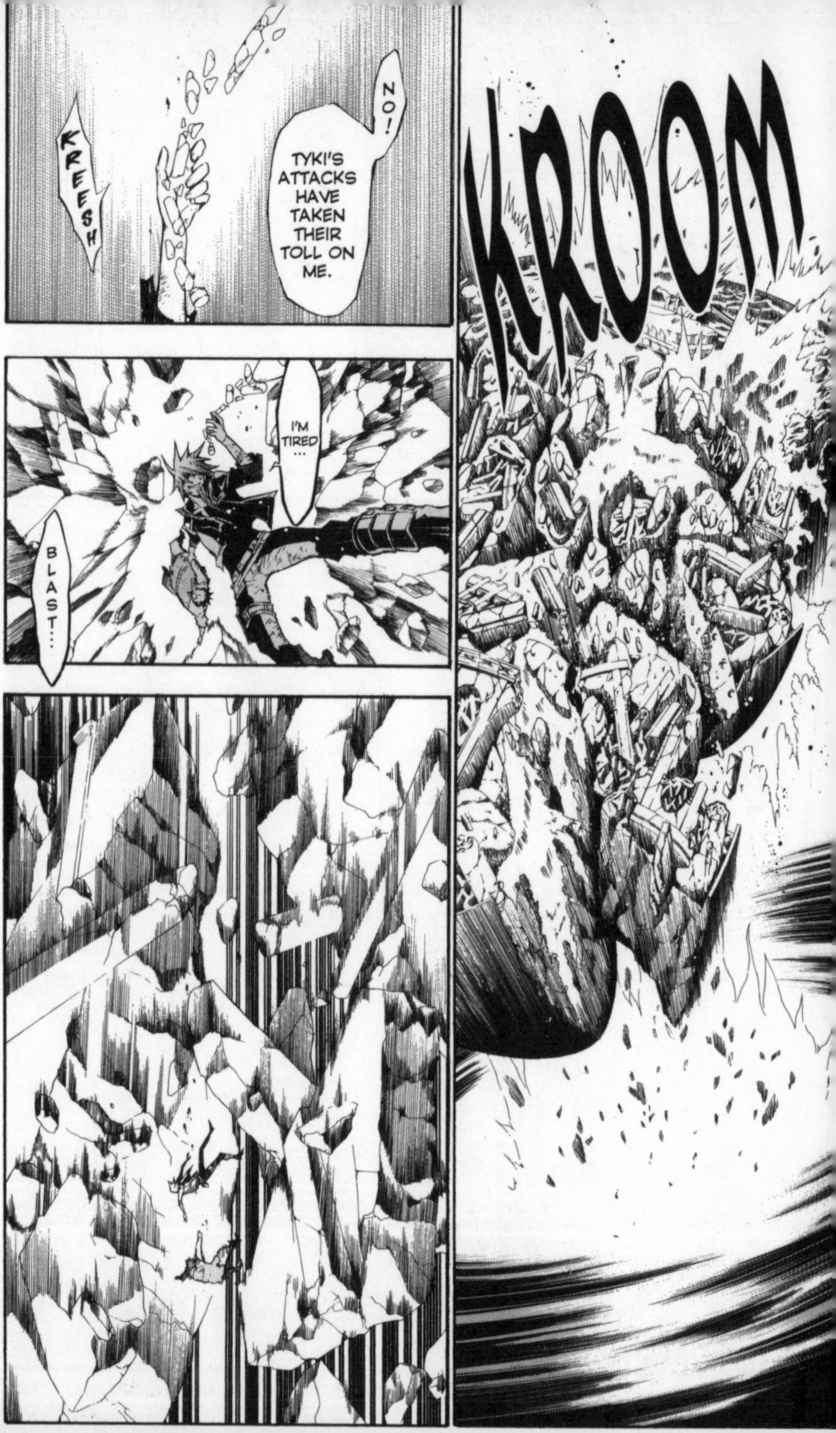
KROOM
NO!
TYKI'S ATTACKS HAVE TAKEN THEIR TOLL ON ME.
KREESH
I'M TIRED...
BLAST...

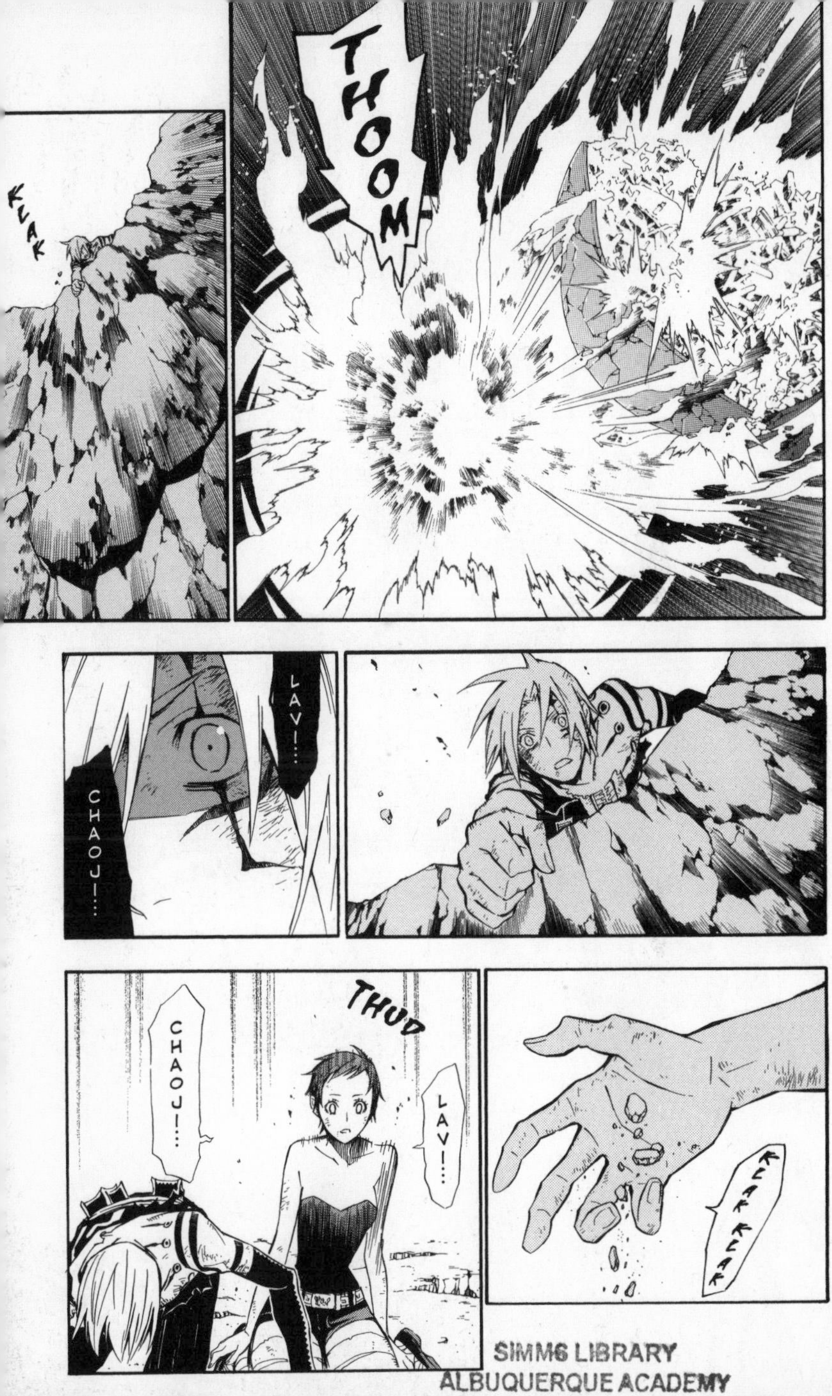
THOOM
KLAK
LAVI...!
CHAOJI...!
KLAK KLAK
THUD
LAVI...!
CHAOJI...!

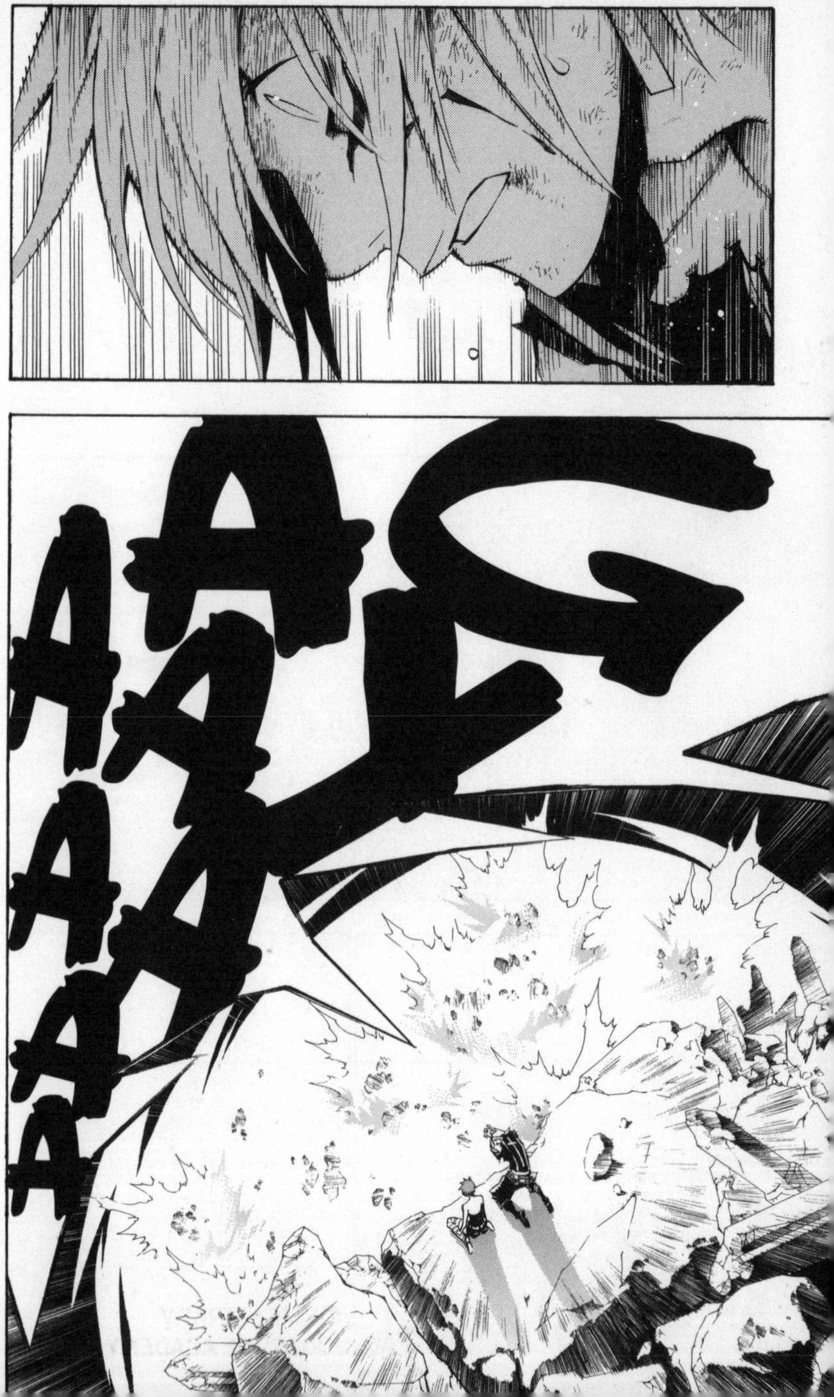

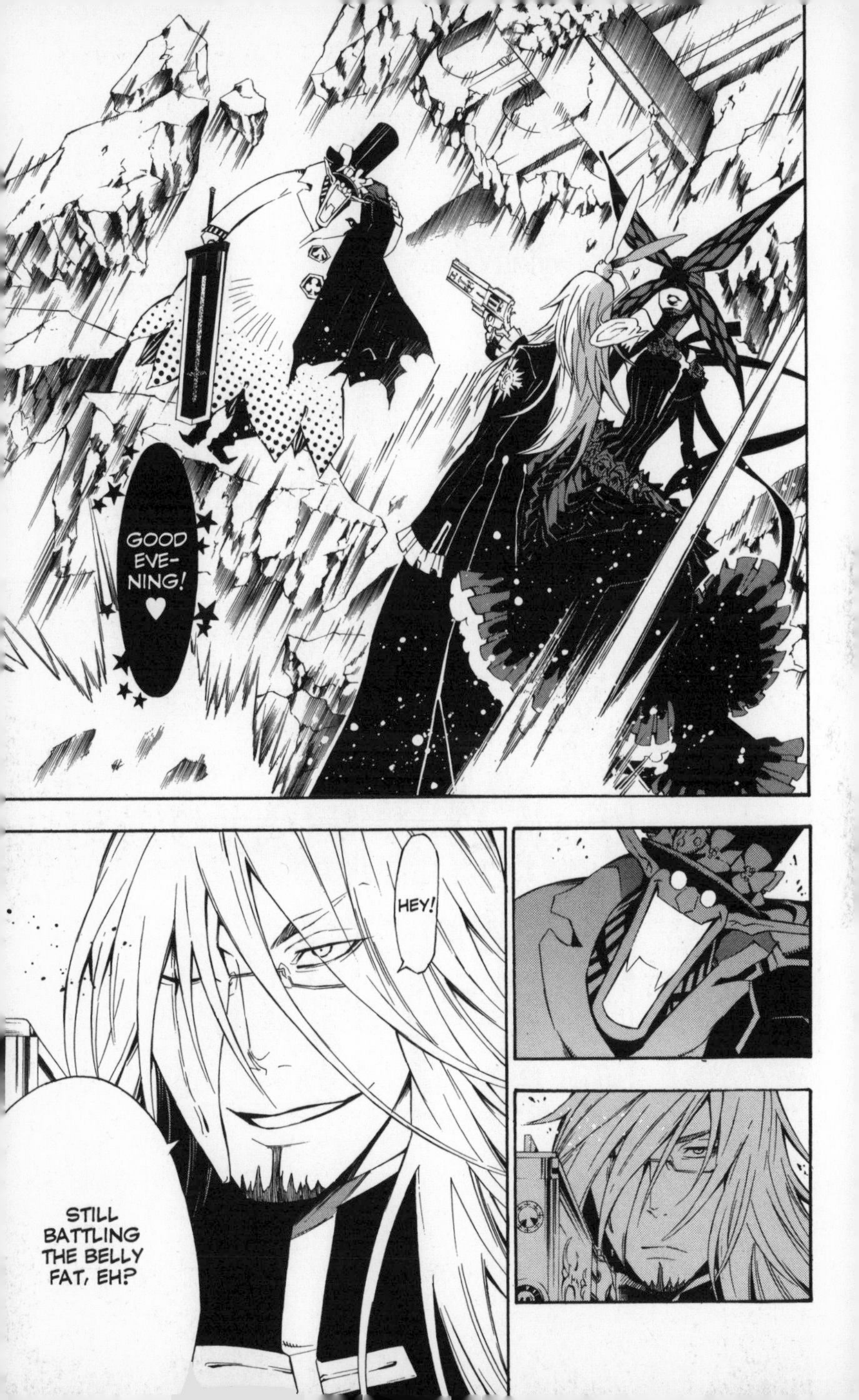
GOOD EVE- NING! ♥
HEY!
STILL BATTLING THE BELLY FAT, EH?

Q. KANDA SEEMS HARD-HEARTED, BUT I THINK HE'S ACTUALLY KIND. AM I RIGHT?

(ERINA SATO, SAITAMA PREFECTURE)

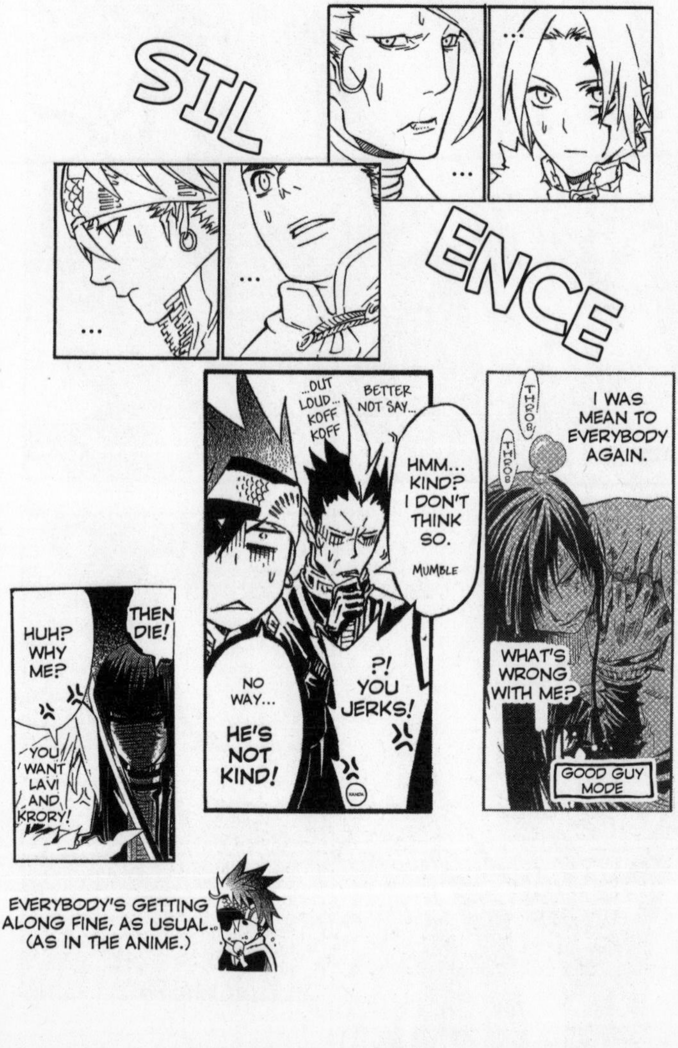

...
...
SIL
...
...
...
ENCE
I WAS MEAN TO EVERYBODY AGAIN.
THROB
THROB
WHAT'S WRONG WITH ME?
GOOD GUY MODE
BETTER NOT SAY...
...OUT LOUD... KOFF KOFF
HMM... KIND? I DON'T THINK SO.
MUMBLE
?! YOU JERKS!
NO WAY...
HE'S NOT KIND!
KANDA
THEN DIE!
HUH? WHY ME?
YOU WANT LAVI AND KRORY!
EVERYBODY'S GETTING ALONG FINE, AS USUAL.
(AS IN THE ANIME.)

# THE 130TH NIGHT: EYES OF HATRED

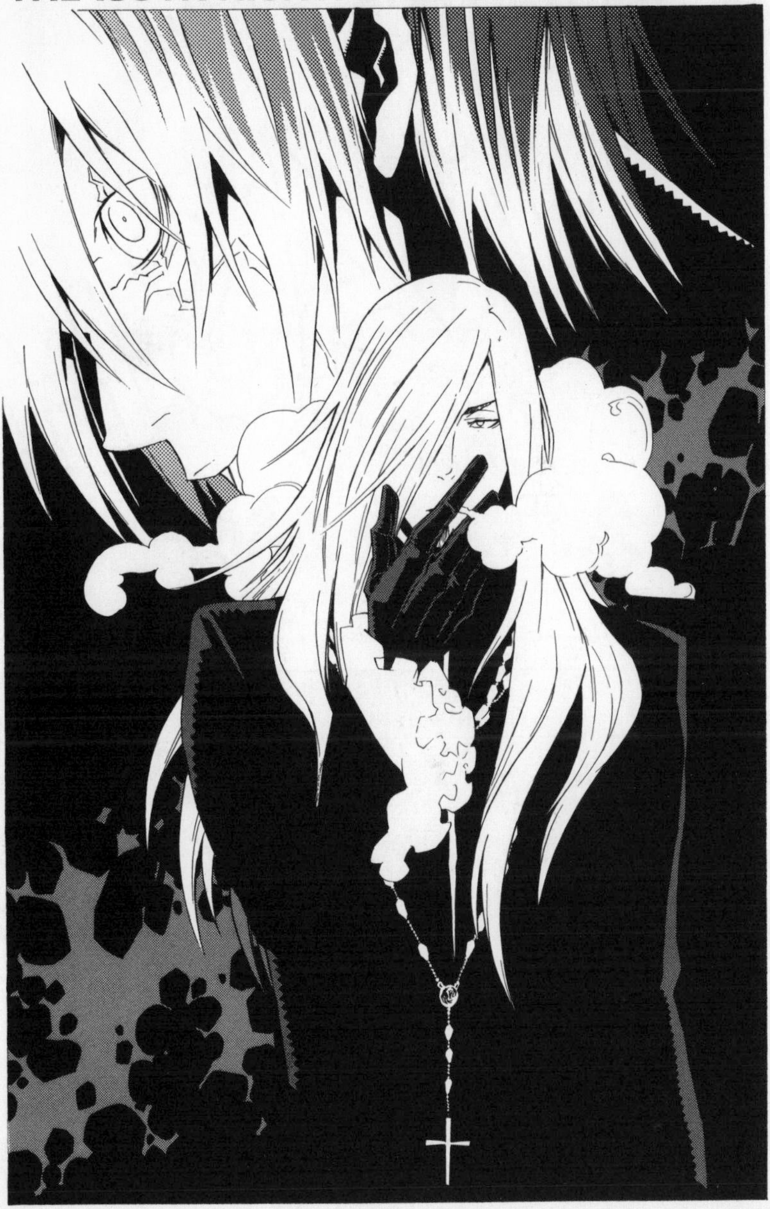

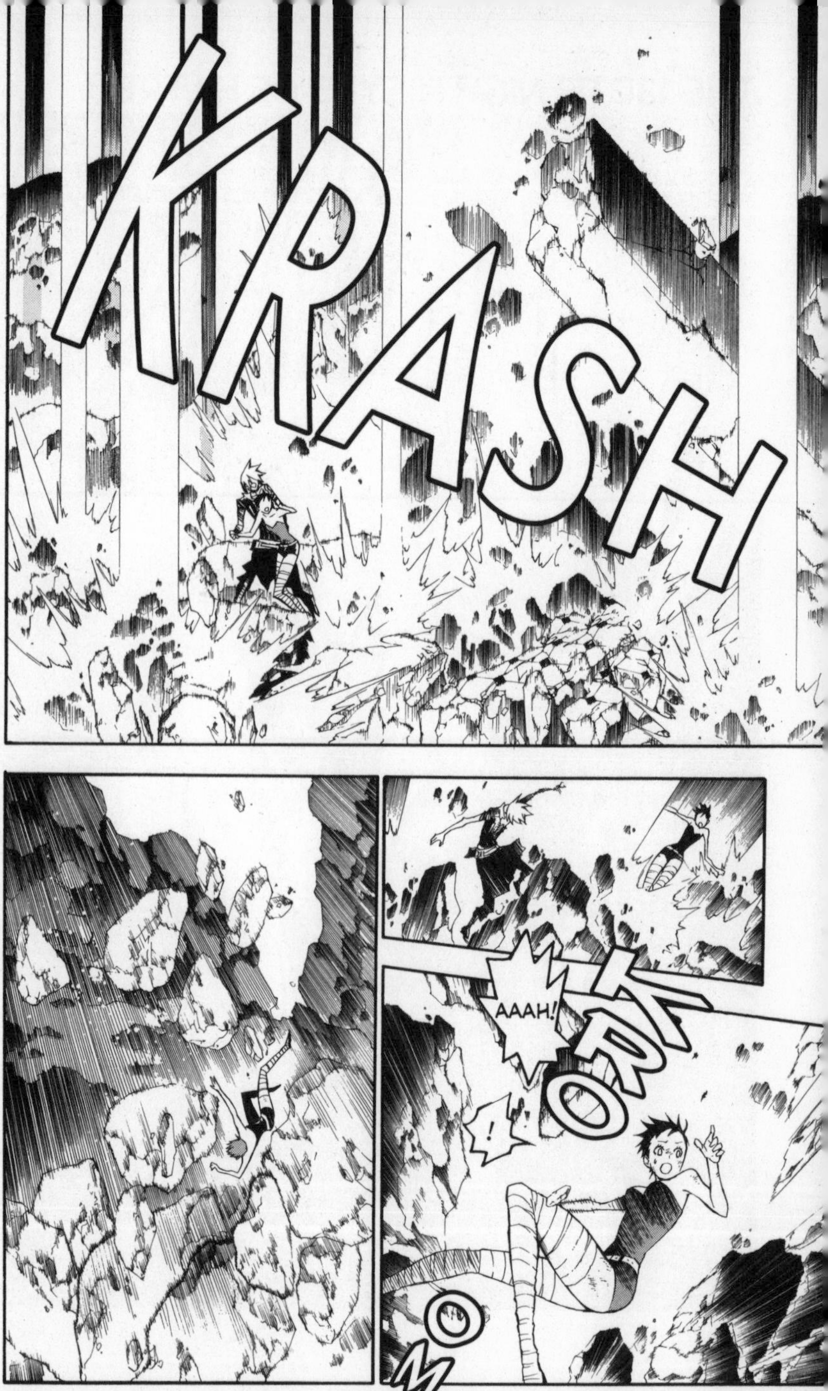
KRASH
AAAH!
KRO
!
OM

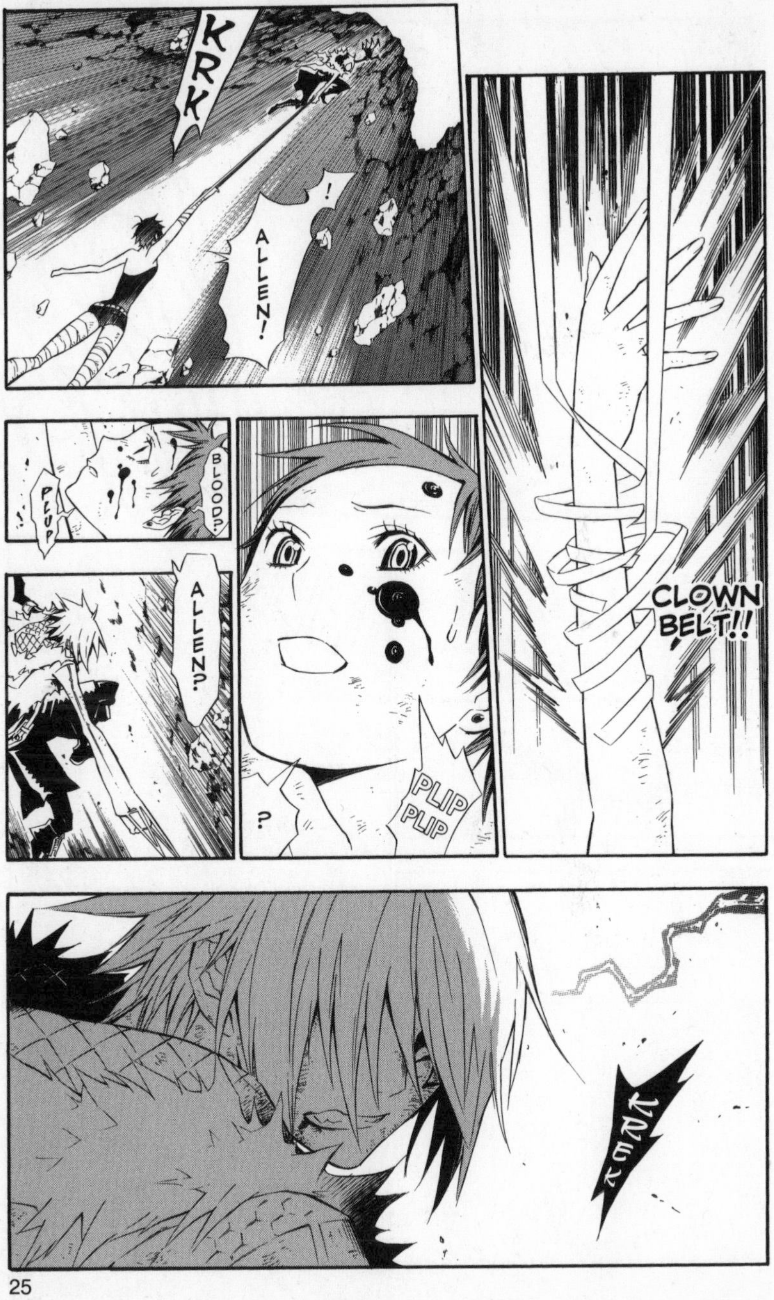
KRK
!
ALLEN!
CLOWN BELT!!
PLIP PLIP
?
BLOOD?
PLUP
ALLEN?
KREK

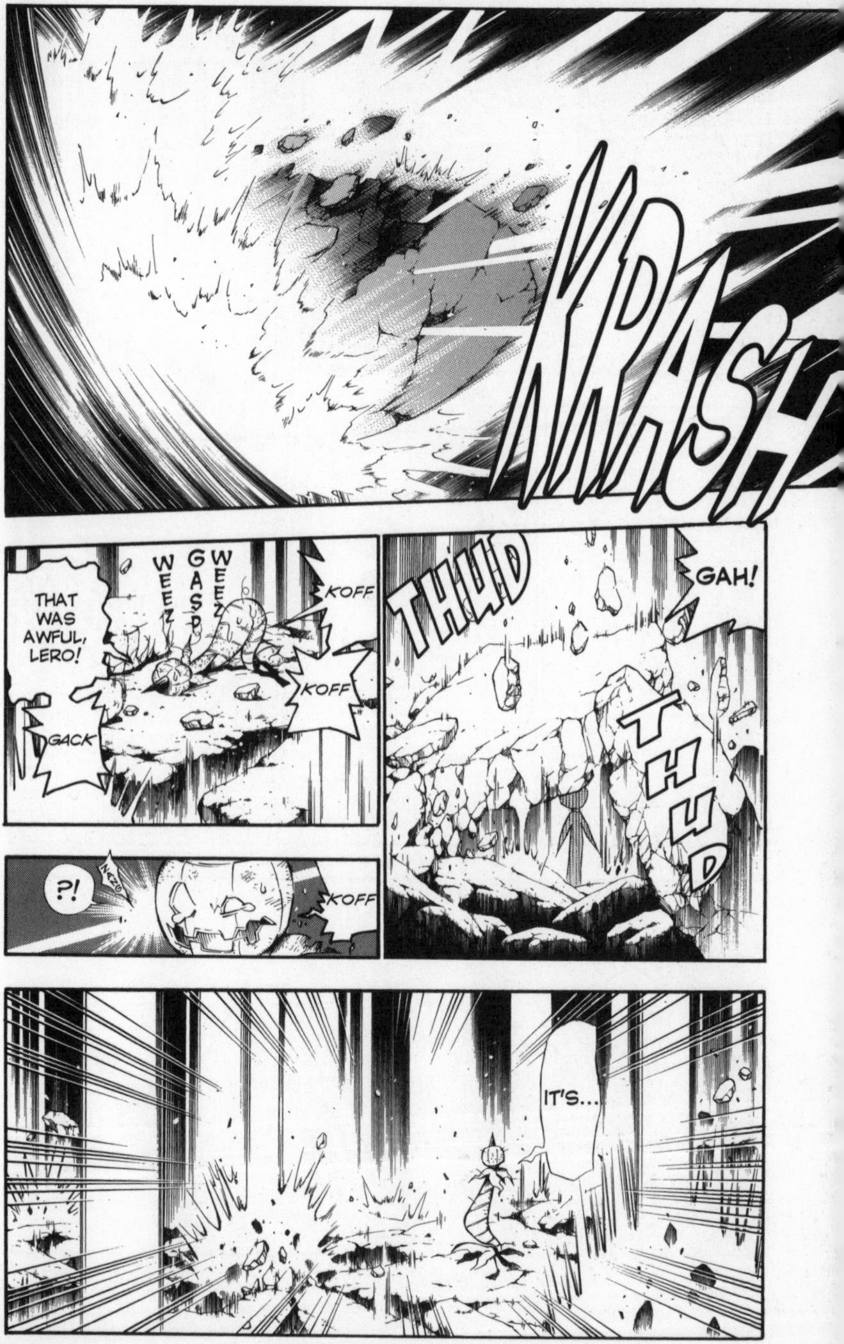
KRASH
THUD
GAH!
THUD
KOFF
WEEZ
GASP
WEEZ
THAT WAS AWFUL, LERO!
KOFF
GACK
KOFF
?!
IT'S...

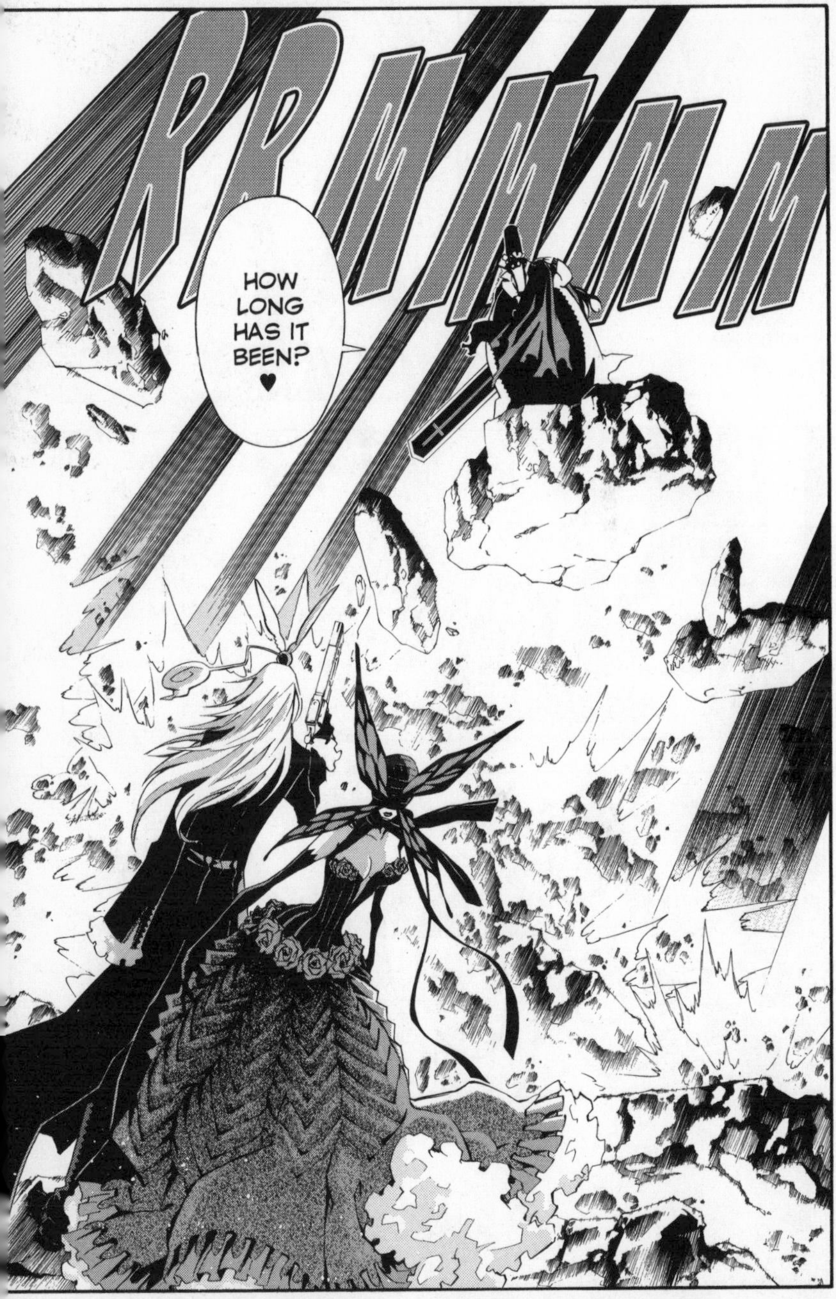

BRMMMMM
HOW LONG HAS IT BEEN? ♥

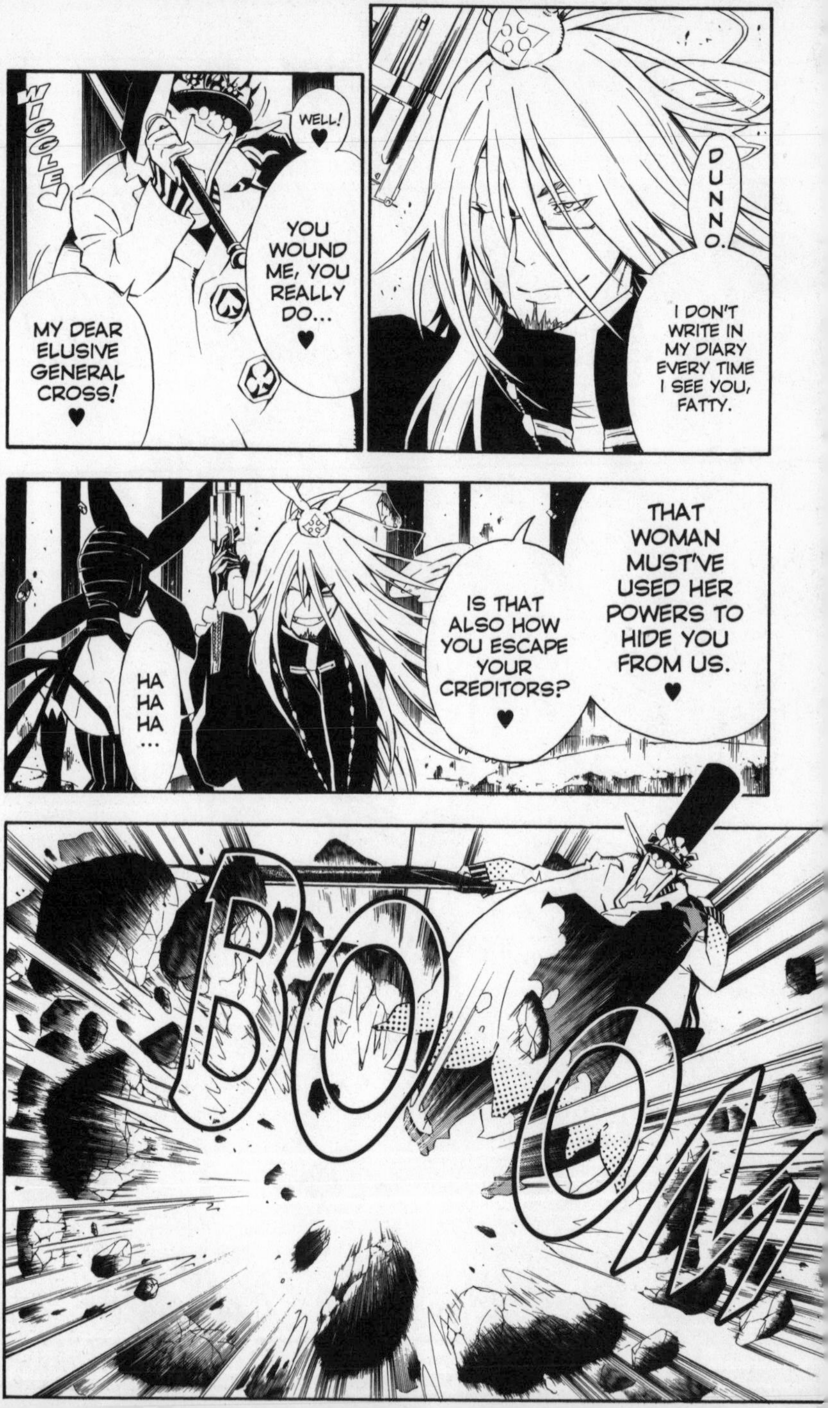
DUNNO.
I DON'T WRITE IN MY DIARY EVERY TIME I SEE YOU, FATTY.
WELL! ♥
YOU WOUND ME, YOU REALLY DO... ♥
WIGGLE ♥
MY DEAR ELUSIVE GENERAL CROSS! ♥
THAT WOMAN MUST'VE USED HER POWERS TO HIDE YOU FROM US. ♥
IS THAT ALSO HOW YOU ESCAPE YOUR CREDITORS? ♥
HA HA HA ...
BOOM

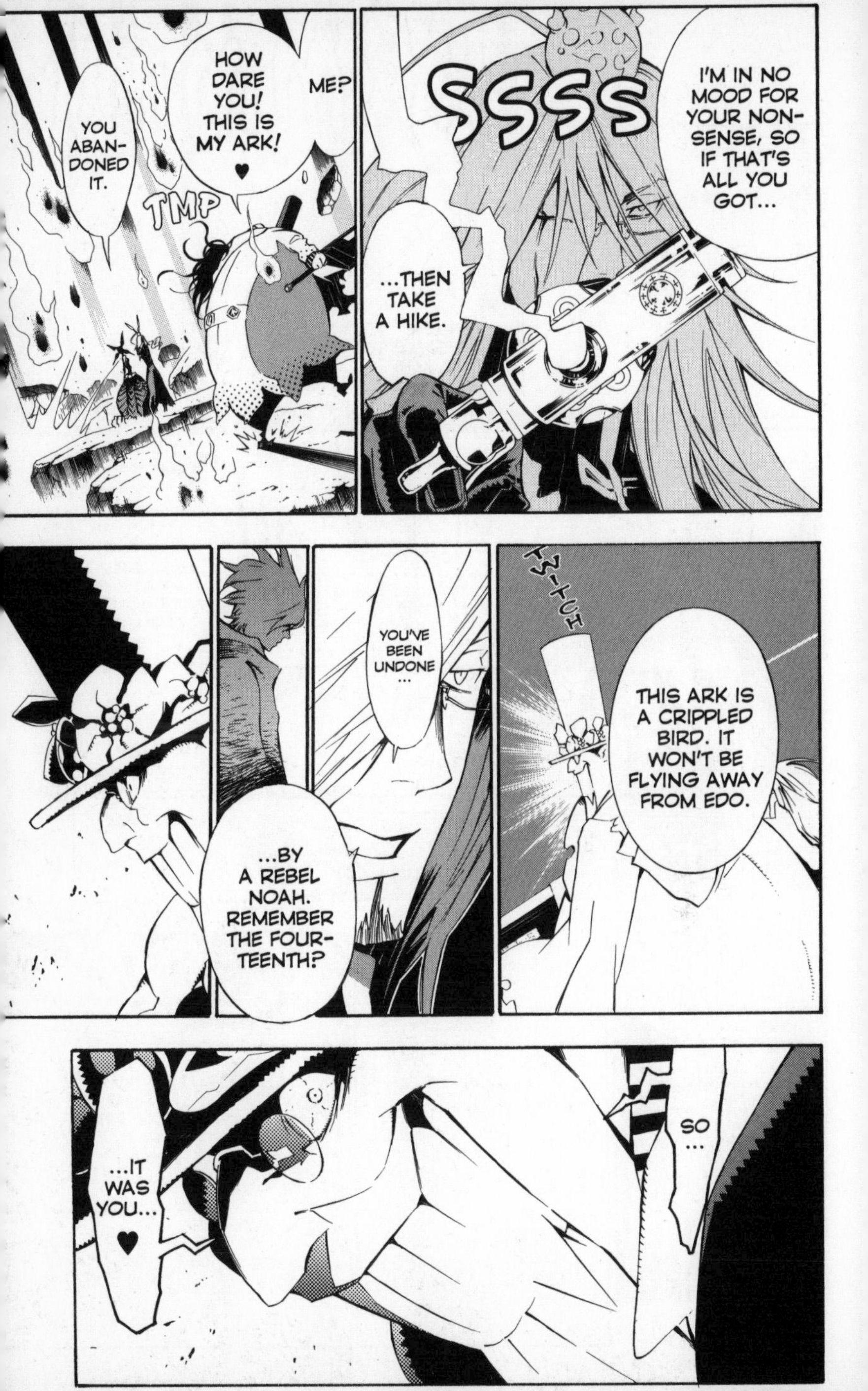
SSSS
I'M IN NO MOOD FOR YOUR NON-SENSE, SO IF THAT'S ALL YOU GOT...
...THEN TAKE A HIKE.
HOW DARE YOU! THIS IS MY ARK! ♥
ME?
TMP
YOU ABAN-DONED IT.
TWITCH
THIS ARK IS A CRIPPLED BIRD. IT WON'T BE FLYING AWAY FROM EDO.
YOU'VE BEEN UNDONE...
...BY A REBEL NOAH. REMEMBER THE FOUR-TEENTH?
SO...
...IT WAS YOU... ♥

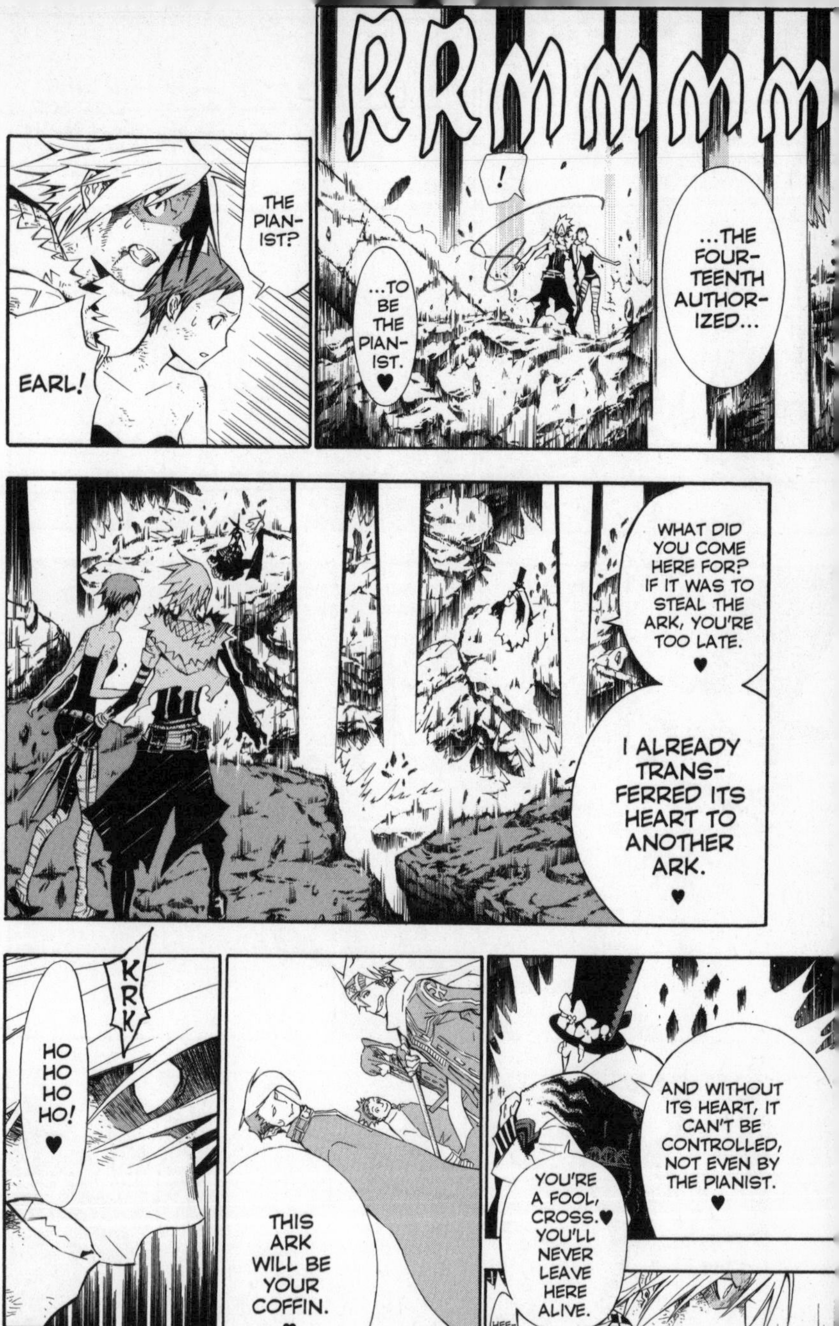
RRMMMMM
!
...THE FOURTEENTH AUTHORIZED...
...TO BE THE PIANIST. ♥
THE PIANIST?
EARL!
WHAT DID YOU COME HERE FOR? IF IT WAS TO STEAL THE ARK, YOU'RE TOO LATE. ♥
I ALREADY TRANSFERRED ITS HEART TO ANOTHER ARK. ♥
AND WITHOUT ITS HEART, IT CAN'T BE CONTROLLED, NOT EVEN BY THE PIANIST. ♥
YOU'RE A FOOL, CROSS. ♥ YOU'LL NEVER LEAVE HERE ALIVE.
HEE-HEE! ♥
THIS ARK WILL BE YOUR COFFIN. ♥
KRK
HO HO HO HO! ♥

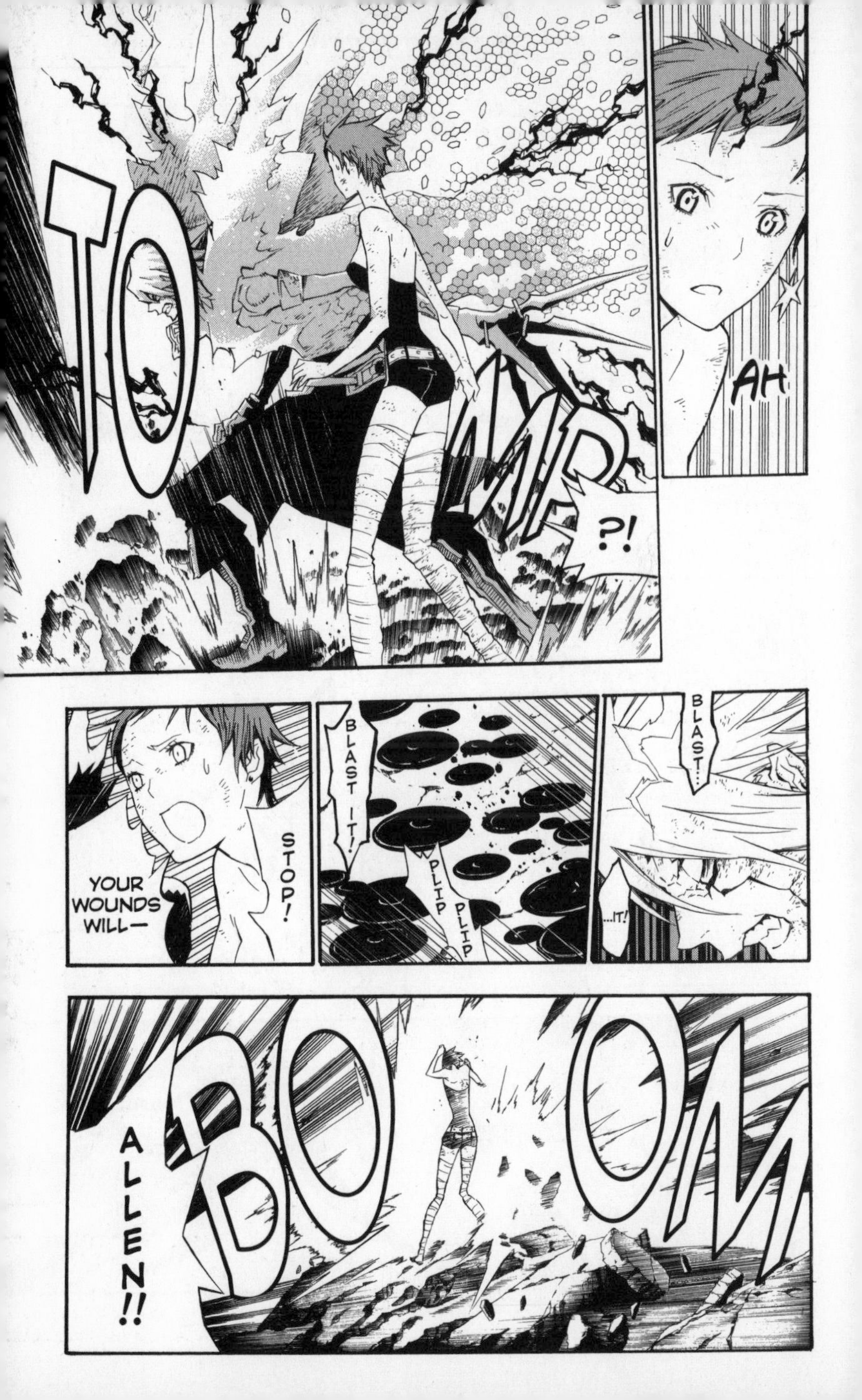
AH
TOMP
?!
BLAST...
...IT!
BLAST IT!
PLIP PLIP
STOP!
YOUR WOUNDS WILL—
BOOM
ALLEN!!

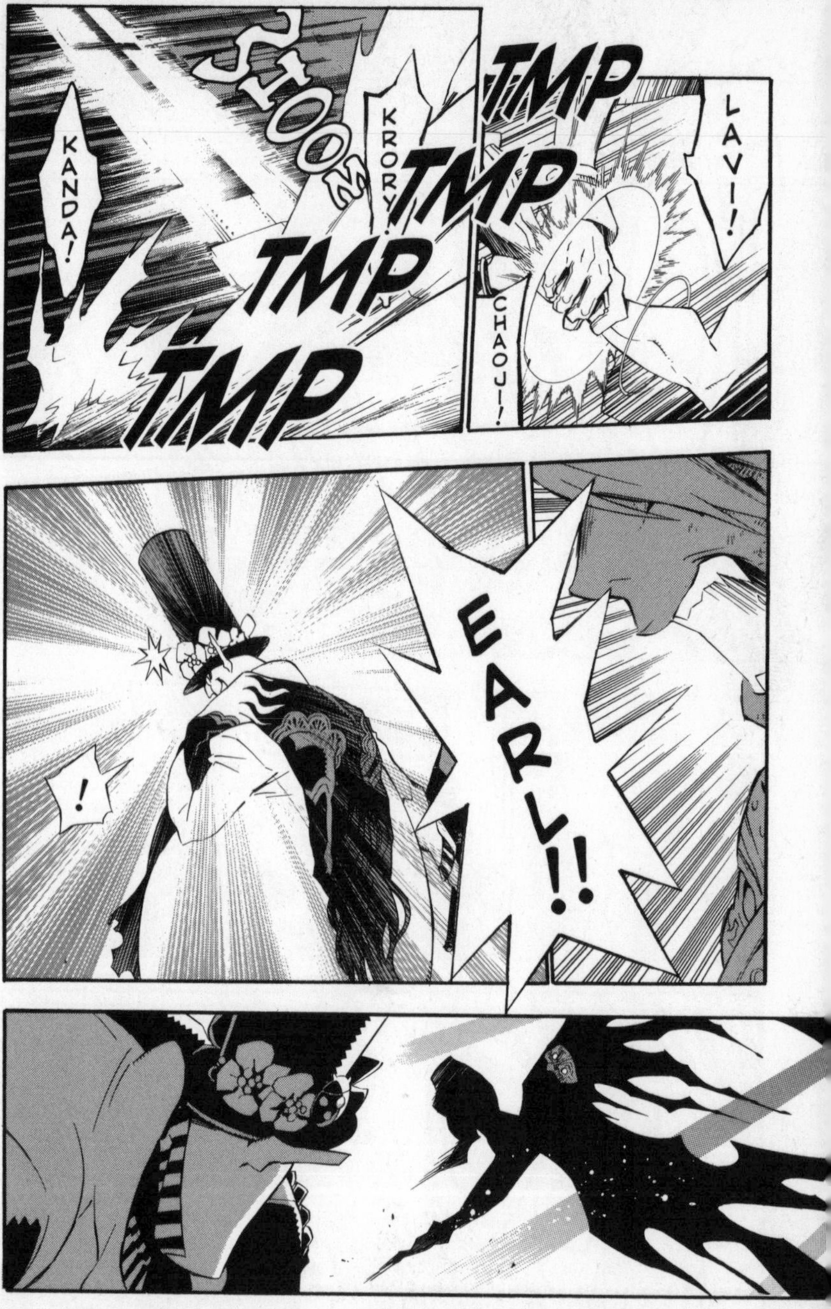
LAVI!
CHAOJI!
TMP
TMP
TMP
TMP
KRORY!
SHOOM
KANDA!
EARL!!
!

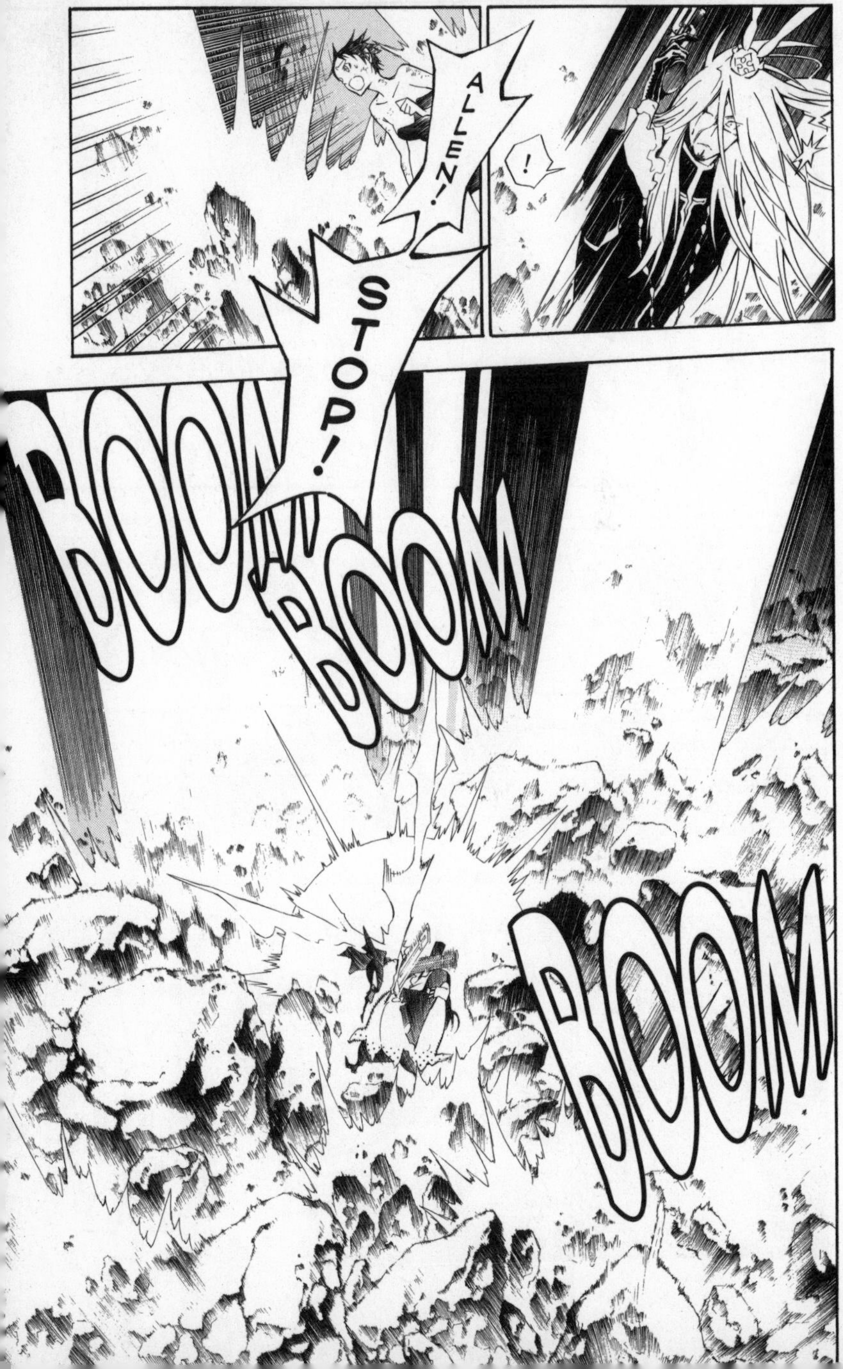
!
ALLEN!
STOP!
BOOM
BOOM
BOOM

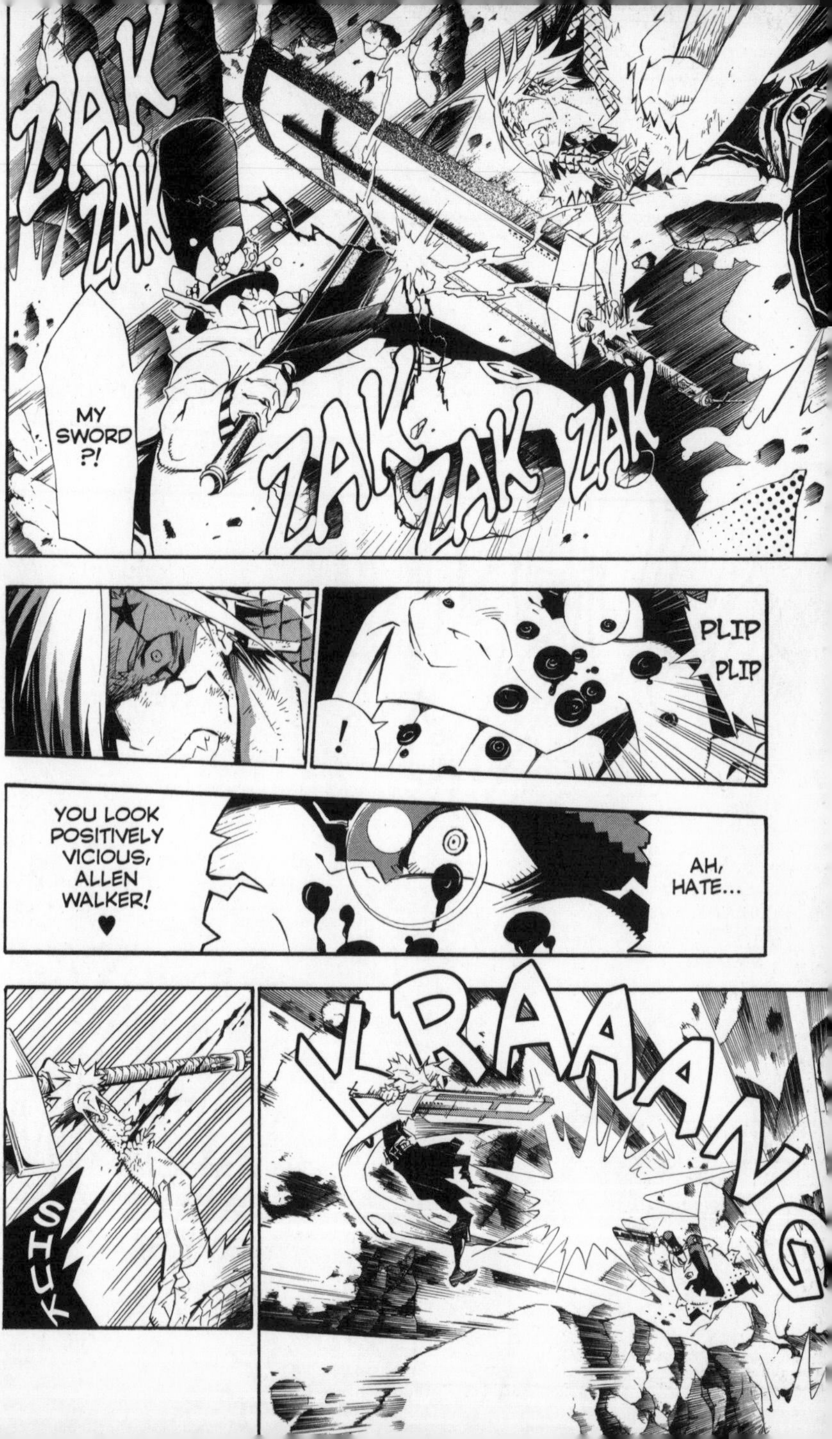
ZAK ZAK
MY SWORD ?!
ZAK ZAK ZAK
PLIP PLIP
!
AH, HATE...
YOU LOOK POSITIVELY VICIOUS, ALLEN WALKER! ♥
KRAAAANG
SHUK

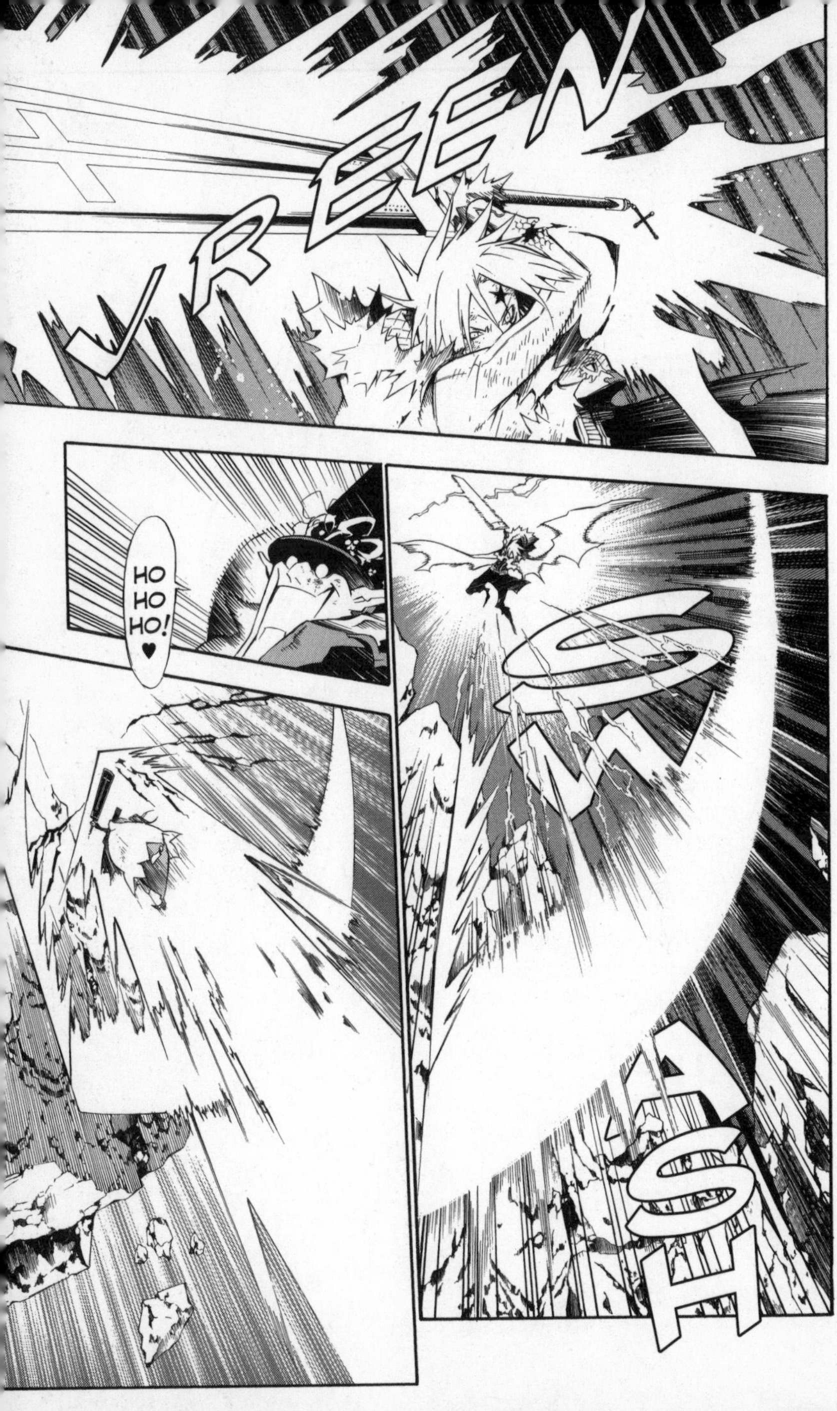
VREEN
SMASH
HO HO HO! ♥

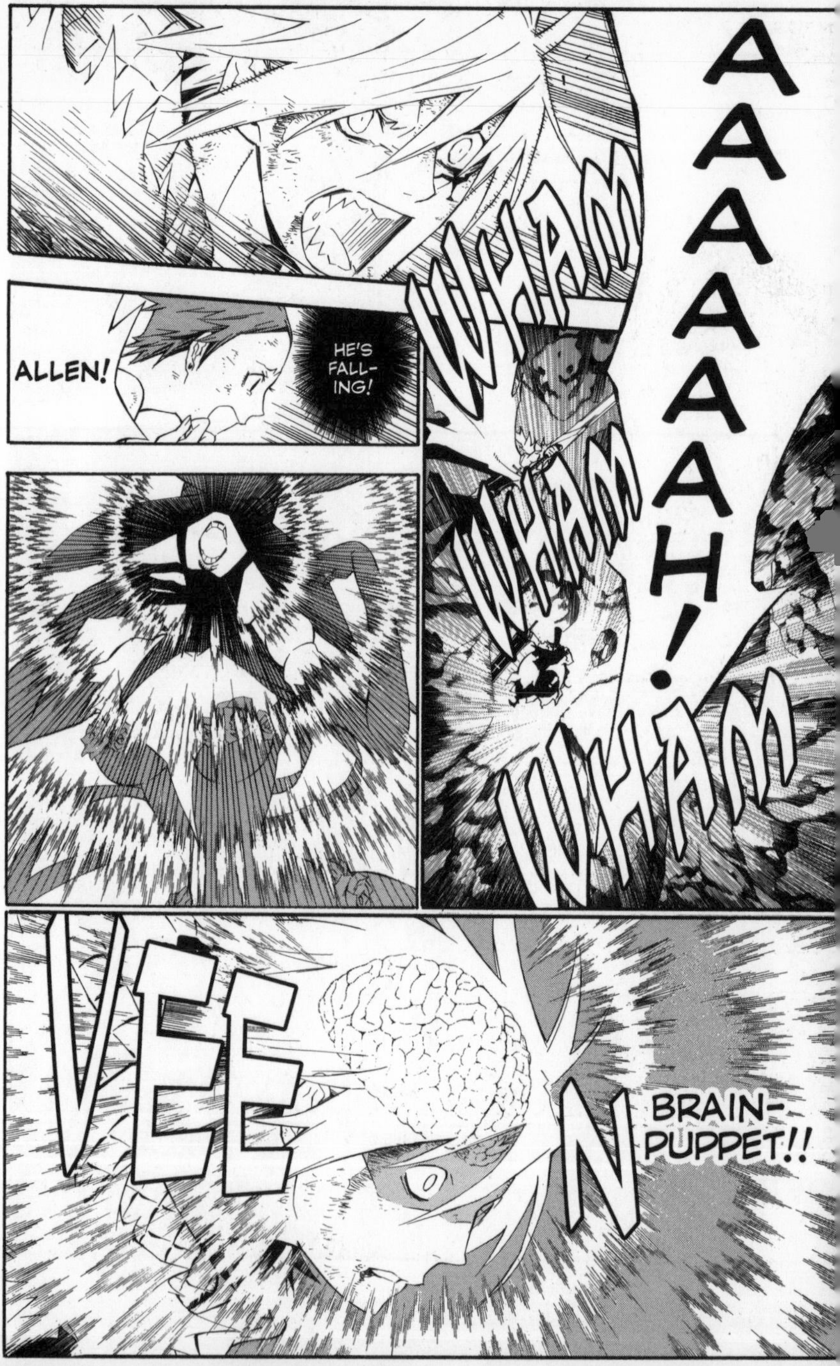
AAAAAH!
WHAM
WHAM
WHAM
HE'S FALLING!
ALLEN!
VEEN
BRAIN-PUPPET!!

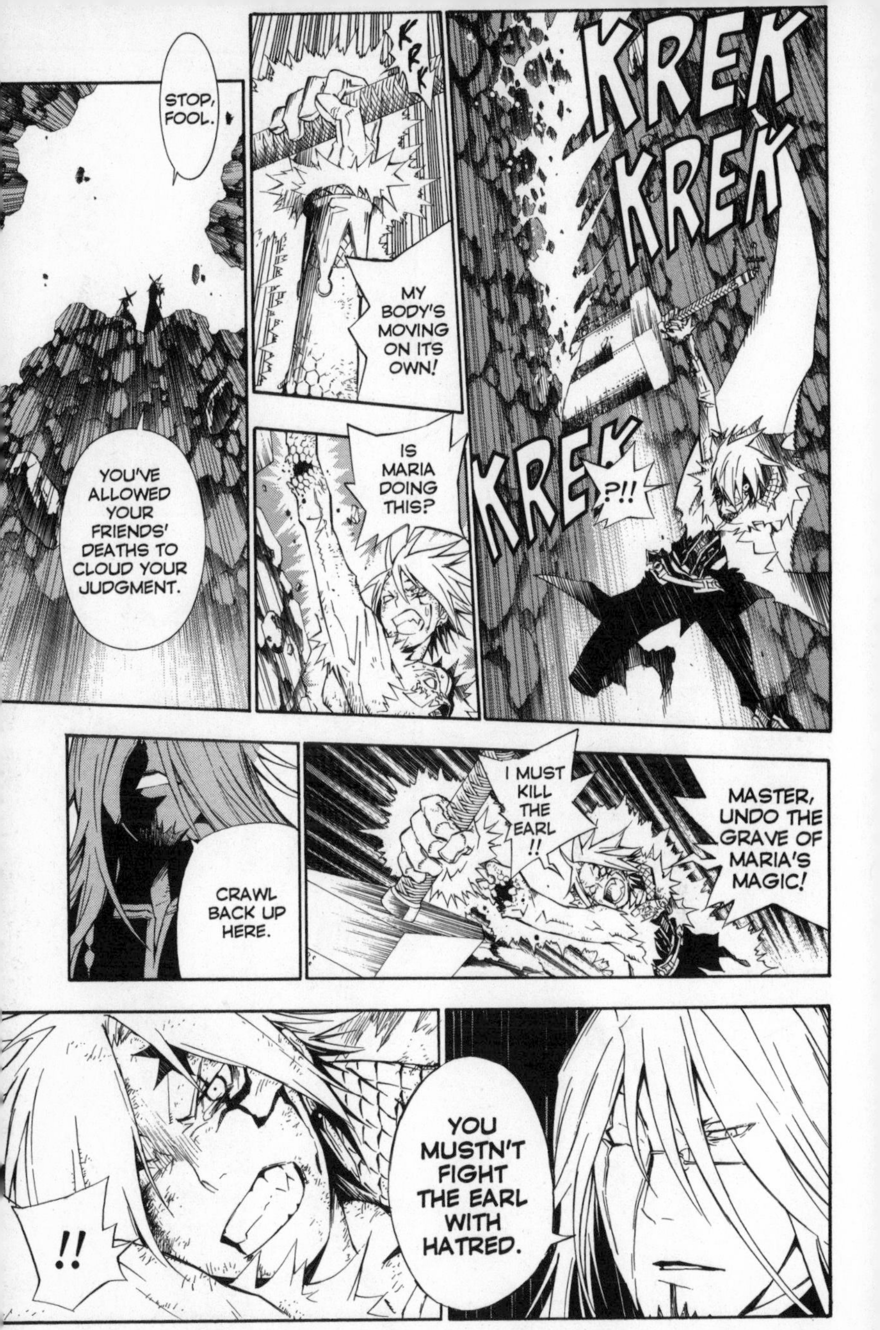
KREK
KREK
KREK
?!!
KRK
MY BODY'S MOVING ON ITS OWN!
IS MARIA DOING THIS?
STOP, FOOL.
YOU'VE ALLOWED YOUR FRIENDS' DEATHS TO CLOUD YOUR JUDGMENT.
MASTER, UNDO THE GRAVE OF MARIA'S MAGIC!
I MUST KILL THE EARL !!
CRAWL BACK UP HERE.
YOU MUSTN'T FIGHT THE EARL WITH HATRED.
!!

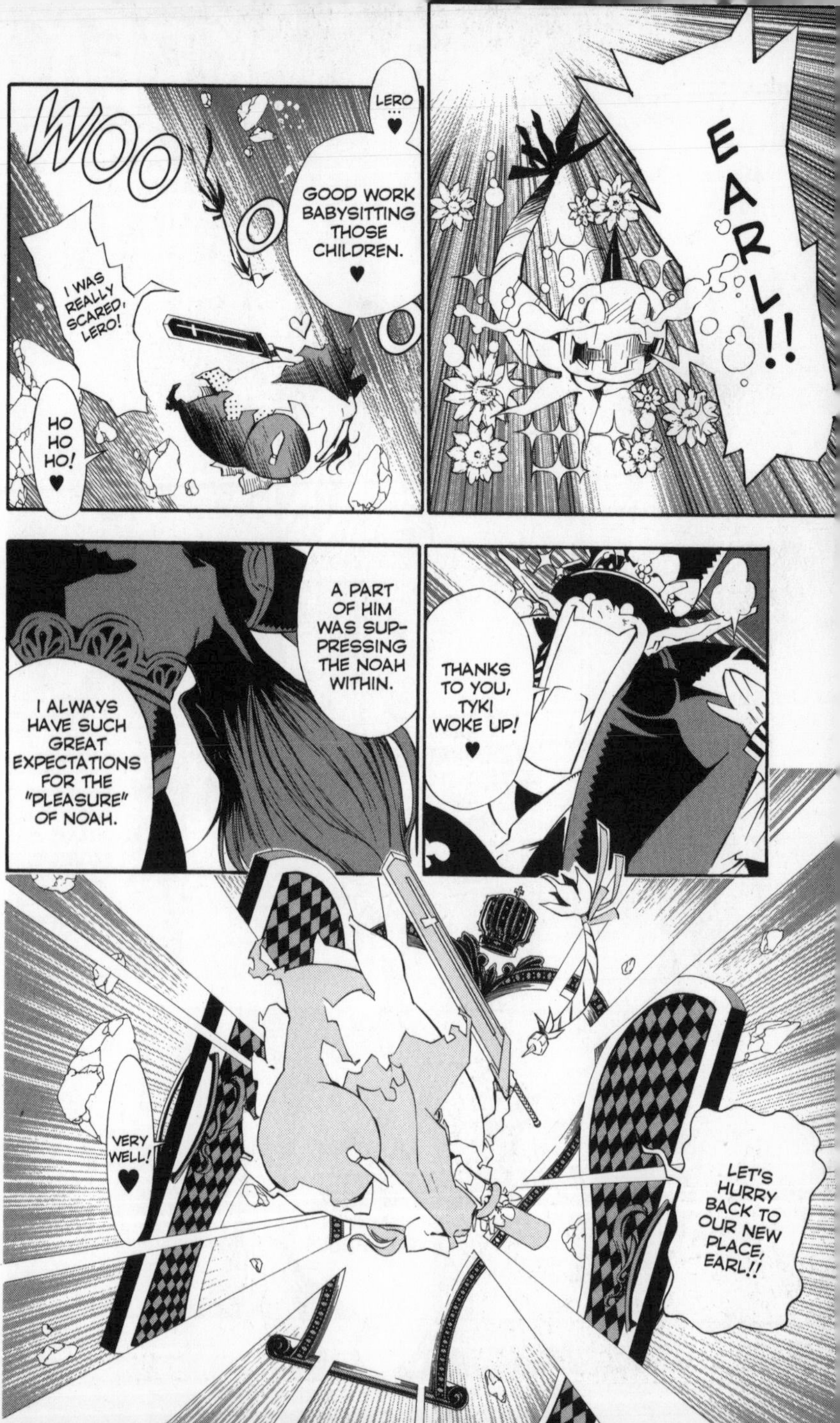
EARL!!
LERO... ♥
GOOD WORK BABYSITTING THOSE CHILDREN. ♥
WOOO
I WAS REALLY SCARED, LERO!
HO HO HO! ♥
THANKS TO YOU, TYKI WOKE UP! ♥
A PART OF HIM WAS SUP-PRESSING THE NOAH WITHIN.
I ALWAYS HAVE SUCH GREAT EXPECTATIONS FOR THE "PLEASURE" OF NOAH.
LET'S HURRY BACK TO OUR NEW PLACE, EARL!!
VERY WELL! ♥

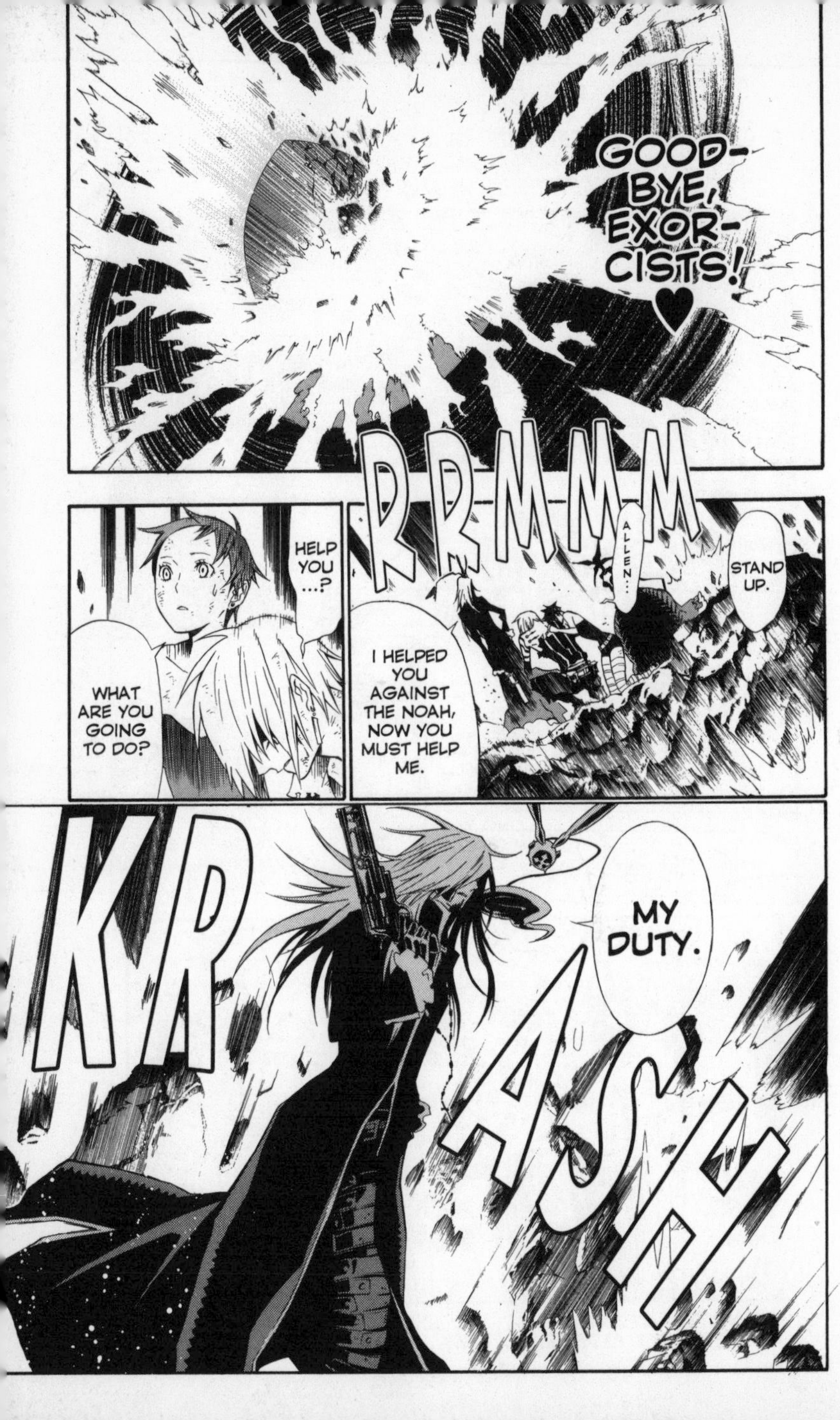
GOOD-BYE, EXORCISTS! ♥
RRMMM
STAND UP.
ALLEN...
I HELPED YOU AGAINST THE NOAH, NOW YOU MUST HELP ME.
HELP YOU ...?
WHAT ARE YOU GOING TO DO?
MY DUTY.
KRASH

Q. RECENTLY I NOTICED THAT KANDA YU'S INITIALS ARE K.Y. DOES THAT STAND FOR KUKI YOMENAI (SOMEONE WHO CAN'T READ THE MOOD OF THE PEOPLE AROUND HIM)?

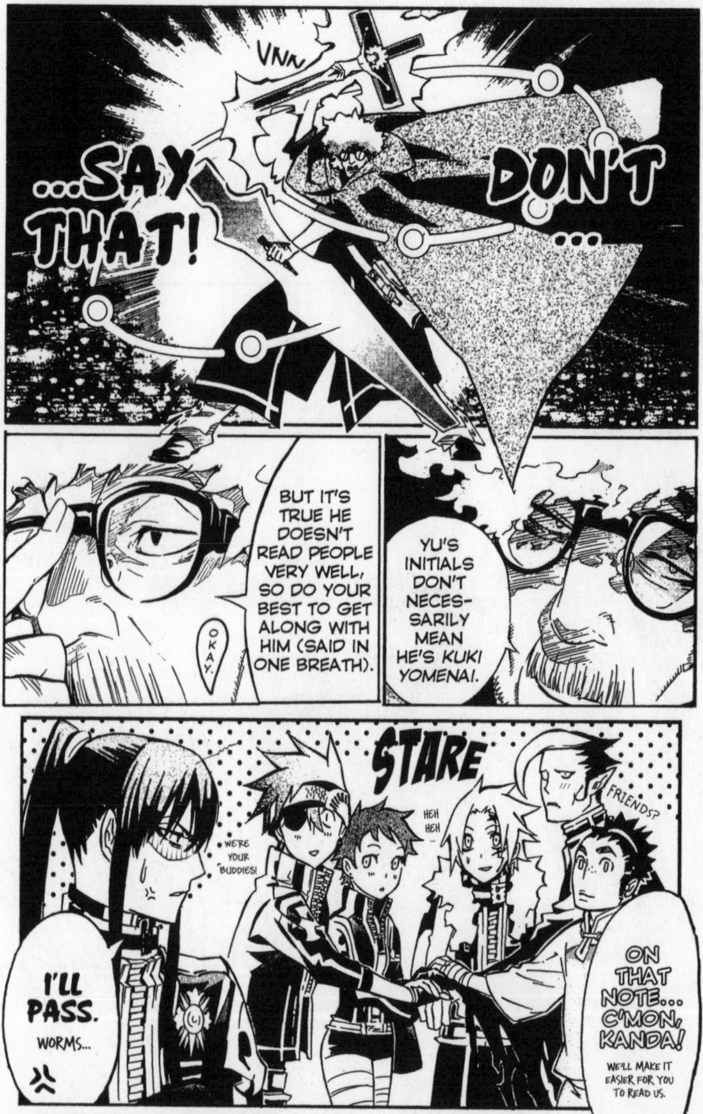
VNN
DON'T...
...SAY THAT!
YU'S INITIALS DON'T NECES-SARILY MEAN HE'S KUKI YOMENAI.
BUT IT'S TRUE HE DOESN'T READ PEOPLE VERY WELL, SO DO YOUR BEST TO GET ALONG WITH HIM (SAID IN ONE BREATH).
OKAY.
ON THAT NOTE... C'MON, KANDA!
WE'LL MAKE IT EASIER FOR YOU TO READ US.
FRIENDS?
STARE
HEH HEH
WE'RE YOUR BUDDIES!
I'LL PASS.
WORMS...

I HEARD THAT SOMEONE EVEN WORSE AT READING PEOPLE IS CALLED A S.K.Y. (SUPER KUKI YOMENAI).

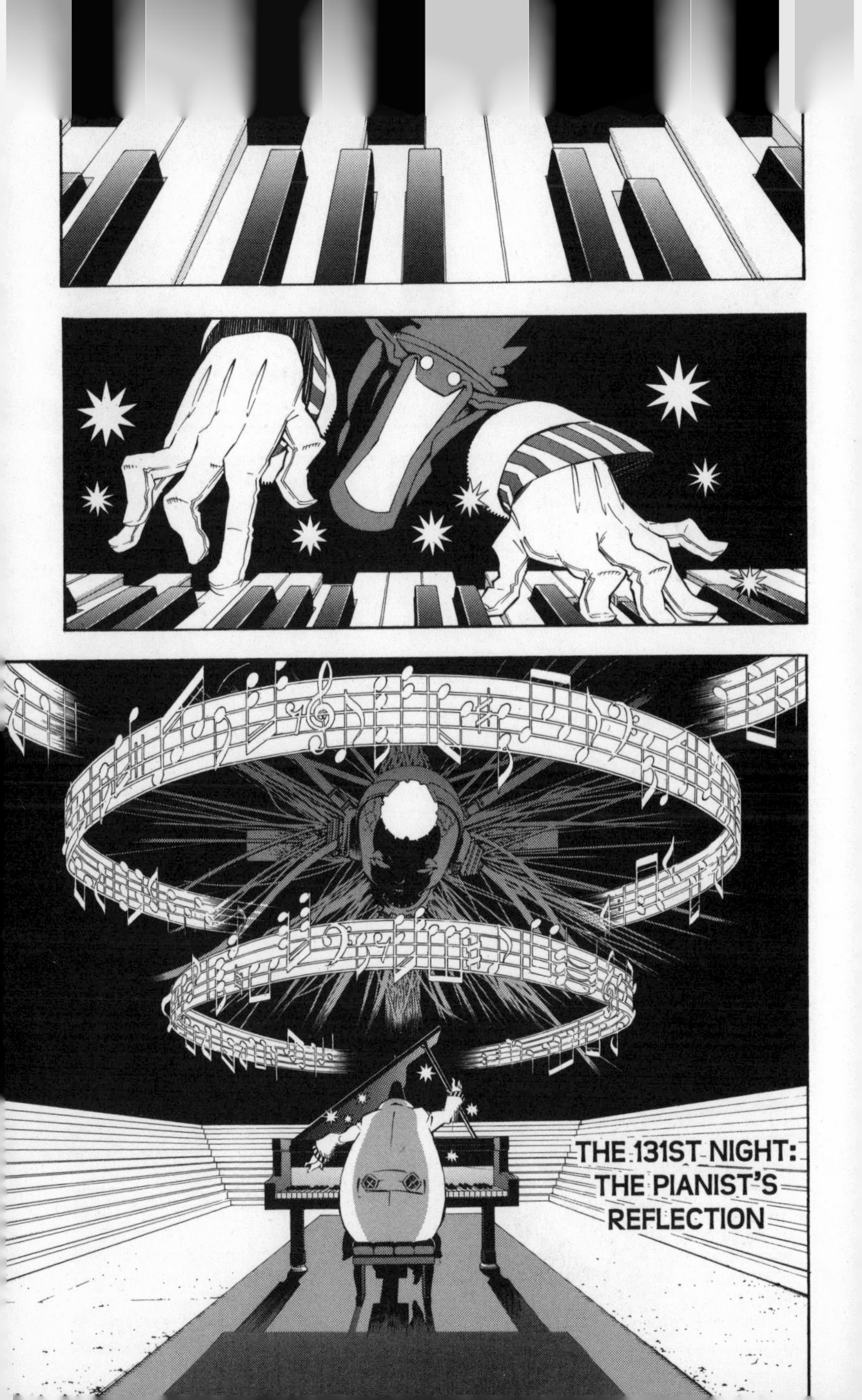
THE 131ST NIGHT: THE PIANIST'S REFLECTION

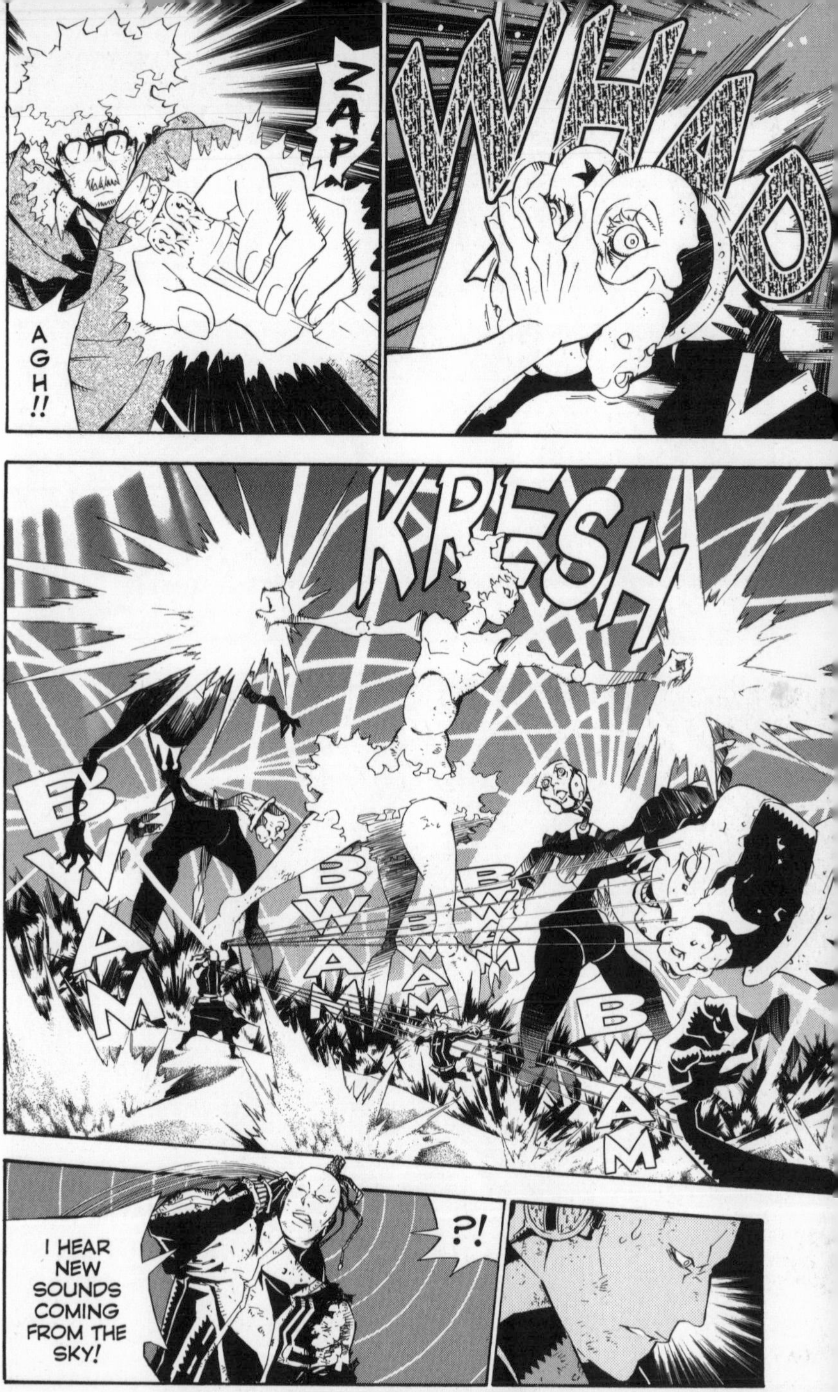

WHAO
ZAP
AGH!!
KRESH
BWAM
BWAM
BWAM
BWAM
BWAM
?!
I HEAR NEW SOUNDS COMING FROM THE SKY!

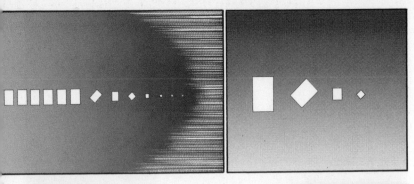

WHAT IS IT?!

?!

WHAT IS IT?
SOME-THING'S...
...UP THERE.

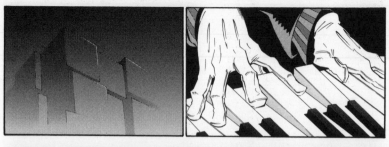

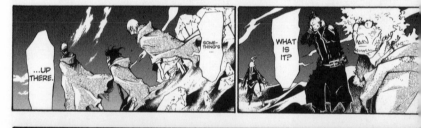

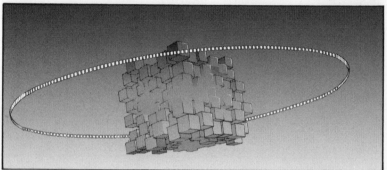

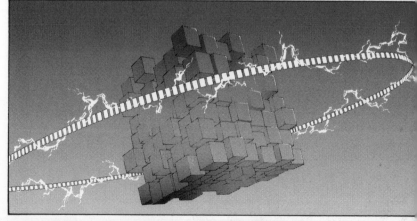

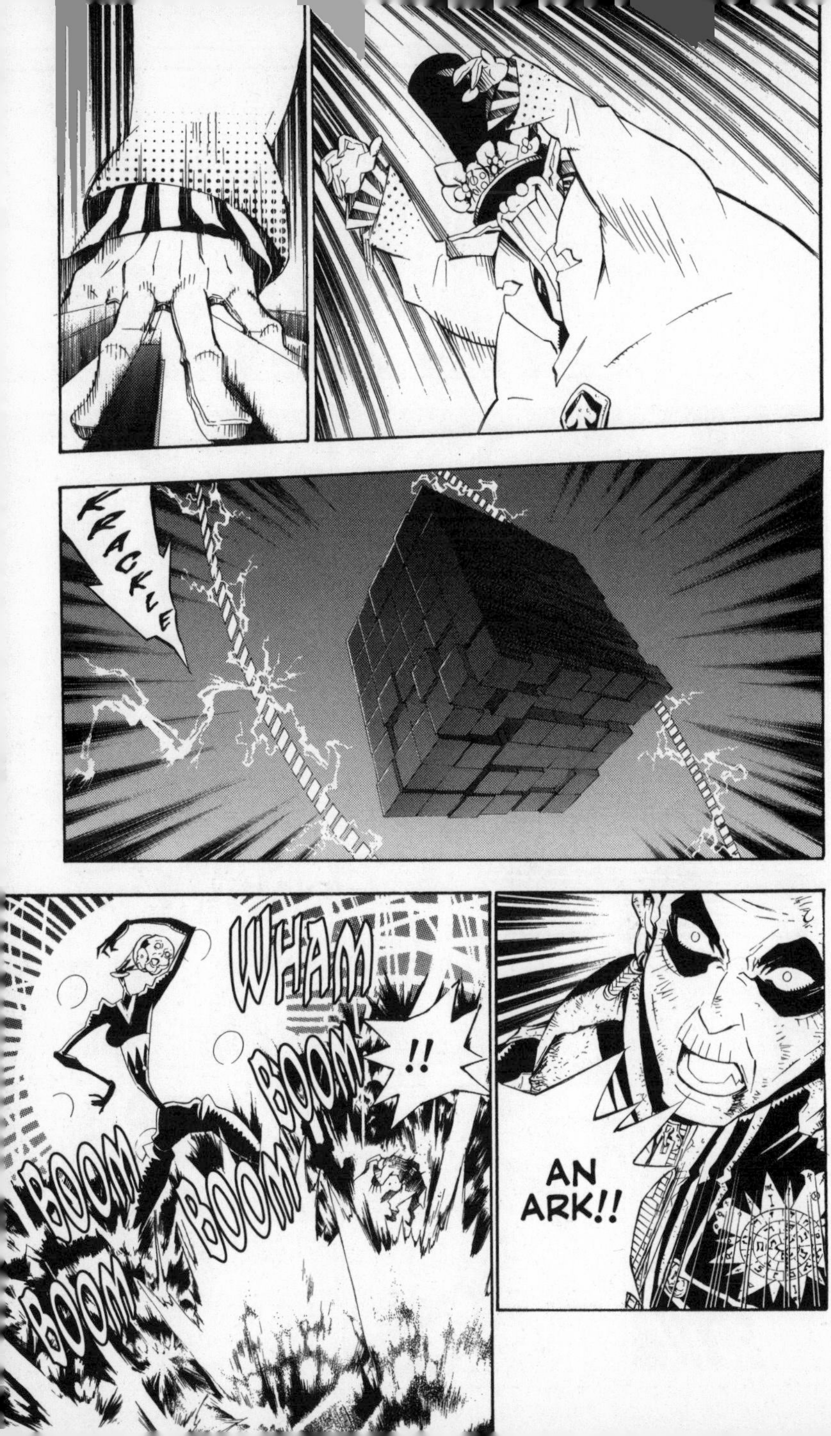
KRACKLE
AN ARK!!
WHAM
!!
BOOM
BOOM
BOOM
BOOM

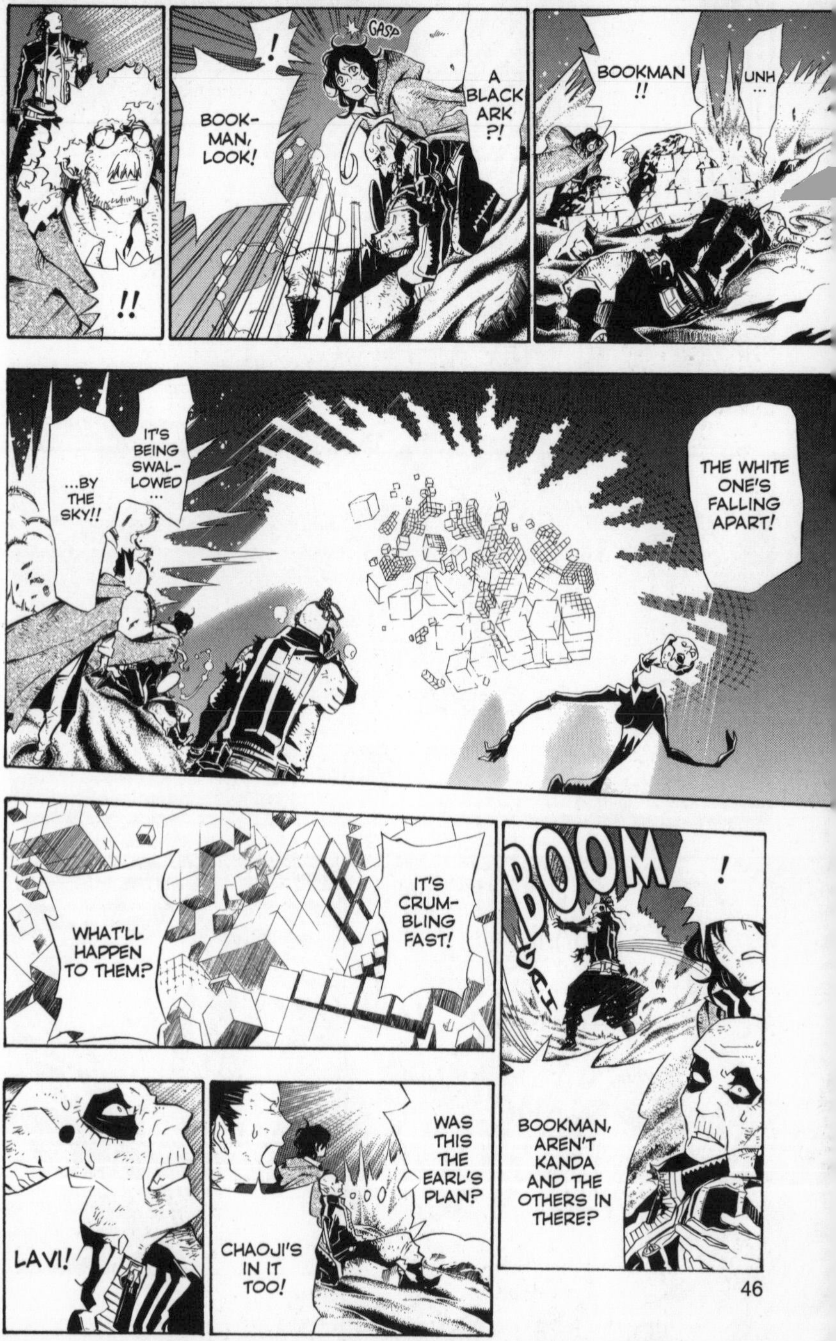
UNH ...
BOOKMAN !!
GASP
A BLACK ARK ?!
!
BOOK-MAN, LOOK!
!!
THE WHITE ONE'S FALLING APART!
IT'S BEING SWAL-LOWED ...
...BY THE SKY!!
!
BOOM
GAH
BOOKMAN, AREN'T KANDA AND THE OTHERS IN THERE?
IT'S CRUM-BLING FAST!
WHAT'LL HAPPEN TO THEM?
WAS THIS THE EARL'S PLAN?
CHAOJI'S IN IT TOO!
LAVI!

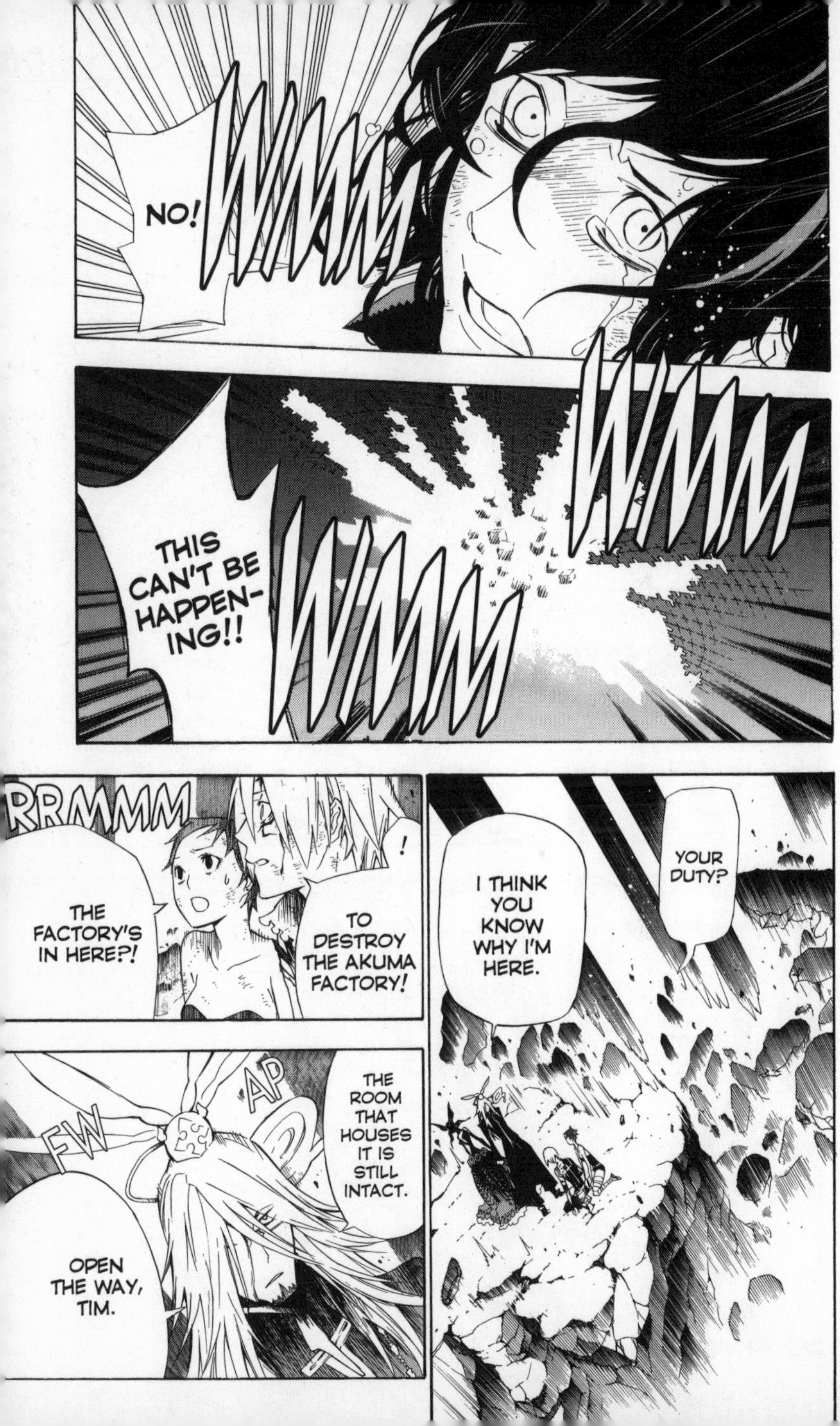
WMM
NO!
WMM
WMM
THIS CAN'T BE HAPPEN-ING!!
YOUR DUTY?
I THINK YOU KNOW WHY I'M HERE.
RRMMM
!
TO DESTROY THE AKUMA FACTORY!
THE FACTORY'S IN HERE?!
AP
FW
THE ROOM THAT HOUSES IT IS STILL INTACT.
OPEN THE WAY, TIM.

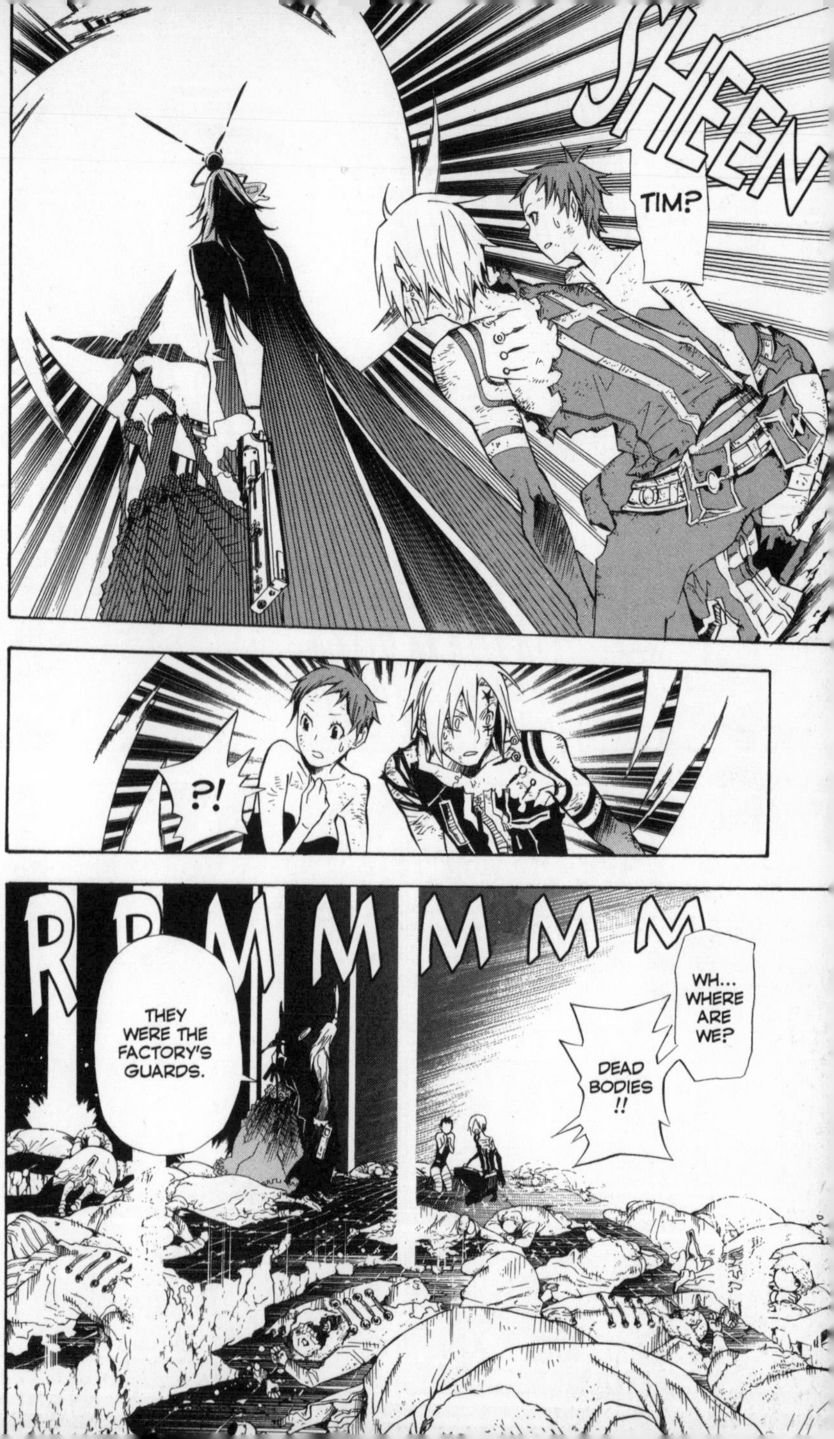
SHEEN
TIM?
?!
RRMMMMM
WH... WHERE ARE WE?
DEAD BODIES !!
THEY WERE THE FACTORY'S GUARDS.

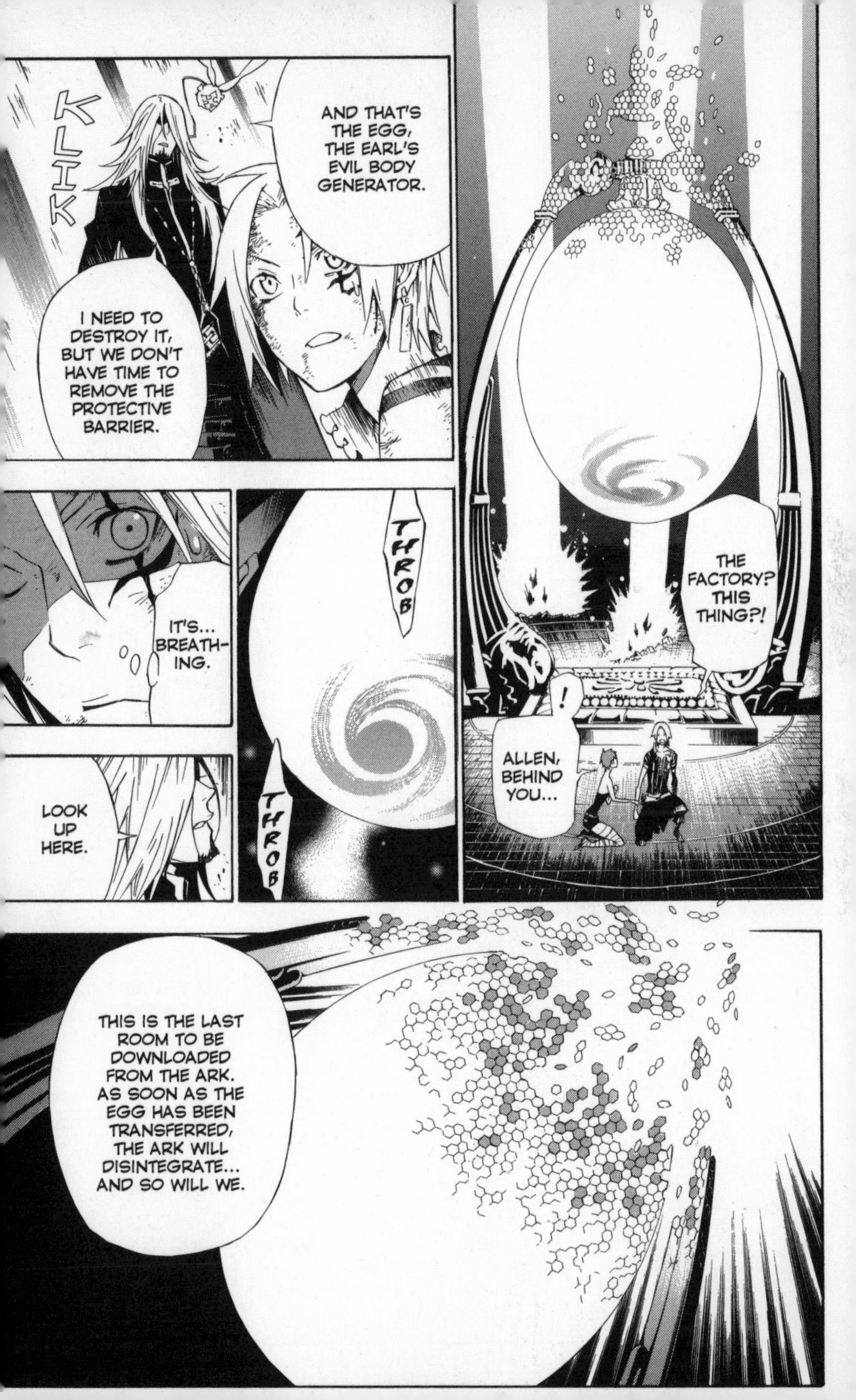
THE FACTORY? THIS THING?!
!
ALLEN, BEHIND YOU...
AND THAT'S THE EGG, THE EARL'S EVIL BODY GENERATOR.
KLIK
I NEED TO DESTROY IT, BUT WE DON'T HAVE TIME TO REMOVE THE PROTECTIVE BARRIER.
THROB
THROB
IT'S... BREATH-ING.
LOOK UP HERE.
THIS IS THE LAST ROOM TO BE DOWNLOADED FROM THE ARK. AS SOON AS THE EGG HAS BEEN TRANSFERRED, THE ARK WILL DISINTEGRATE... AND SO WILL WE.

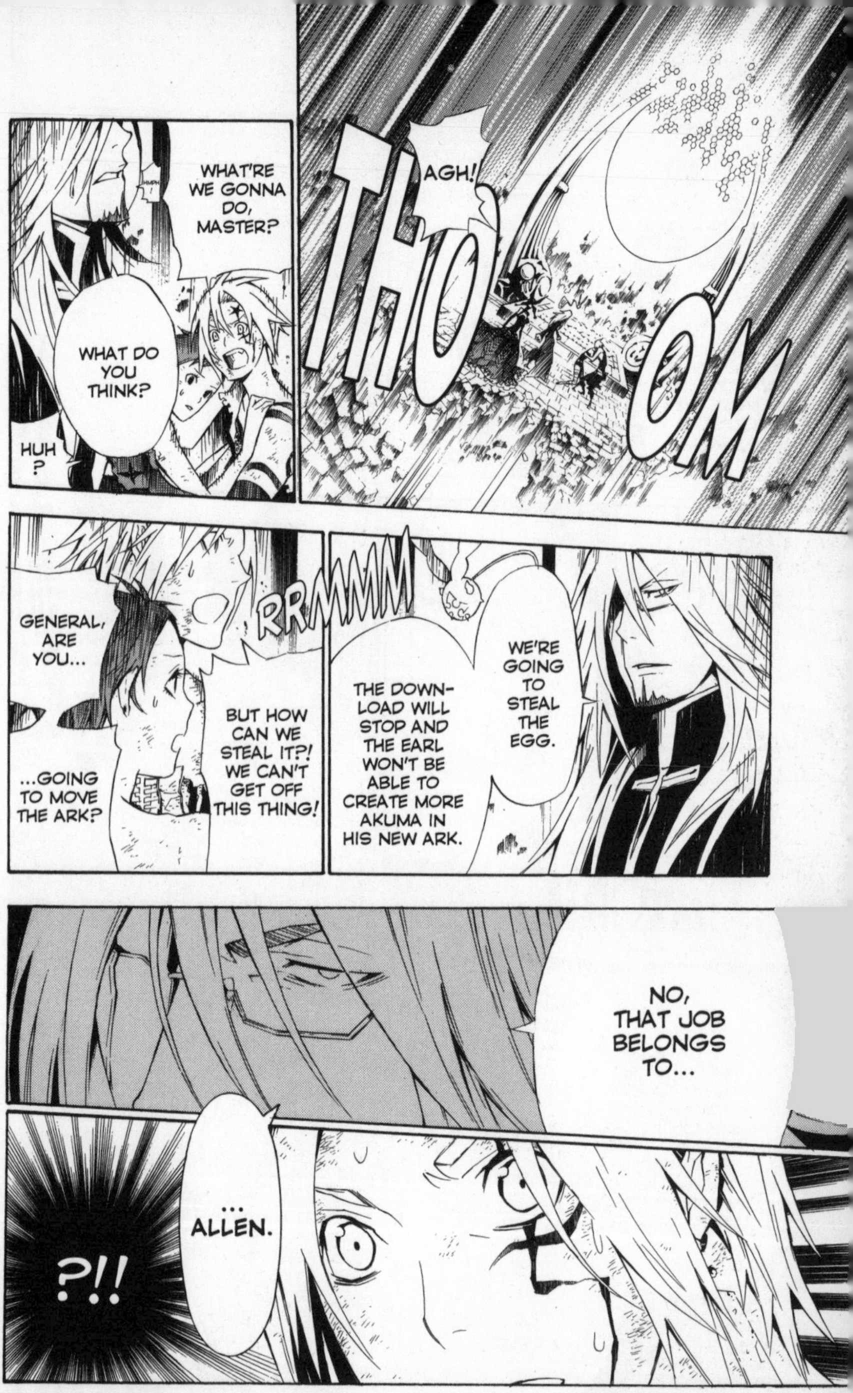
AGH!
THOOOM
WHAT'RE WE GONNA DO, MASTER?
HMPH
WHAT DO YOU THINK?
HUH?
RRMMM
WE'RE GOING TO STEAL THE EGG.
THE DOWN-LOAD WILL STOP AND THE EARL WON'T BE ABLE TO CREATE MORE AKUMA IN HIS NEW ARK.
BUT HOW CAN WE STEAL IT?! WE CAN'T GET OFF THIS THING!
GENERAL, ARE YOU...
...GOING TO MOVE THE ARK?
NO, THAT JOB BELONGS TO...
... ALLEN.
?!!

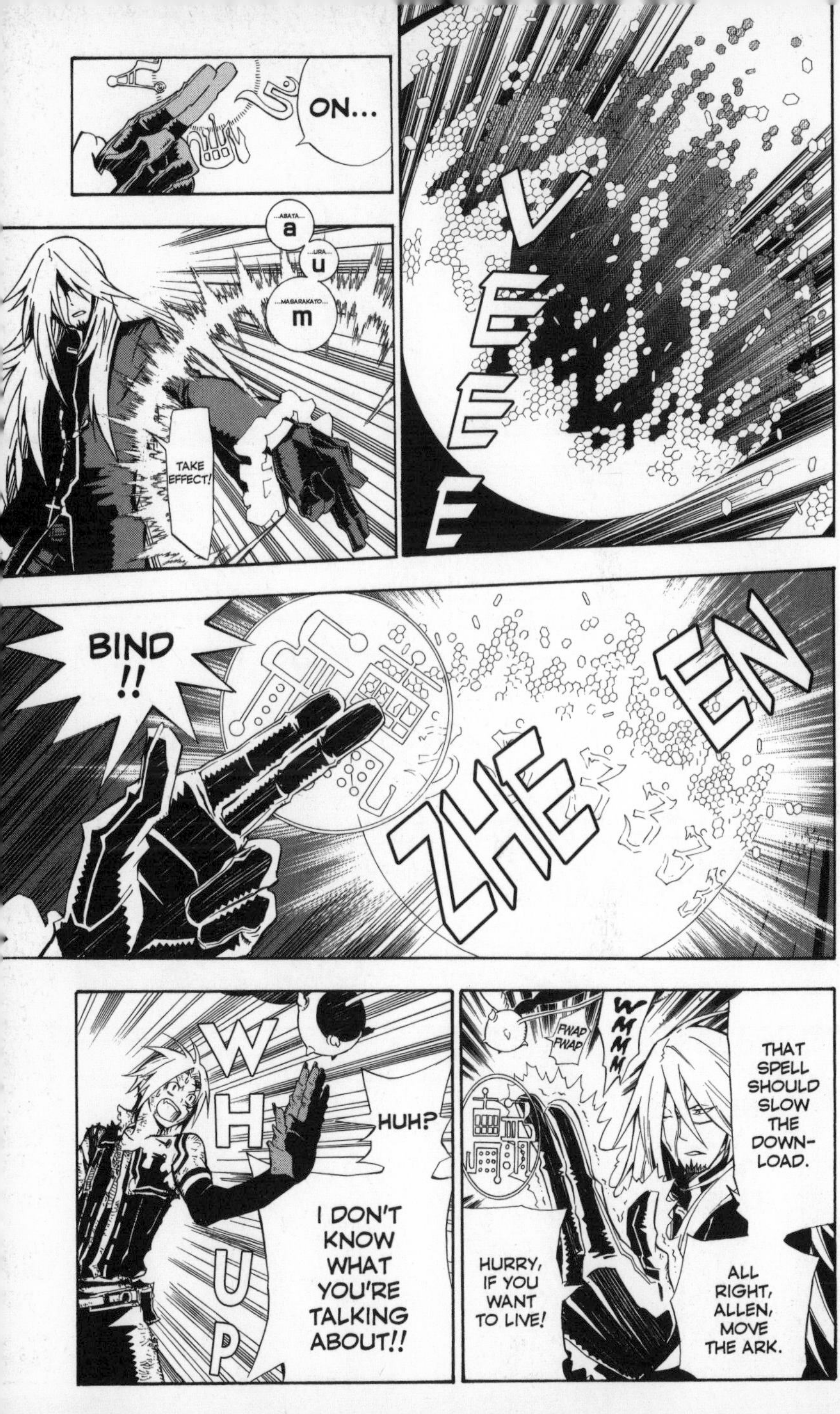
VEEEE
ON...
...ABATA...
a
...URA...
u
...MASARAKATO...
m
TAKE EFFECT!
BIND!!
ZHE EN
THAT SPELL SHOULD SLOW THE DOWN-LOAD.
ALL RIGHT, ALLEN, MOVE THE ARK.
WMMM
FWAP FWAP
HURRY, IF YOU WANT TO LIVE!
HUH?
WHUP
I DON'T KNOW WHAT YOU'RE TALKING ABOUT!!

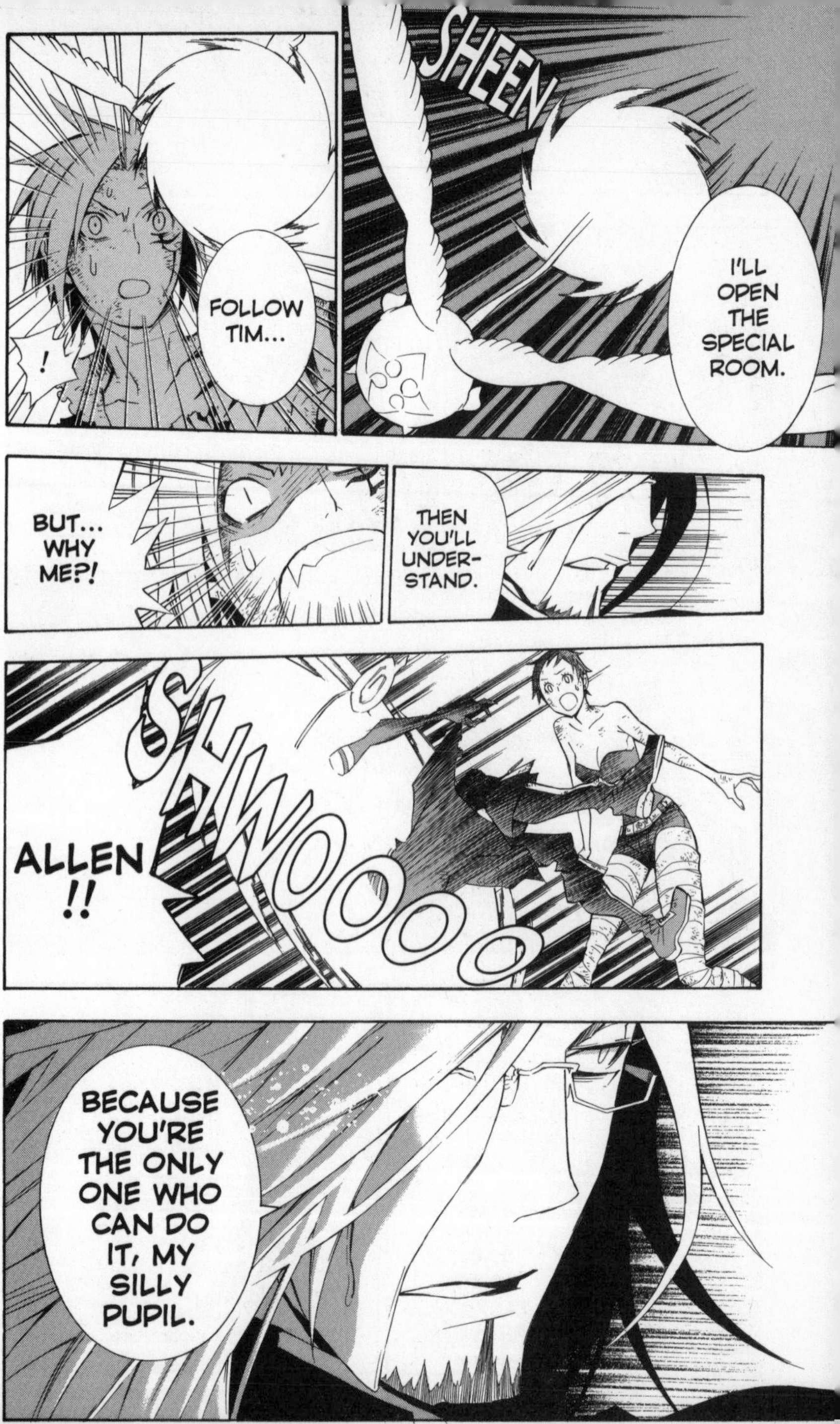
SHEEN
I'LL OPEN THE SPECIAL ROOM.
FOLLOW TIM...
!
THEN YOU'LL UNDER-STAND.
BUT... WHY ME?!
SHWOOOO
ALLEN!!
BECAUSE YOU'RE THE ONLY ONE WHO CAN DO IT, MY SILLY PUPIL.

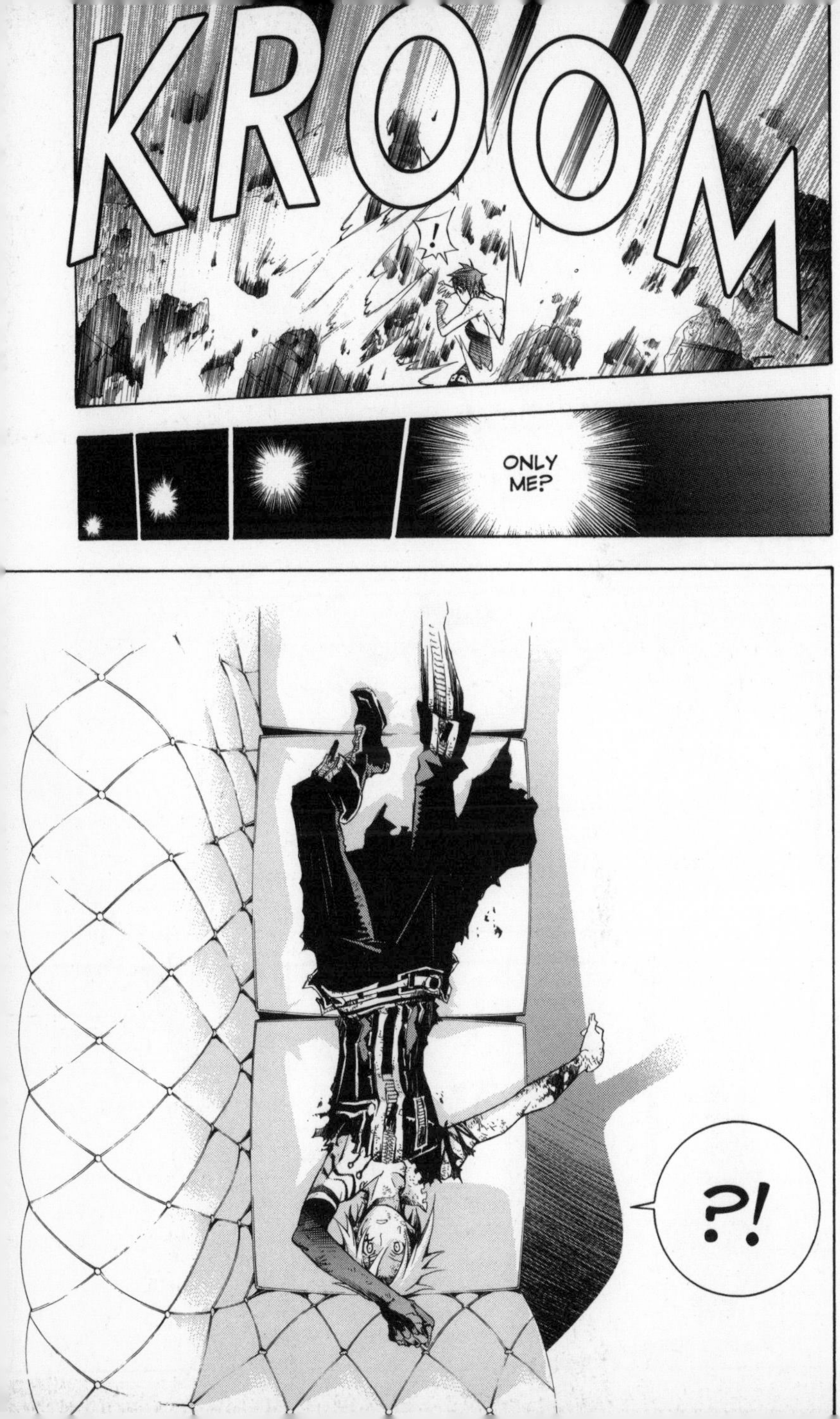
KROOM
!
ONLY ME?
?!

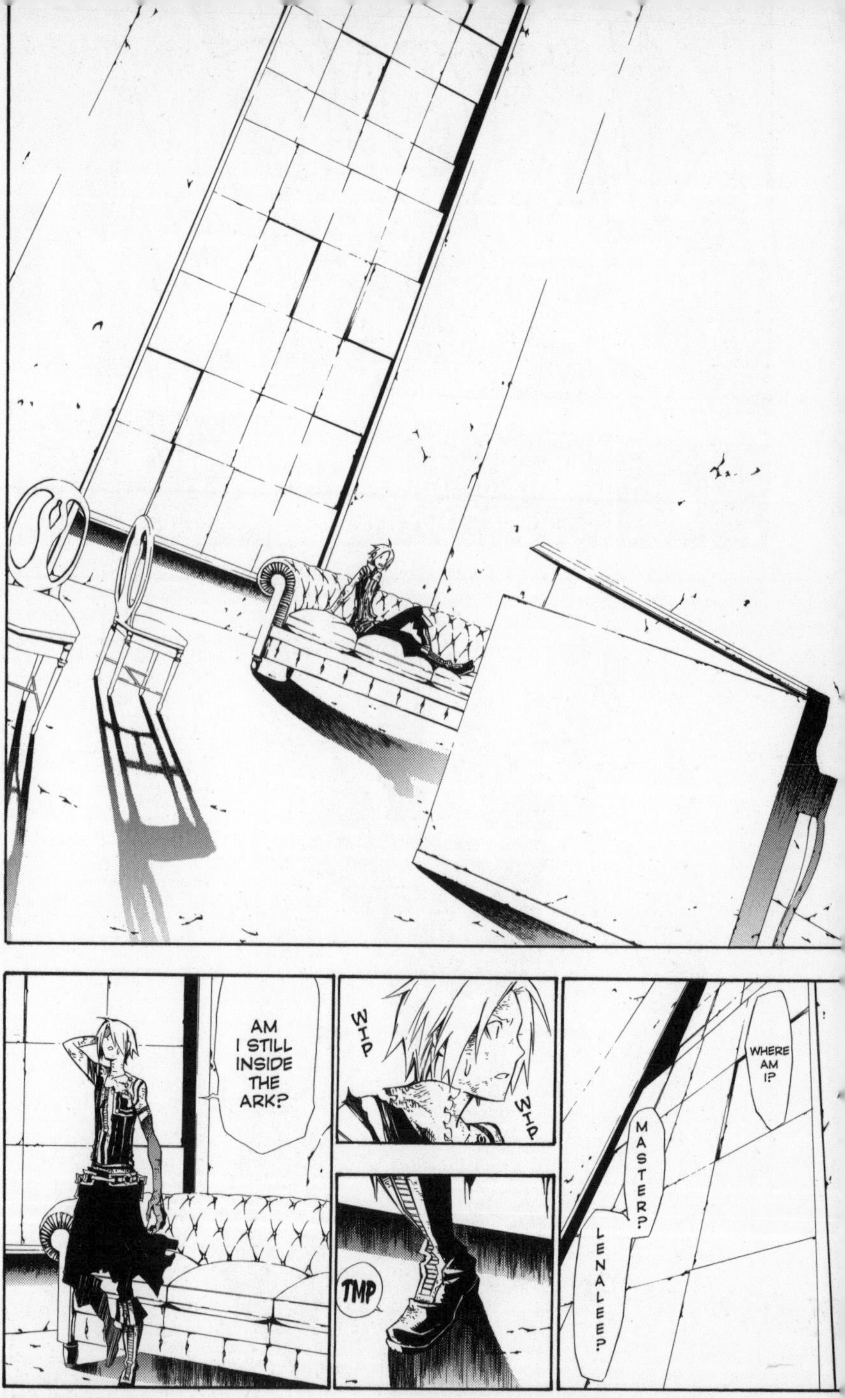
WHERE AM I?
MASTER?
LENALEE?
WIP
WIP
TMP
AM I STILL INSIDE THE ARK?

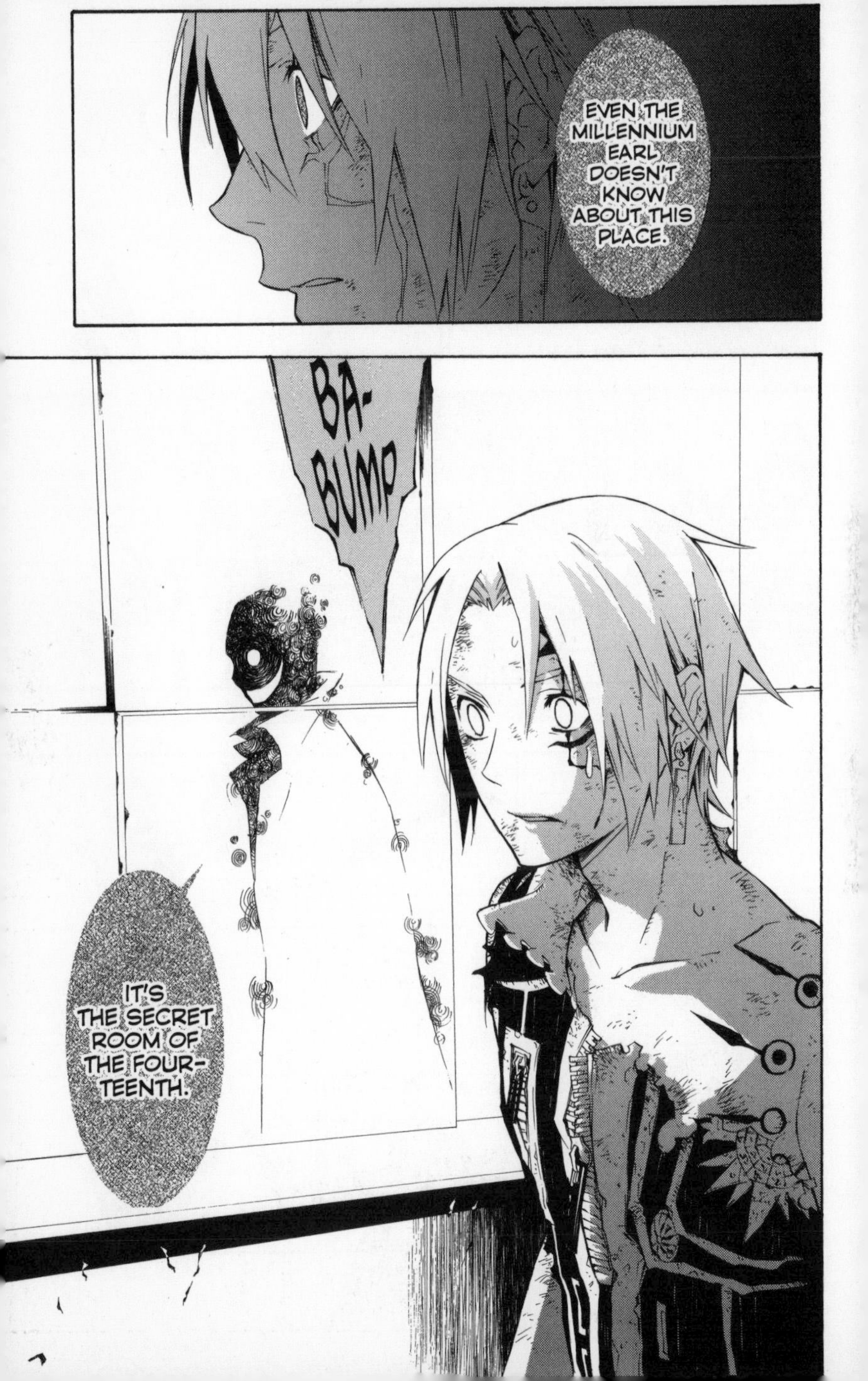
EVEN THE MILLENNIUM EARL DOESN'T KNOW ABOUT THIS PLACE.
BA-BUMP
IT'S THE SECRET ROOM OF THE FOUR-TEENTH.

BA-BUMP

NO...

WHO ARE YOU?!

THE DREAM I HAD WHERE LENALEE WAS CRYING?

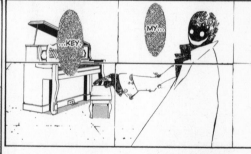

...KEY.

MY...

KEY?

?

MY...

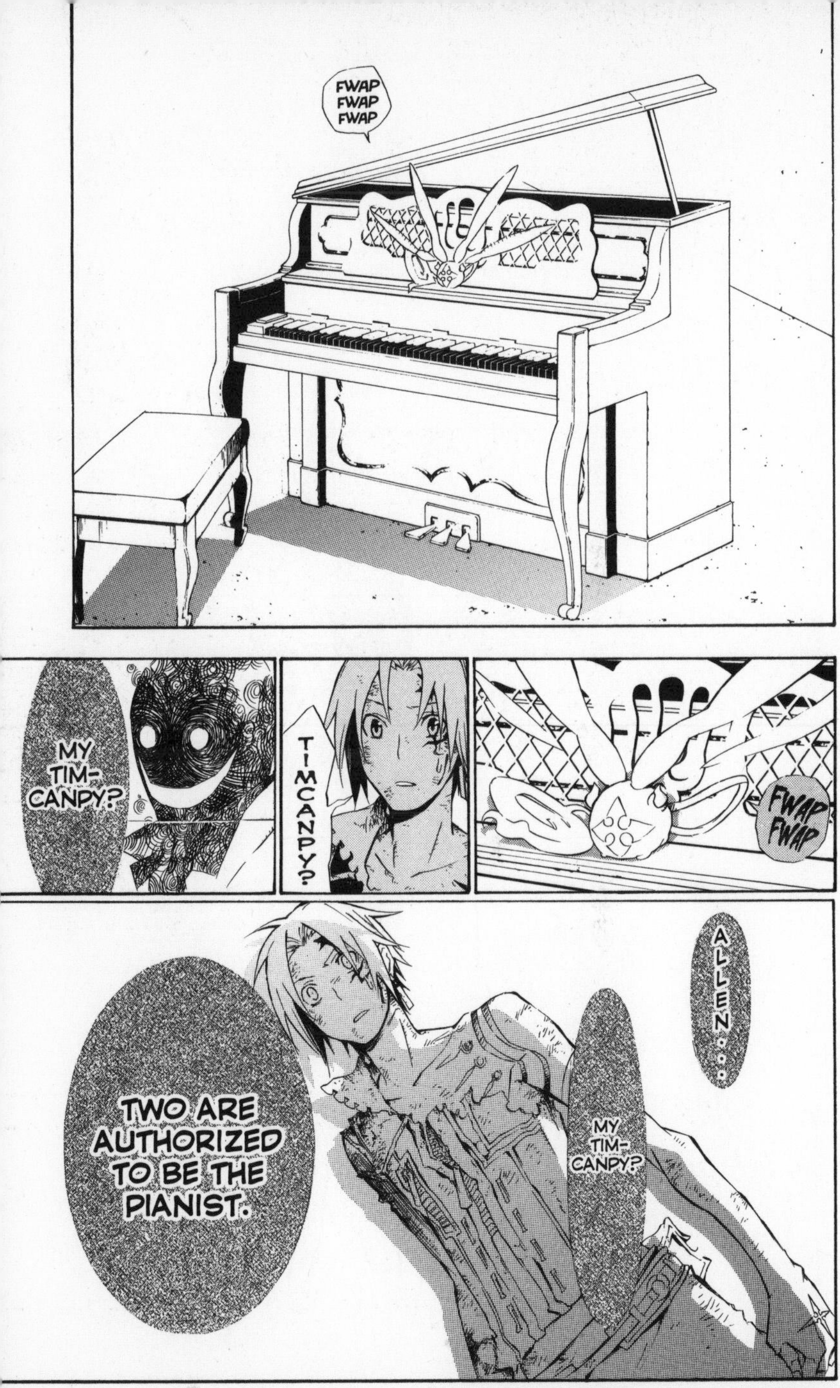
FWAP FWAP FWAP
FWAP FWAP
TIMCANPY?
MY TIM-CANPY?
ALLEN...
MY TIM-CANPY?
TWO ARE AUTHORIZED TO BE THE PIANIST.

## THE 132ND NIGHT: PIANIST?!!

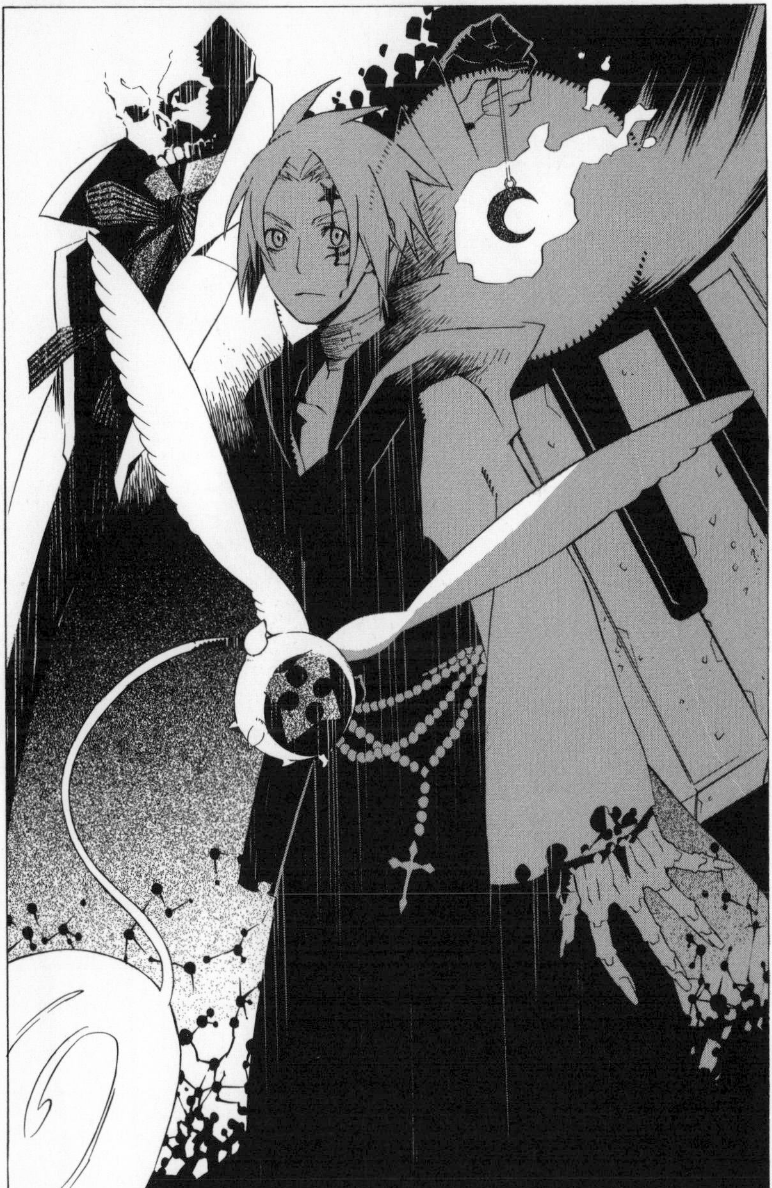

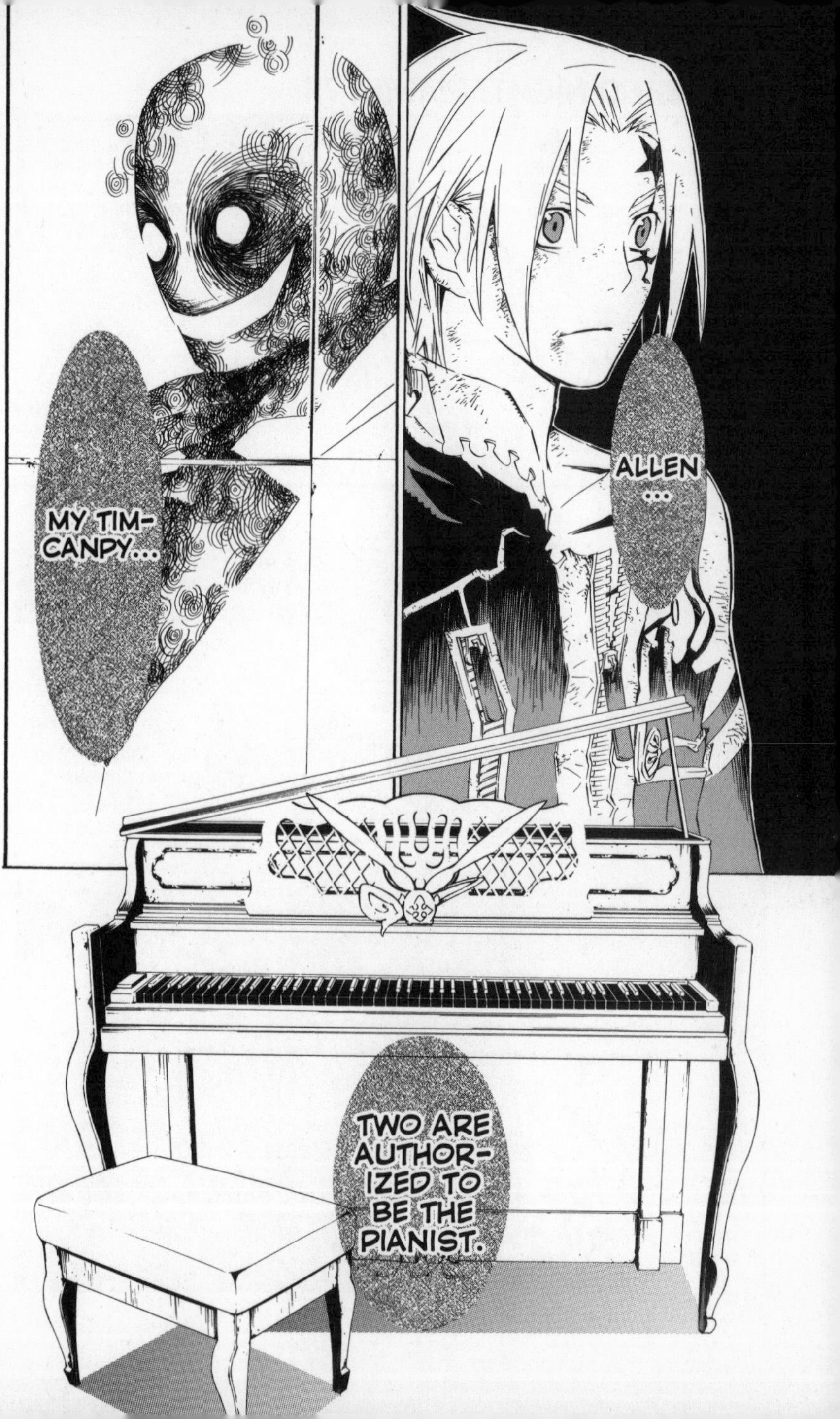
ALLEN ...
MY TIM-CANPY...
TWO ARE AUTHOR-IZED TO BE THE PIANIST.

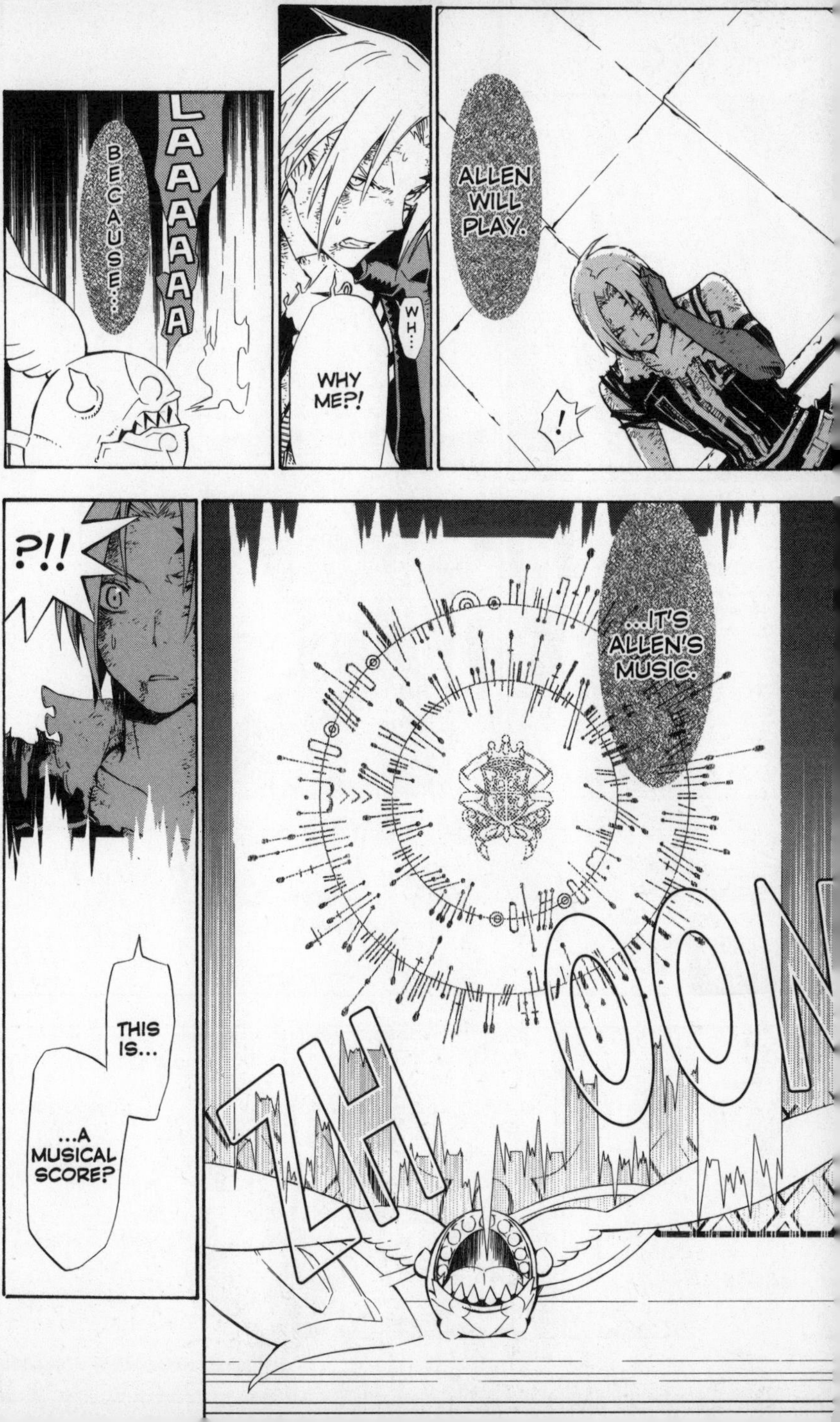
ALLEN WILL PLAY.
!
WH...
WHY ME?!
LAAAAAAA
BECAUSE...
...IT'S ALLEN'S MUSIC.
ZHOON
?!!
THIS IS...
...A MUSICAL SCORE?

READ THIS WAY

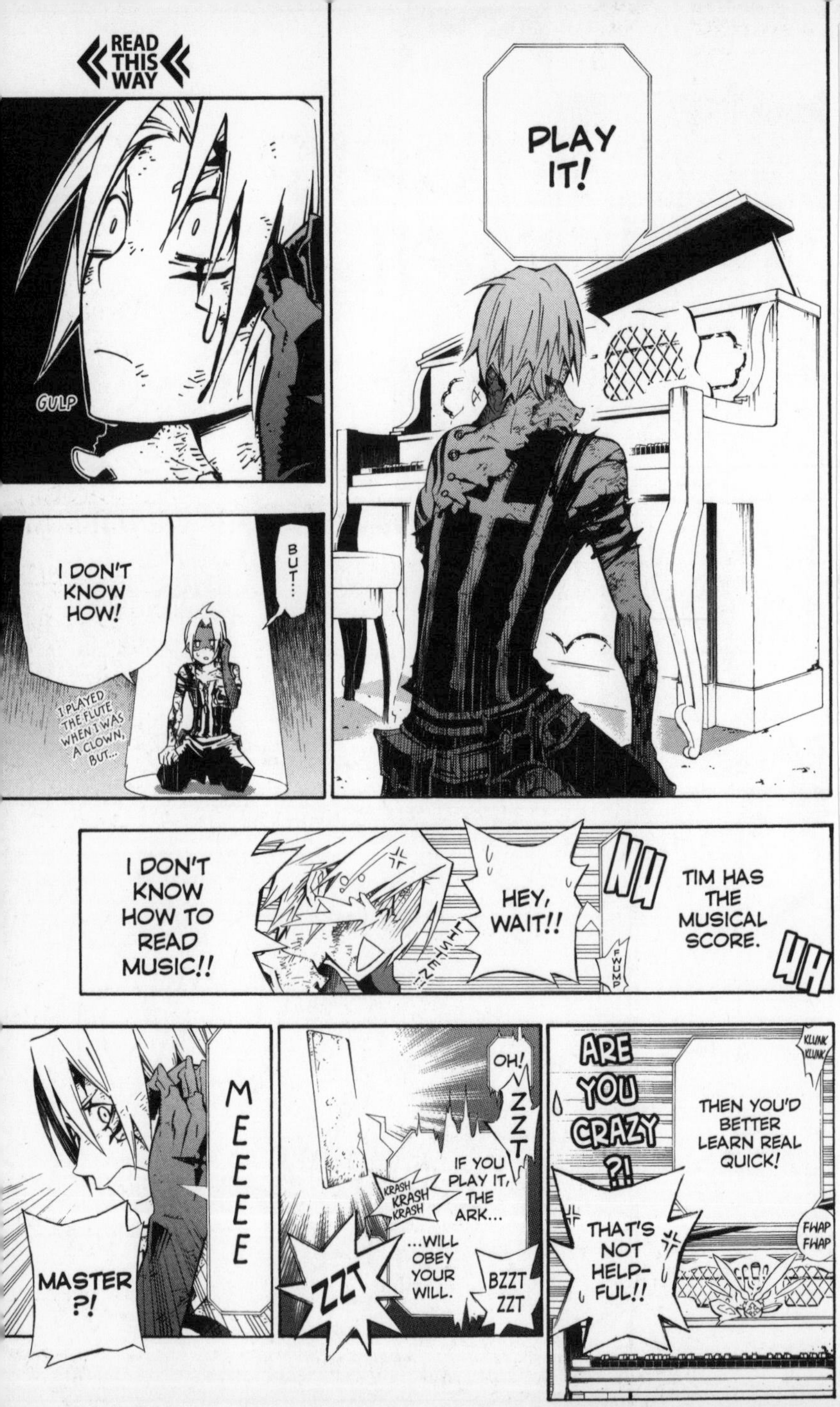
PLAY IT!
GULP
BUT...
I DON'T KNOW HOW!
I PLAYED THE FLUTE WHEN I WAS A CLOWN, BUT...
NUH UH
TIM HAS THE MUSICAL SCORE.
FWUMP
HEY, WAIT!!
I DON'T KNOW HOW TO READ MUSIC!!
KLUNK KLUNK
THEN YOU'D BETTER LEARN REAL QUICK!
ARE YOU CRAZY?!
FWAP FWAP
THAT'S NOT HELPFUL!!
OH!
ZZT
IF YOU PLAY IT, THE ARK...
KRASH KRASH KRASH
...WILL OBEY YOUR WILL.
BZZT ZZT
ZZT
MEEEE
MASTER?!

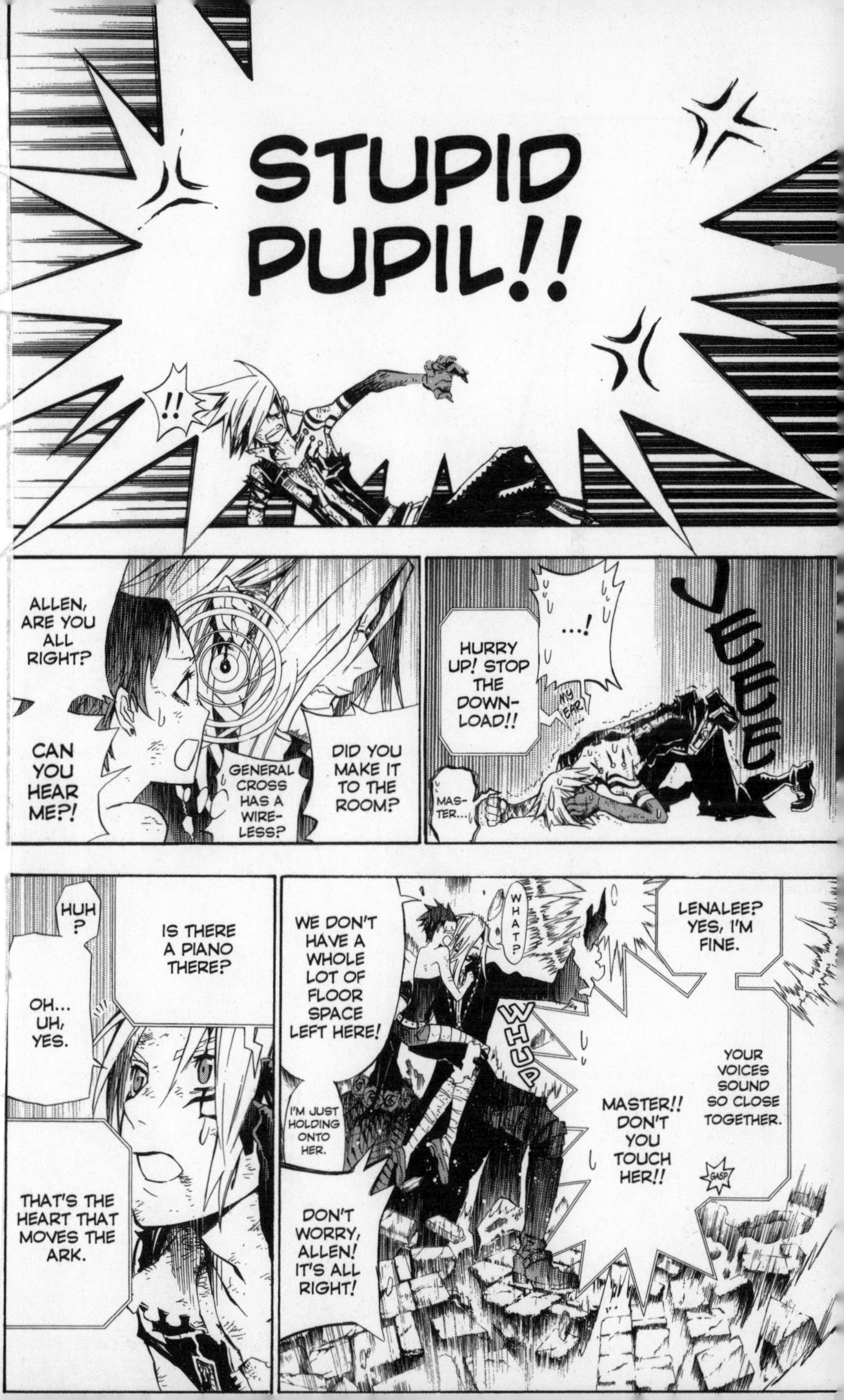
!!
STUPID PUPIL!!
JEEE
...!
HURRY UP! STOP THE DOWN-LOAD!!
MY EAR...
MAS-TER...
ALLEN, ARE YOU ALL RIGHT?
CAN YOU HEAR ME?!
GENERAL CROSS HAS A WIRE-LESS?
DID YOU MAKE IT TO THE ROOM?
LENALEE? YES, I'M FINE.
YOUR VOICES SOUND SO CLOSE TOGETHER.
GASP
WHAT?
WHUP
MASTER!! DON'T YOU TOUCH HER!!
WE DON'T HAVE A WHOLE LOT OF FLOOR SPACE LEFT HERE!
I'M JUST HOLDING ONTO HER.
DON'T WORRY, ALLEN! IT'S ALL RIGHT!
IS THERE A PIANO THERE?
HUH?
OH... UH, YES.
THAT'S THE HEART THAT MOVES THE ARK.

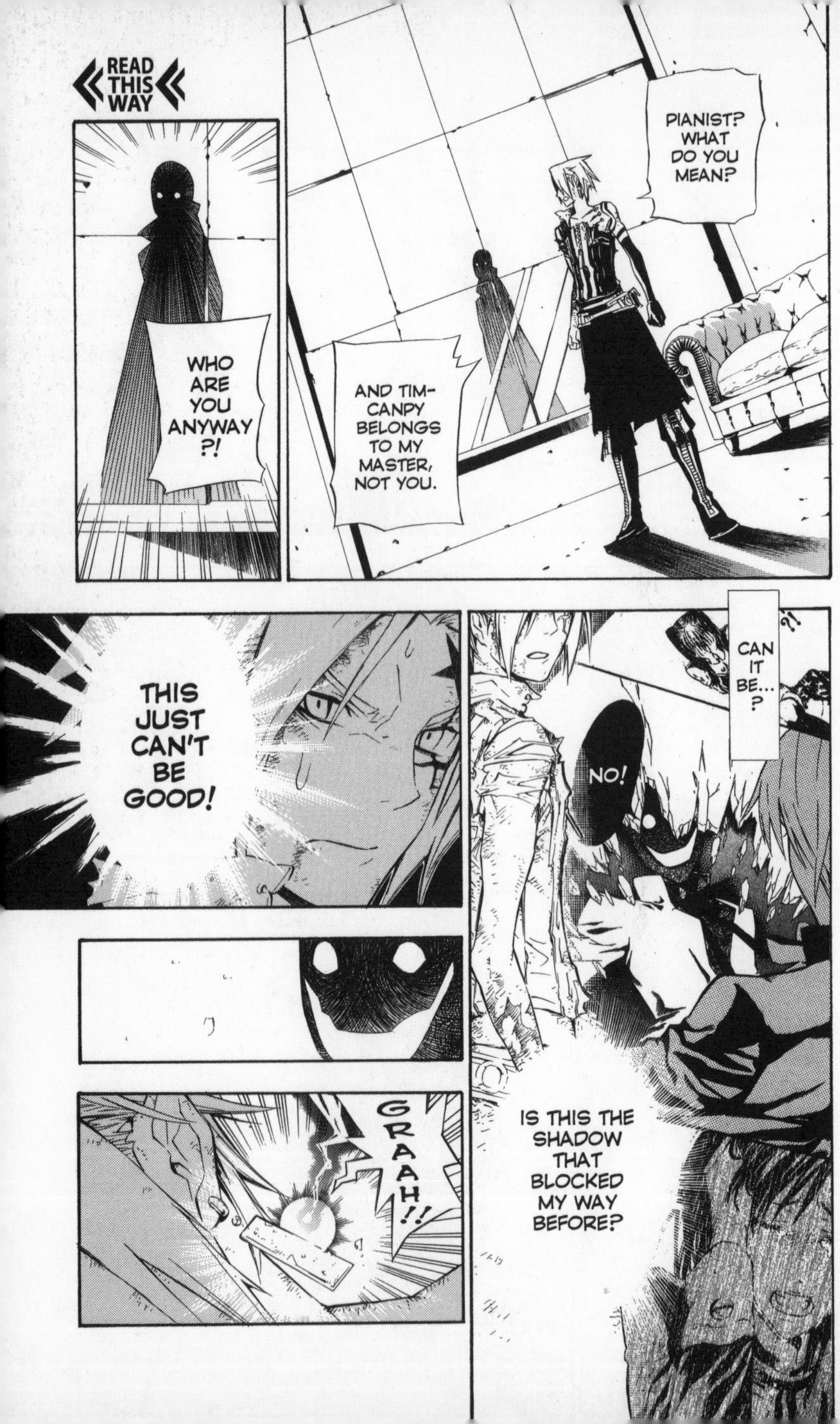
READ THIS WAY
PIANIST? WHAT DO YOU MEAN?
AND TIM-CANPY BELONGS TO MY MASTER, NOT YOU.
WHO ARE YOU ANYWAY ?!
?!
CAN IT BE...?
NO!
IS THIS THE SHADOW THAT BLOCKED MY WAY BEFORE?
THIS JUST CAN'T BE GOOD!
GRAAAH!!

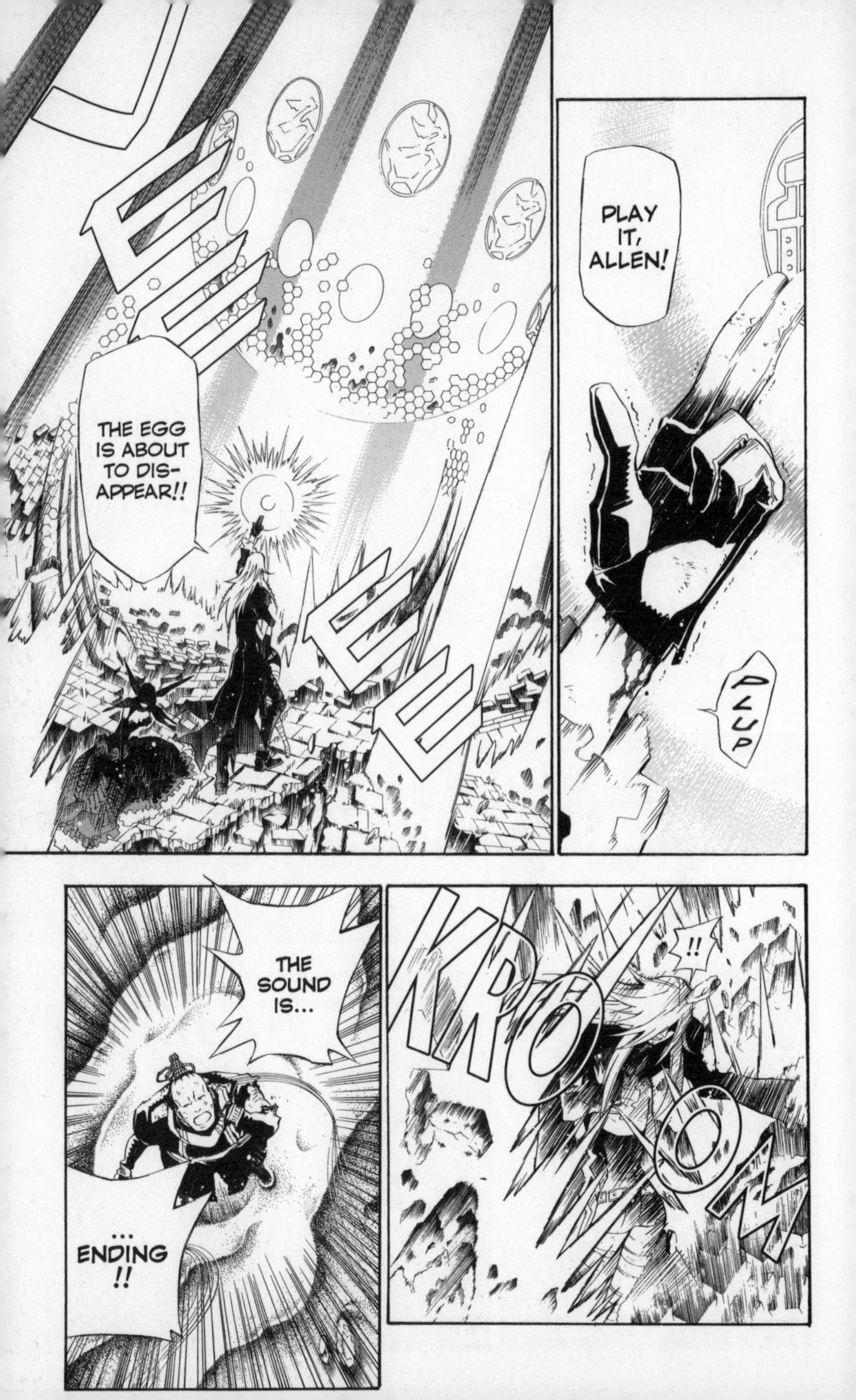
PLAY IT, ALLEN!
PLUP
THE EGG IS ABOUT TO DIS-APPEAR!!
KROOOM
!!
THE SOUND IS...
...ENDING!!

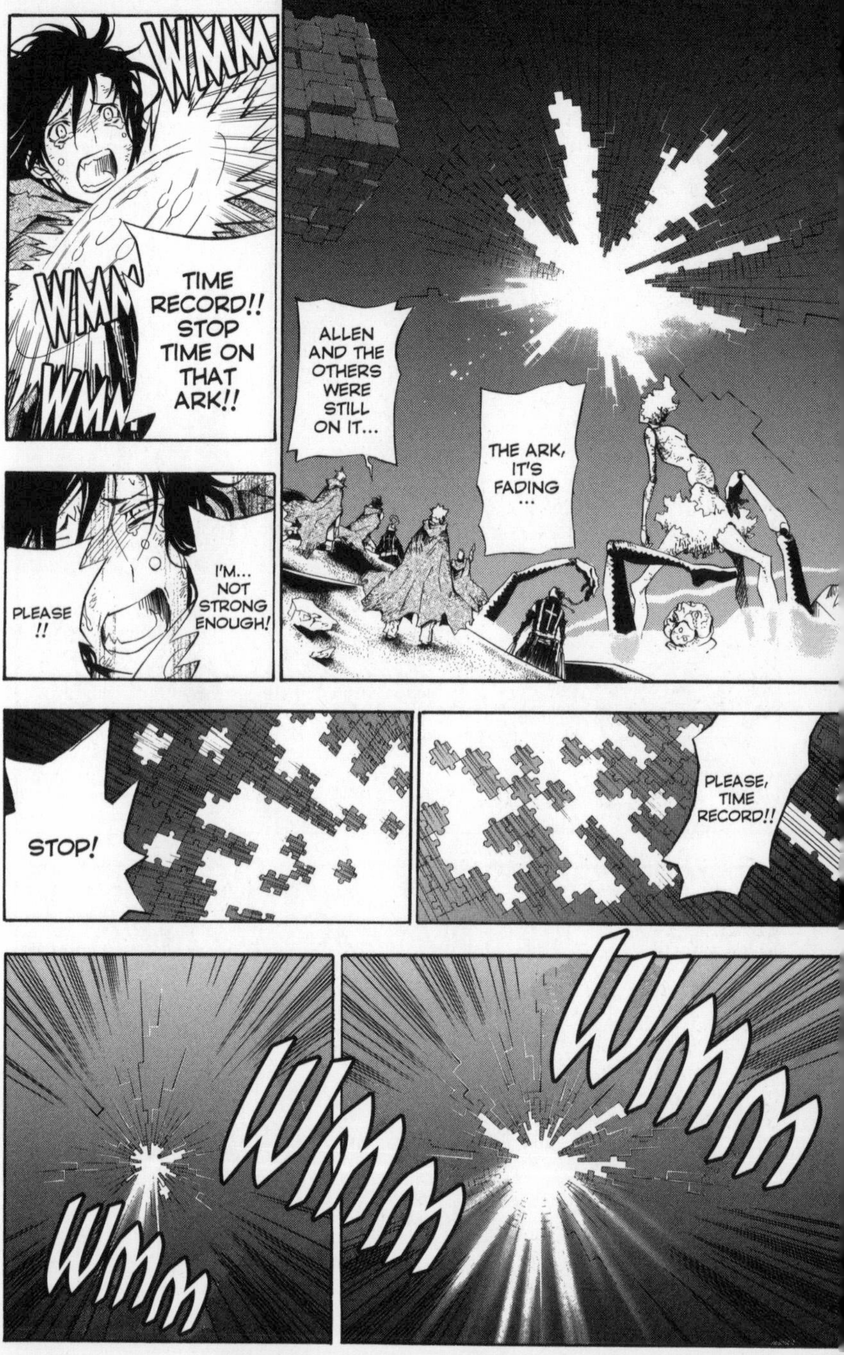
THE ARK, IT'S FADING ...
ALLEN AND THE OTHERS WERE STILL ON IT...
WMM
TIME RECORD!! STOP TIME ON THAT ARK!!
WMM
WMM
I'M... NOT STRONG ENOUGH!
PLEASE !!
PLEASE, TIME RECORD!!
STOP!
WMM
WMM
WMM
WMM

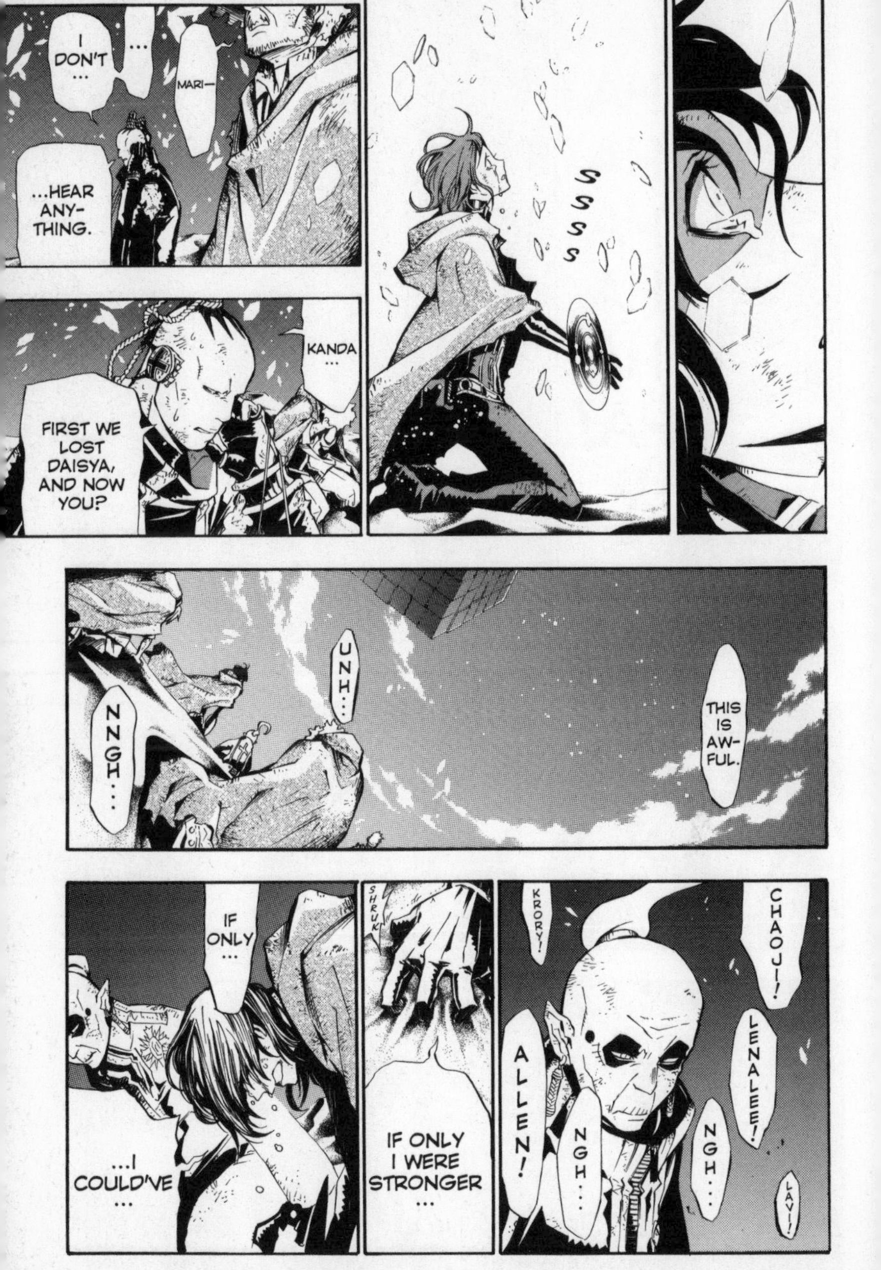
SSSS
...
MARI—
I DON'T ...
...HEAR ANYTHING.
KANDA ...
FIRST WE LOST DAISYA, AND NOW YOU?
THIS IS AWFUL.
UNH...
NNGH...
CHAOJI!
KRORY!
LENALEE!
NGH...
ALLEN!
NGH...
LAVI!
SHRUK
IF ONLY I WERE STRONGER ...
IF ONLY ...
...I COULD'VE ...

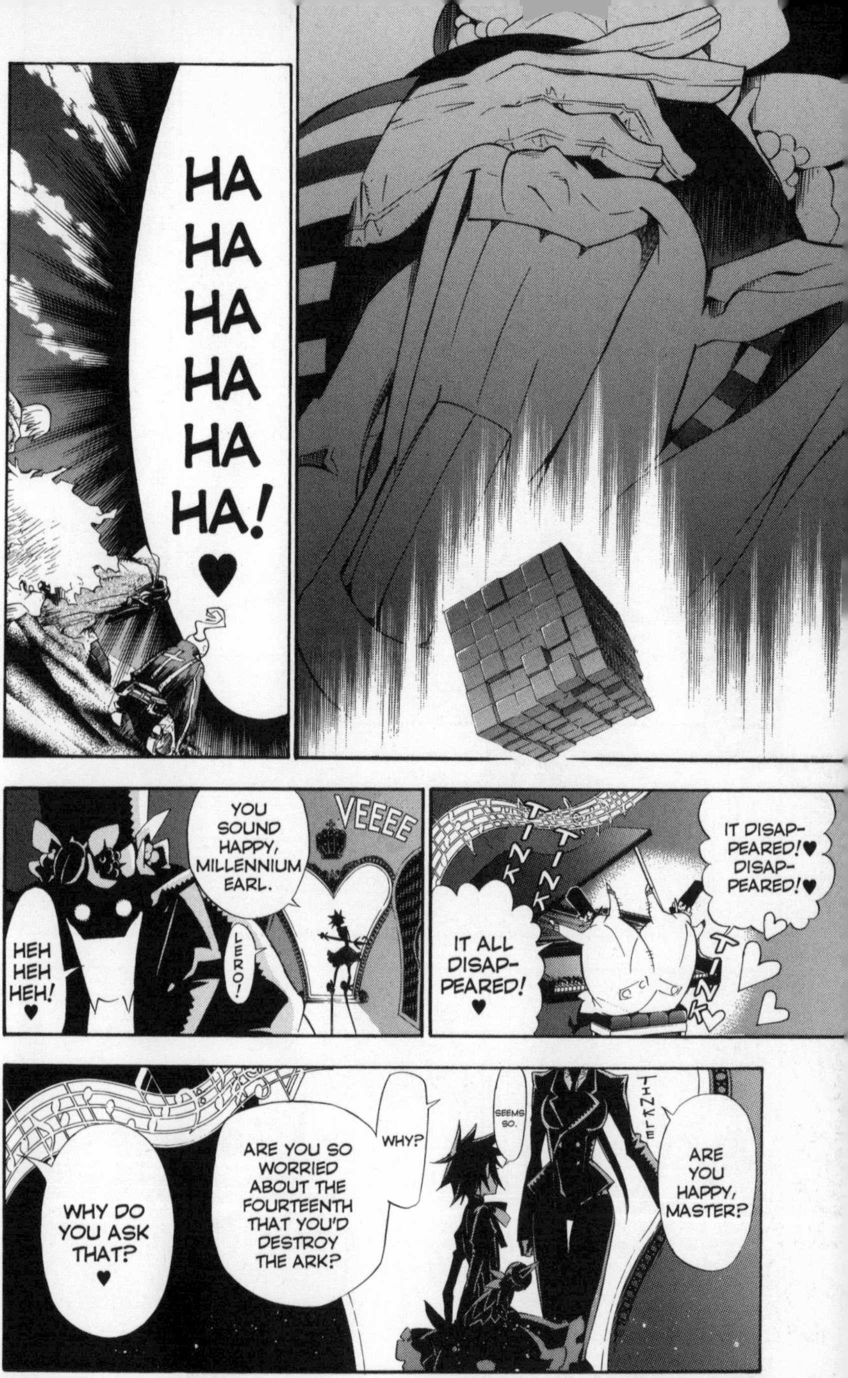
HA HA HA HA HA HA! ♥
IT DISAP-PEARED! ♥ DISAP-PEARED! ♥
TINK
TINK
IT ALL DISAP-PEARED! ♥
TINK
YOU SOUND HAPPY, MILLENNIUM EARL.
VEEEE
LERO!
HEH HEH HEH! ♥
TINKLE
ARE YOU HAPPY, MASTER?
SEEMS SO.
WHY?
ARE YOU SO WORRIED ABOUT THE FOURTEENTH THAT YOU'D DESTROY THE ARK?
WHY DO YOU ASK THAT? ♥

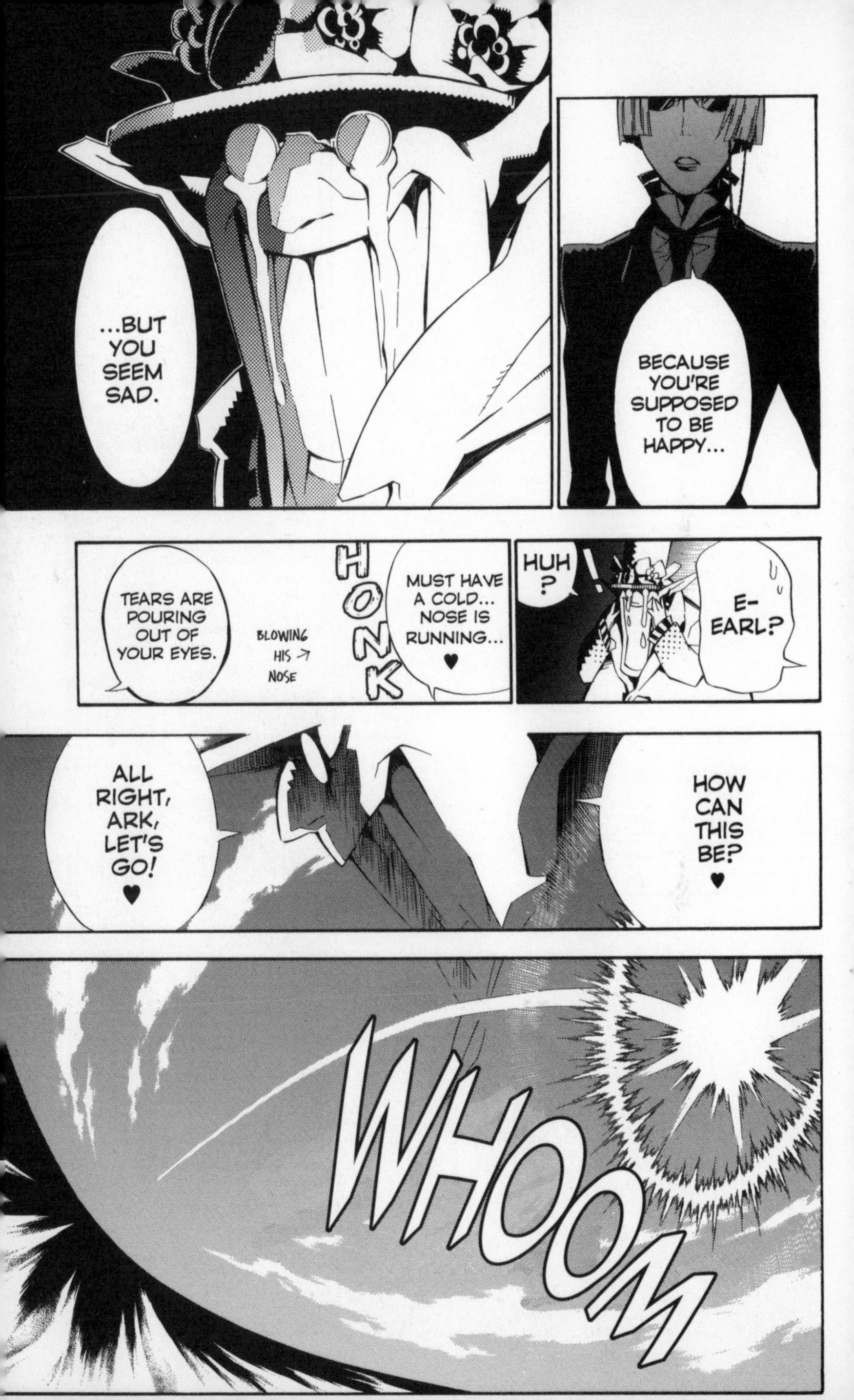
BECAUSE YOU'RE SUPPOSED TO BE HAPPY...
...BUT YOU SEEM SAD.
E-EARL?
HUH?
MUST HAVE A COLD... NOSE IS RUNNING... ♥
HONK
BLOWING HIS NOSE
TEARS ARE POURING OUT OF YOUR EYES.
HOW CAN THIS BE? ♥
ALL RIGHT, ARK, LET'S GO! ♥
WHOOM

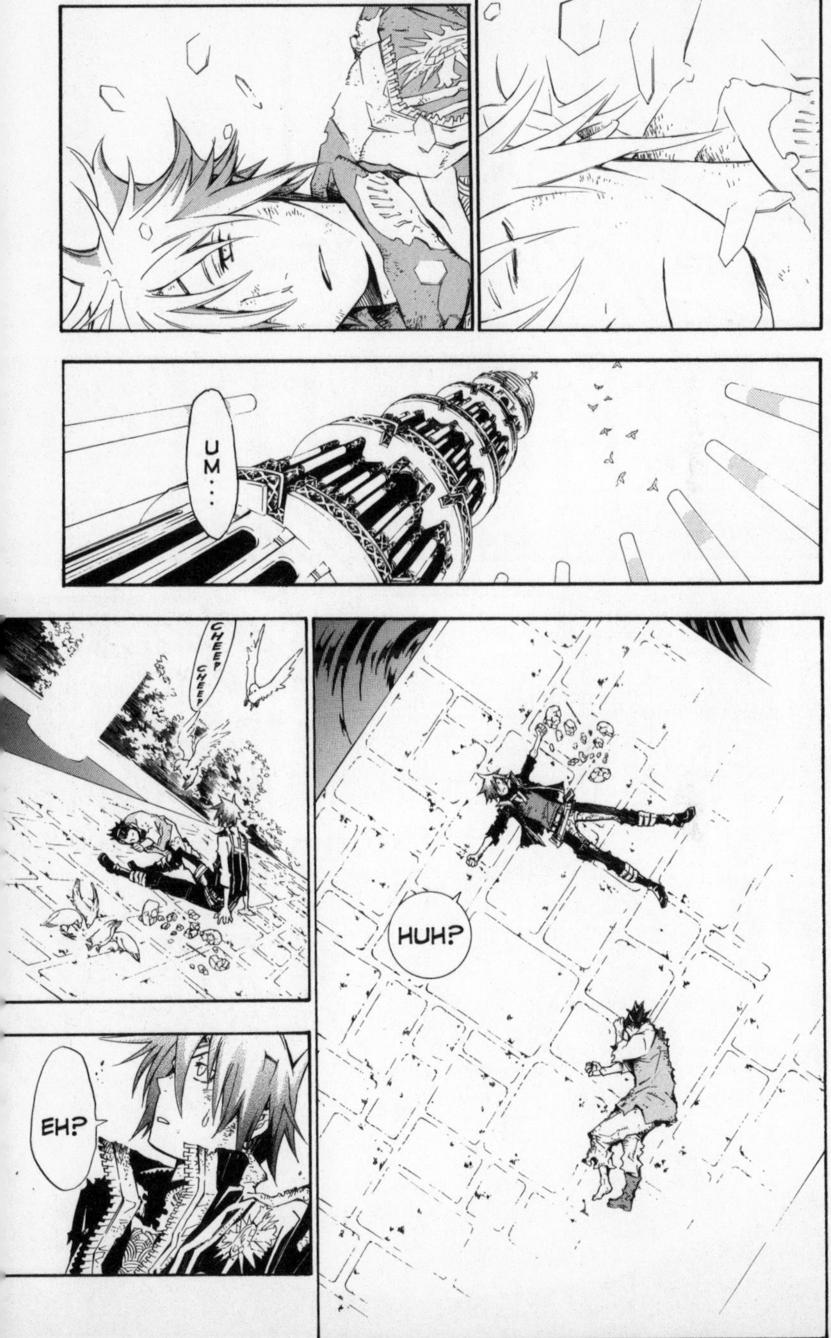
UM...
HUH?
CHEEP CHEEP
EH?

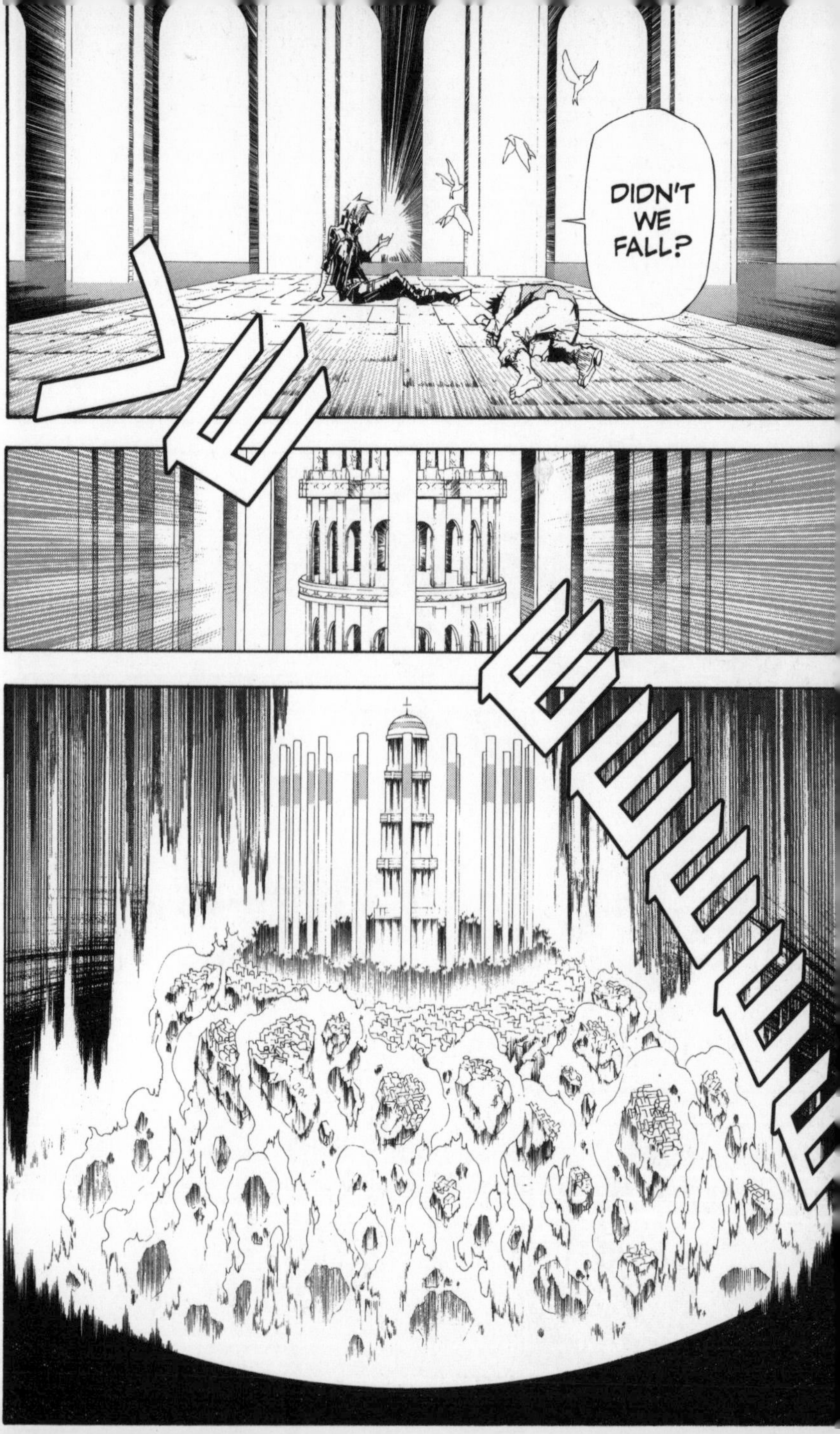
DIDN'T WE FALL?

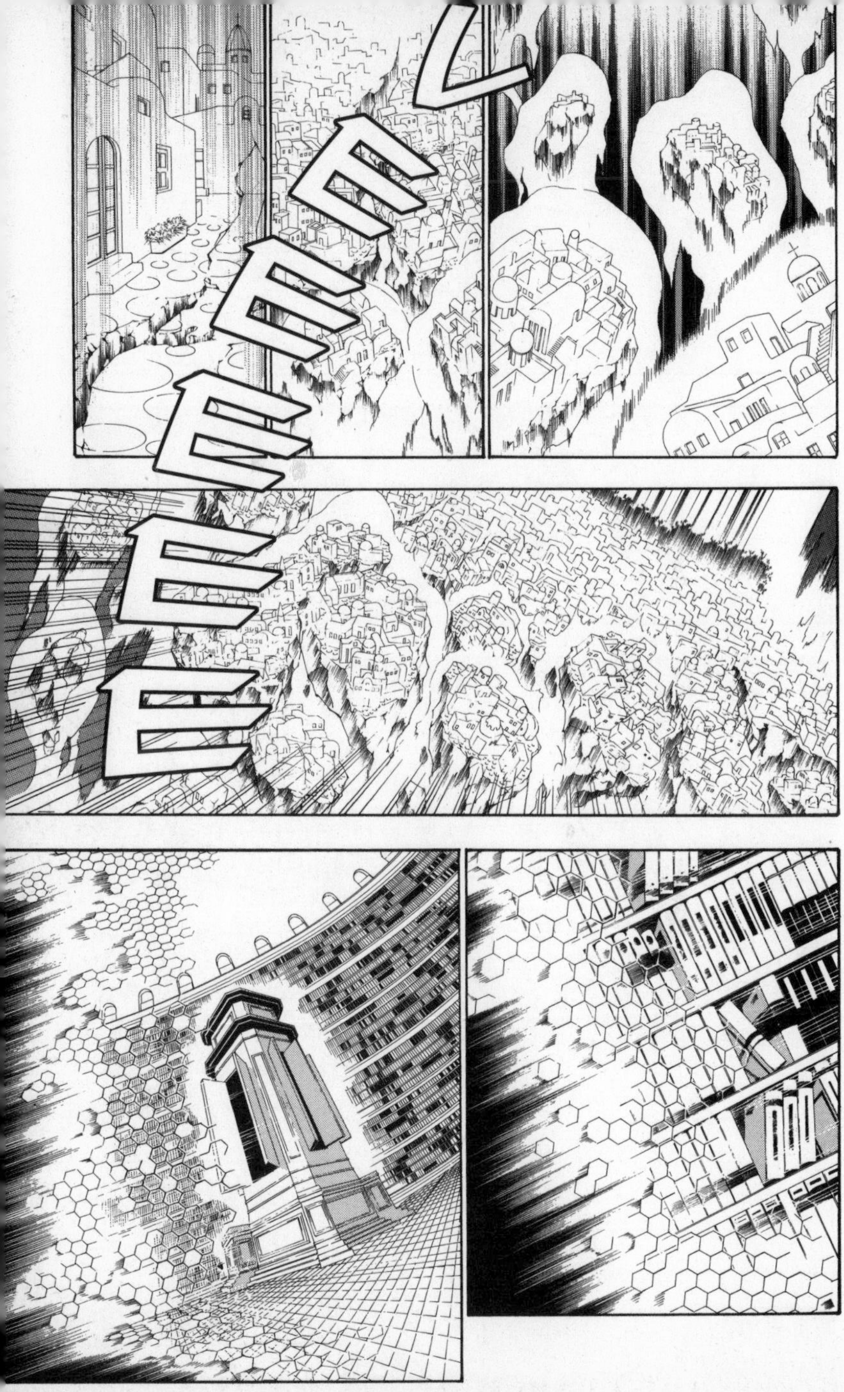
VEEEEEE

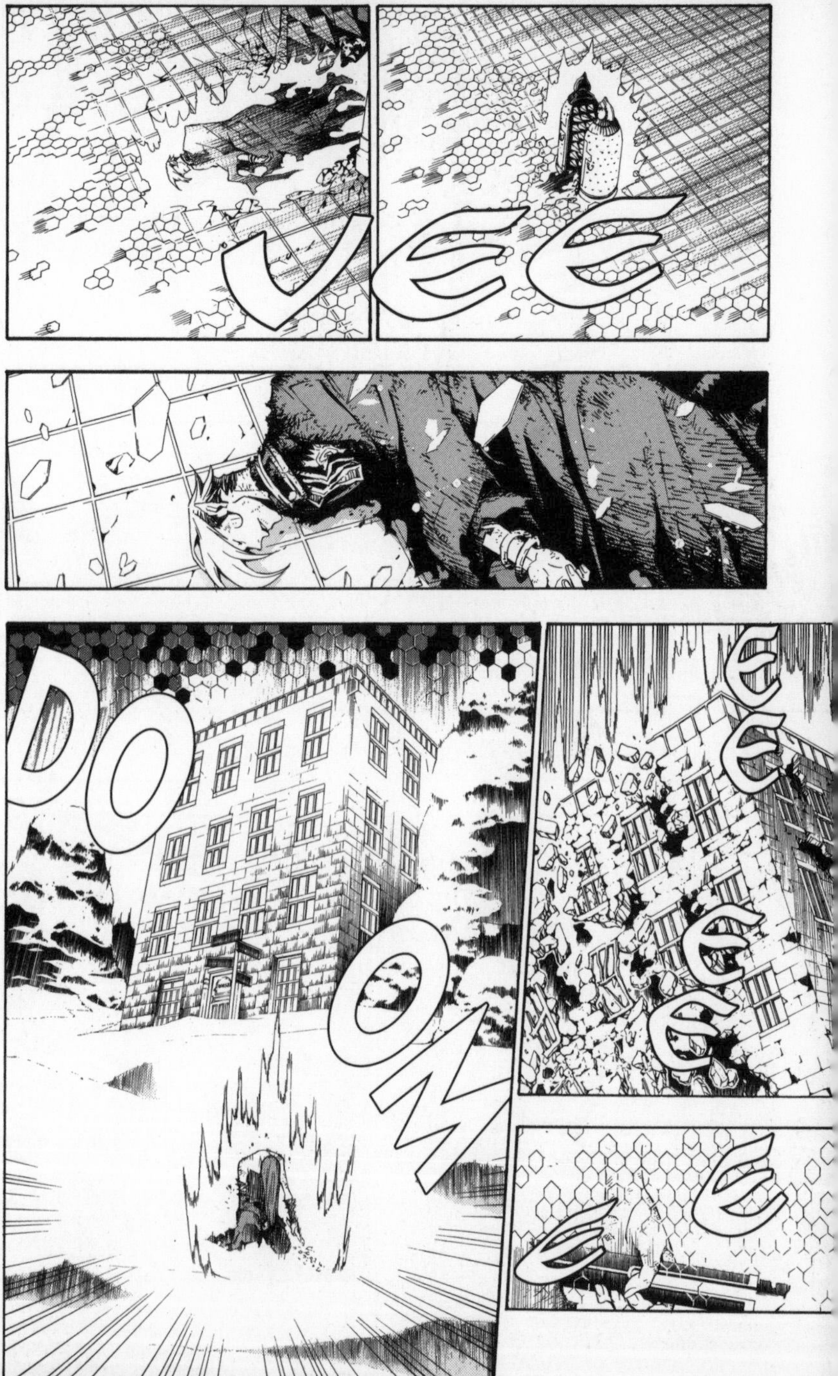
VEE
EEEE
EE
DOOM

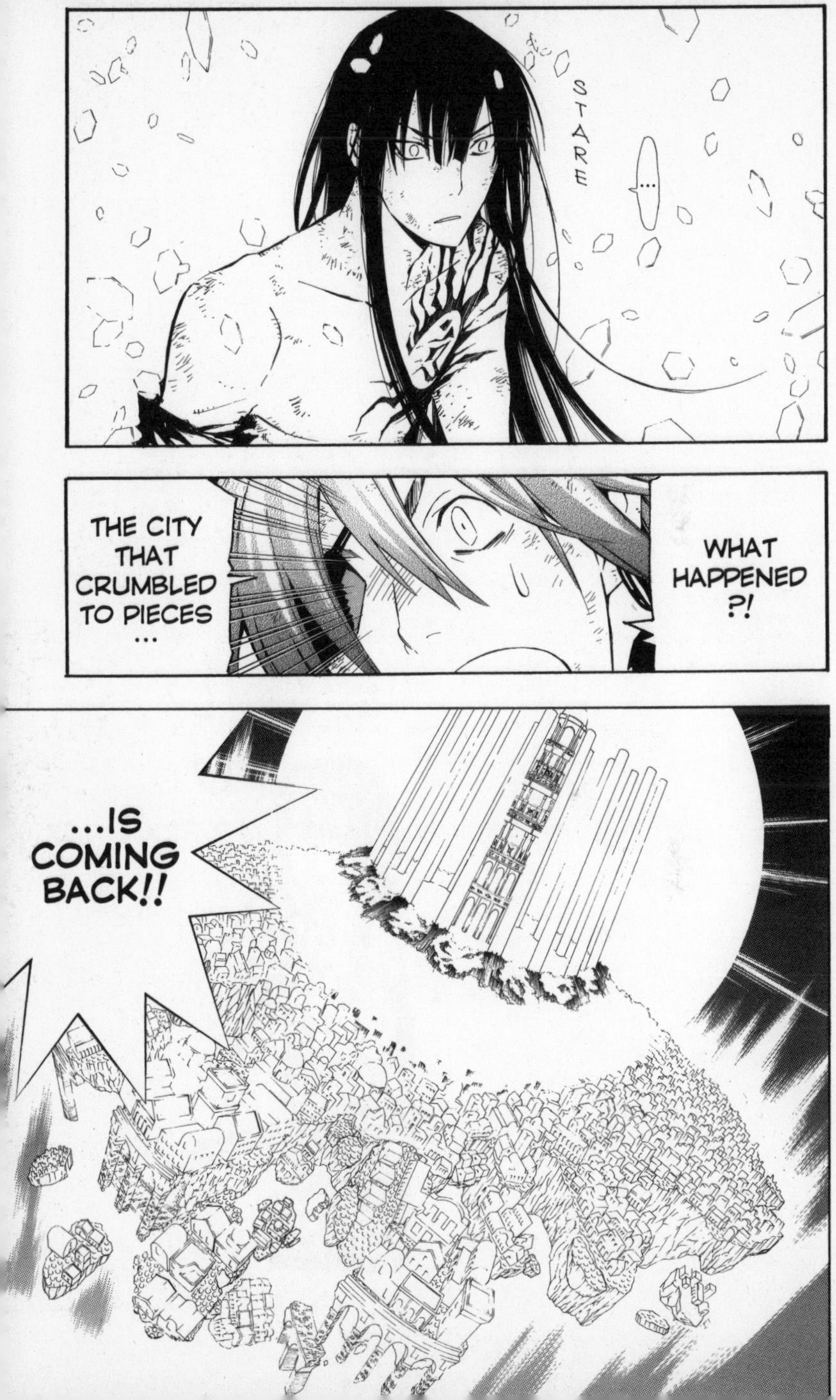
STARE
....
WHAT HAPPENED ?!
THE CITY THAT CRUMBLED TO PIECES ...
...IS COMING BACK!!

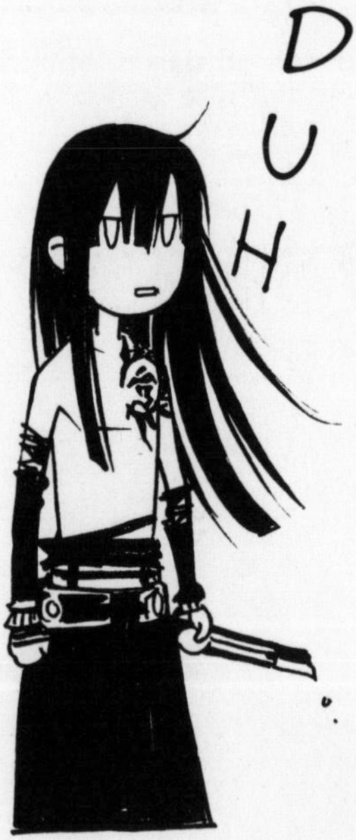
DUH

# THE 133RD NIGHT: HOMECOMING

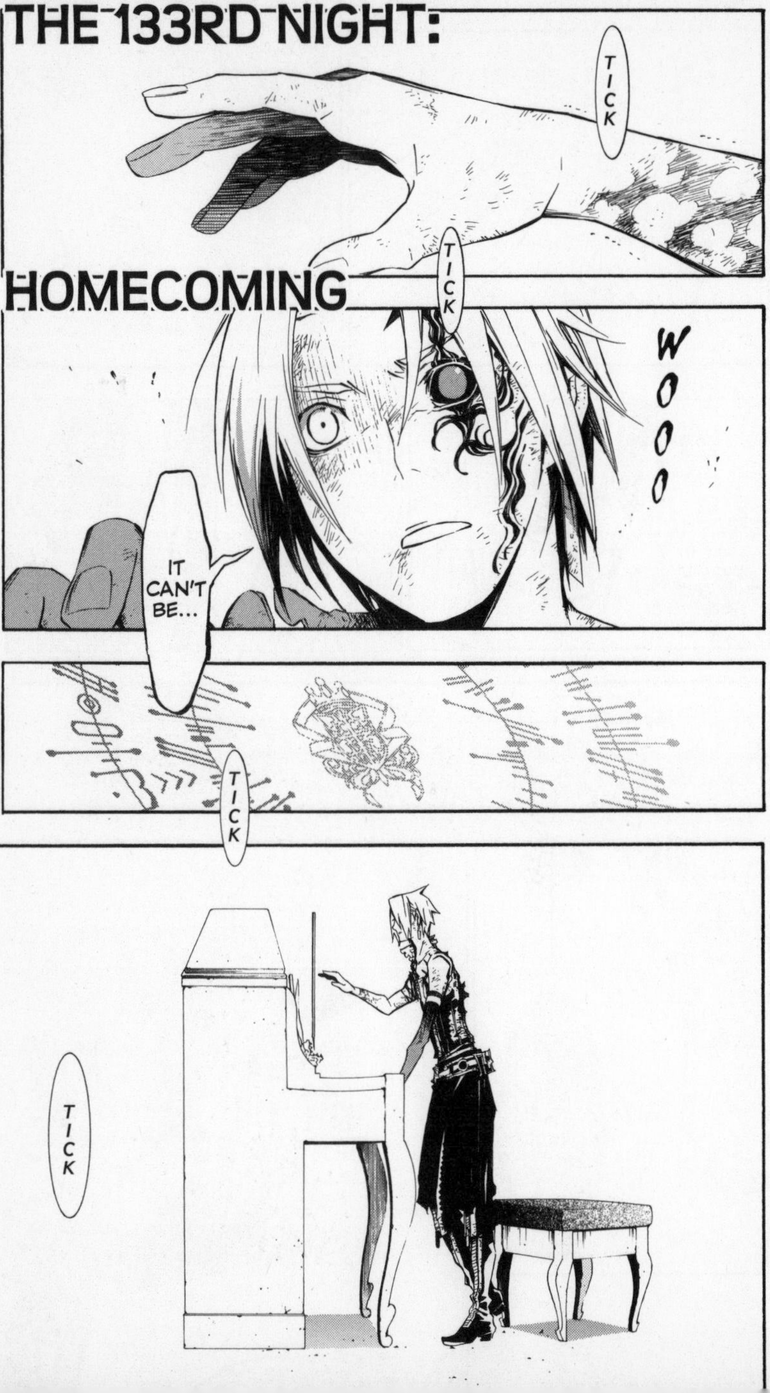
TICK
WOOO
TICK
IT CAN'T BE...
TICK
TICK

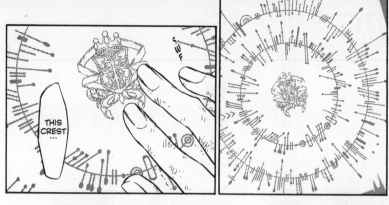

THIS CREST...

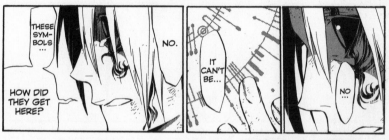

THESE SYMBOLS...

HOW DID THEY GET HERE?

NO.

IT CAN'T BE...

NO ...

THAT'S A SONG.

THE MELODY ...

READ THIS WAY

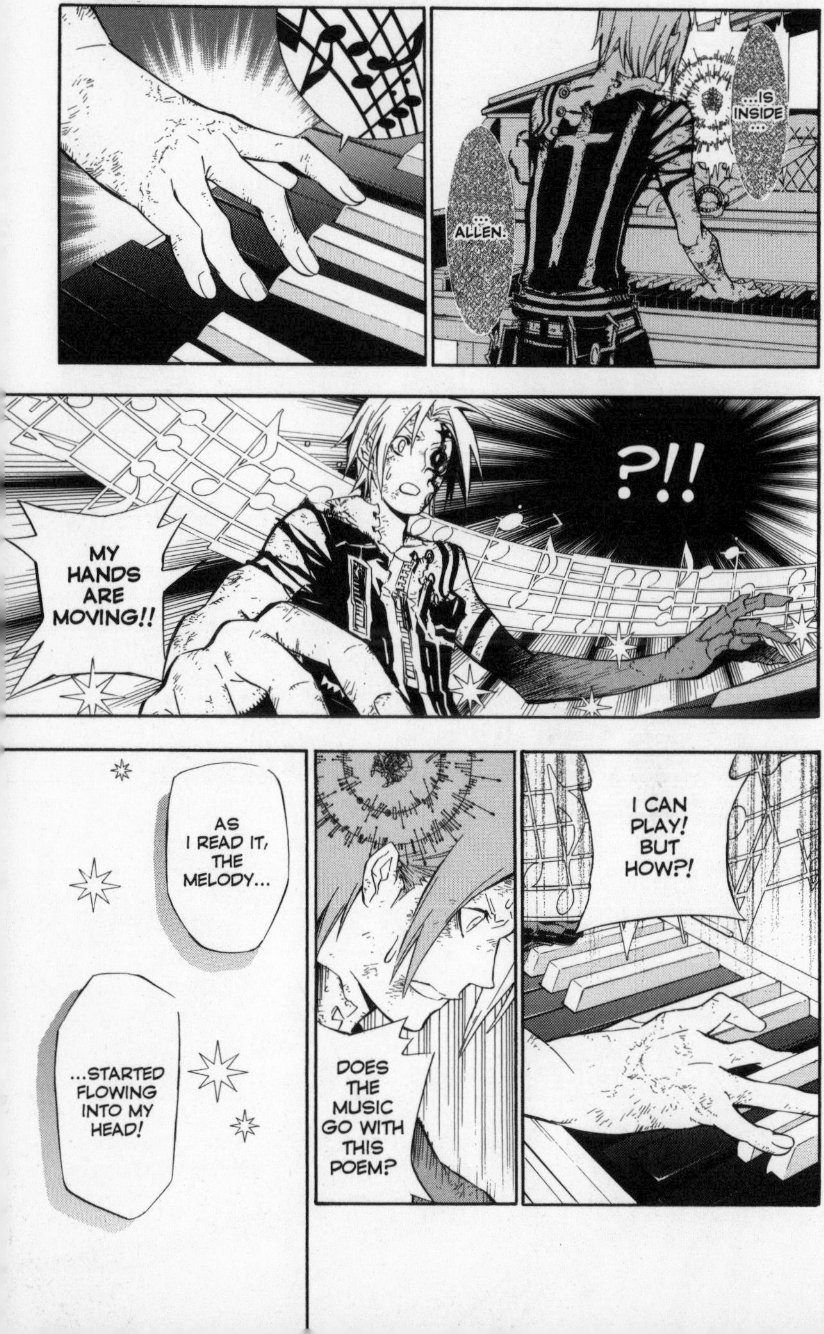
...IS INSIDE...
...ALLEN.
?!!
MY HANDS ARE MOVING!!
I CAN PLAY! BUT HOW?!
DOES THE MUSIC GO WITH THIS POEM?
AS I READ IT, THE MELODY...
...STARTED FLOWING INTO MY HEAD!

WHO'S SINGING INSIDE MY HEAD?!

MELODY?

HEY!

THEN THE BOY WENT TO SLEEP...

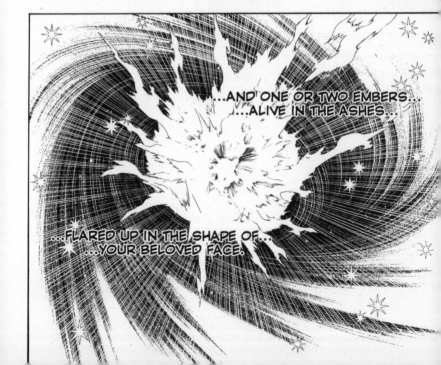

...AND ONE OR TWO EMBERS...
...ALIVE IN THE ASHES...

...FLARED UP IN THE SHAPE OF...
...YOUR BELOVED FACE.

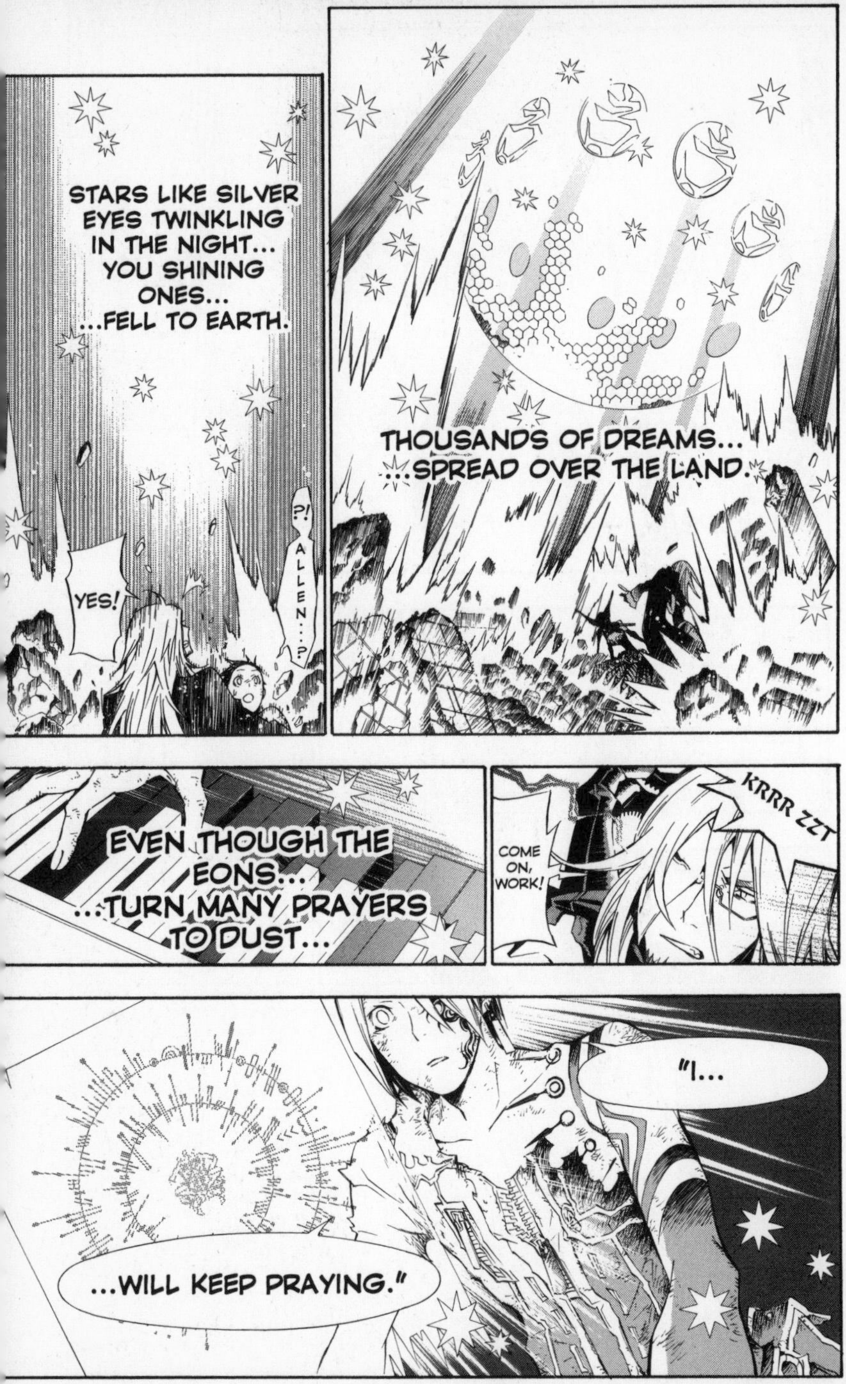
THOUSANDS OF DREAMS... ...SPREAD OVER THE LAND.
STARS LIKE SILVER EYES TWINKLING IN THE NIGHT... YOU SHINING ONES... ...FELL TO EARTH.
?! ALLEN...?
YES!
KRRR ZZT
COME ON, WORK!
EVEN THOUGH THE EONS... ...TURN MANY PRAYERS TO DUST...
"I...
...WILL KEEP PRAYING."

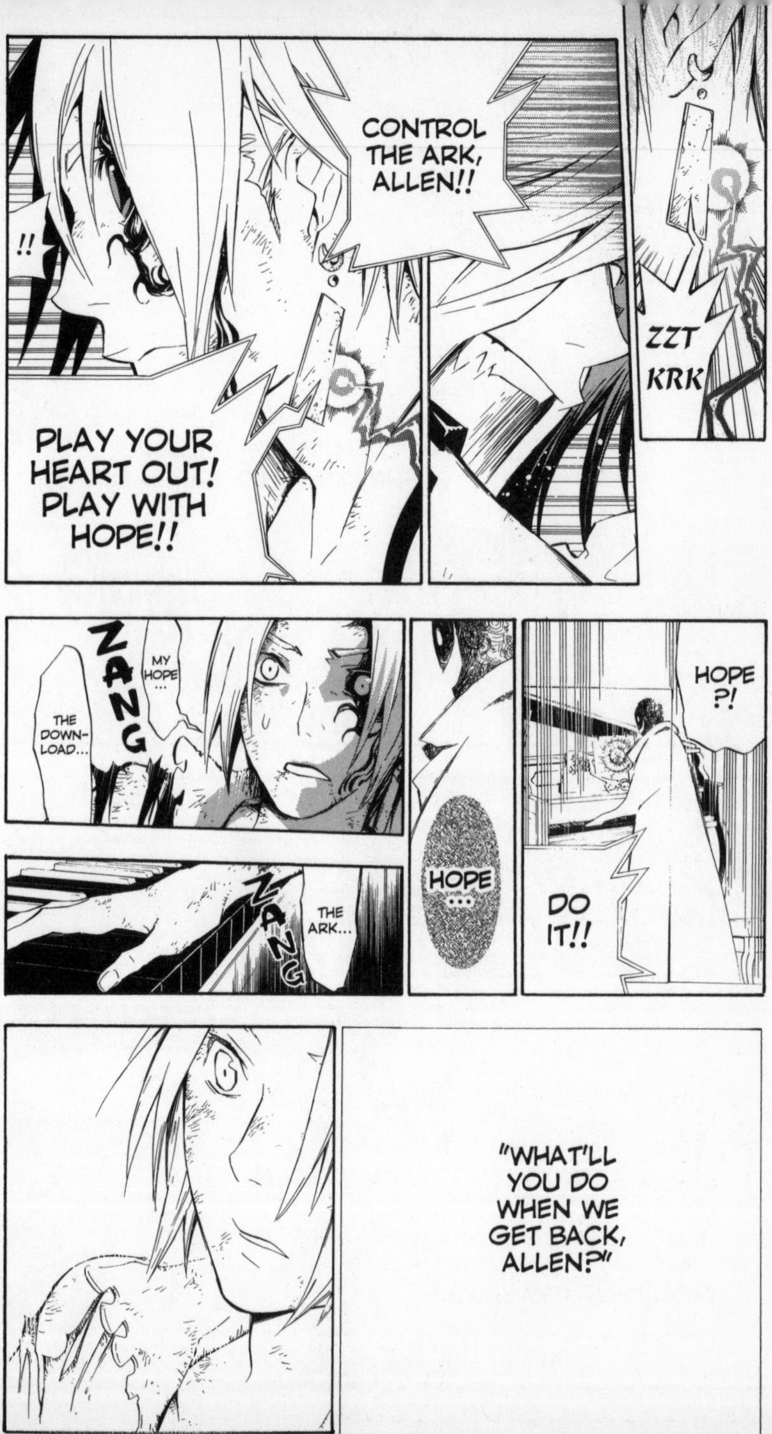
ZZT KRK
CONTROL THE ARK, ALLEN!!
!!
PLAY YOUR HEART OUT! PLAY WITH HOPE!!
HOPE?!
DO IT!!
HOPE...
ZANG
MY HOPE...
THE DOWN-LOAD...
ZANG
THE ARK...
"WHAT'LL YOU DO WHEN WE GET BACK, ALLEN?"

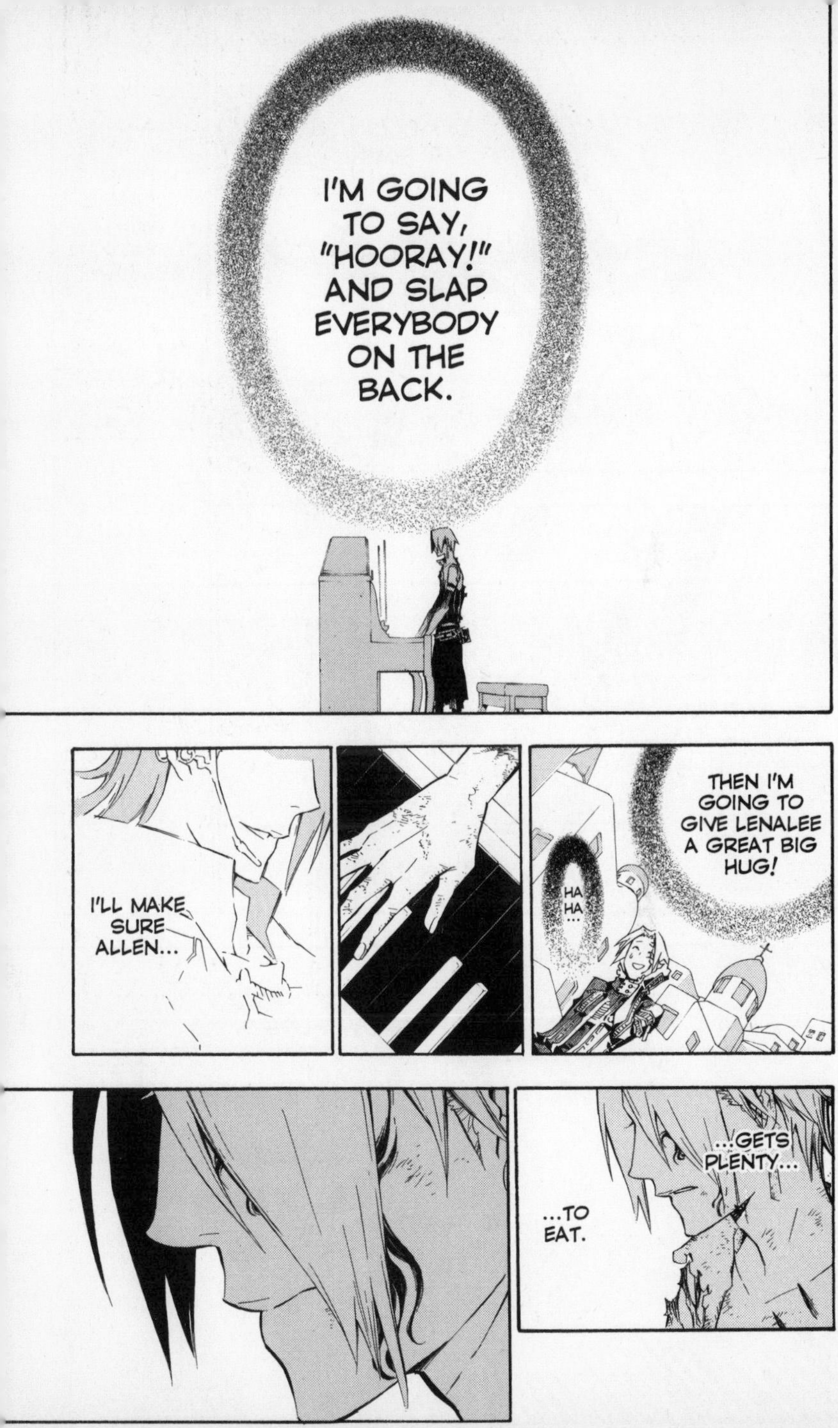
I'M GOING TO SAY, "HOORAY!" AND SLAP EVERYBODY ON THE BACK.
THEN I'M GOING TO GIVE LENALEE A GREAT BIG HUG!
HA HA...
I'LL MAKE SURE ALLEN...
...GETS PLENTY...
...TO EAT.

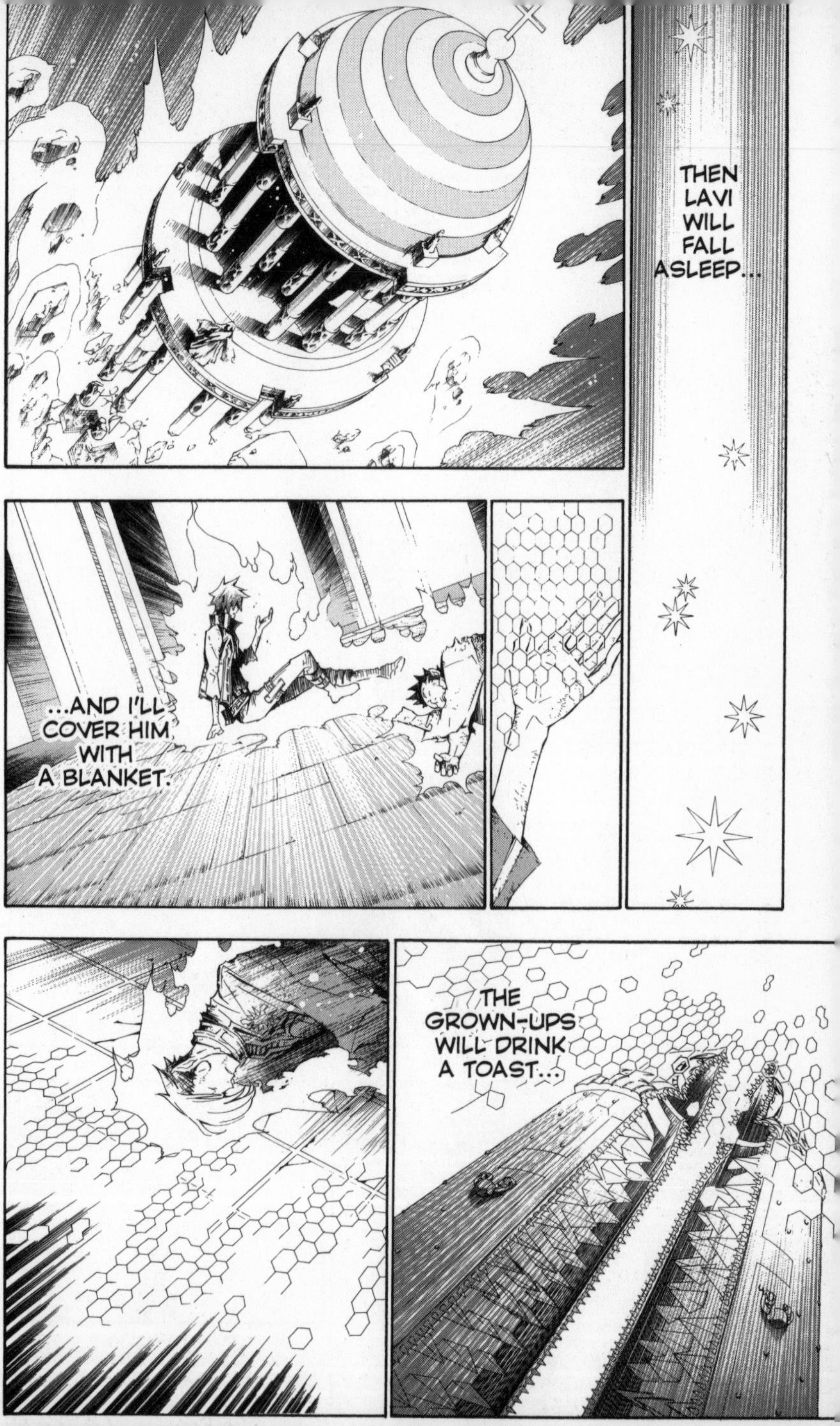
THEN LAVI WILL FALL ASLEEP...
...AND I'LL COVER HIM WITH A BLANKET.
THE GROWN-UPS WILL DRINK A TOAST...

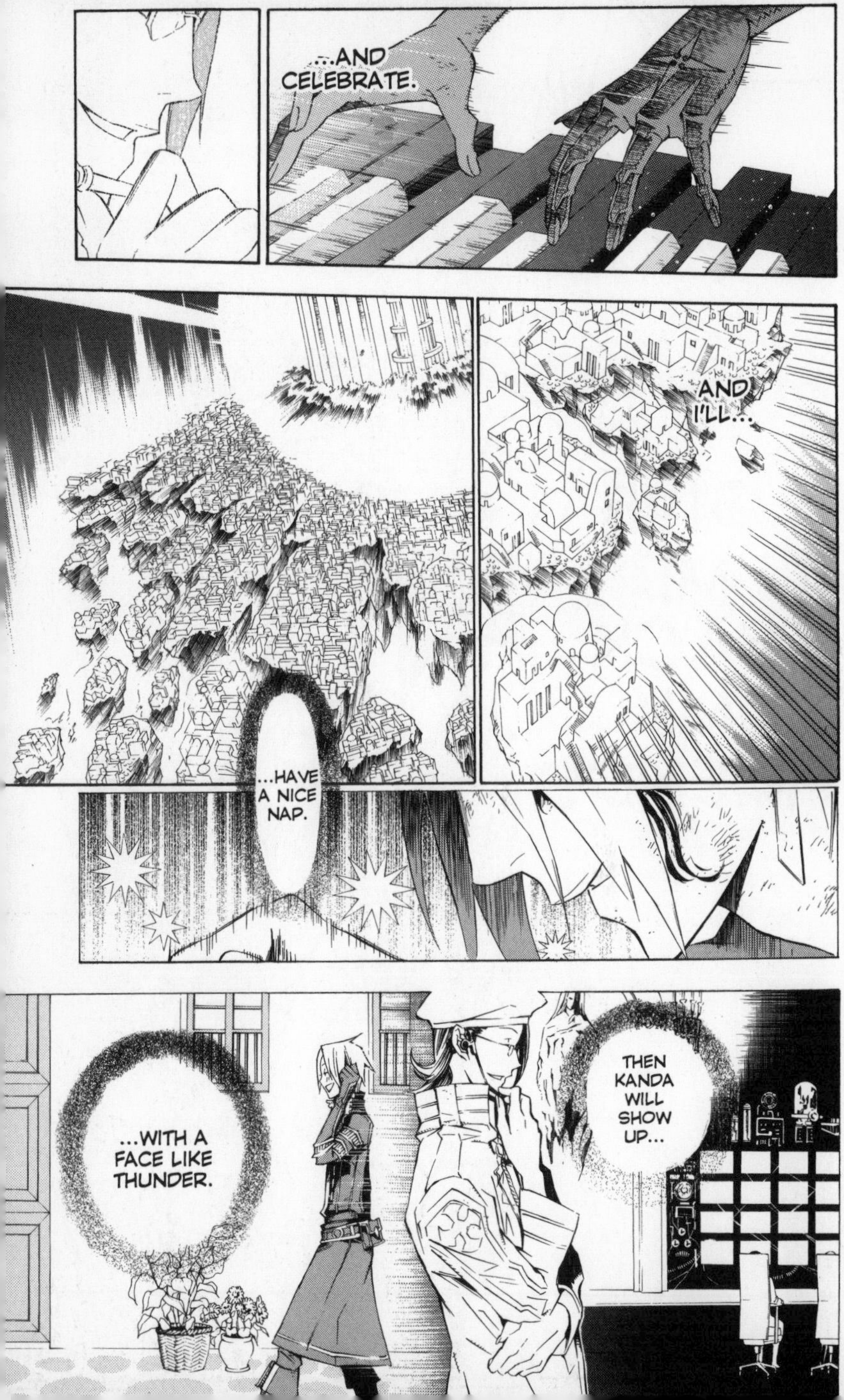
...AND CELEBRATE.
AND I'LL...
...HAVE A NICE NAP.
THEN KANDA WILL SHOW UP...
...WITH A FACE LIKE THUNDER.

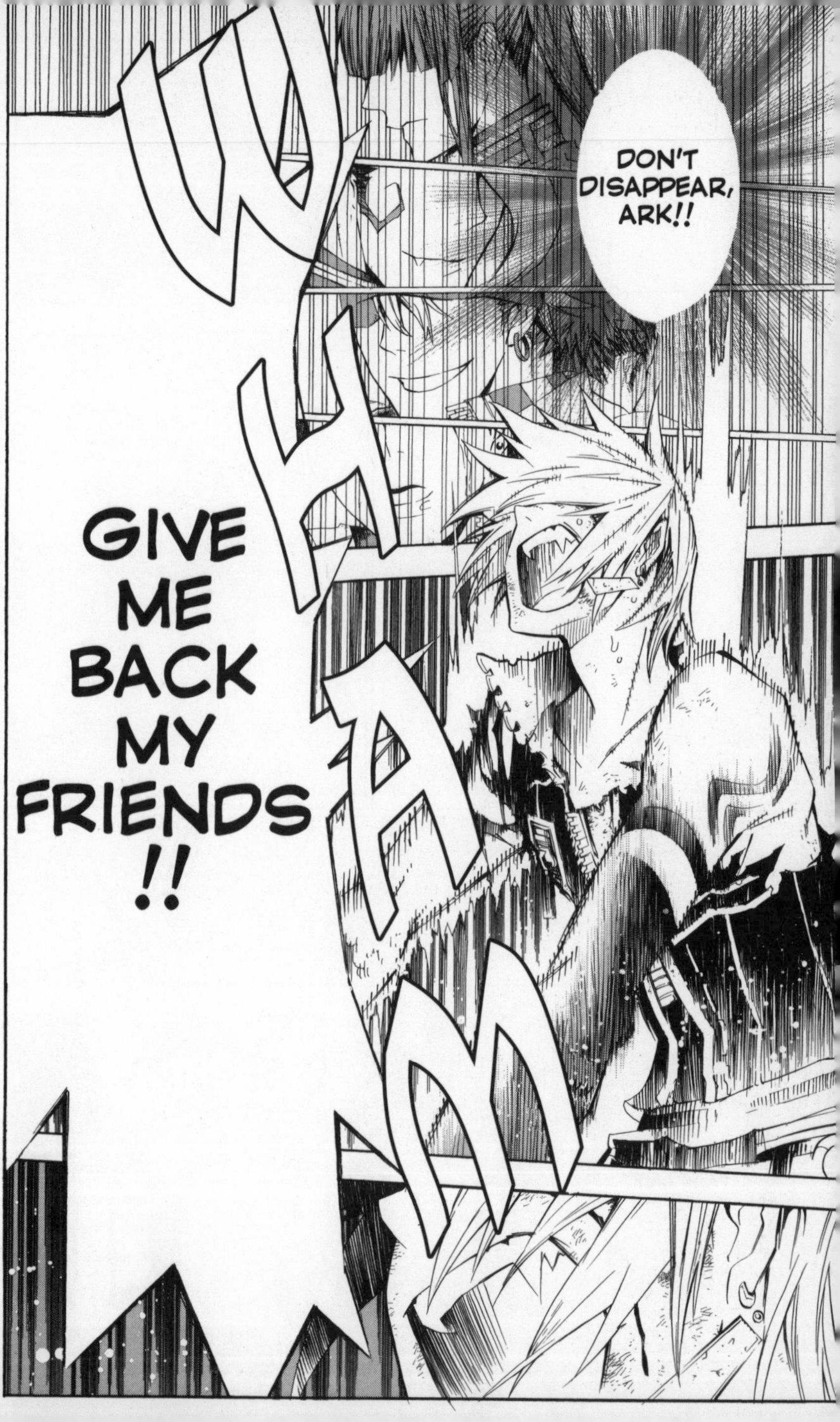
DON'T DISAPPEAR, ARK!!
WHAM
GIVE ME BACK MY FRIENDS!!

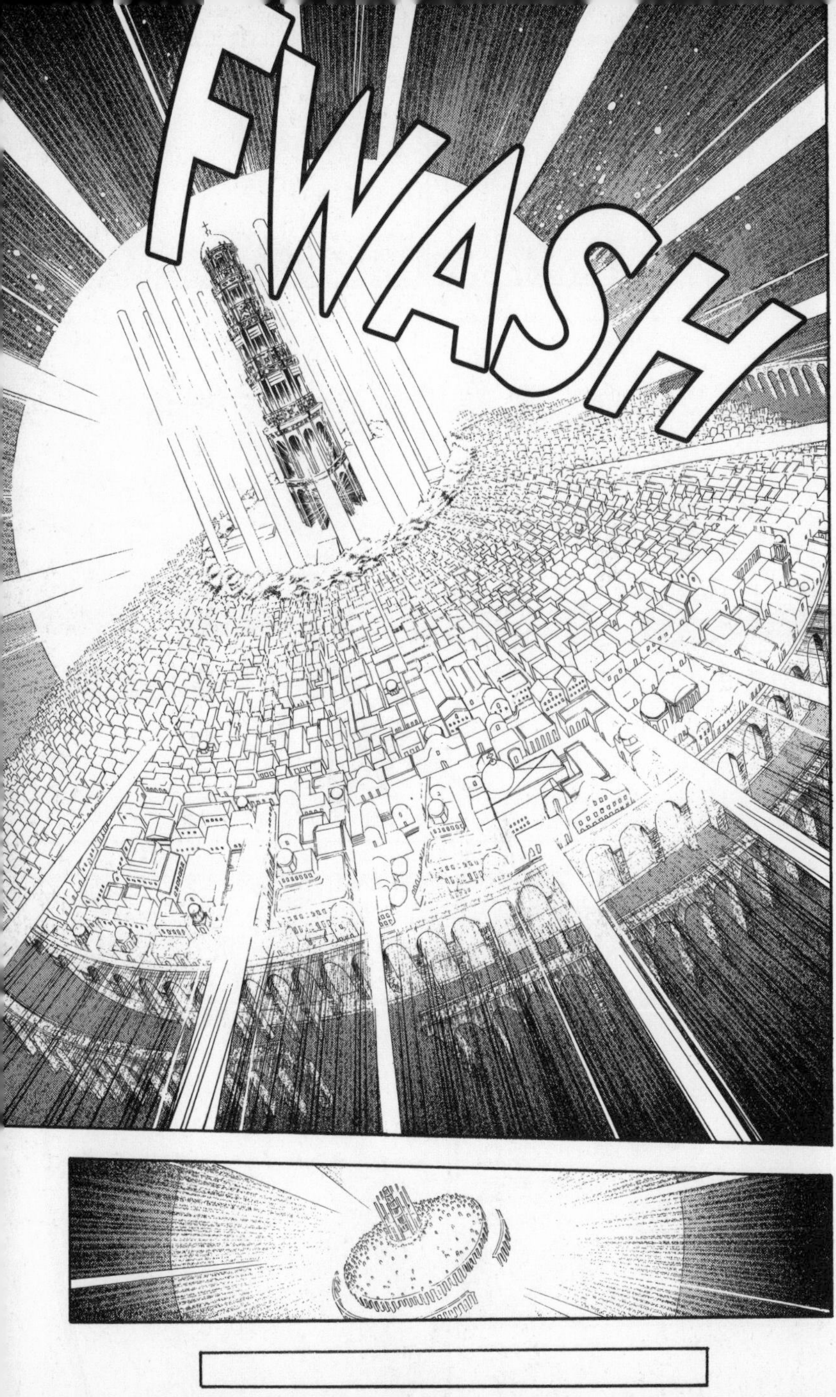
FWASH

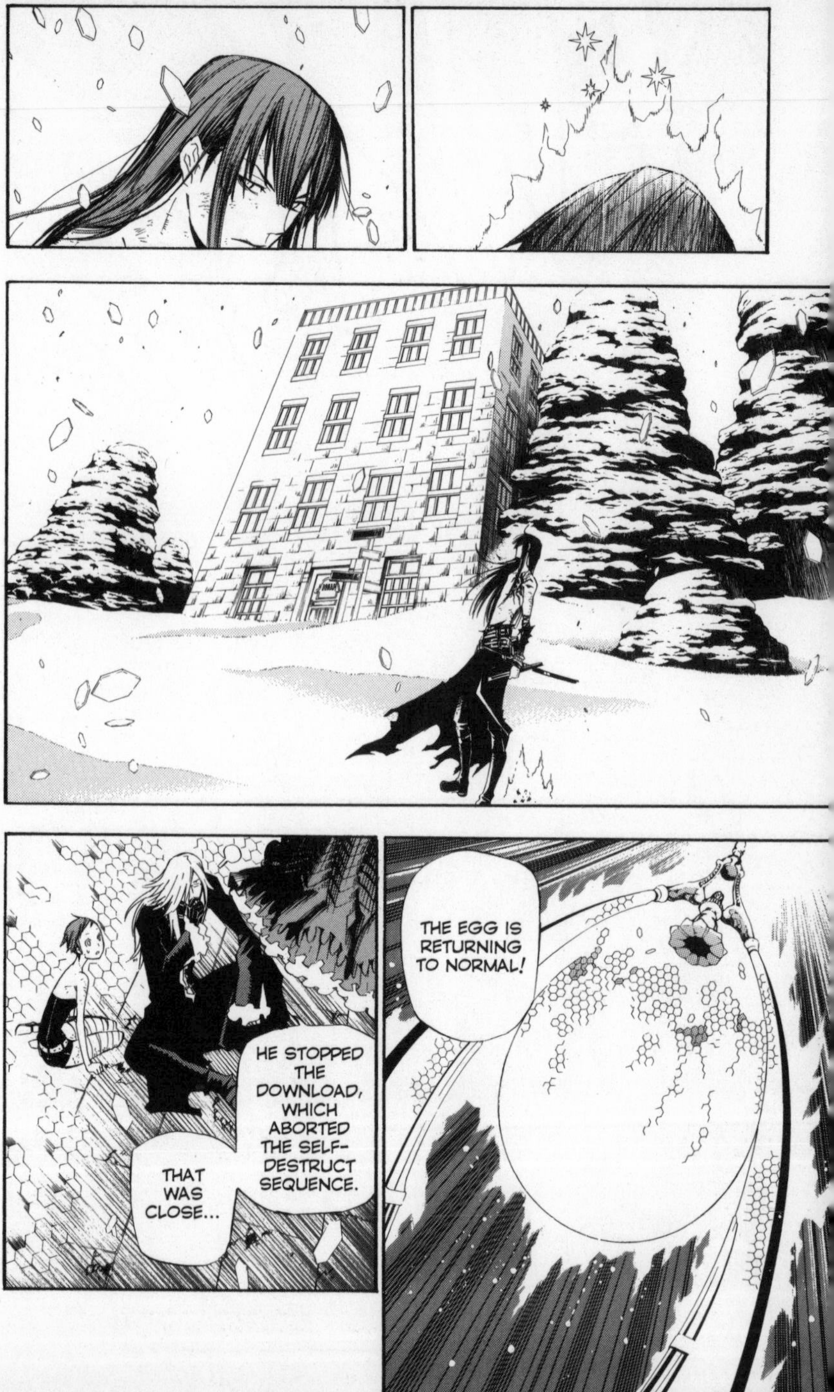
THE EGG IS RETURNING TO NORMAL!
HE STOPPED THE DOWNLOAD, WHICH ABORTED THE SELF-DESTRUCT SEQUENCE.
THAT WAS CLOSE...

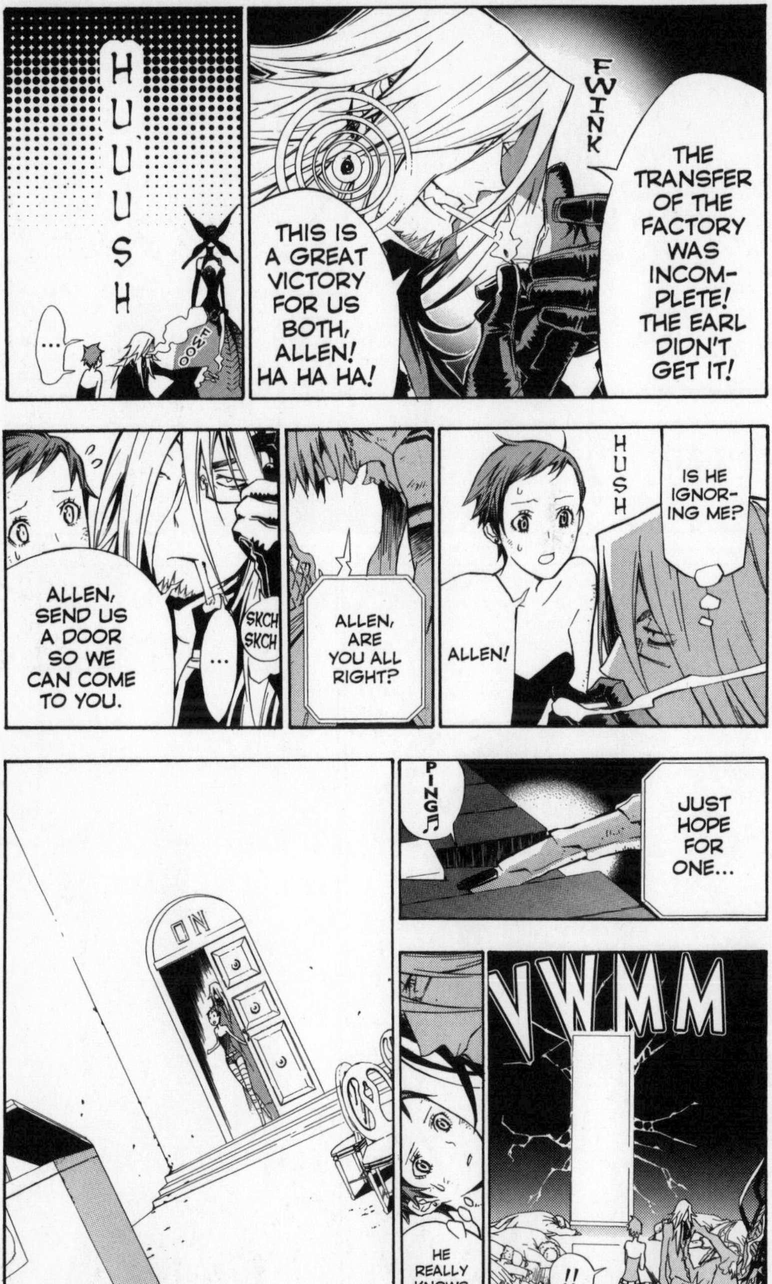
FWINK
THE TRANSFER OF THE FACTORY WAS INCOMPLETE! THE EARL DIDN'T GET IT!
THIS IS A GREAT VICTORY FOR US BOTH, ALLEN! HA HA HA!
HUUUSH
FWOO
...
HUSH
IS HE IGNORING ME?
ALLEN!
ALLEN, ARE YOU ALL RIGHT?
SKCH SKCH
ALLEN, SEND US A DOOR SO WE CAN COME TO YOU.
...
JUST HOPE FOR ONE...
PING♫
VWMM
!!
HE REALLY KNOWS THE ARK.
ON

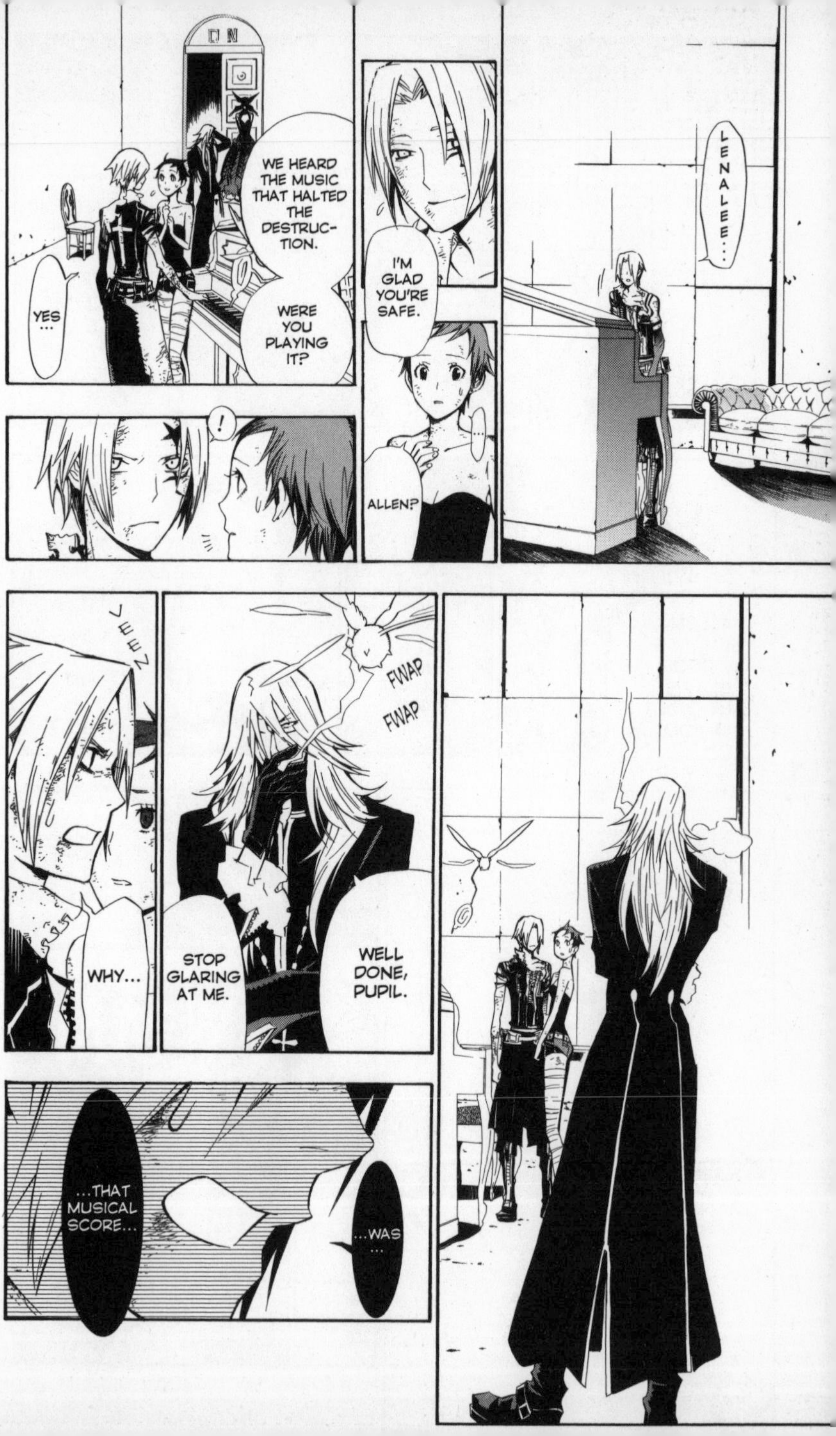
LENALEE...
I'M GLAD YOU'RE SAFE.
...
ALLEN?
WE HEARD THE MUSIC THAT HALTED THE DESTRUCTION.
WERE YOU PLAYING IT?
YES...
!
FWAP
FWAP
WELL DONE, PUPIL.
STOP GLARING AT ME.
VEEN
WHY...
...THAT MUSICAL SCORE...
...WAS...

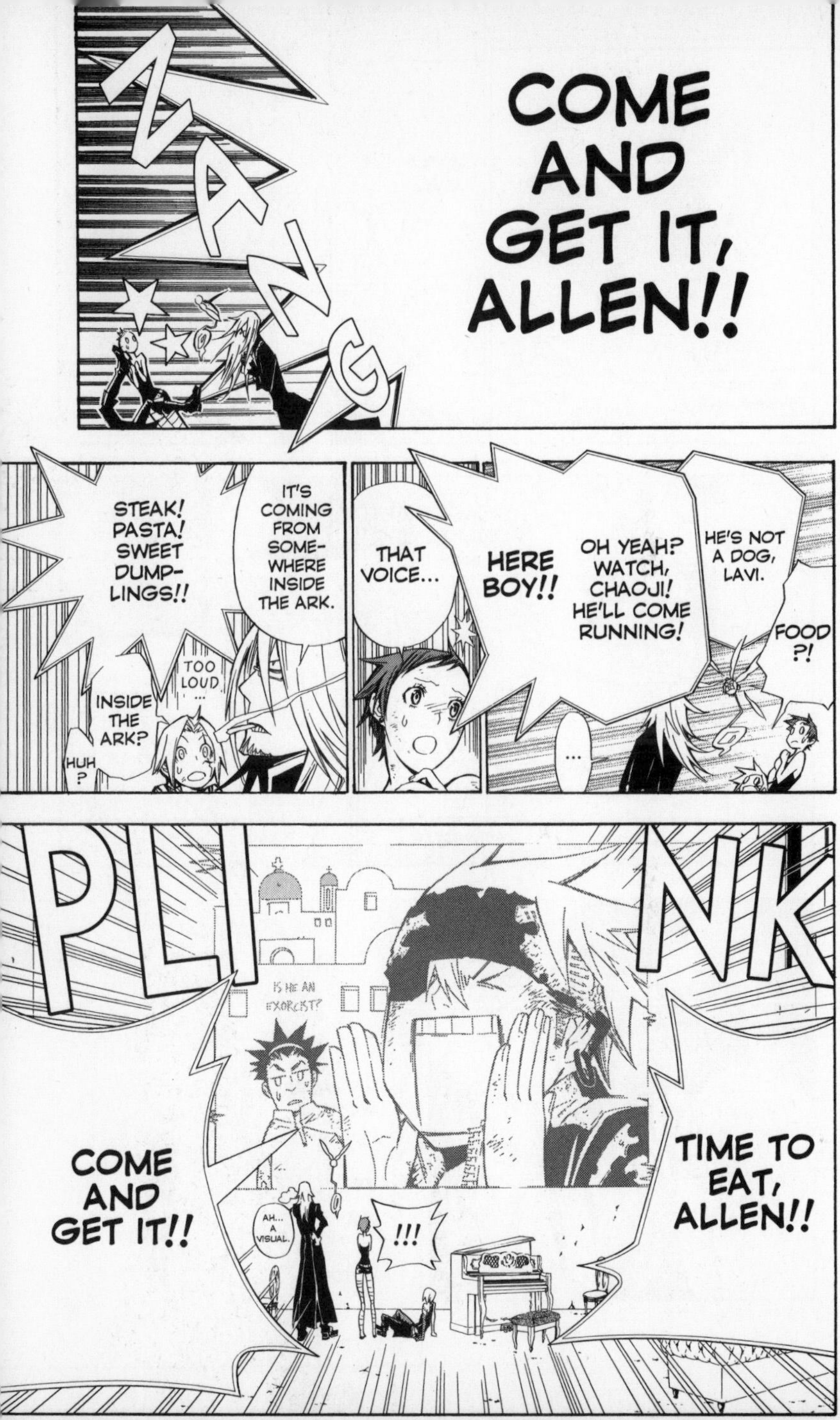
ZANG
COME AND GET IT, ALLEN!!
HE'S NOT A DOG, LAVI.
OH YEAH? WATCH, CHAOJI! HE'LL COME RUNNING!
HERE BOY!!
FOOD ?!
...
THAT VOICE...
IT'S COMING FROM SOME-WHERE INSIDE THE ARK.
STEAK! PASTA! SWEET DUMP-LINGS!!
TOO LOUD ...
INSIDE THE ARK?
HUH ?
PLINK
TIME TO EAT, ALLEN!!
IS HE AN EXORCIST?
COME AND GET IT!!
!!!
AH... A VISUAL.

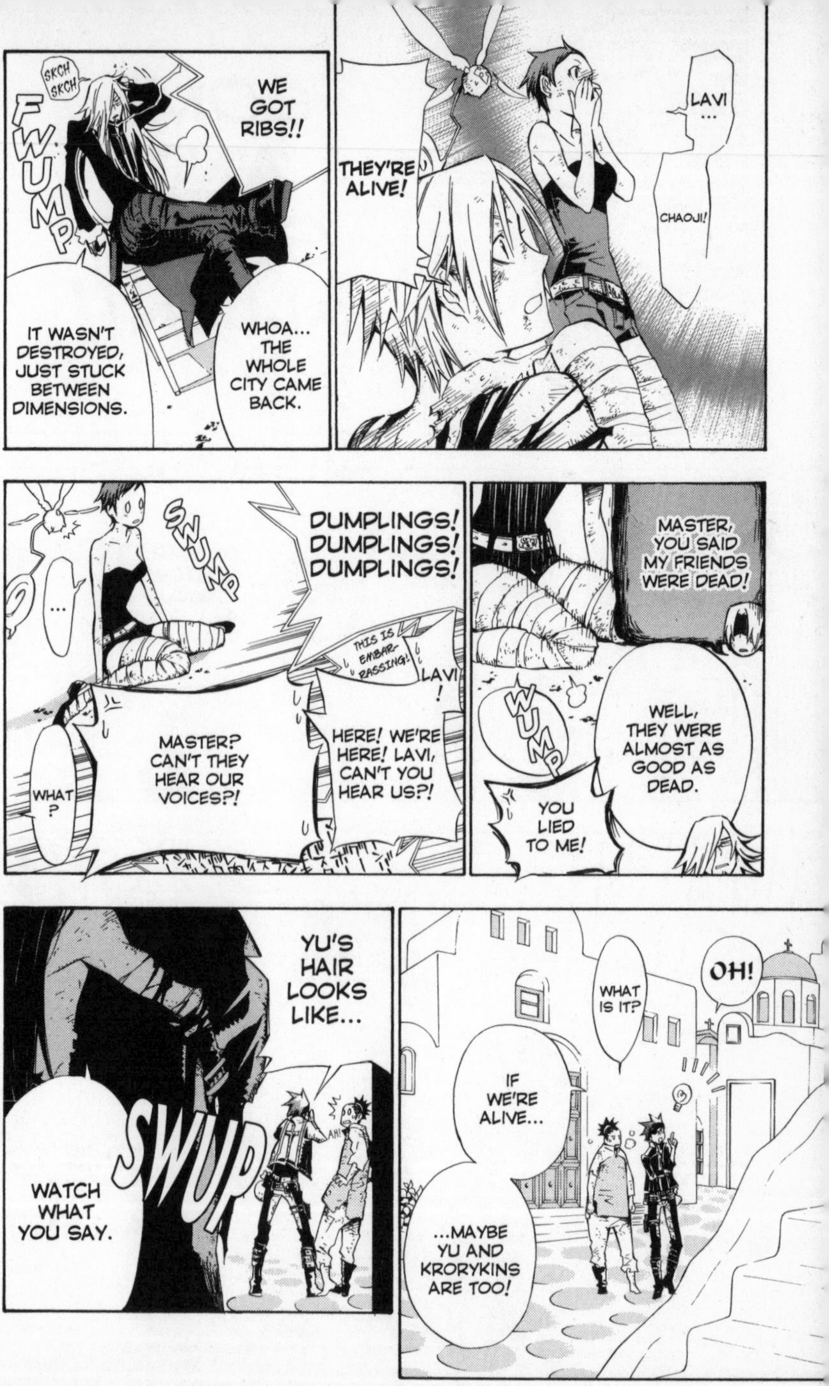
LAVI ...
CHAOJI!
THEY'RE ALIVE!
WE GOT RIBS!!
SKCH SKCH
FWUMP
WHOA... THE WHOLE CITY CAME BACK.
IT WASN'T DESTROYED, JUST STUCK BETWEEN DIMENSIONS.
MASTER, YOU SAID MY FRIENDS WERE DEAD!
WELL, THEY WERE ALMOST AS GOOD AS DEAD.
WUMP
YOU LIED TO ME!
DUMPLINGS! DUMPLINGS! DUMPLINGS!
SWUMP
LAVI!
THIS IS EMBARRASSING!
HERE! WE'RE HERE! LAVI, CAN'T YOU HEAR US?!
MASTER? CAN'T THEY HEAR OUR VOICES?!
...
WHAT?
OH!
WHAT IS IT?
IF WE'RE ALIVE...
...MAYBE YU AND KRORYKINS ARE TOO!
YU'S HAIR LOOKS LIKE...
AH!
SWUP
WATCH WHAT YOU SAY.

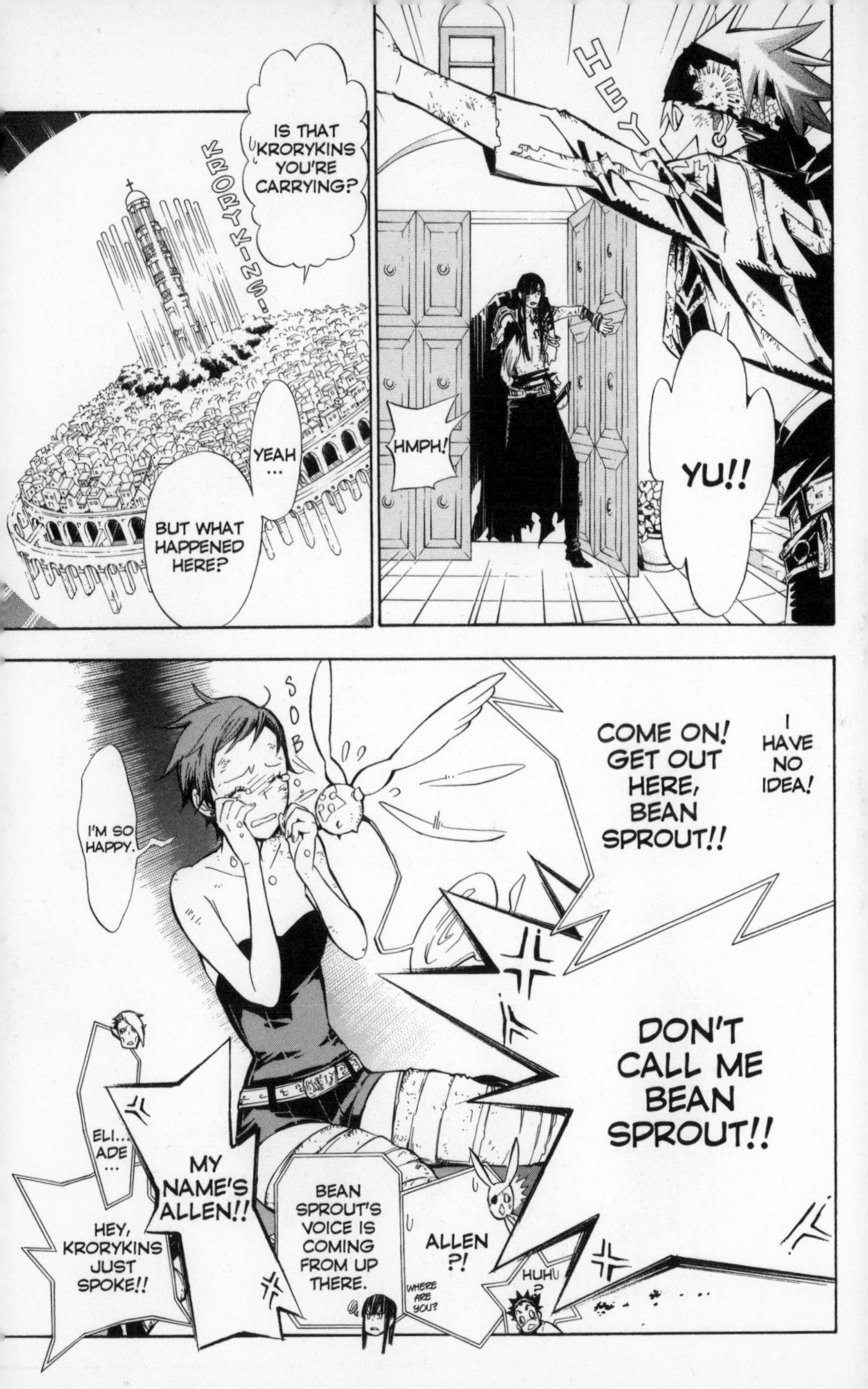
HEY
YU!!
HMPH!
KRORYKINS!
IS THAT KRORYKINS YOU'RE CARRYING?
YEAH...
BUT WHAT HAPPENED HERE?
I HAVE NO IDEA!
COME ON! GET OUT HERE, BEAN SPROUT!!
SOB
I'M SO HAPPY.
DON'T CALL ME BEAN SPROUT!!
HUH?
ALLEN?!
WHERE ARE YOU?
BEAN SPROUT'S VOICE IS COMING FROM UP THERE.
MY NAME'S ALLEN!!
ELI... ADE...
HEY, KRORYKINS JUST SPOKE!!

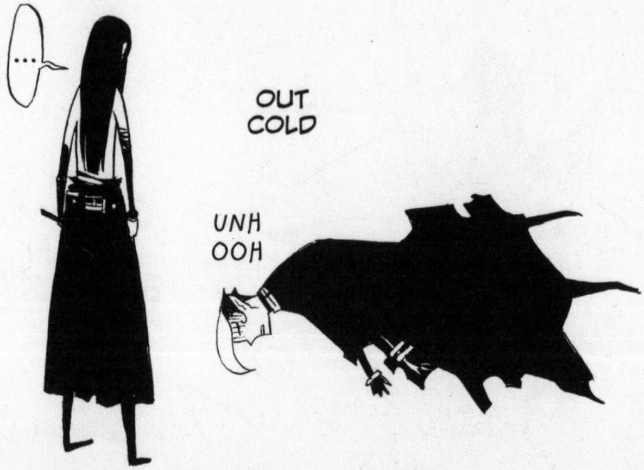
...
OUT
COLD
UNH
OOH

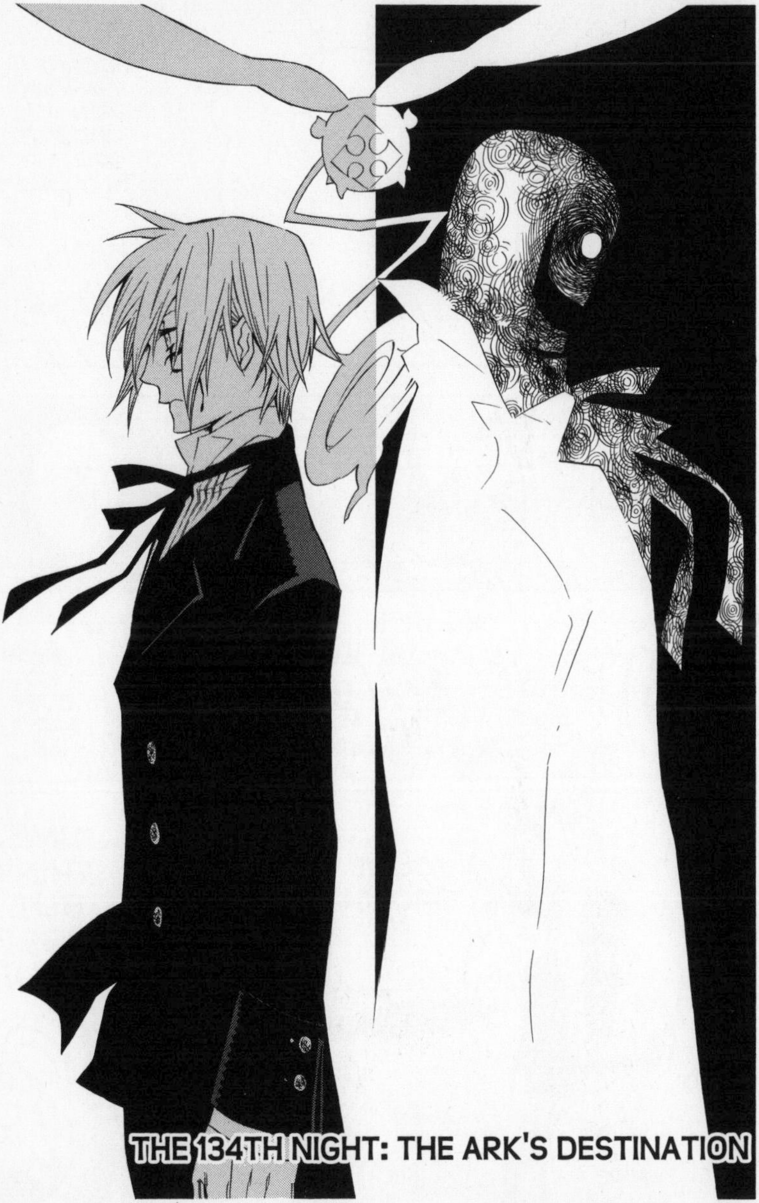

# THE 134TH NIGHT: THE ARK'S DESTINATION

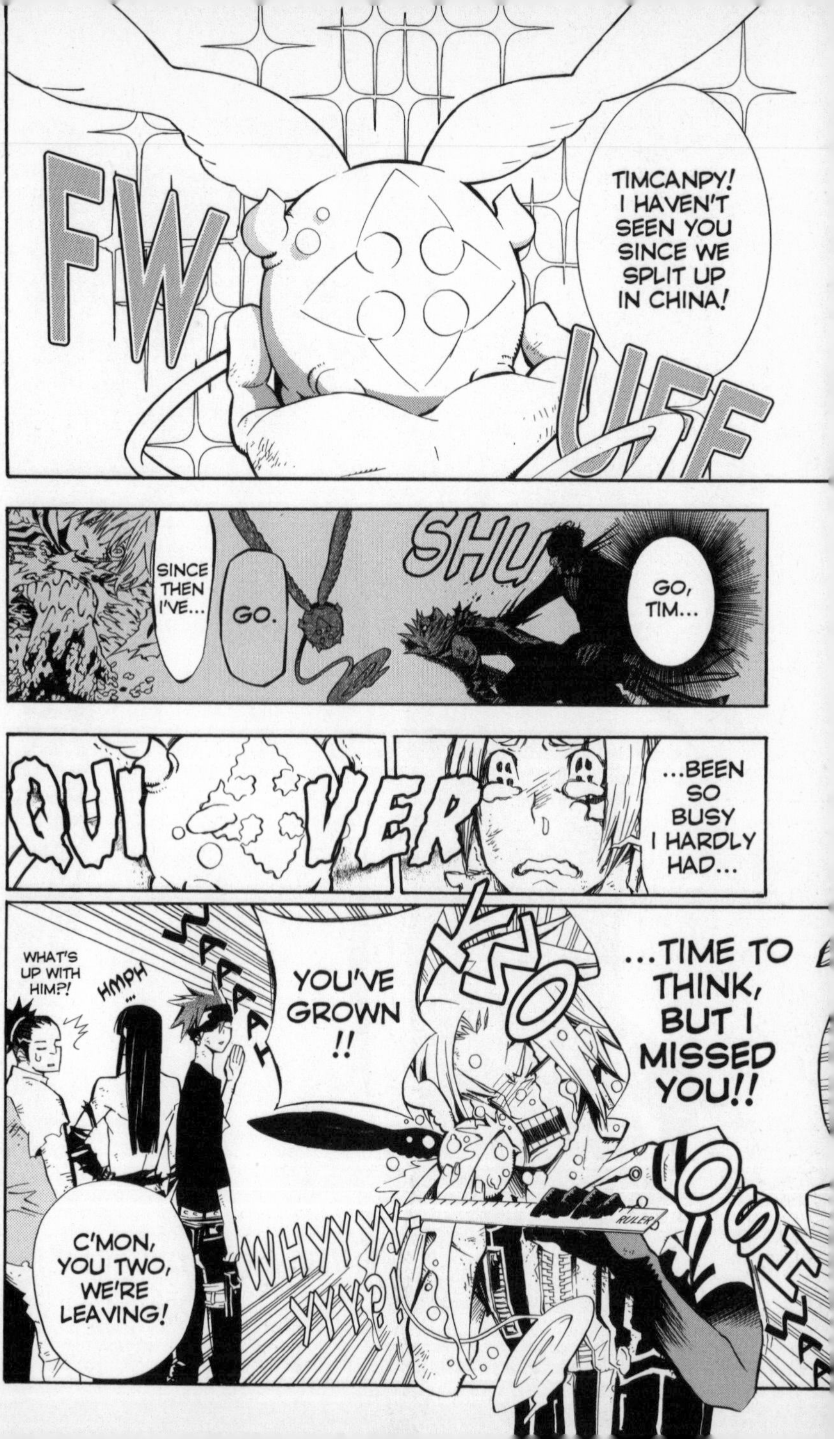
FWUFF
TIMCANPY! I HAVEN'T SEEN YOU SINCE WE SPLIT UP IN CHINA!
GO, TIM...
SHU
GO.
SINCE THEN I'VE...
...BEEN SO BUSY I HARDLY HAD...
QUIVER
...TIME TO THINK, BUT I MISSED YOU!!
YOU'VE GROWN !!
RULER
WHYYYY YYY?!
HMPH...
WHAT'S UP WITH HIM?!
C'MON, YOU TWO, WE'RE LEAVING!

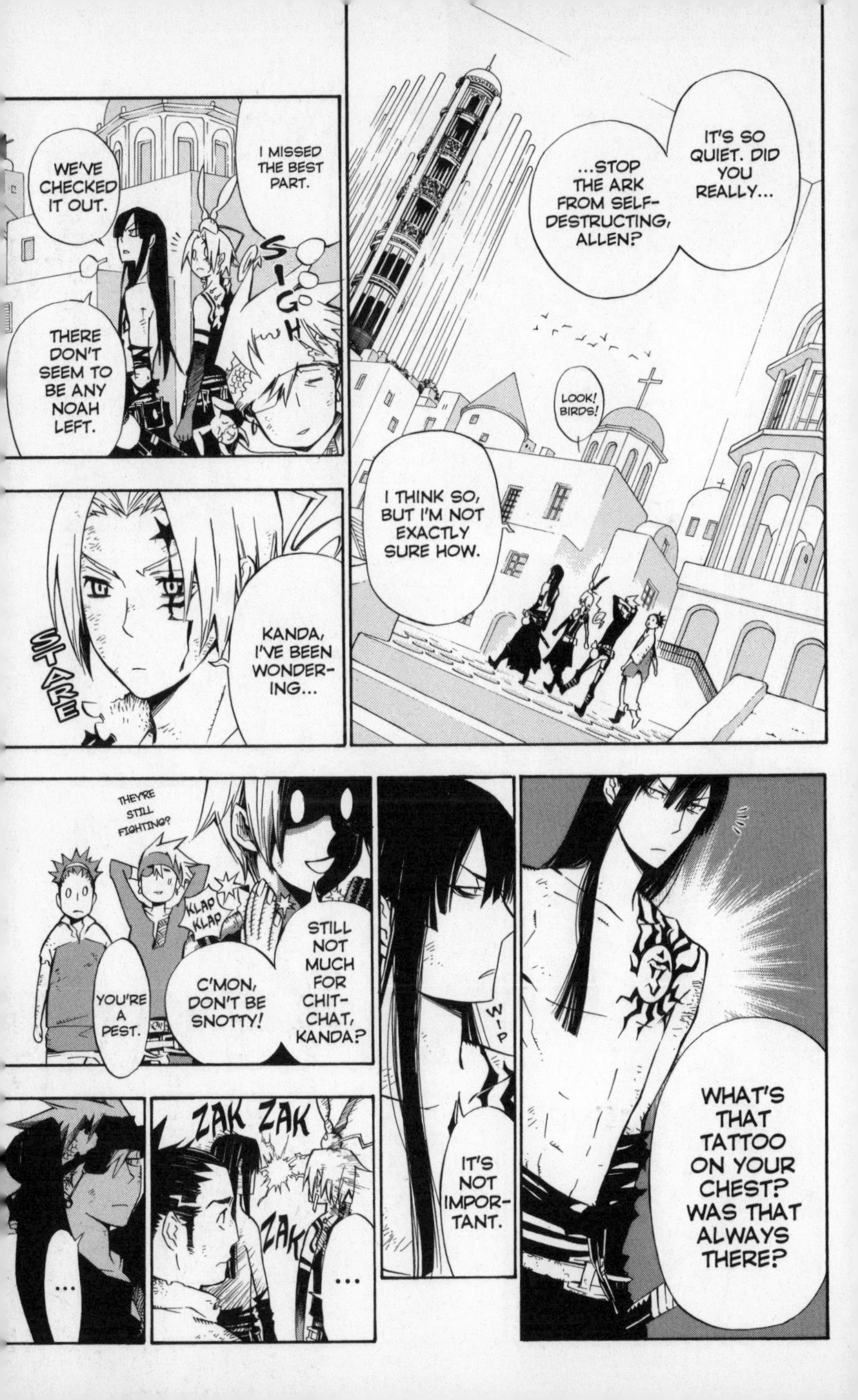
IT'S SO QUIET. DID YOU REALLY...
...STOP THE ARK FROM SELF-DESTRUCTING, ALLEN?
LOOK! BIRDS!
I THINK SO, BUT I'M NOT EXACTLY SURE HOW.
I MISSED THE BEST PART.
WE'VE CHECKED IT OUT.
SIGH
THERE DON'T SEEM TO BE ANY NOAH LEFT.
KANDA, I'VE BEEN WONDERING...
STARE
WHAT'S THAT TATTOO ON YOUR CHEST? WAS THAT ALWAYS THERE?
WIP
IT'S NOT IMPORTANT.
STILL NOT MUCH FOR CHIT-CHAT, KANDA?
C'MON, DON'T BE SNOTTY!
KLAP KLAP
YOU'RE A PEST.
THEY'RE STILL FIGHTING?
ZAK ZAK
ZAK
...
...

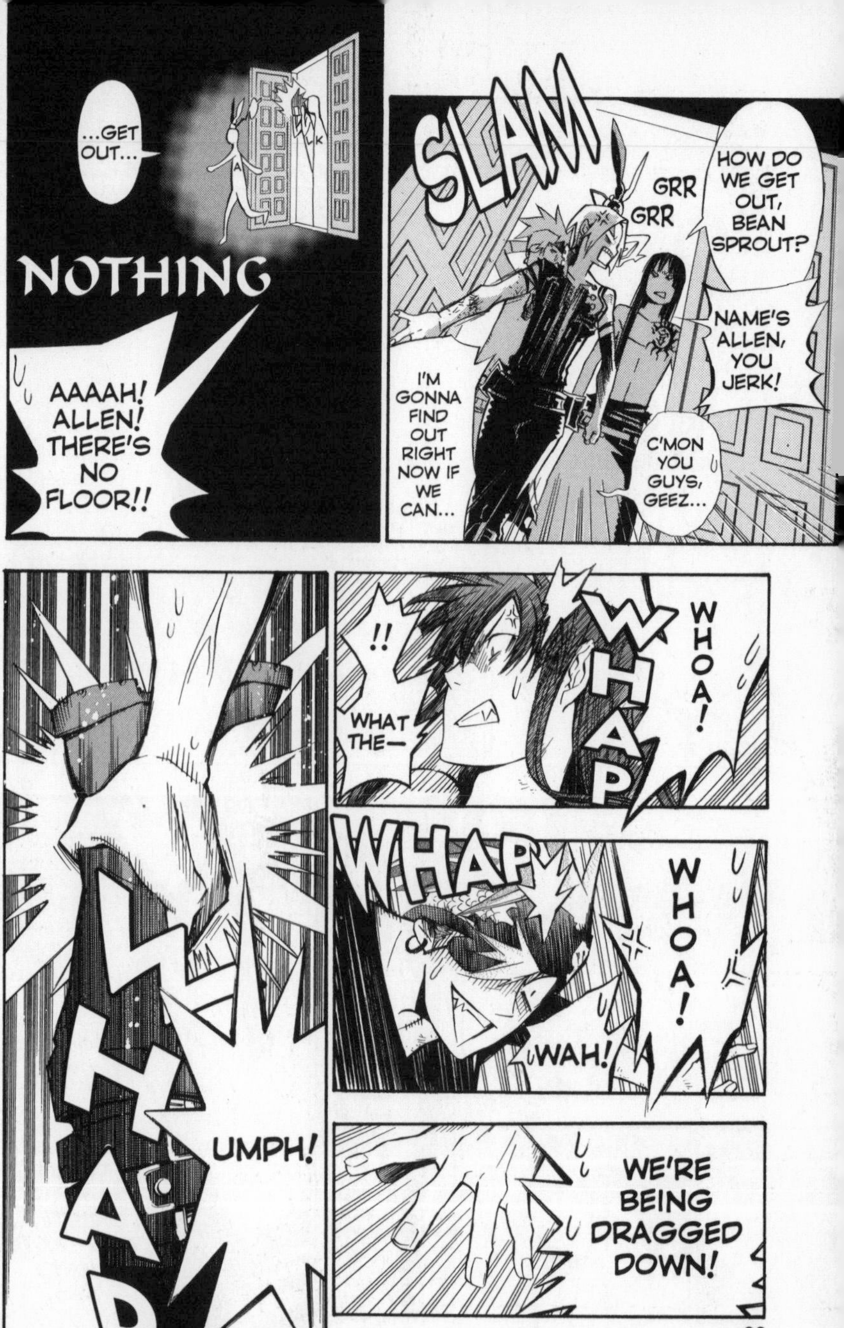

SLAM
HOW DO WE GET OUT, BEAN SPROUT?
GRR
GRR
NAME'S ALLEN, YOU JERK!
I'M GONNA FIND OUT RIGHT NOW IF WE CAN...
C'MON YOU GUYS, GEEZ...
...GET OUT...
NOTHING
AAAAH! ALLEN! THERE'S NO FLOOR!!
WHOA!
WHAP
!!
WHAT THE—
WHOA!
WHAP
WAH!
WE'RE BEING DRAGGED DOWN!
WHAP
UMPH!

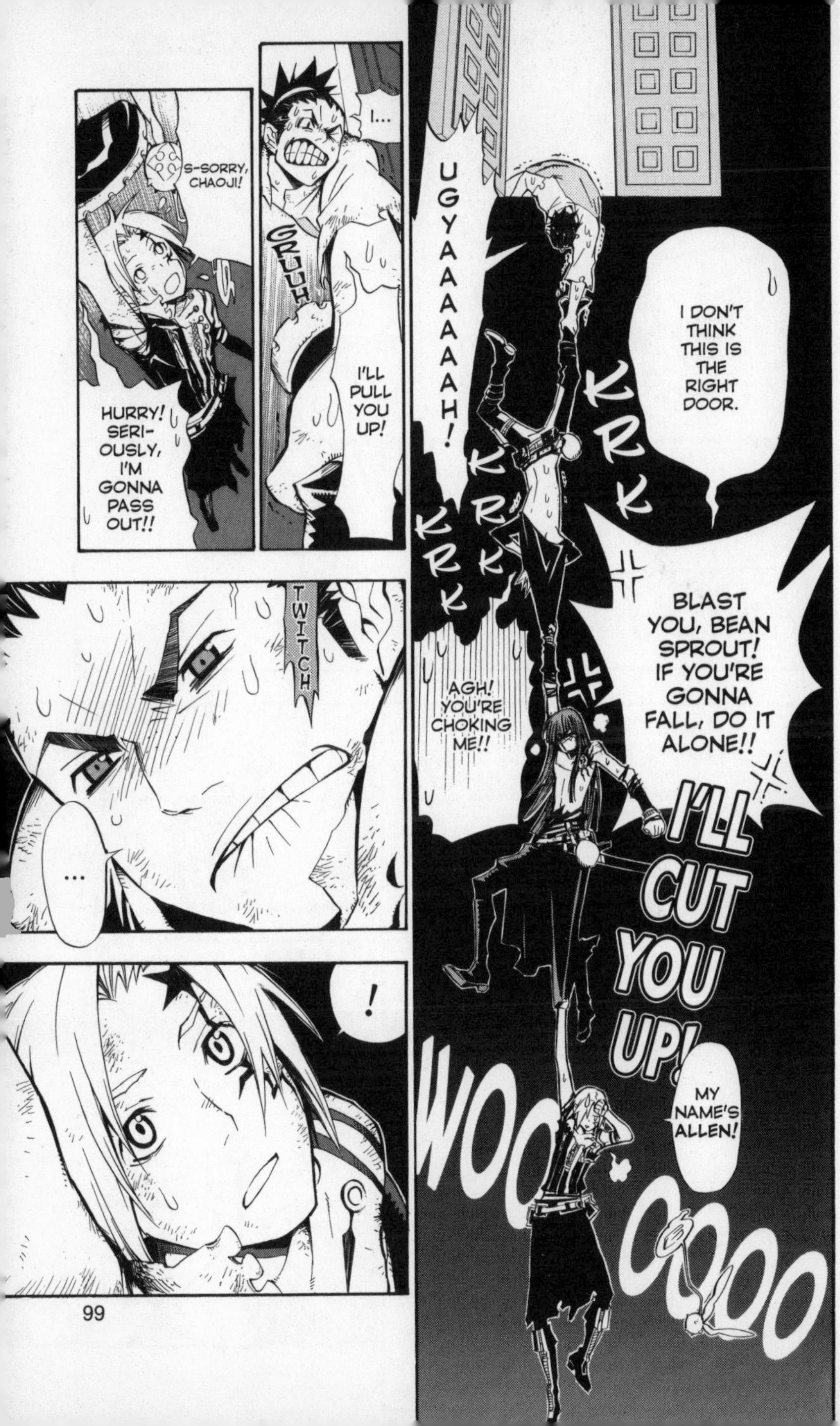
UGYAAAAAAAH!
I DON'T THINK THIS IS THE RIGHT DOOR.
KRK KRK KRK KRK
BLAST YOU, BEAN SPROUT! IF YOU'RE GONNA FALL, DO IT ALONE!!
AGH! YOU'RE CHOKING ME!!
I'LL CUT YOU UP!
MY NAME'S ALLEN!
WOOOOOOO
I...
GRUUH
I'LL PULL YOU UP!
S-SORRY, CHAOJI!
HURRY! SERI-OUSLY, I'M GONNA PASS OUT!!
TWITCH
...
!

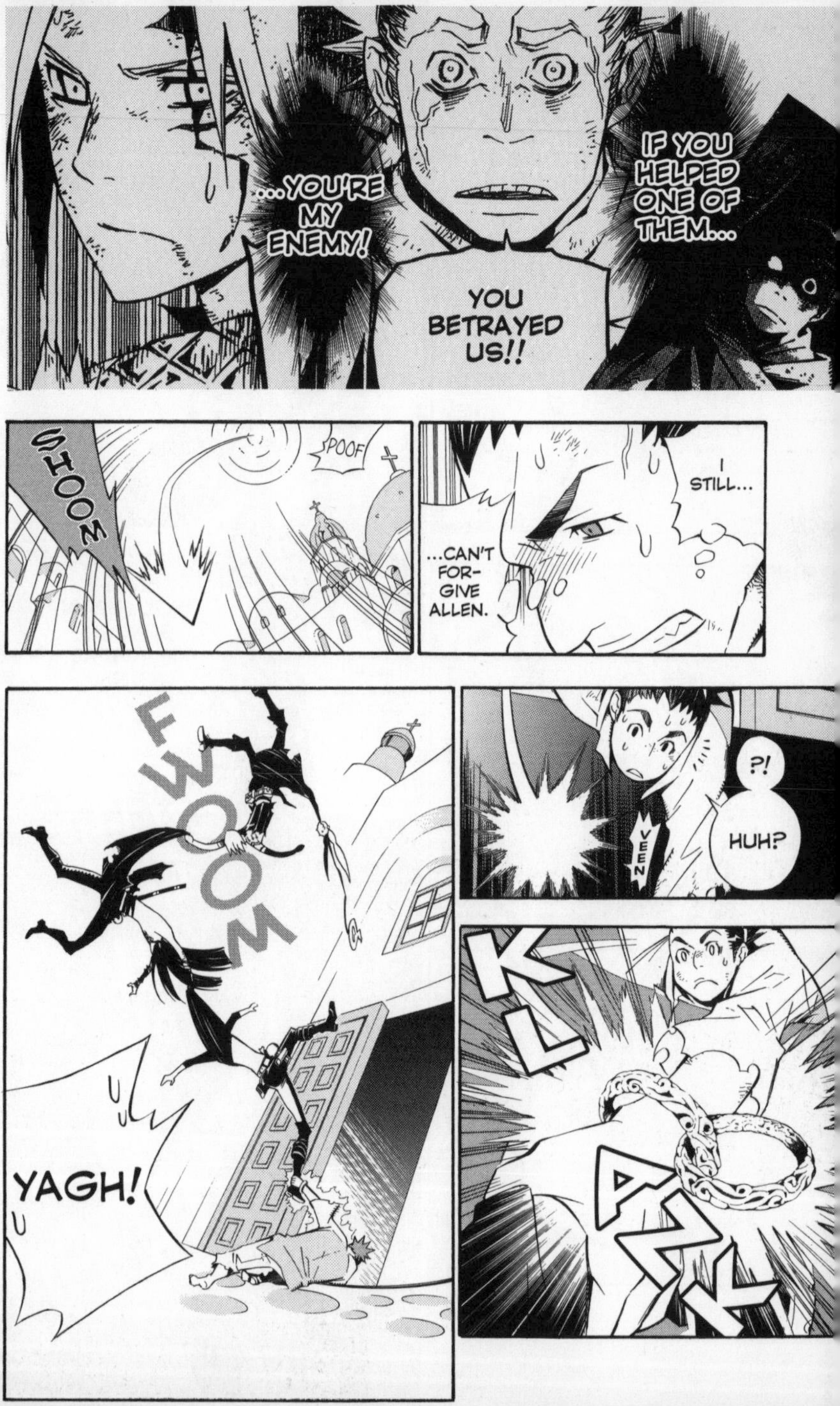
IF YOU HELPED ONE OF THEM...
YOU BETRAYED US!!
...YOU'RE MY ENEMY!
I STILL...
...CAN'T FORGIVE ALLEN.
SHOOM
POOF
?!
HUH?
VEEN
KLAZZK
FWOOM
YAGH!

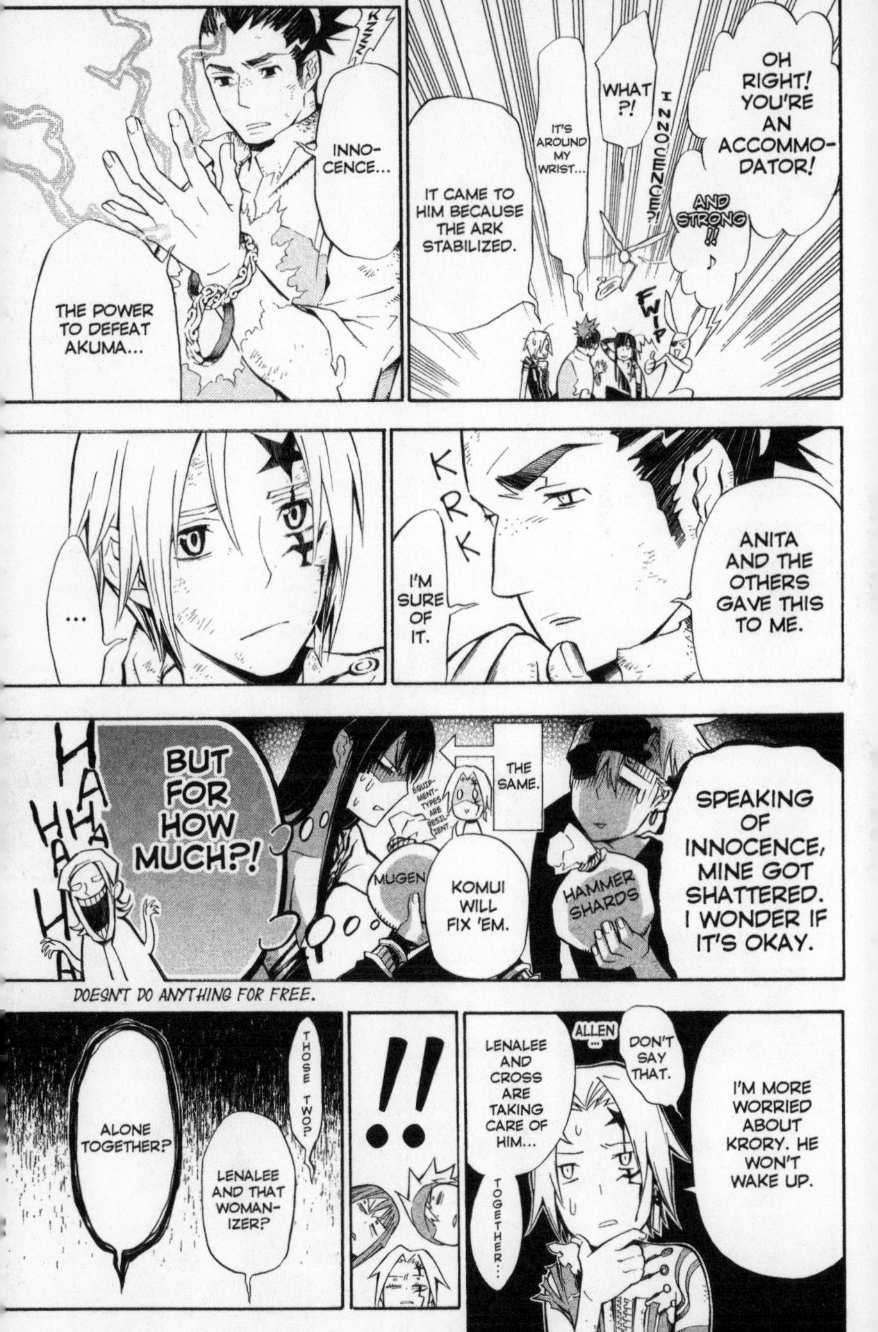
OH RIGHT! YOU'RE AN ACCOMMO-DATOR!
AND STRONG!! ♪
INNOCENCE?!
WHAT?!
IT'S AROUND MY WRIST...
IT CAME TO HIM BECAUSE THE ARK STABILIZED.
FWIP
KNNN
INNO-CENCE...
THE POWER TO DEFEAT AKUMA...
ANITA AND THE OTHERS GAVE THIS TO ME.
I'M SURE OF IT.
KRK
...
SPEAKING OF INNOCENCE, MINE GOT SHATTERED. I WONDER IF IT'S OKAY.
HAMMER SHARDS
THE SAME.
EQUIPMENT-TYPES ARE RESILIENT
KOMUI WILL FIX 'EM.
MUGEN
BUT FOR HOW MUCH?!
HAHAHAHA
DOESN'T DO ANYTHING FOR FREE.
I'M MORE WORRIED ABOUT KRORY. HE WON'T WAKE UP.
DON'T SAY THAT.
ALLEN...
LENALEE AND CROSS ARE TAKING CARE OF HIM...
TOGETHER...
!!
THOSE TWO?
LENALEE AND THAT WOMAN-IZER?
ALONE TOGETHER?

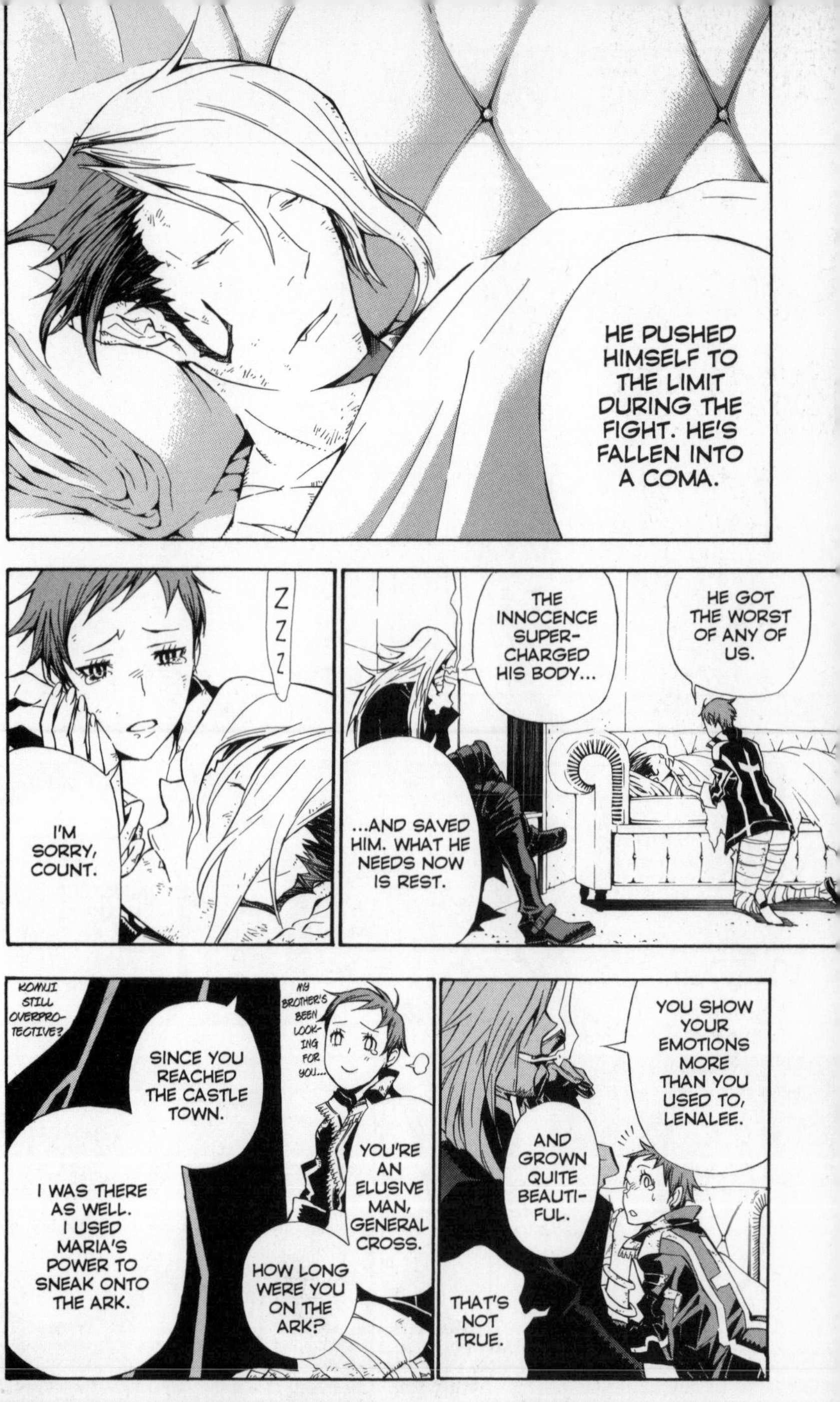
HE PUSHED HIMSELF TO THE LIMIT DURING THE FIGHT. HE'S FALLEN INTO A COMA.
HE GOT THE WORST OF ANY OF US.
THE INNOCENCE SUPER-CHARGED HIS BODY...
...AND SAVED HIM. WHAT HE NEEDS NOW IS REST.
ZZZ
I'M SORRY, COUNT.
YOU SHOW YOUR EMOTIONS MORE THAN YOU USED TO, LENALEE.
AND GROWN QUITE BEAUTI-FUL.
THAT'S NOT TRUE.
MY BROTHER'S BEEN LOOK-ING FOR YOU...
YOU'RE AN ELUSIVE MAN, GENERAL CROSS.
HOW LONG WERE YOU ON THE ARK?
KOMUI STILL OVERPRO-TECTIVE?
SINCE YOU REACHED THE CASTLE TOWN.
I WAS THERE AS WELL. I USED MARIA'S POWER TO SNEAK ONTO THE ARK.

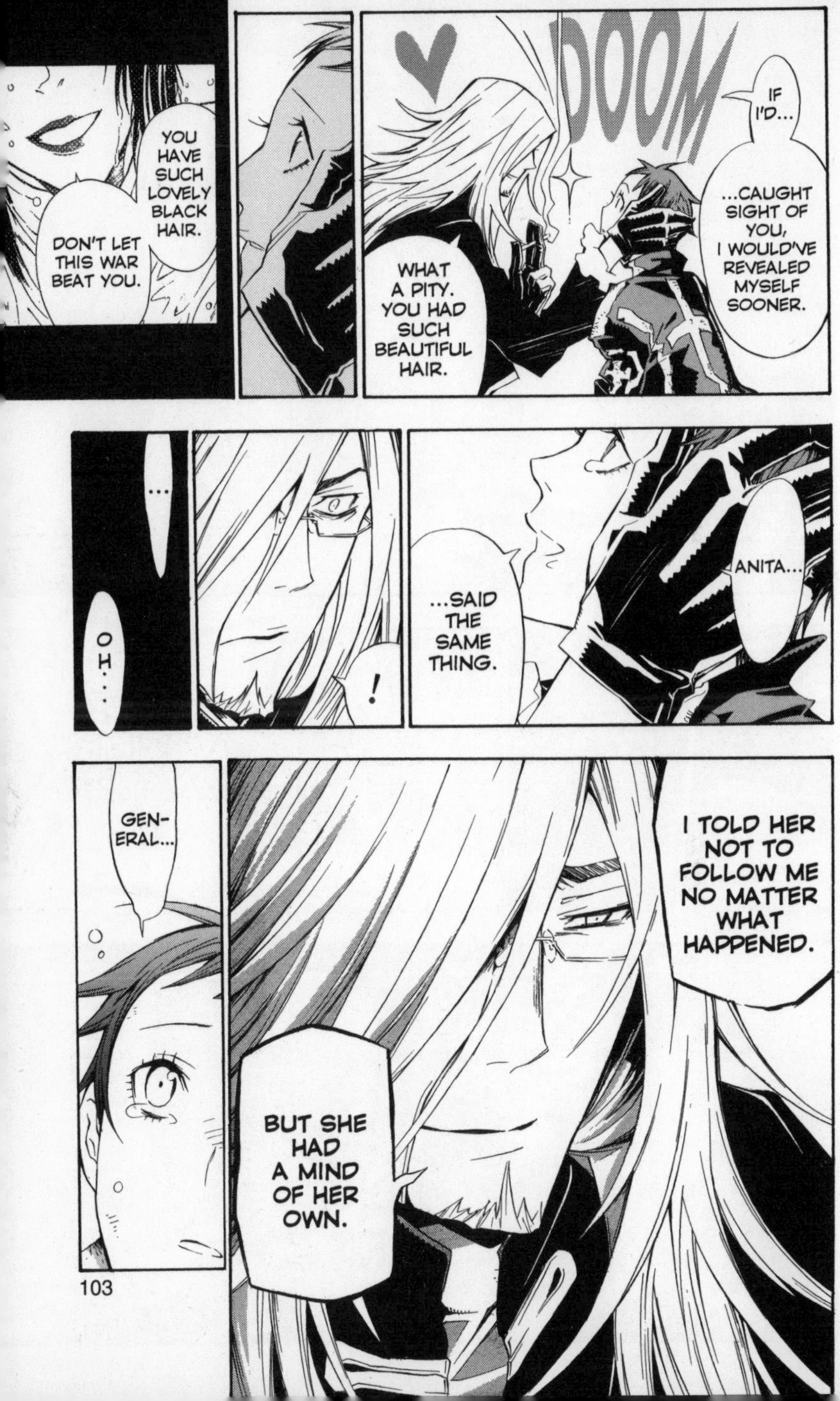
DOOM
IF I'D...
...CAUGHT SIGHT OF YOU, I WOULD'VE REVEALED MYSELF SOONER.
WHAT A PITY. YOU HAD SUCH BEAUTIFUL HAIR.
YOU HAVE SUCH LOVELY BLACK HAIR.
DON'T LET THIS WAR BEAT YOU.
ANITA...
...SAID THE SAME THING.
!
...
OH...
I TOLD HER NOT TO FOLLOW ME NO MATTER WHAT HAPPENED.
BUT SHE HAD A MIND OF HER OWN.
GEN-ERAL...

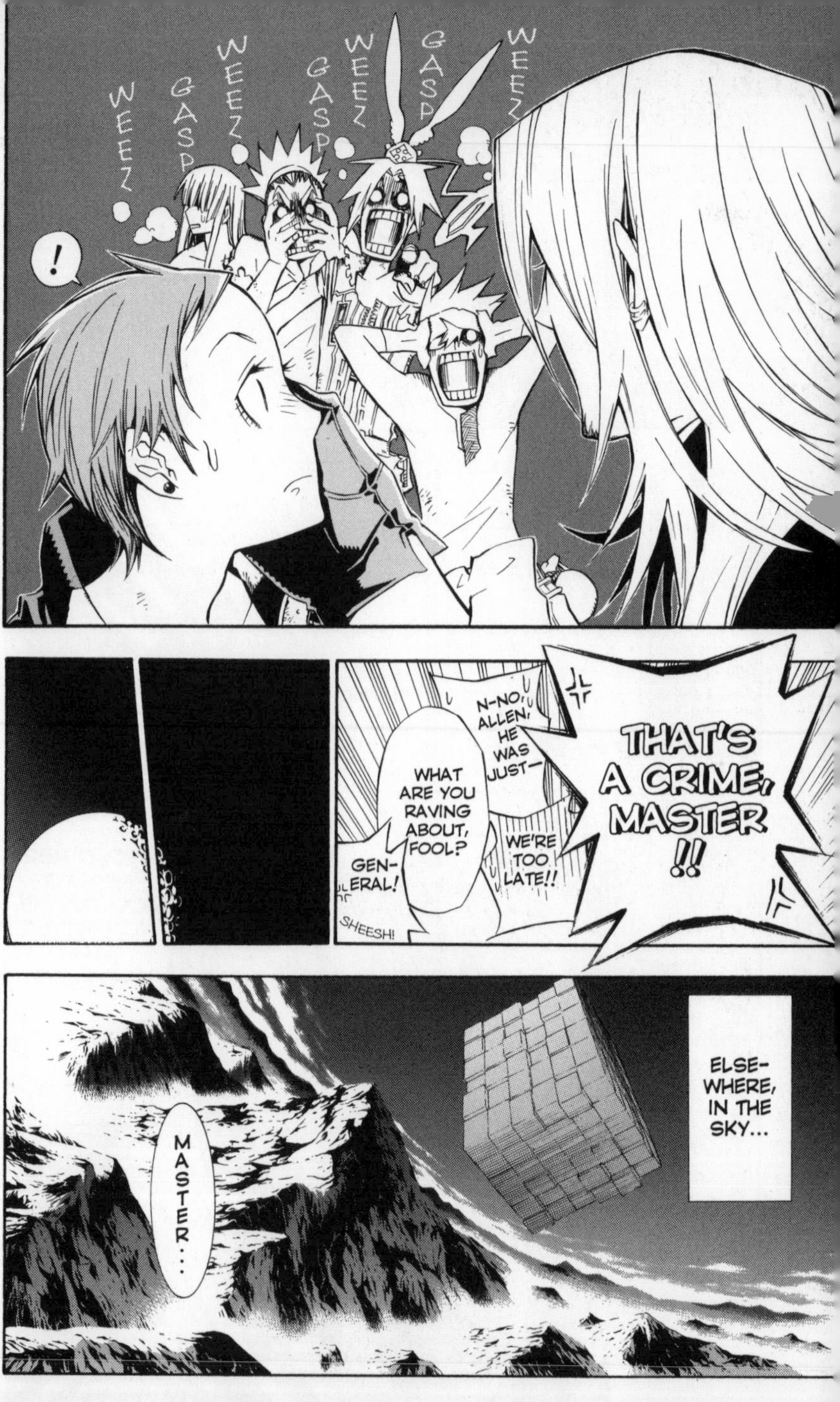
WEEZ
GASP
WEEZ
GASP
WEEZ
GASP
WEEZ
!
THAT'S A CRIME, MASTER!!
N-NO, ALLEN, HE WAS JUST—
WE'RE TOO LATE!!
WHAT ARE YOU RAVING ABOUT, FOOL?
GEN-ERAL!
SHEESH!
ELSE-WHERE, IN THE SKY...
MASTER...

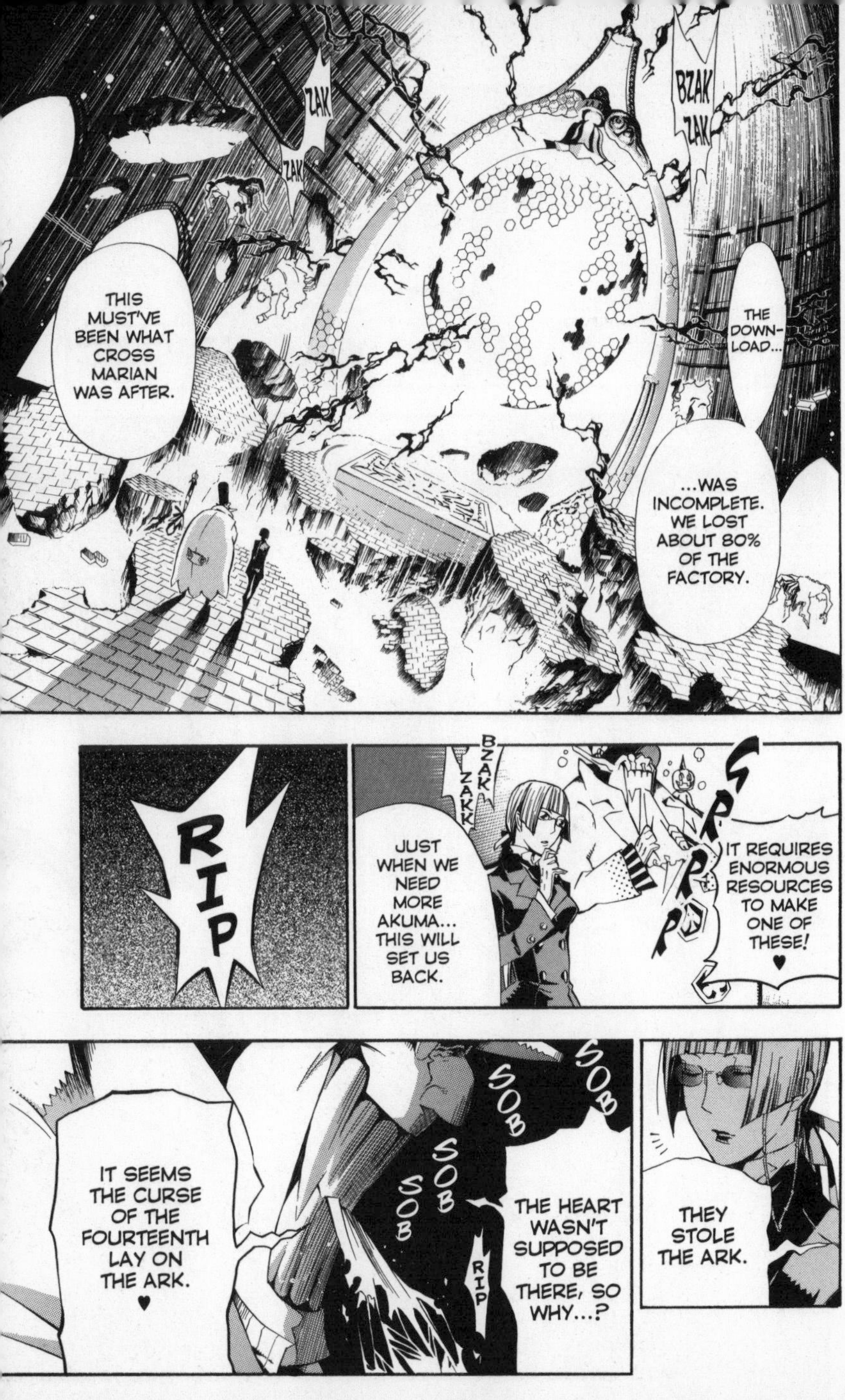
BZAK
ZAK
THE DOWN-LOAD...
...WAS INCOMPLETE. WE LOST ABOUT 80% OF THE FACTORY.
ZAK
ZAK
THIS MUST'VE BEEN WHAT CROSS MARIAN WAS AFTER.
BZAK
ZAKK
SPRRP
IT REQUIRES ENORMOUS RESOURCES TO MAKE ONE OF THESE! ♥
JUST WHEN WE NEED MORE AKUMA... THIS WILL SET US BACK.
RIP
THEY STOLE THE ARK.
SOB
SOB
THE HEART WASN'T SUPPOSED TO BE THERE, SO WHY...?
RIP
SOB
SOB
SOB
IT SEEMS THE CURSE OF THE FOURTEENTH LAY ON THE ARK. ♥

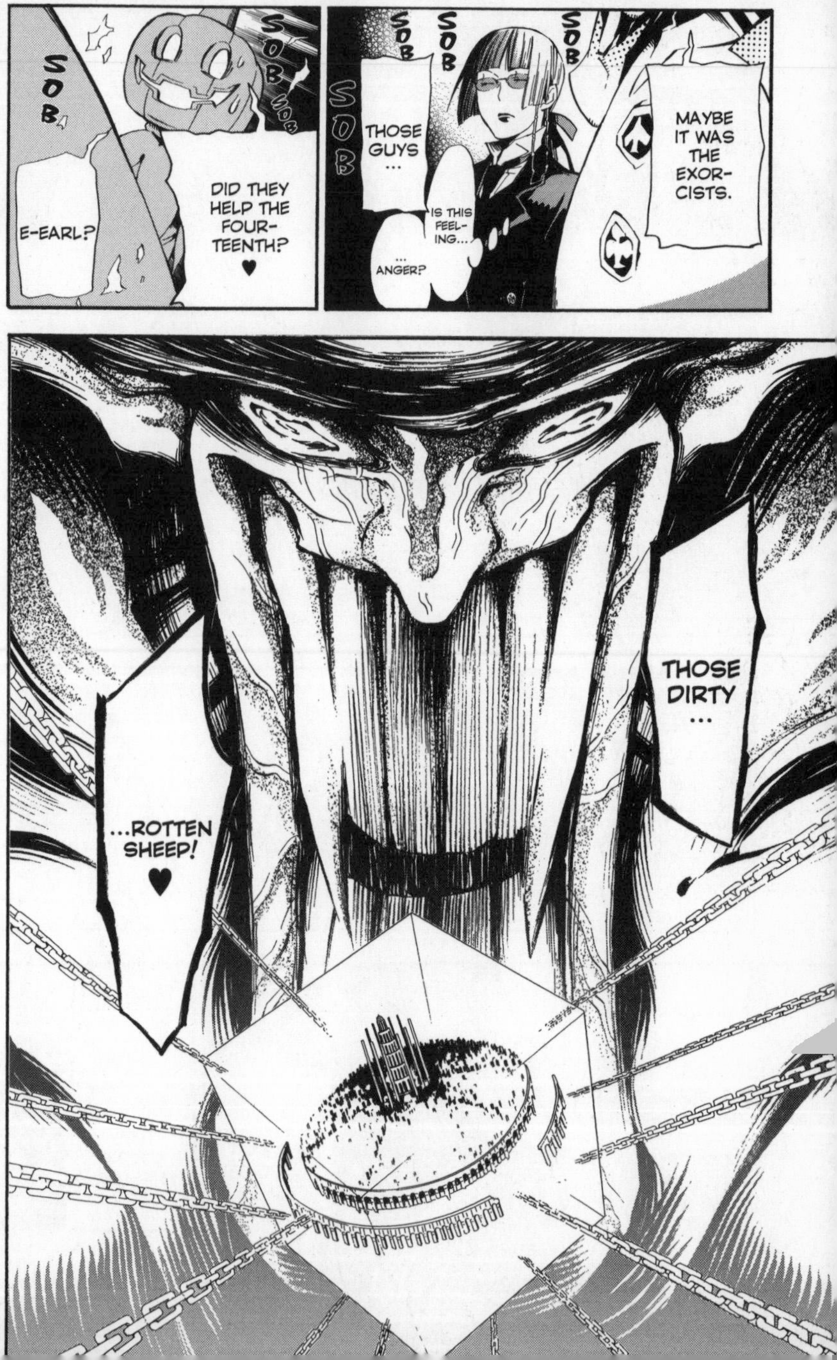
SOB
MAYBE IT WAS THE EXORCISTS.
SOB
SOB
SOB
SOB
THOSE GUYS ...
IS THIS FEELING...
... ANGER?
SOB SOB
SOB
DID THEY HELP THE FOUR-TEENTH? ♥
SOB
E-EARL?
THOSE DIRTY ...
...ROTTEN SHEEP! ♥

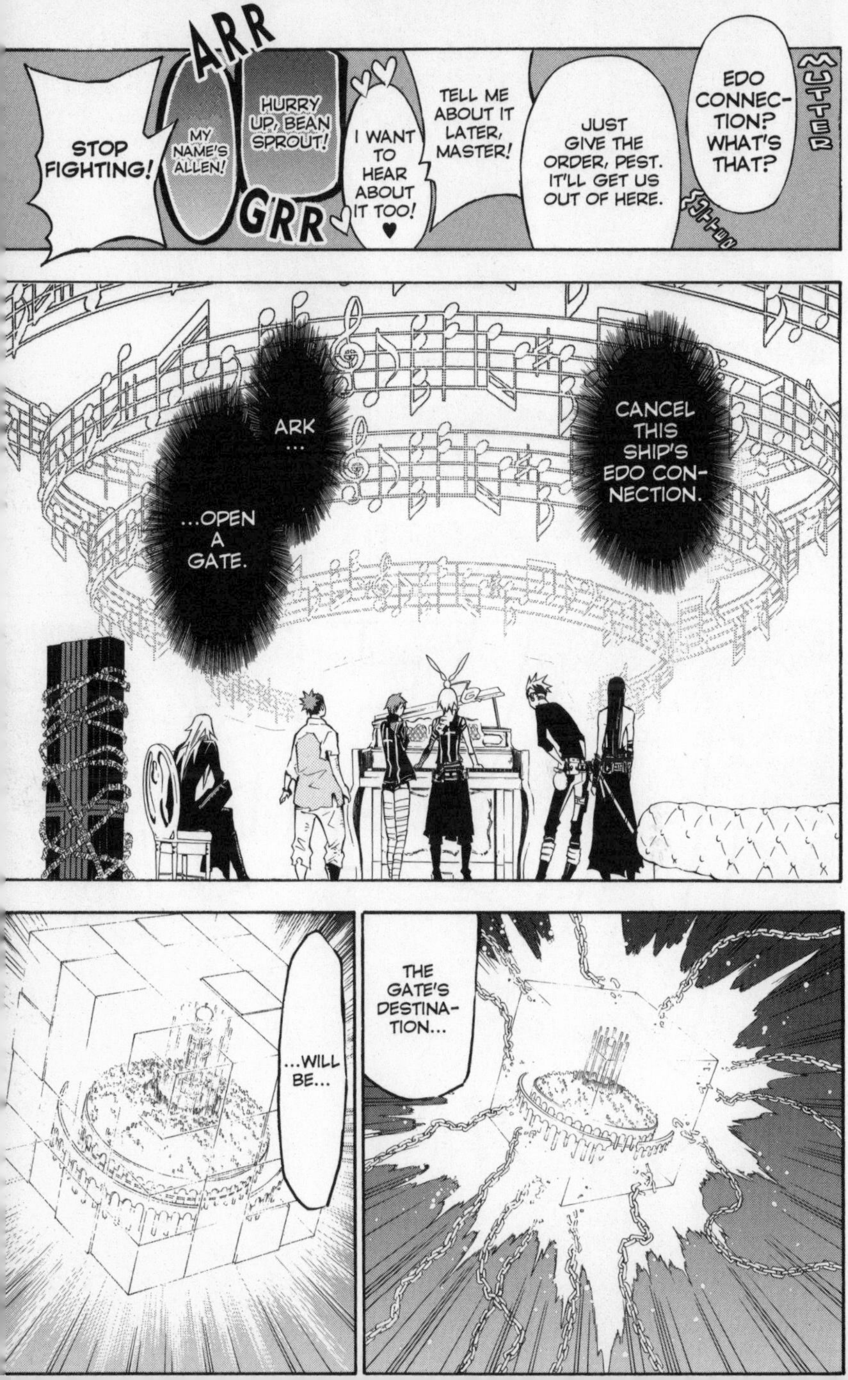
MUTTER
EDO CONNECTION? WHAT'S THAT?
JUST GIVE THE ORDER, PEST. IT'LL GET US OUT OF HERE.
TELL ME ABOUT IT LATER, MASTER!
I WANT TO HEAR ABOUT IT TOO! ♥
HURRY UP, BEAN SPROUT!
ARR
MY NAME'S ALLEN!
GRR
STOP FIGHTING!
CANCEL THIS SHIP'S EDO CONNECTION.
ARK...
...OPEN A GATE.
THE GATE'S DESTINATION...
...WILL BE...

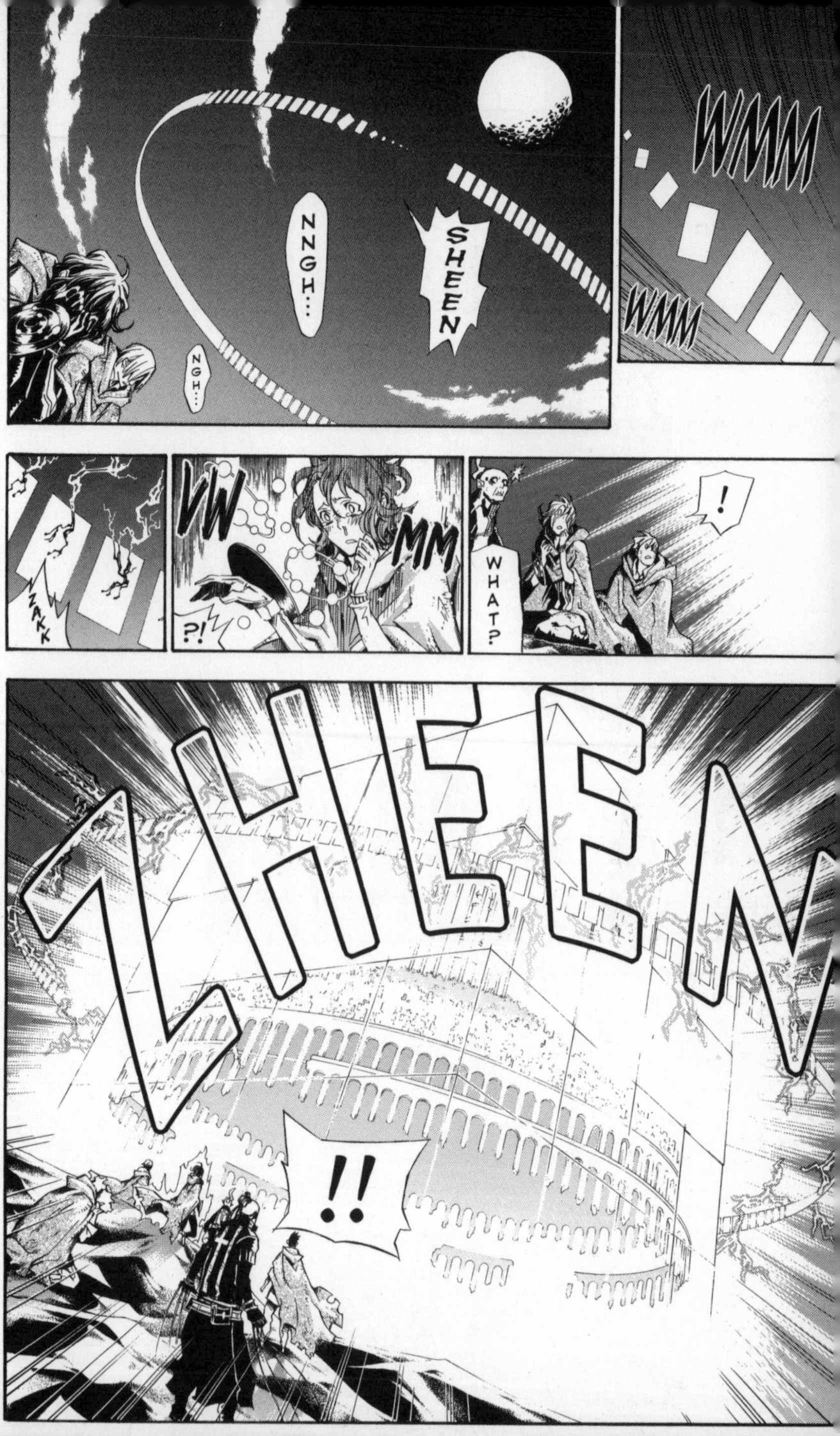
WMM
WMM
SHEEN
NNGH...
NGH...
!
WHAT?
VW
MM
?!
ZAKK
ZHEEN
!!

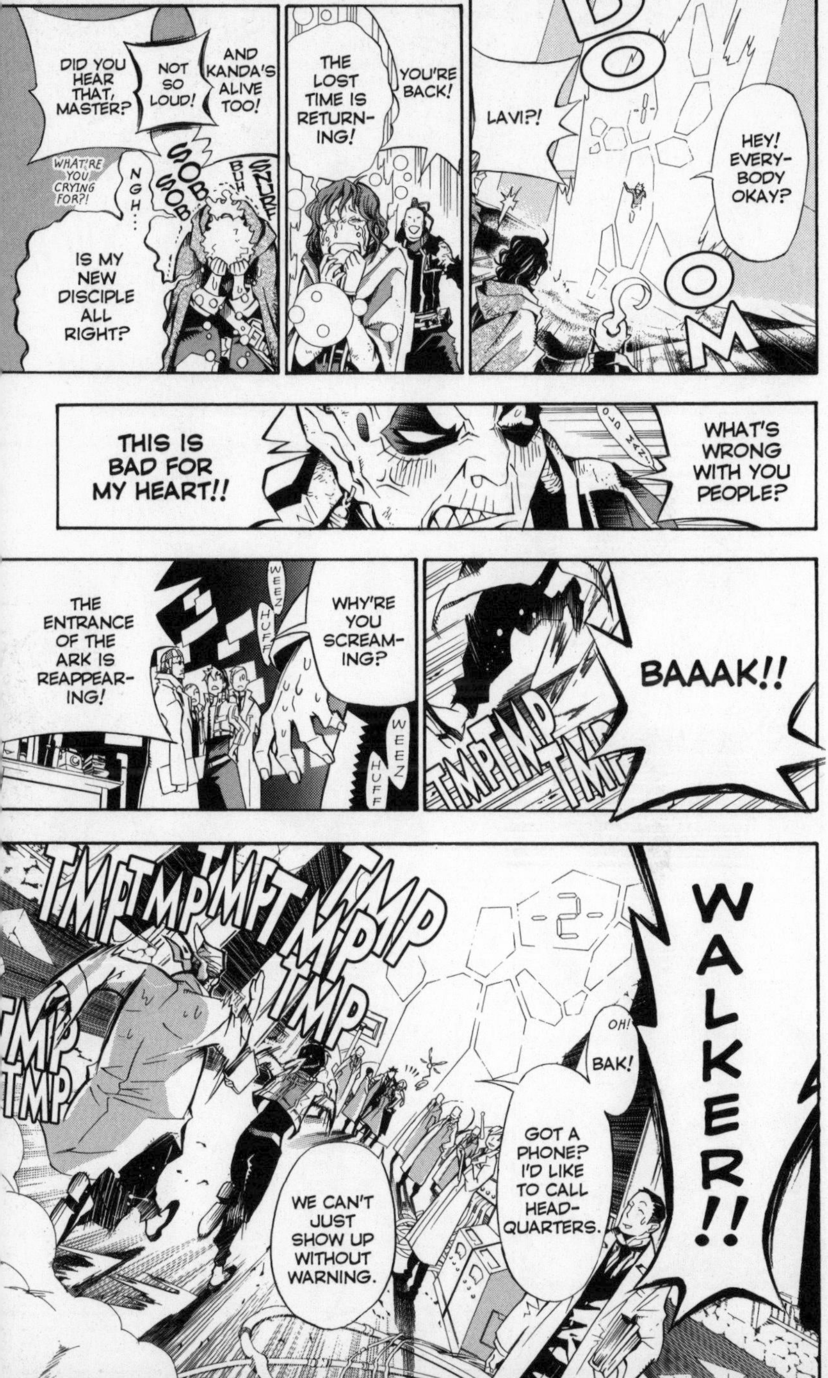
DOOM
HEY! EVERYBODY OKAY?
LAVI?!
YOU'RE BACK!
THE LOST TIME IS RETURNING!
AND KANDA'S ALIVE TOO!
NOT SO LOUD!
DID YOU HEAR THAT, MASTER?
SNURF
BUH
SOB SOB
NGH...
WHAT'RE YOU CRYING FOR?!
IS MY NEW DISCIPLE ALL RIGHT?
WHAT'S WRONG WITH YOU PEOPLE?
OLD MAN...
THIS IS BAD FOR MY HEART!!
BAAAK!!
TMP TMP TMP TMP
WHY'RE YOU SCREAMING?
WEEZ HUFF
WEEZ HUFF
THE ENTRANCE OF THE ARK IS REAPPEARING!
WALKER!!
OH!
BAK!
GOT A PHONE? I'D LIKE TO CALL HEADQUARTERS.
WE CAN'T JUST SHOW UP WITHOUT WARNING.
TMP TMP TMP TMP TMP TMP TMP
TMP TMP

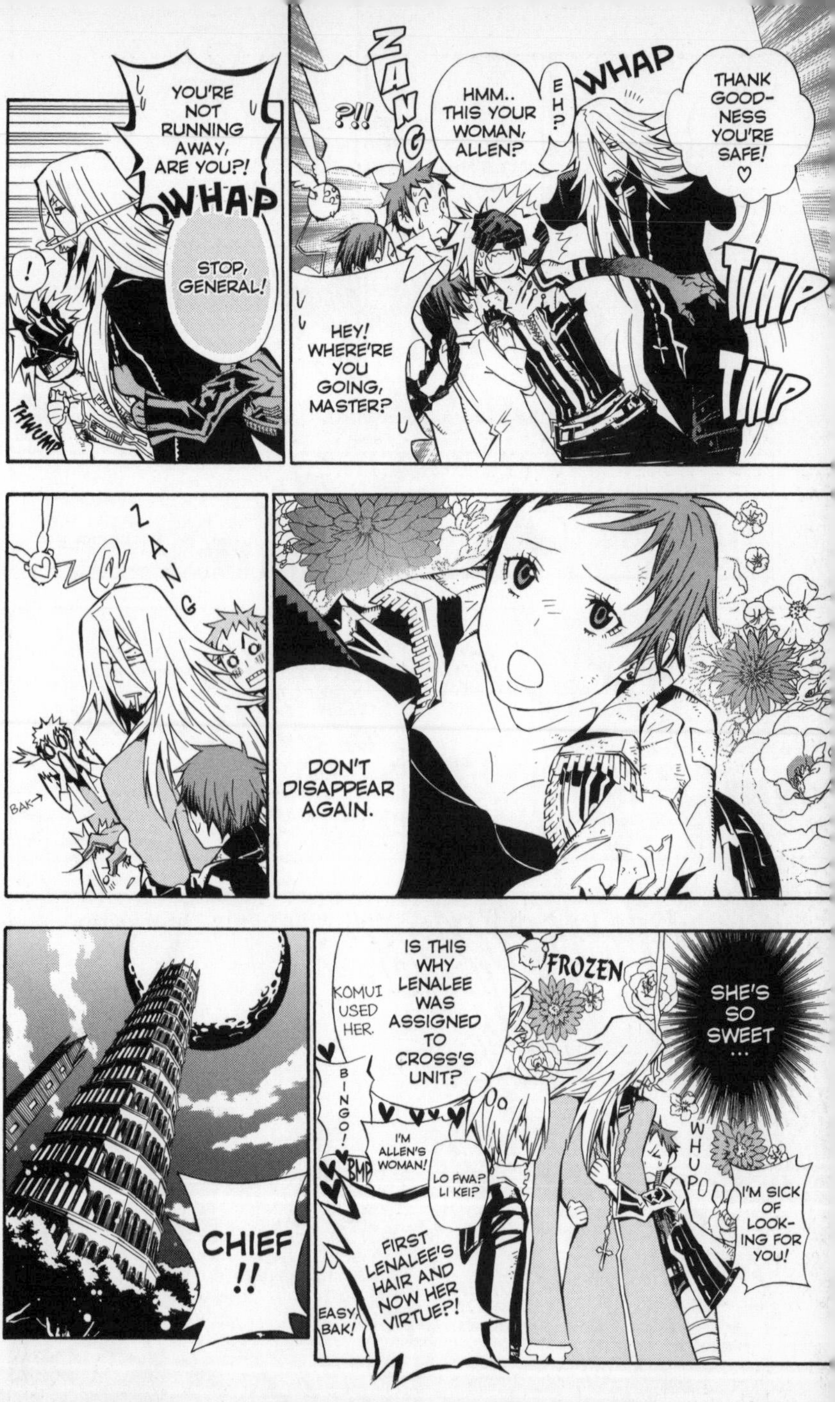
THANK GOODNESS YOU'RE SAFE! ♡
WHAP
EH?
HMM.. THIS YOUR WOMAN, ALLEN?
ZANG
?!!
TMP
TMP
HEY! WHERE'RE YOU GOING, MASTER?
YOU'RE NOT RUNNING AWAY, ARE YOU?!
WHAP
STOP, GENERAL!
!
THWUMP
DON'T DISAPPEAR AGAIN.
ZANG
BAK→
SHE'S SO SWEET...
FROZEN
IS THIS WHY LENALEE WAS ASSIGNED TO CROSS'S UNIT?
KOMUI USED HER.
BINGO!
WHUP
I'M SICK OF LOOKING FOR YOU!
I'M ALLEN'S WOMAN!
LO FWA? LI KEI?
BMP
FIRST LENALEE'S HAIR AND NOW HER VIRTUE?!
EASY, BAK!
CHIEF!!

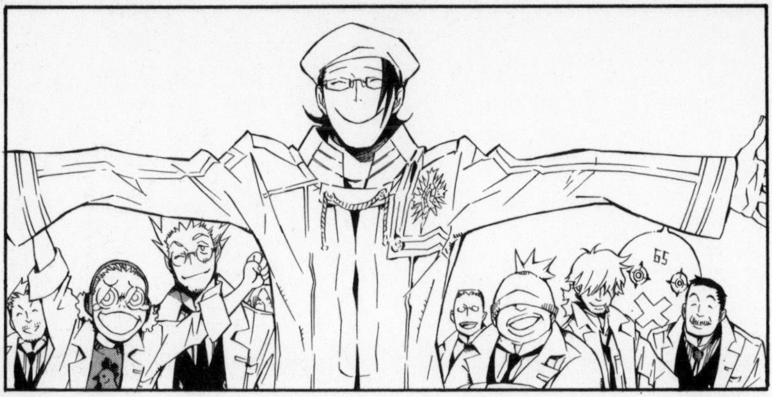
65
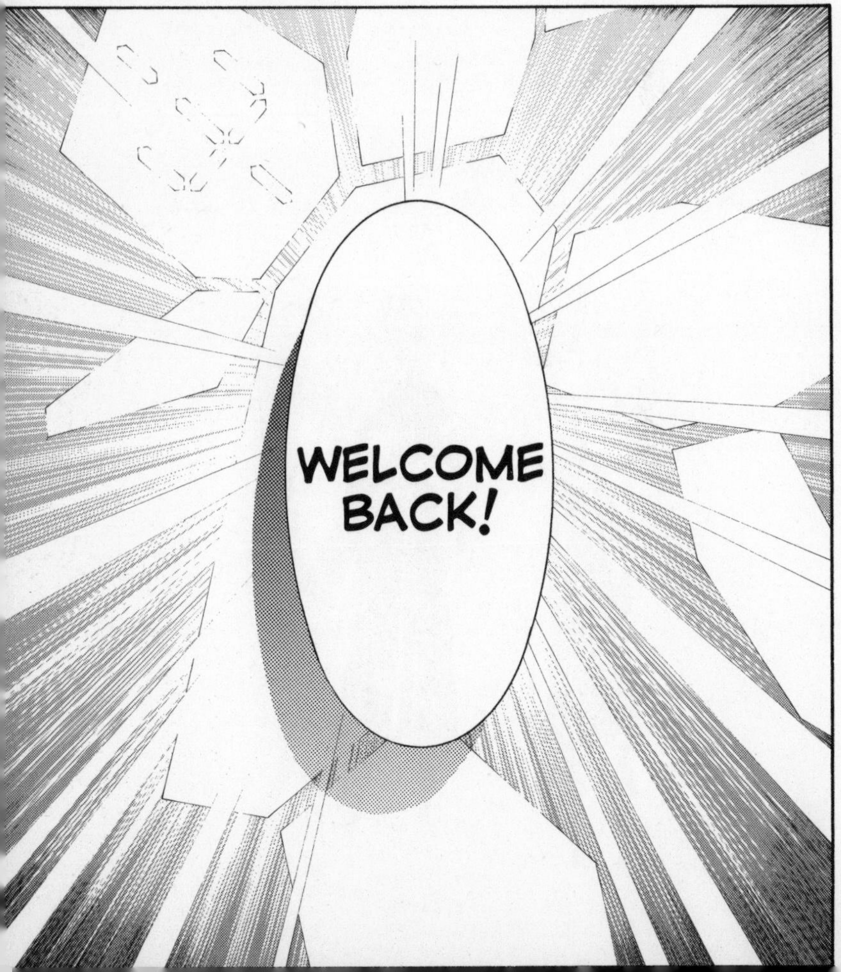
WELCOME BACK!

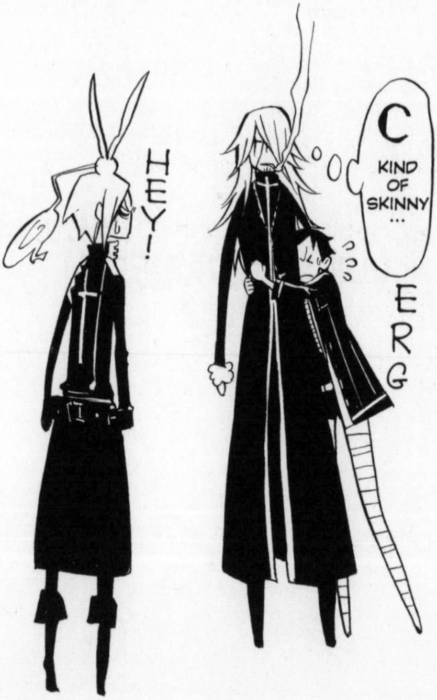
C
KIND OF SKINNY...
ERG
HEY!

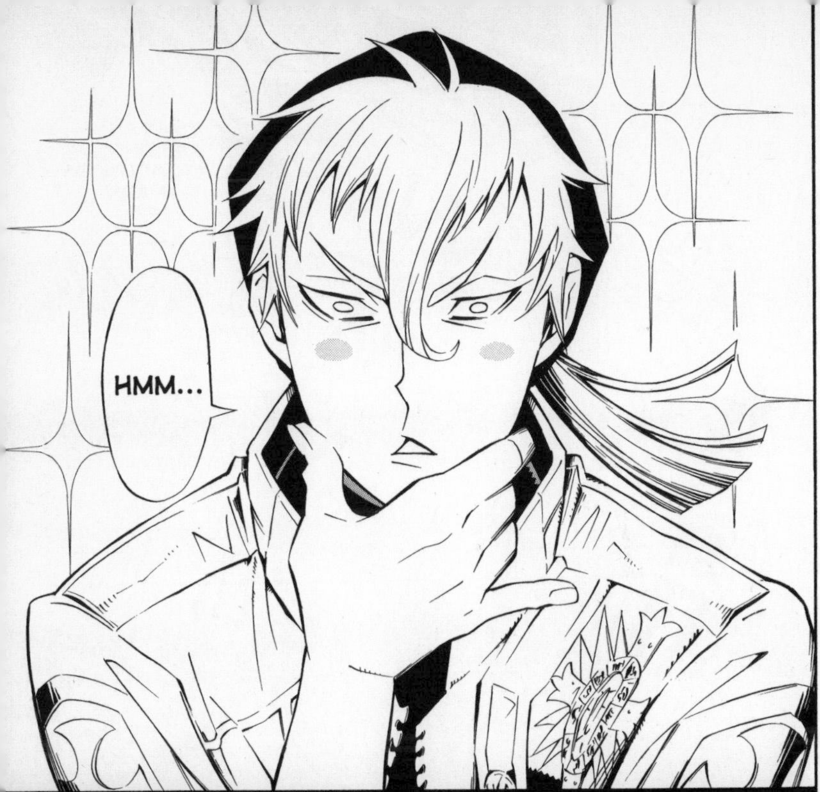
HMM...

# THE 135TH NIGHT: REPOSE, PARTLY CLOUDY

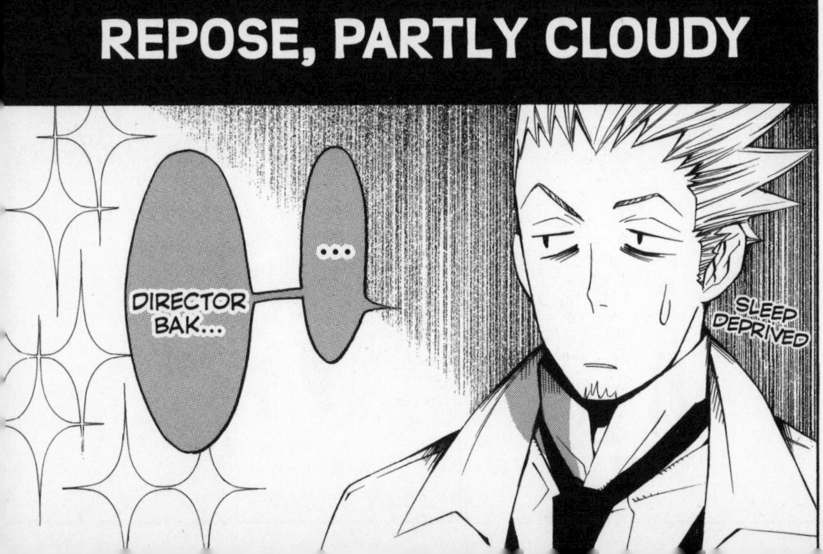
SLEEP DEPRIVED
...
DIRECTOR BAK...

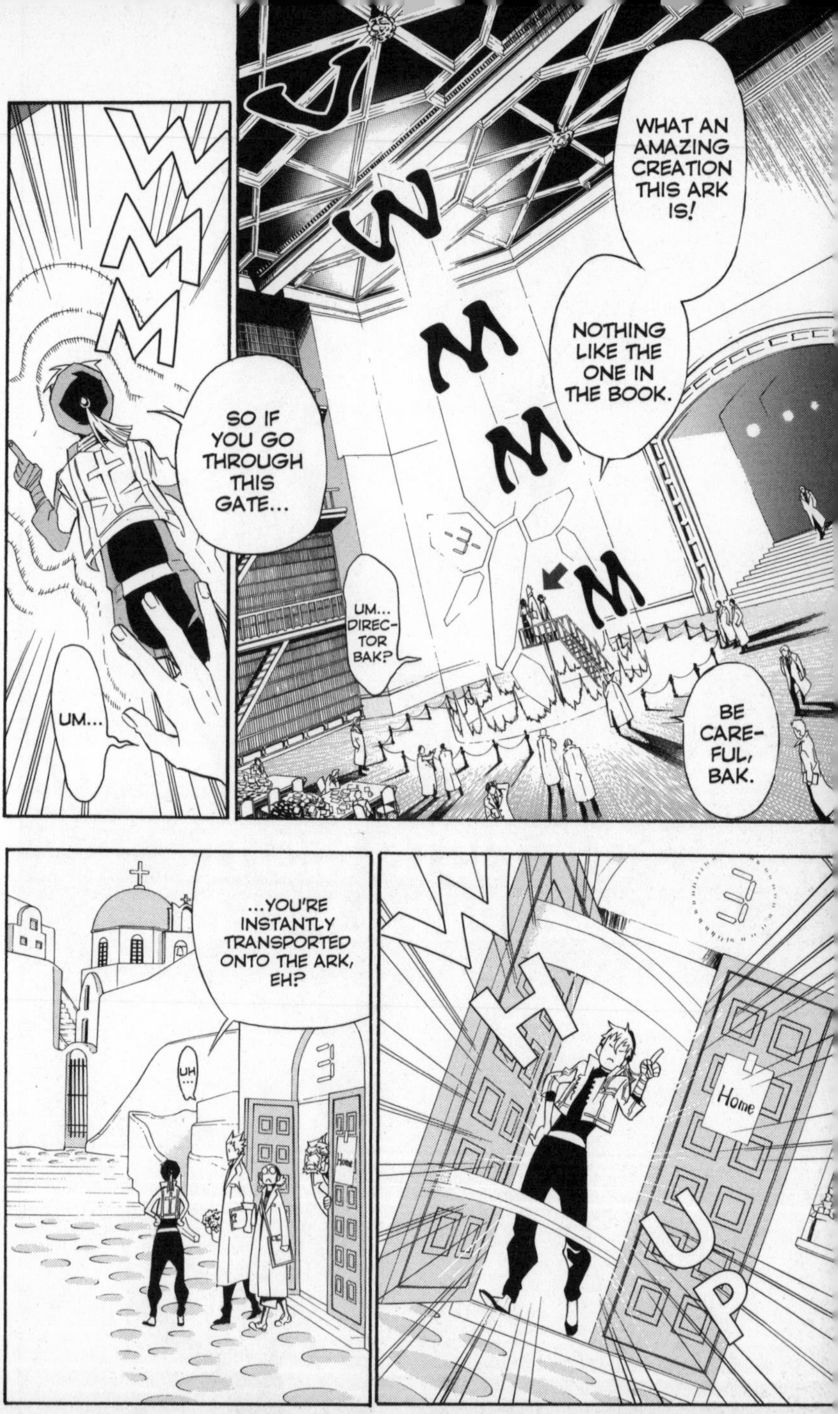
WHAT AN AMAZING CREATION THIS ARK IS!
NOTHING LIKE THE ONE IN THE BOOK.
WMMMM
BE CAREFUL, BAK.
UM... DIRECTOR BAK?
WMMM
SO IF YOU GO THROUGH THIS GATE...
UM...
WHUP
Home
...YOU'RE INSTANTLY TRANSPORTED ONTO THE ARK, EH?
UH...
Home

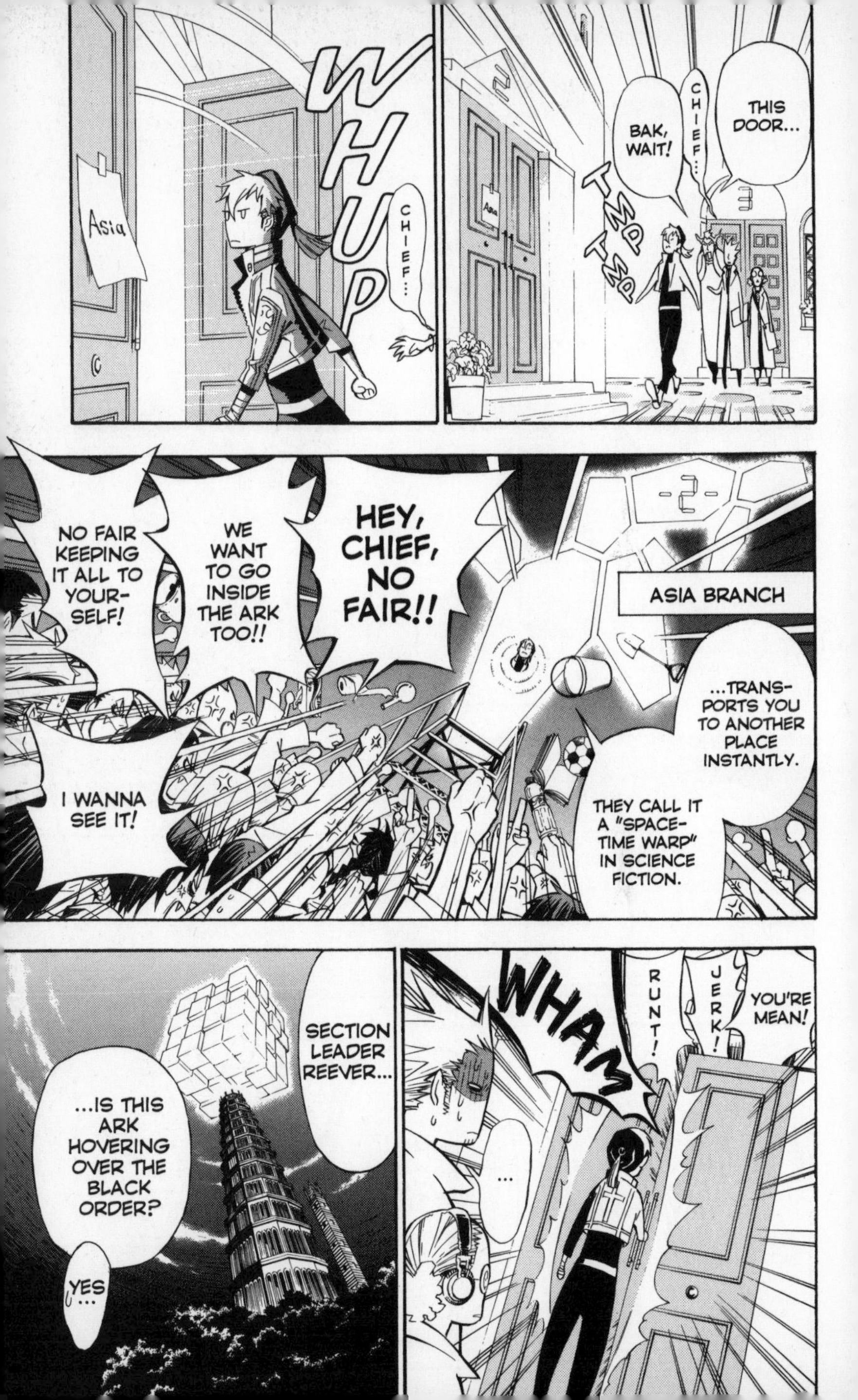
THIS DOOR...
CHIEF...
BAK, WAIT!
TMP TMP TMP
WHUP
CHIEF...
Asia
Asia
ASIA BRANCH
...TRANSPORTS YOU TO ANOTHER PLACE INSTANTLY.
THEY CALL IT A "SPACE-TIME WARP" IN SCIENCE FICTION.
HEY, CHIEF, NO FAIR!!
WE WANT TO GO INSIDE THE ARK TOO!!
NO FAIR KEEPING IT ALL TO YOUR-SELF!
I WANNA SEE IT!
YOU'RE MEAN!
JERK!
RUNT!
WHAM
...
SECTION LEADER REEVER...
...IS THIS ARK HOVERING OVER THE BLACK ORDER?
YES...

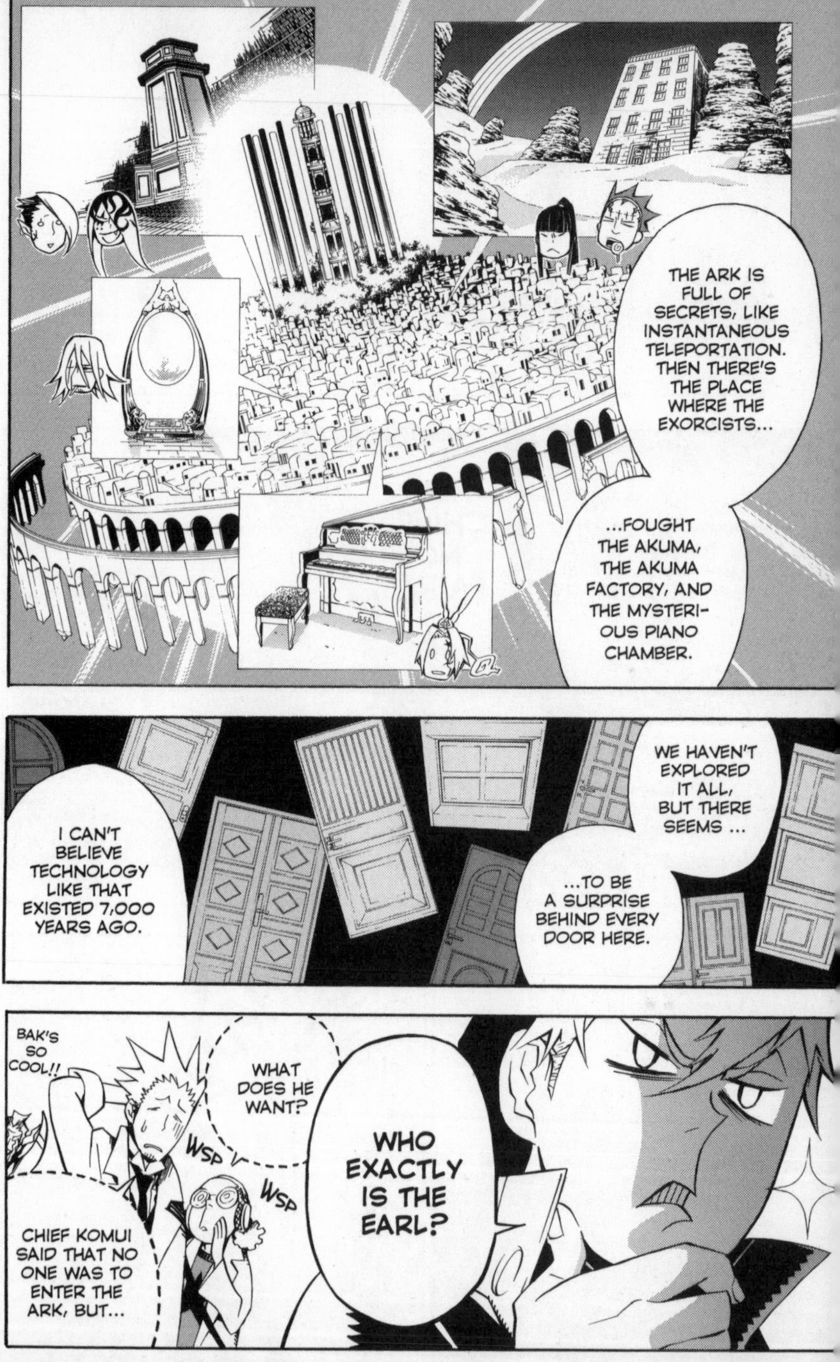
THE ARK IS FULL OF SECRETS, LIKE INSTANTANEOUS TELEPORTATION. THEN THERE'S THE PLACE WHERE THE EXORCISTS...
...FOUGHT THE AKUMA, THE AKUMA FACTORY, AND THE MYSTERI-OUS PIANO CHAMBER.
WE HAVEN'T EXPLORED IT ALL, BUT THERE SEEMS ...
...TO BE A SURPRISE BEHIND EVERY DOOR HERE.
I CAN'T BELIEVE TECHNOLOGY LIKE THAT EXISTED 7,000 YEARS AGO.
WHO EXACTLY IS THE EARL?
WHAT DOES HE WANT?
BAK'S SO COOL!!
WSP
WSP
CHIEF KOMUI SAID THAT NO ONE WAS TO ENTER THE ARK, BUT...

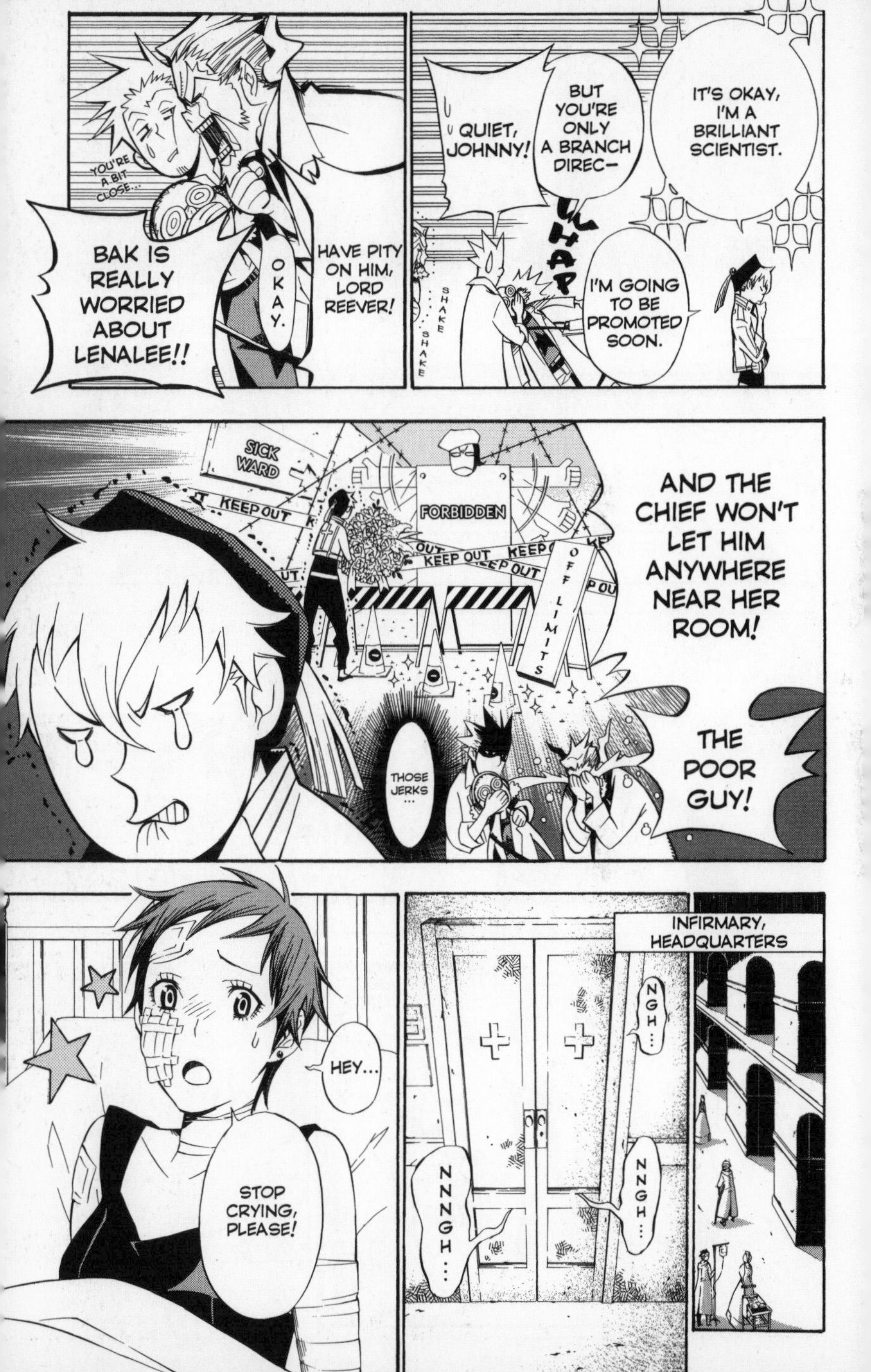
IT'S OKAY, I'M A BRILLIANT SCIENTIST.
BUT YOU'RE ONLY A BRANCH DIREC—
QUIET, JOHNNY!
WHAP
I'M GOING TO BE PROMOTED SOON.
SHAKE SHAKE
HAVE PITY ON HIM, LORD REEVER!
OKAY.
YOU'RE A BIT CLOSE...
BAK IS REALLY WORRIED ABOUT LENALEE!!
AND THE CHIEF WON'T LET HIM ANYWHERE NEAR HER ROOM!
SICK WARD
FORBIDDEN
KEEP OUT
OFF LIMITS
THE POOR GUY!
THOSE JERKS...
INFIRMARY, HEADQUARTERS
NGH...
NNGH...
NNNGH...
HEY...
STOP CRYING, PLEASE!

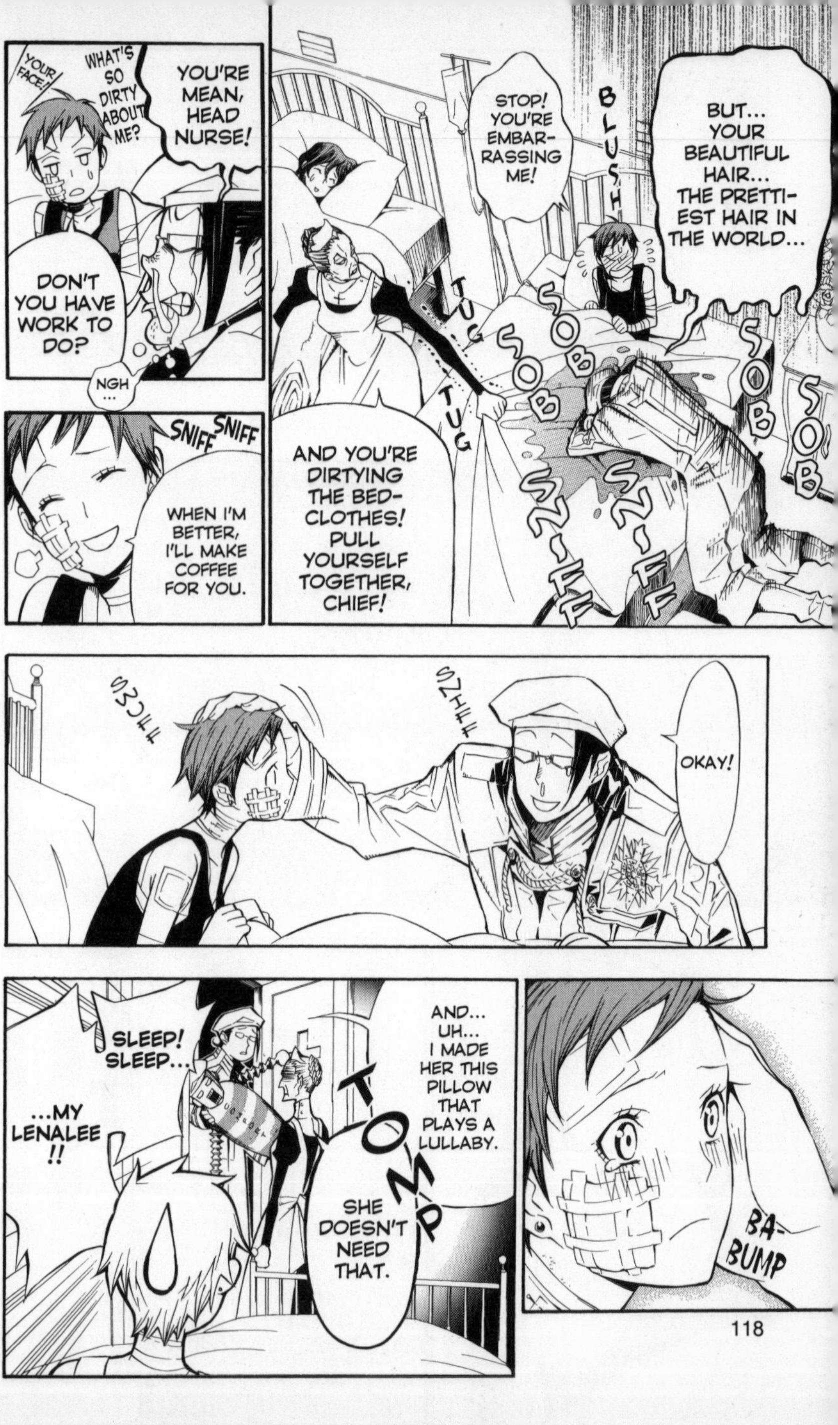
BUT... YOUR BEAUTIFUL HAIR... THE PRETTI-EST HAIR IN THE WORLD...
SOB SOB
BLUSH
STOP! YOU'RE EMBAR-RASSING ME!
SOB SOB
SNIFF SNIFF
TUG TUG
AND YOU'RE DIRTYING THE BED-CLOTHES! PULL YOURSELF TOGETHER, CHIEF!
YOU'RE MEAN, HEAD NURSE!
WHAT'S SO DIRTY ABOUT ME?
YOUR FACE!
DON'T YOU HAVE WORK TO DO?
NGH...
SNIFF SNIFF
WHEN I'M BETTER, I'LL MAKE COFFEE FOR YOU.
OKAY!
SNIFF
SNIFF
BA-BUMP
AND... UH... I MADE HER THIS PILLOW THAT PLAYS A LULLABY.
TOMP
SHE DOESN'T NEED THAT.
SLEEP! SLEEP...
...MY LENALEE!!

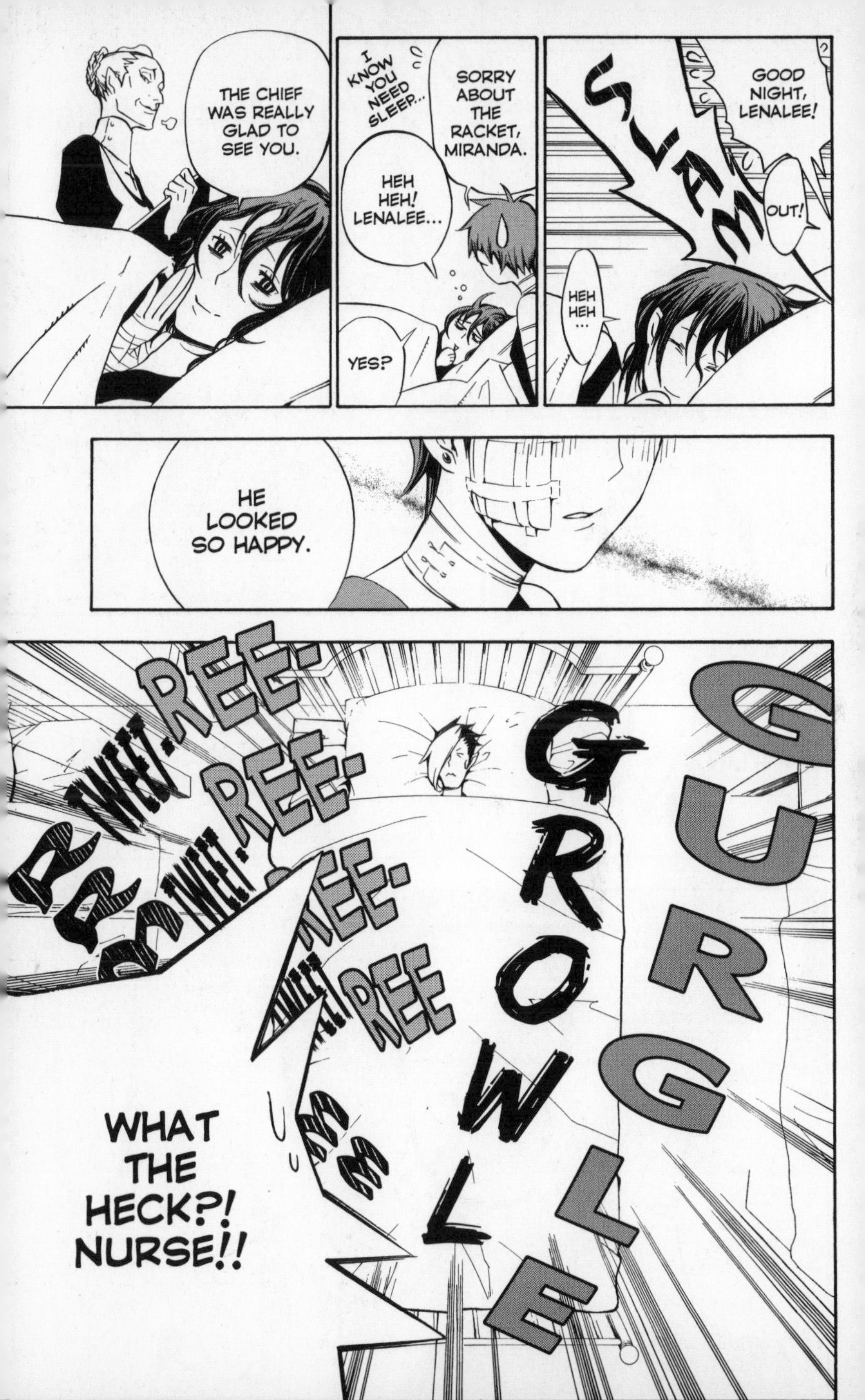
GOOD NIGHT, LENALEE!
SLAM
OUT!
HEH HEH ...
SORRY ABOUT THE RACKET, MIRANDA.
I KNOW YOU NEED SLEEP...
HEH HEH! LENALEE...
YES?
THE CHIEF WAS REALLY GLAD TO SEE YOU.
HE LOOKED SO HAPPY.
GURGLE
GROWL
TWEET-REE-REE-
TWEET-REE-
TWEET REE
WHAT THE HECK?! NURSE!!

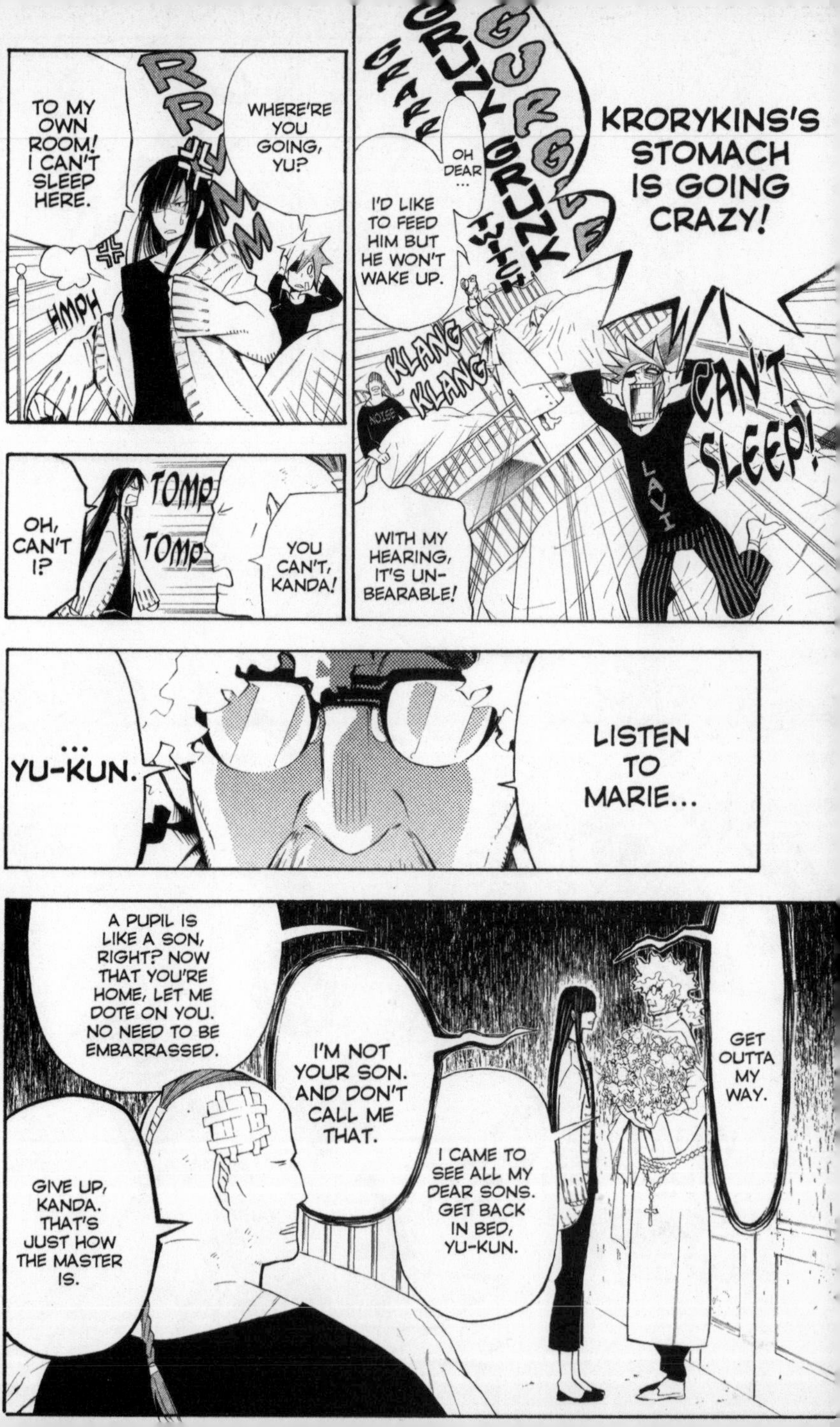

KRORYKINS'S STOMACH IS GOING CRAZY!
GRUNK GRUNK
OH DEAR ...
I'D LIKE TO FEED HIM BUT HE WON'T WAKE UP.
TWITCH
KLANG KLANG
NOISE
CAN'T SLEEP!
LAVI
WITH MY HEARING, IT'S UN-BEARABLE!
WHERE'RE YOU GOING, YU?
RRUMM
TO MY OWN ROOM! I CAN'T SLEEP HERE.
HMPH
YOU CAN'T, KANDA!
TOMP TOMP
OH, CAN'T I?
LISTEN TO MARIE...
... YU-KUN.
GET OUTTA MY WAY.
I CAME TO SEE ALL MY DEAR SONS. GET BACK IN BED, YU-KUN.
I'M NOT YOUR SON. AND DON'T CALL ME THAT.
A PUPIL IS LIKE A SON, RIGHT? NOW THAT YOU'RE HOME, LET ME DOTE ON YOU. NO NEED TO BE EMBARRASSED.
GIVE UP, KANDA. THAT'S JUST HOW THE MASTER IS.

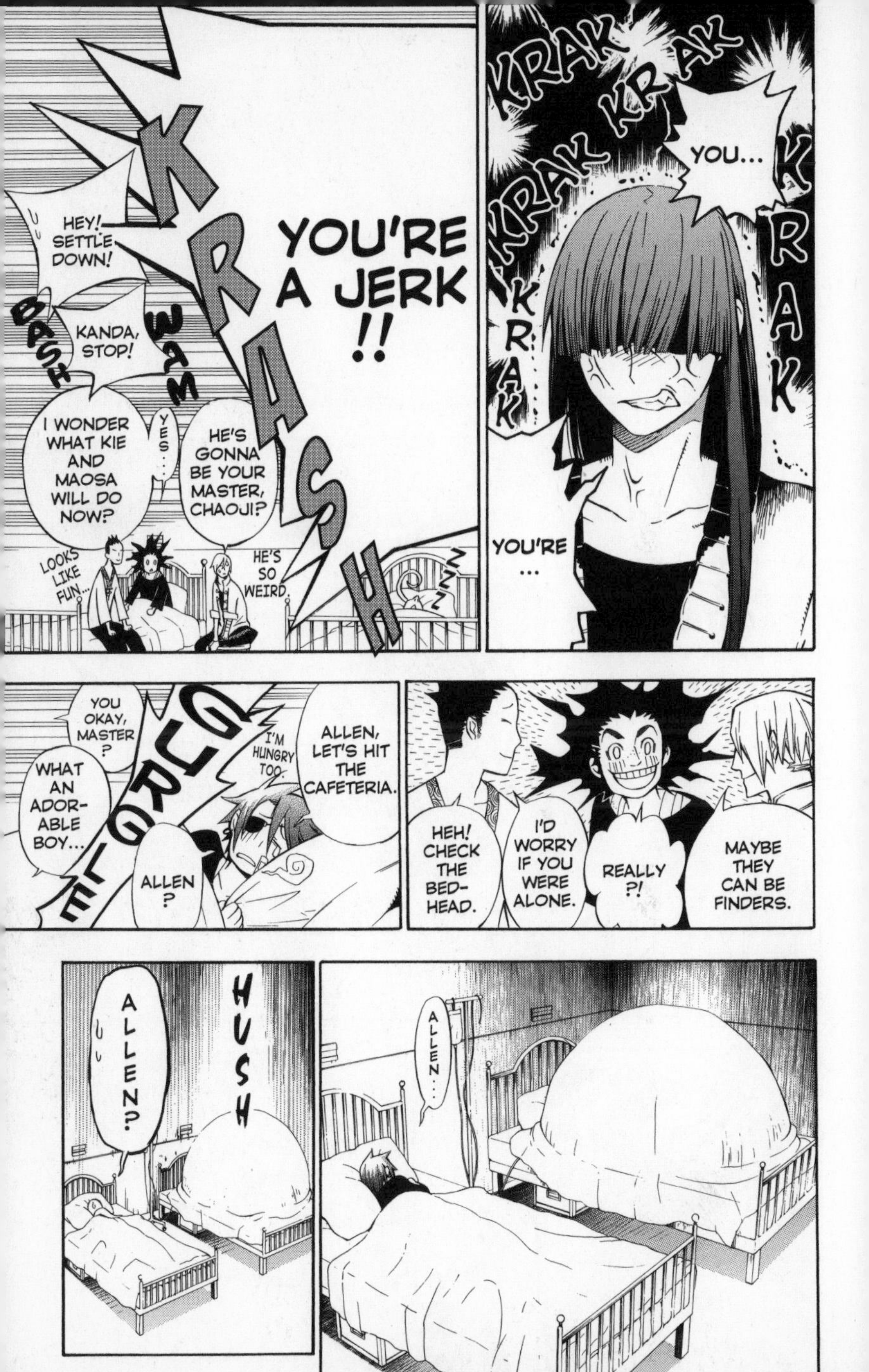
KRAK KRAK KRAK
KRAK KRAK KRAK
YOU...
YOU'RE ...
YOU'RE A JERK!!
KRASH
HEY! SETTLE DOWN!
BASH
WAM
KANDA, STOP!
HE'S GONNA BE YOUR MASTER, CHAOJI?
YES...
I WONDER WHAT KIE AND MAOSA WILL DO NOW?
HE'S SO WEIRD.
LOOKS LIKE FUN...
ZZZ
MAYBE THEY CAN BE FINDERS.
REALLY?!
I'D WORRY IF YOU WERE ALONE.
HEH! CHECK THE BED-HEAD.
ALLEN, LET'S HIT THE CAFETERIA.
I'M HUNGRY TOO.
GURGLE
YOU OKAY, MASTER?
WHAT AN ADORABLE BOY...
ALLEN?
ALLEN...
HUSH
ALLEN?

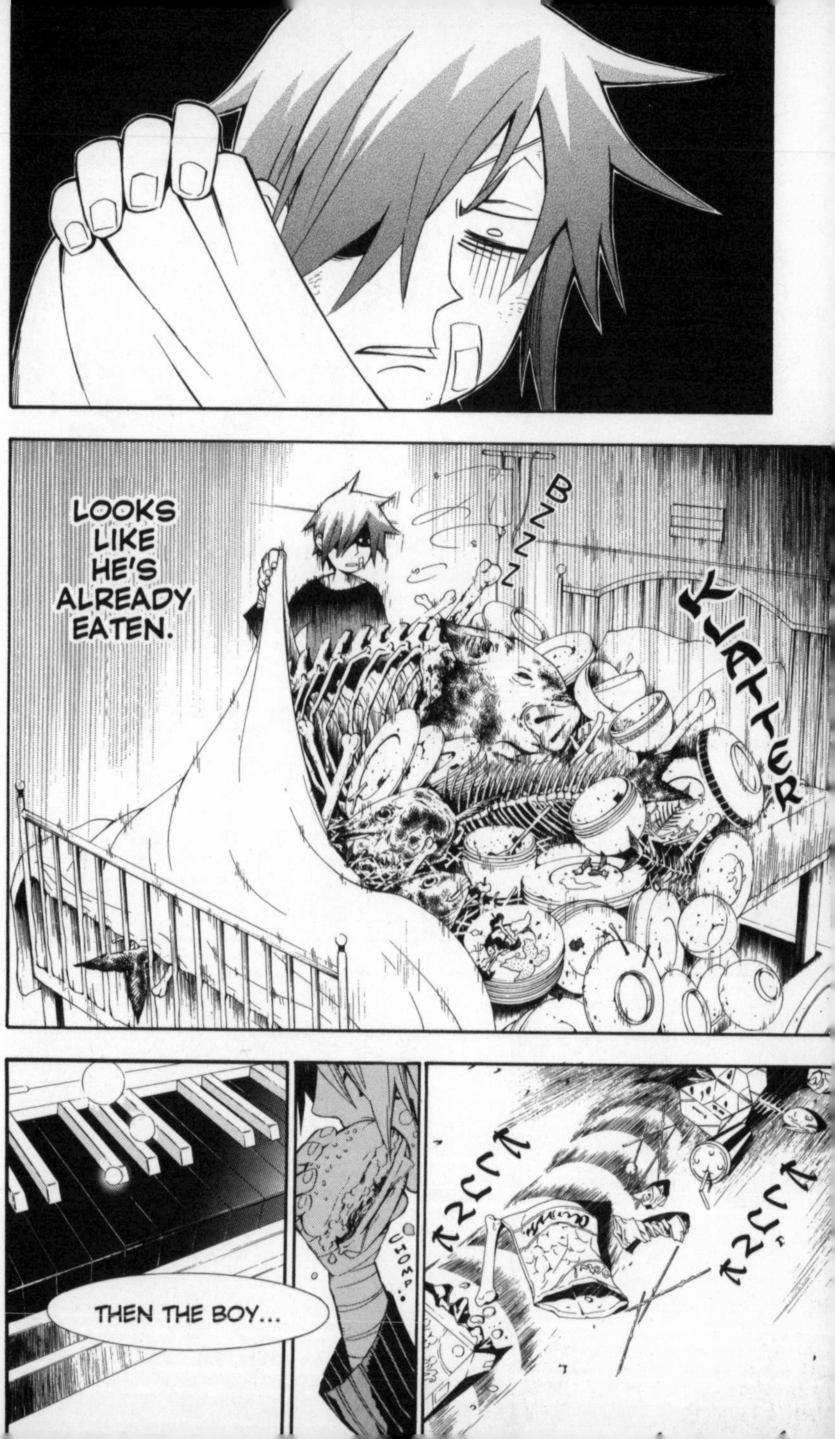
KLATTER
BZZZZ
LOOKS LIKE HE'S ALREADY EATEN.
CHOMP...
THEN THE BOY...

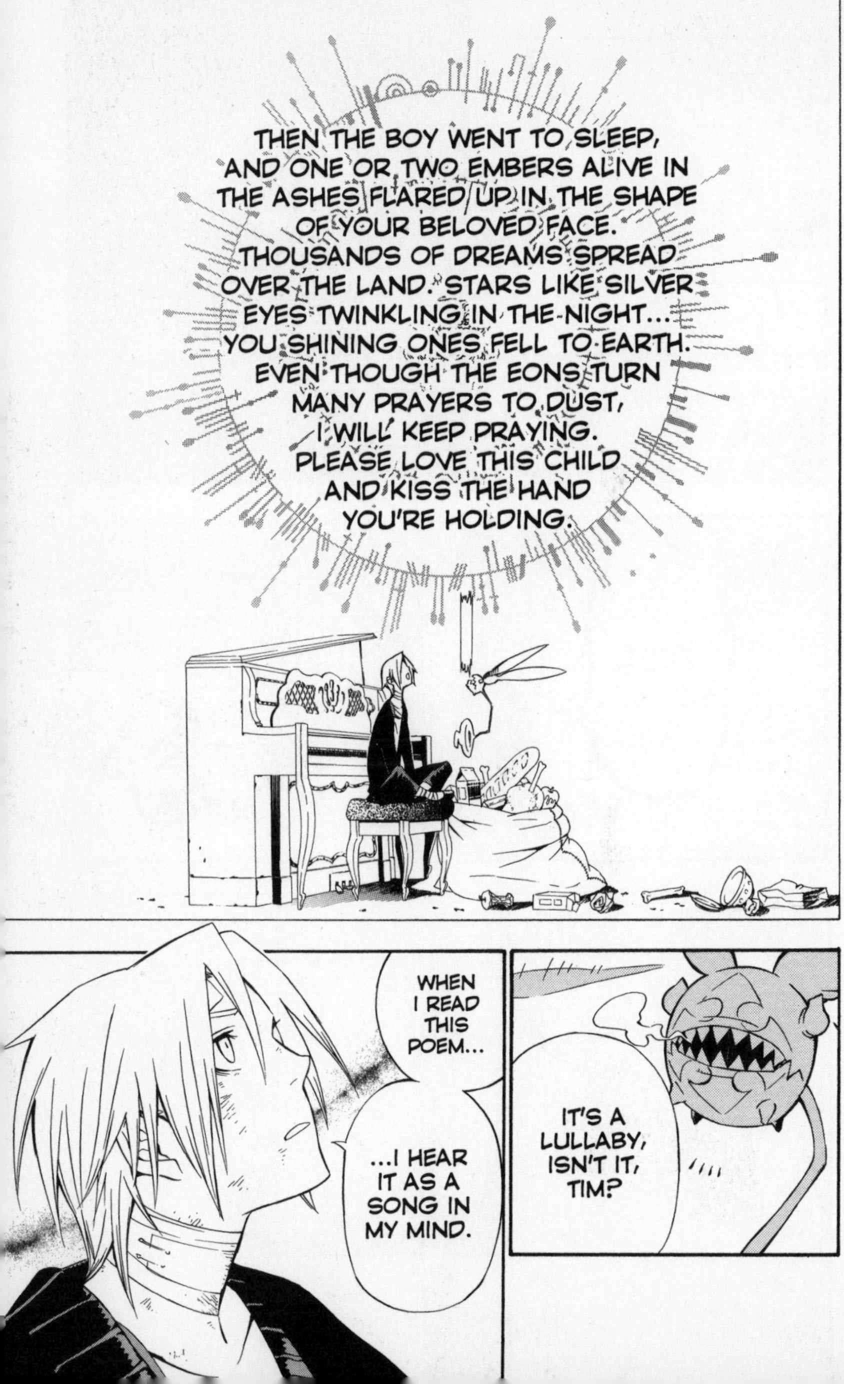
THEN THE BOY WENT TO SLEEP, AND ONE OR TWO EMBERS ALIVE IN THE ASHES FLARED UP IN THE SHAPE OF YOUR BELOVED FACE. THOUSANDS OF DREAMS SPREAD OVER THE LAND. STARS LIKE SILVER EYES TWINKLING IN THE NIGHT... YOU SHINING ONES FELL TO EARTH. EVEN THOUGH THE EONS TURN MANY PRAYERS TO DUST, I WILL KEEP PRAYING. PLEASE LOVE THIS CHILD AND KISS THE HAND YOU'RE HOLDING.
IT'S A LULLABY, ISN'T IT, TIM?
WHEN I READ THIS POEM...
...I HEAR IT AS A SONG IN MY MIND.

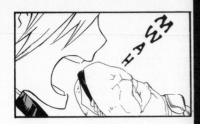

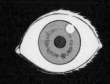

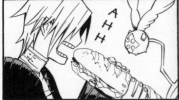

I FEEL LIKE...
...THERE'S SOMEONE INSIDE MY HEAD.
MNAH
AHH
I FEEL SICK...
URRP
CHOMPCHOMP
CHOMP
...
CHOMP
IS THIS ...
MUNCH
MUNCH MUNCH
...THE PATH I'VE CHOSEN?

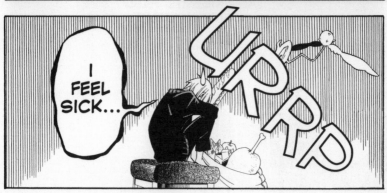

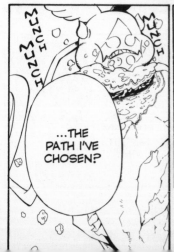

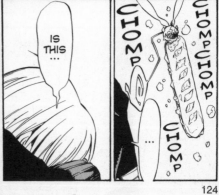

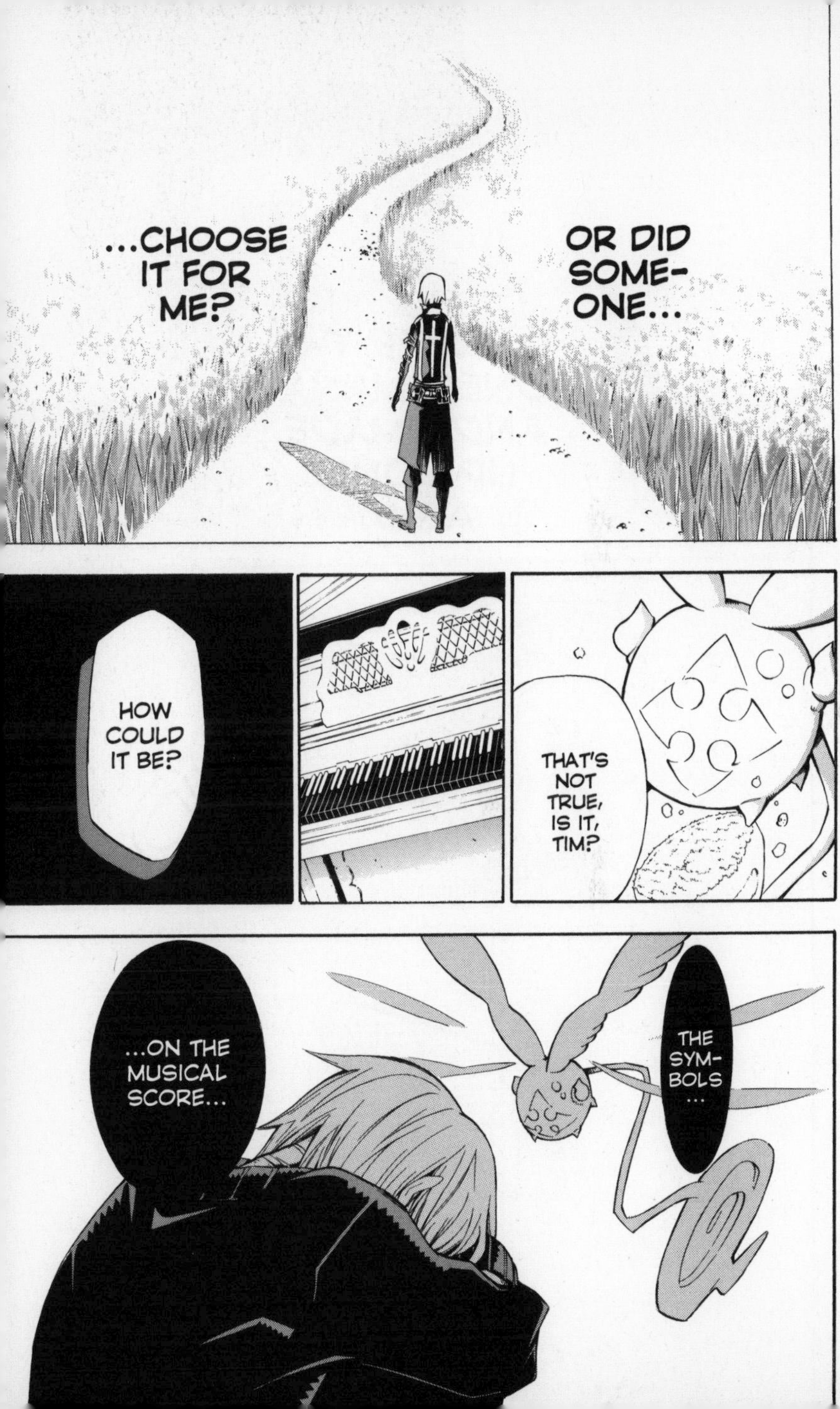
OR DID SOME-ONE...
...CHOOSE IT FOR ME?
THAT'S NOT TRUE, IS IT, TIM?
HOW COULD IT BE?
THE SYM-BOLS...
...ON THE MUSICAL SCORE...

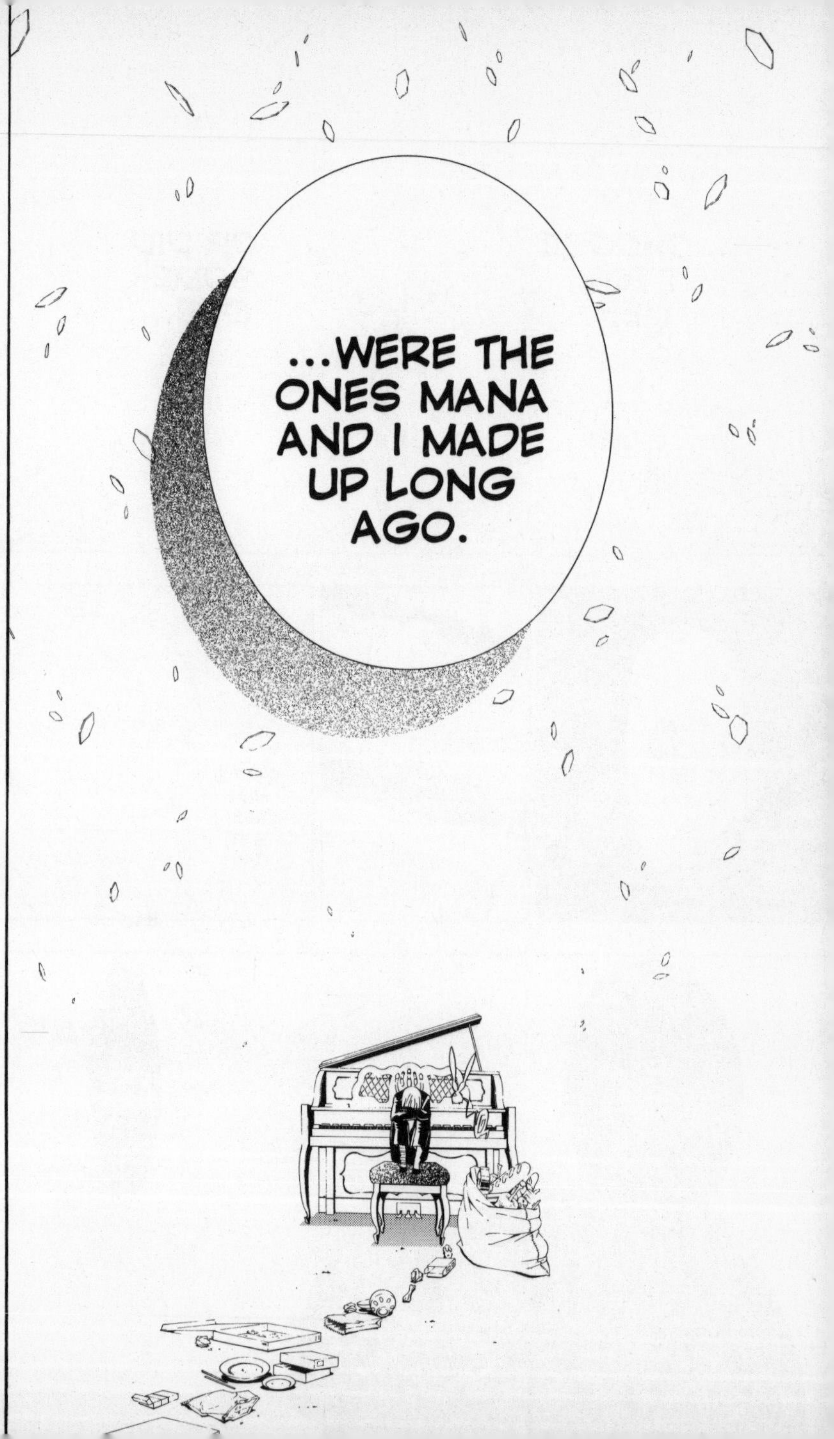
...WERE THE ONES MANA AND I MADE UP LONG AGO.

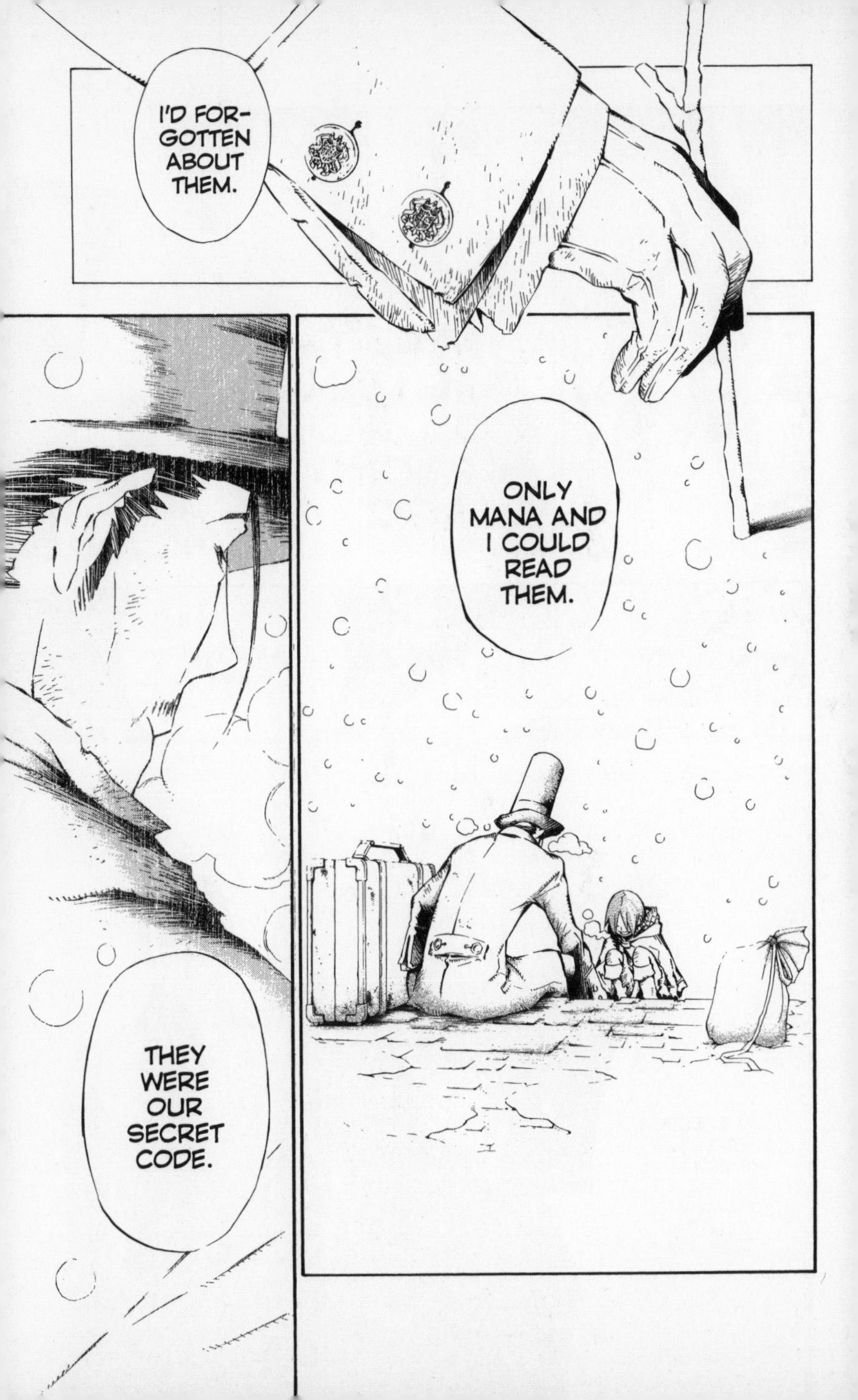
I'D FOR-GOTTEN ABOUT THEM.
ONLY MANA AND I COULD READ THEM.
THEY WERE OUR SECRET CODE.

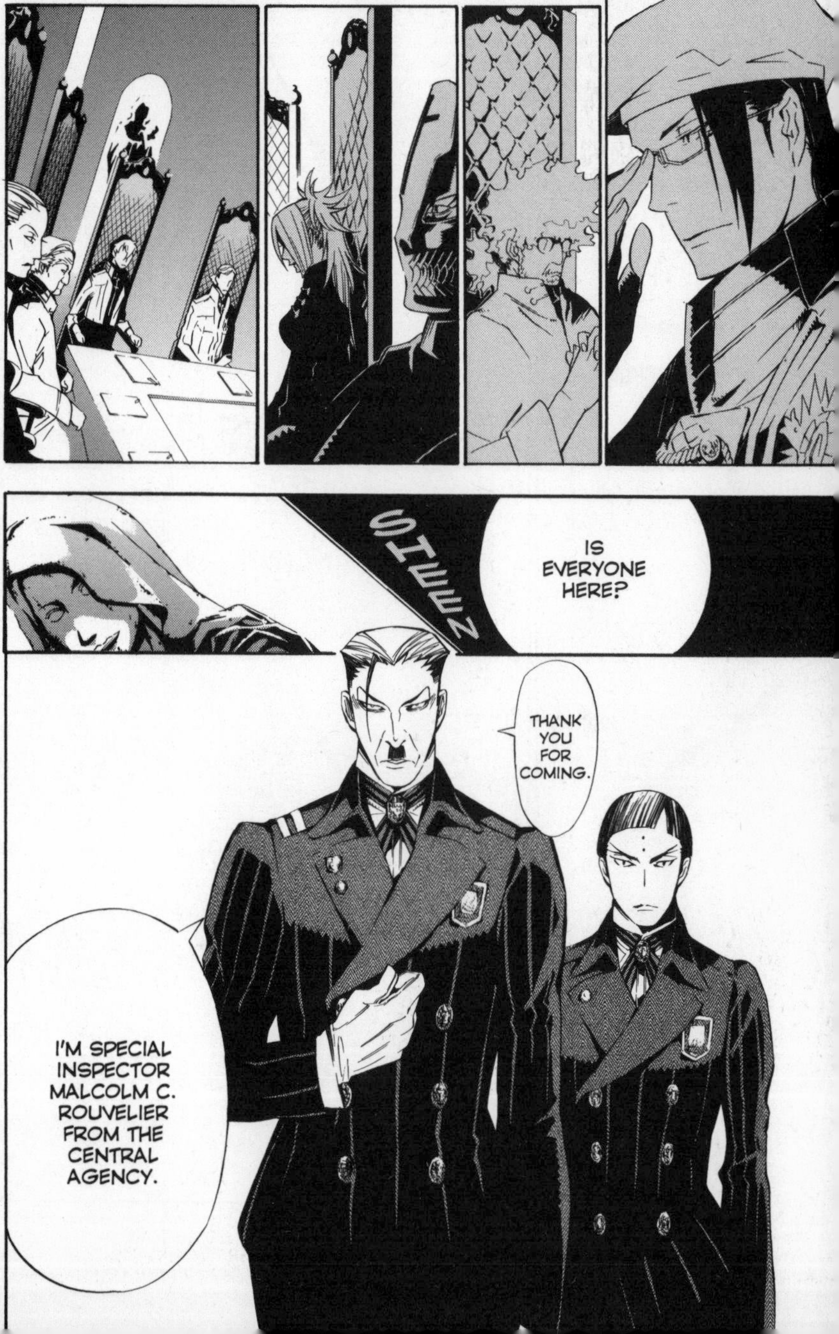
IS EVERYONE HERE?
SHEEN
THANK YOU FOR COMING.
I'M SPECIAL INSPECTOR MALCOLM C. ROUVELIER FROM THE CENTRAL AGENCY.

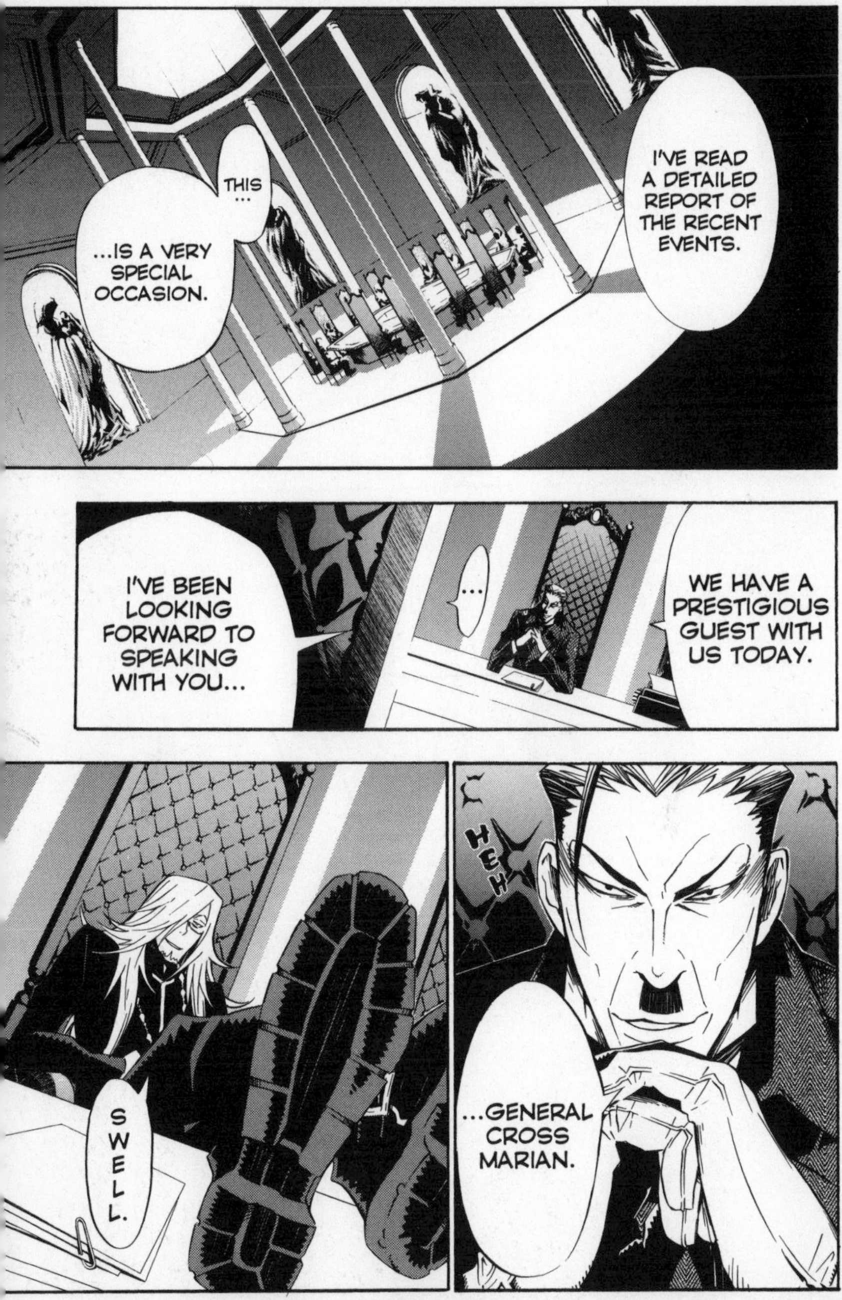
I'VE READ A DETAILED REPORT OF THE RECENT EVENTS.
THIS...
...IS A VERY SPECIAL OCCASION.
WE HAVE A PRESTIGIOUS GUEST WITH US TODAY.
...
I'VE BEEN LOOKING FORWARD TO SPEAKING WITH YOU...
HEH
...GENERAL CROSS MARIAN.
SWELL.

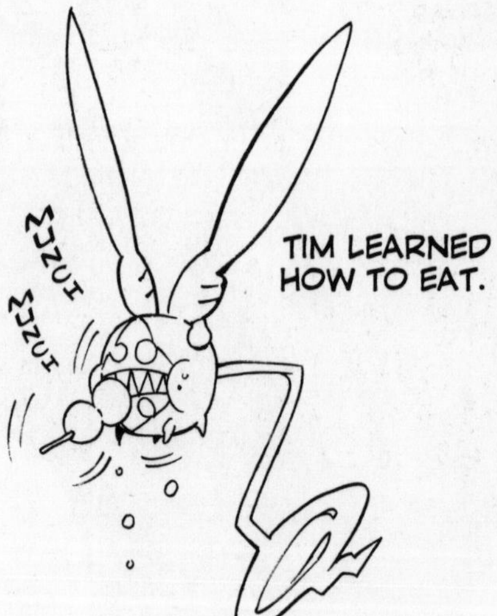
TIM LEARNED HOW TO EAT.
MUNCH
MUNCH

# THE 136TH NIGHT: SHEEP AND DOG

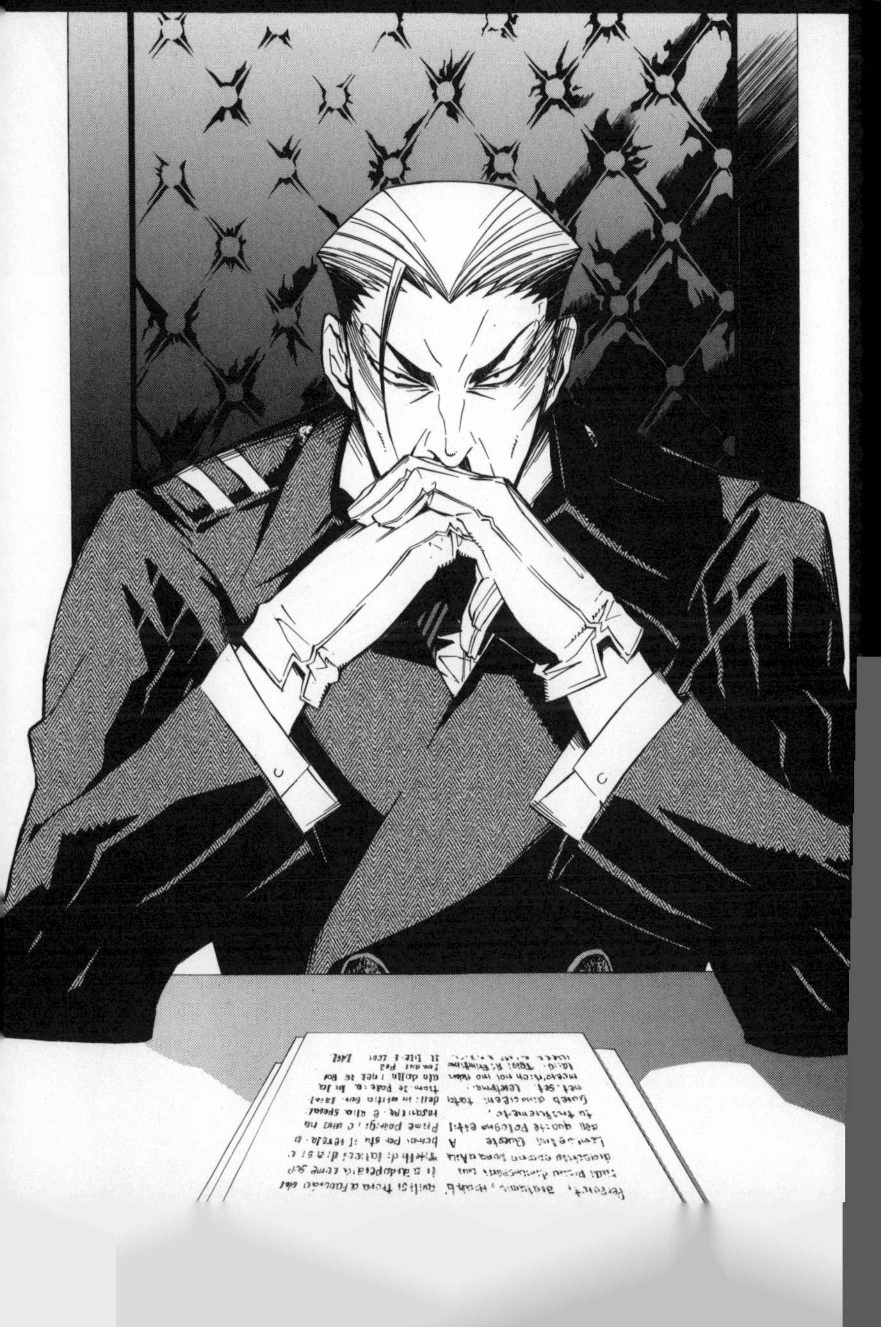

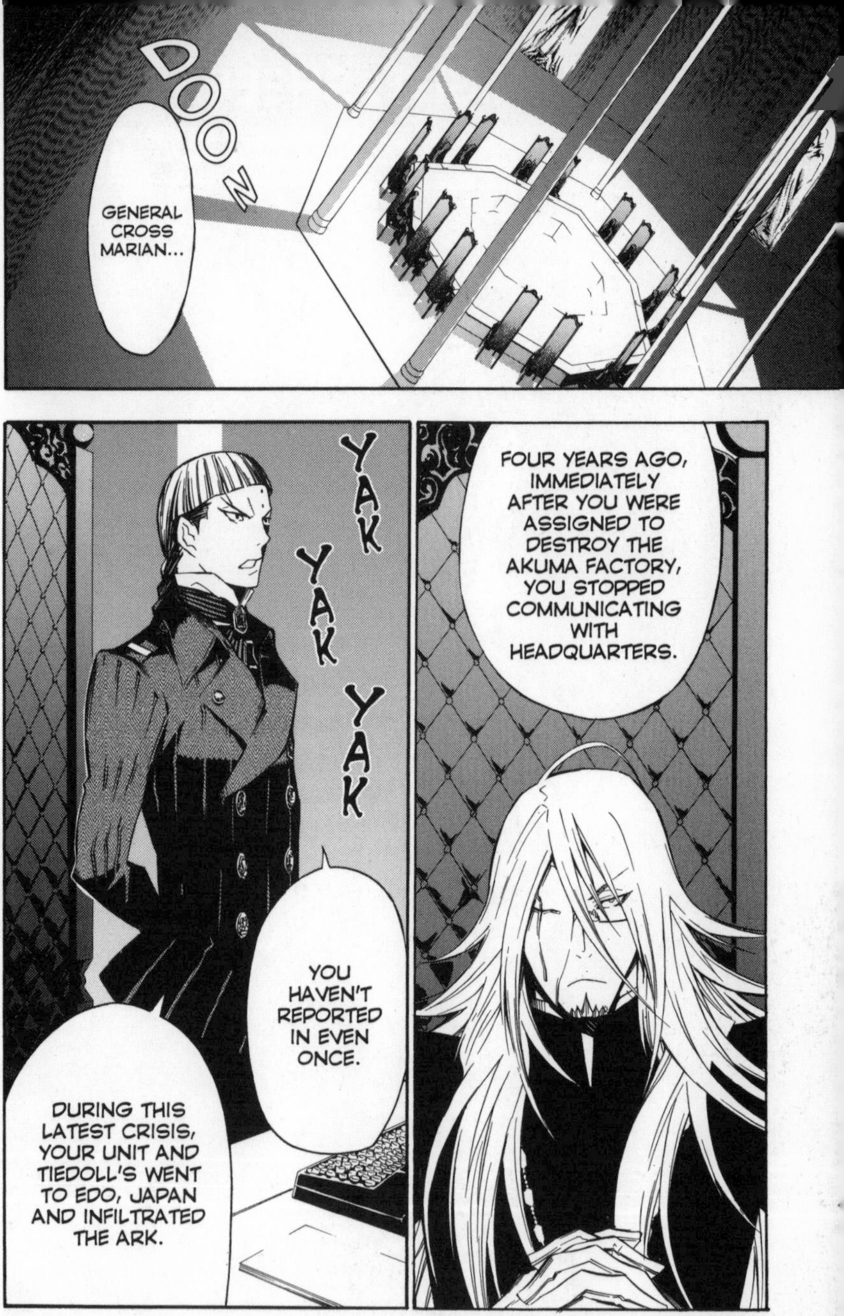
DOOON
GENERAL CROSS MARIAN...
FOUR YEARS AGO, IMMEDIATELY AFTER YOU WERE ASSIGNED TO DESTROY THE AKUMA FACTORY, YOU STOPPED COMMUNICATING WITH HEADQUARTERS.
YAK YAK YAK
YOU HAVEN'T REPORTED IN EVEN ONCE.
DURING THIS LATEST CRISIS, YOUR UNIT AND TIEDOLL'S WENT TO EDO, JAPAN AND INFILTRATED THE ARK.

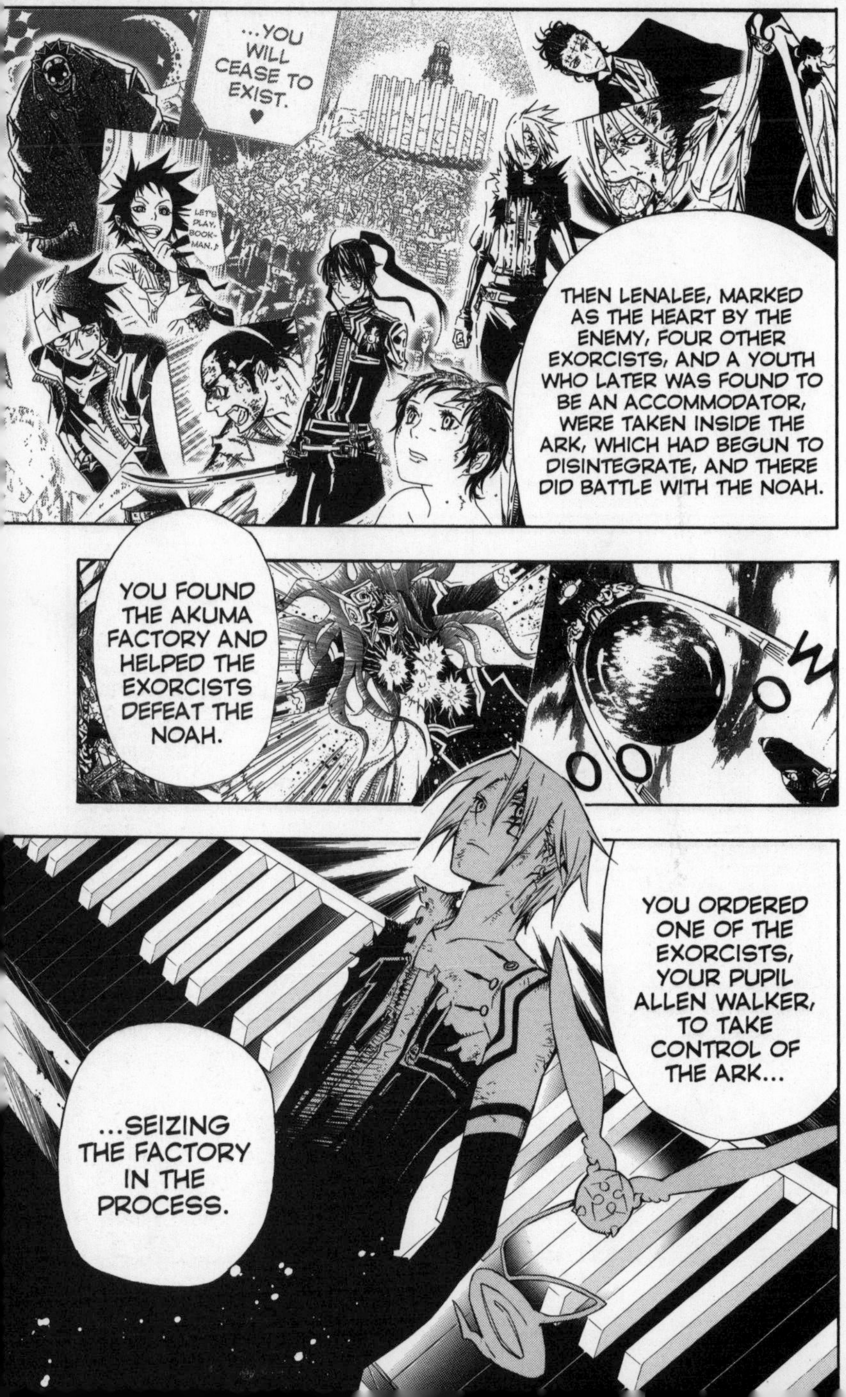
THEN LENALEE, MARKED AS THE HEART BY THE ENEMY, FOUR OTHER EXORCISTS, AND A YOUTH WHO LATER WAS FOUND TO BE AN ACCOMMODATOR, WERE TAKEN INSIDE THE ARK, WHICH HAD BEGUN TO DISINTEGRATE, AND THERE DID BATTLE WITH THE NOAH.
...YOU WILL CEASE TO EXIST. ♥
LET'S PLAY, BOOK-MAN.♪
WOOO
YOU FOUND THE AKUMA FACTORY AND HELPED THE EXORCISTS DEFEAT THE NOAH.
YOU ORDERED ONE OF THE EXORCISTS, YOUR PUPIL ALLEN WALKER, TO TAKE CONTROL OF THE ARK...
...SEIZING THE FACTORY IN THE PROCESS.

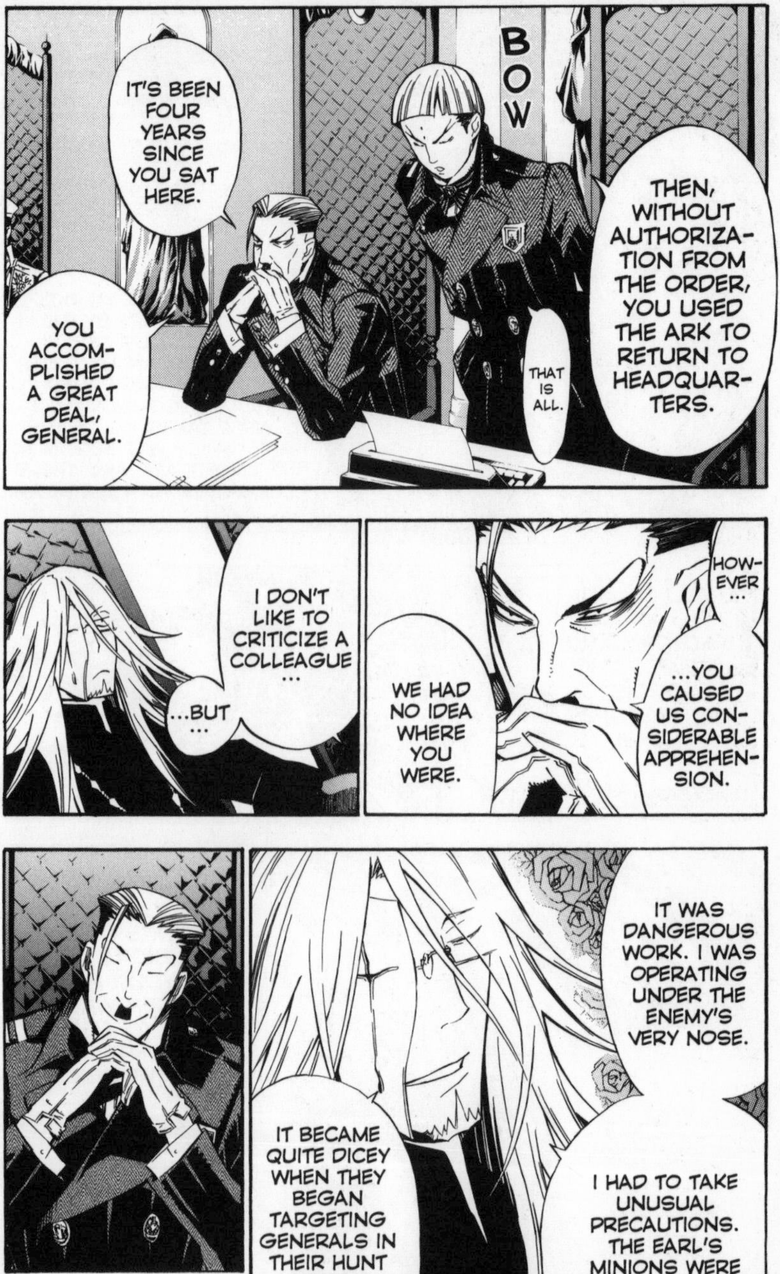
BOW
THEN, WITHOUT AUTHORIZATION FROM THE ORDER, YOU USED THE ARK TO RETURN TO HEADQUARTERS.
THAT IS ALL.
IT'S BEEN FOUR YEARS SINCE YOU SAT HERE.
YOU ACCOMPLISHED A GREAT DEAL, GENERAL.
HOWEVER...
...YOU CAUSED US CONSIDERABLE APPREHENSION.
WE HAD NO IDEA WHERE YOU WERE.
I DON'T LIKE TO CRITICIZE A COLLEAGUE...
...BUT...
IT WAS DANGEROUS WORK. I WAS OPERATING UNDER THE ENEMY'S VERY NOSE.
I HAD TO TAKE UNUSUAL PRECAUTIONS. THE EARL'S MINIONS WERE EVERYWHERE.
IT BECAME QUITE DICEY WHEN THEY BEGAN TARGETING GENERALS IN THEIR HUNT FOR THE HEART.

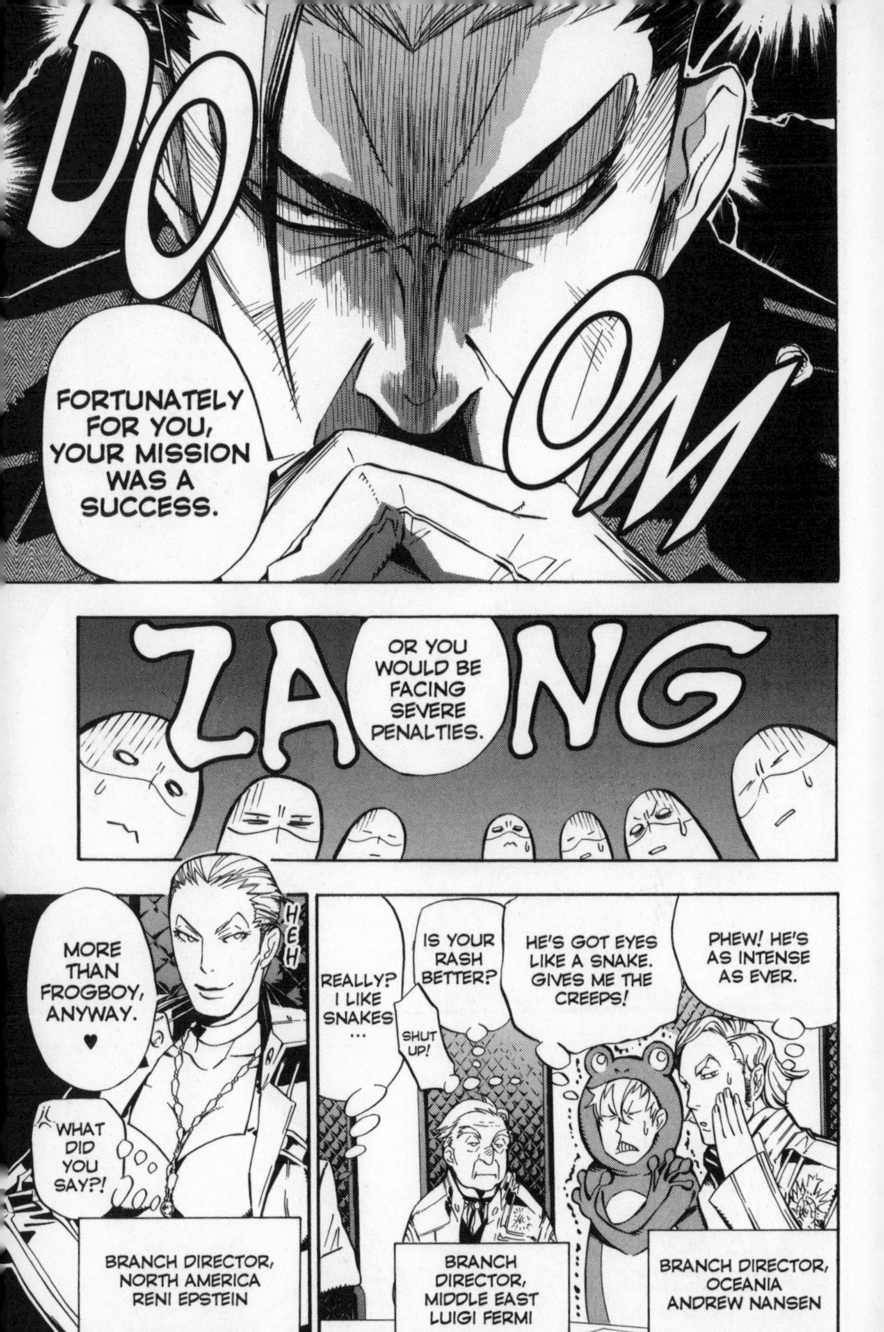
DOOM
FORTUNATELY FOR YOU, YOUR MISSION WAS A SUCCESS.
ZANG
OR YOU WOULD BE FACING SEVERE PENALTIES.
PHEW! HE'S AS INTENSE AS EVER.
HE'S GOT EYES LIKE A SNAKE. GIVES ME THE CREEPS!
IS YOUR RASH BETTER?
REALLY? I LIKE SNAKES...
SHUT UP!
BRANCH DIRECTOR, OCEANIA ANDREW NANSEN
BRANCH DIRECTOR, MIDDLE EAST LUIGI FERMI
HEH
MORE THAN FROGBOY, ANYWAY. ♥
WHAT DID YOU SAY?!
BRANCH DIRECTOR, NORTH AMERICA RENI EPSTEIN

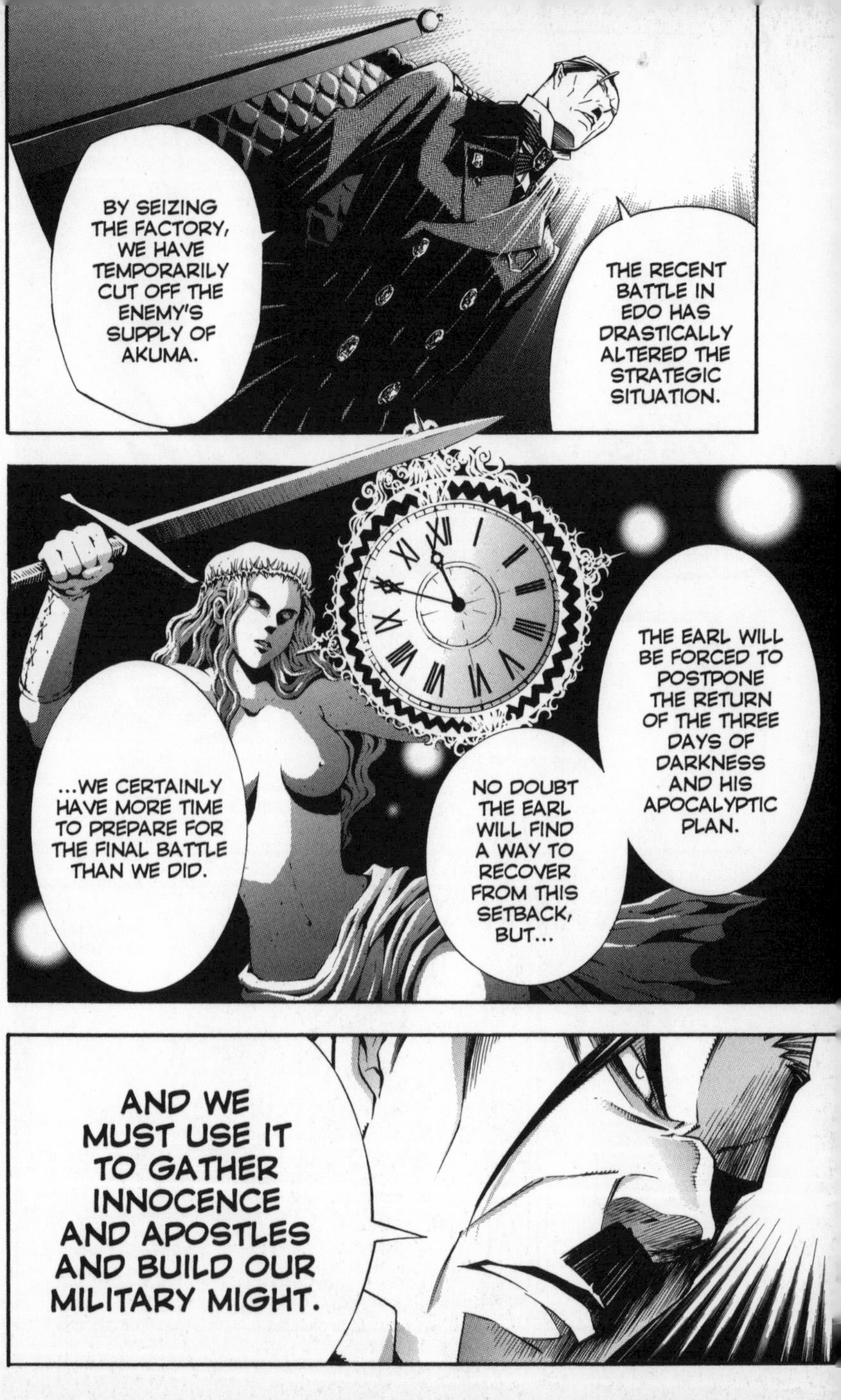
THE RECENT BATTLE IN EDO HAS DRASTICALLY ALTERED THE STRATEGIC SITUATION.
BY SEIZING THE FACTORY, WE HAVE TEMPORARILY CUT OFF THE ENEMY'S SUPPLY OF AKUMA.
THE EARL WILL BE FORCED TO POSTPONE THE RETURN OF THE THREE DAYS OF DARKNESS AND HIS APOCALYPTIC PLAN.
NO DOUBT THE EARL WILL FIND A WAY TO RECOVER FROM THIS SETBACK, BUT...
...WE CERTAINLY HAVE MORE TIME TO PREPARE FOR THE FINAL BATTLE THAN WE DID.
AND WE MUST USE IT TO GATHER INNOCENCE AND APOSTLES AND BUILD OUR MILITARY MIGHT.

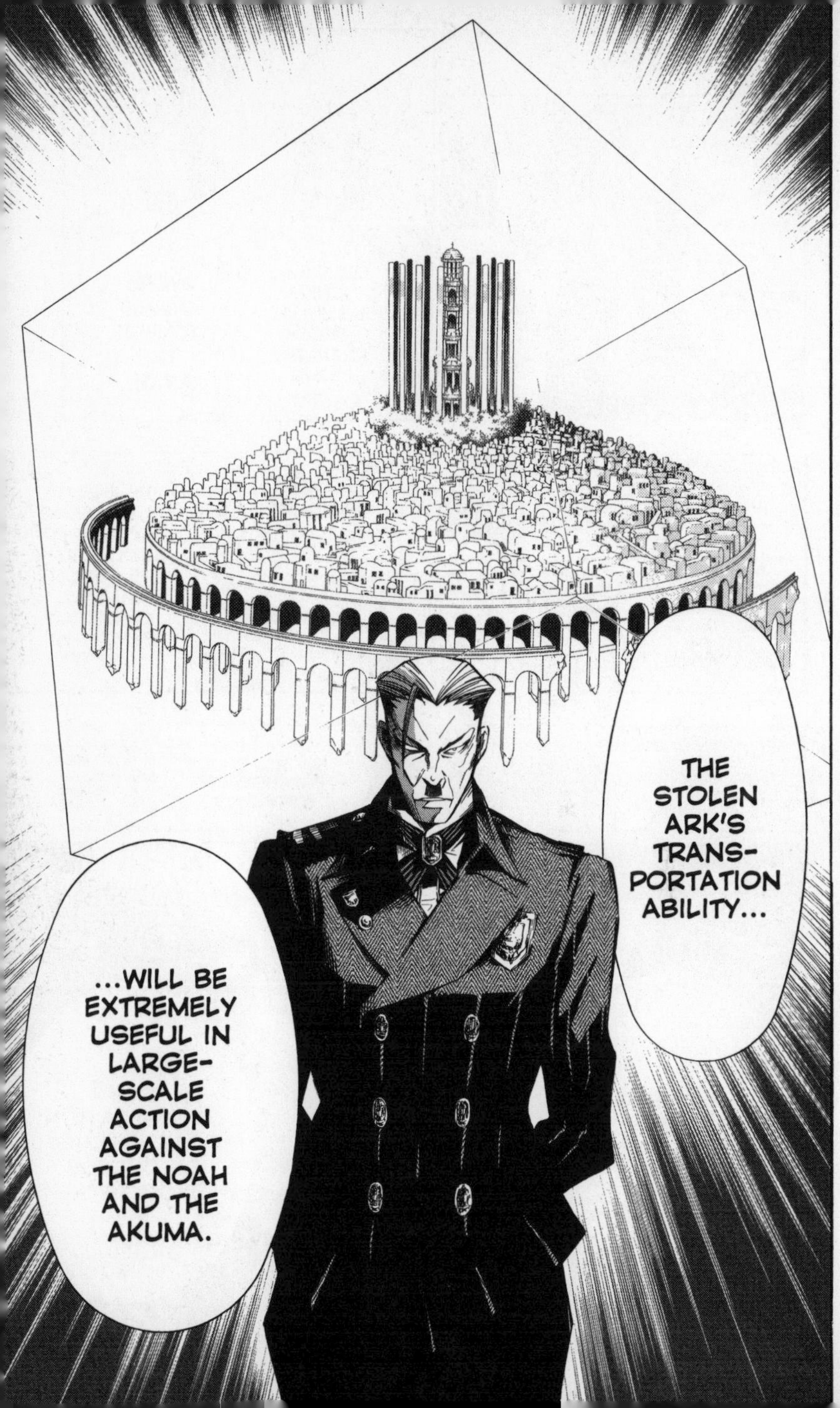
THE STOLEN ARK'S TRANS-PORTATION ABILITY...
...WILL BE EXTREMELY USEFUL IN LARGE-SCALE ACTION AGAINST THE NOAH AND THE AKUMA.

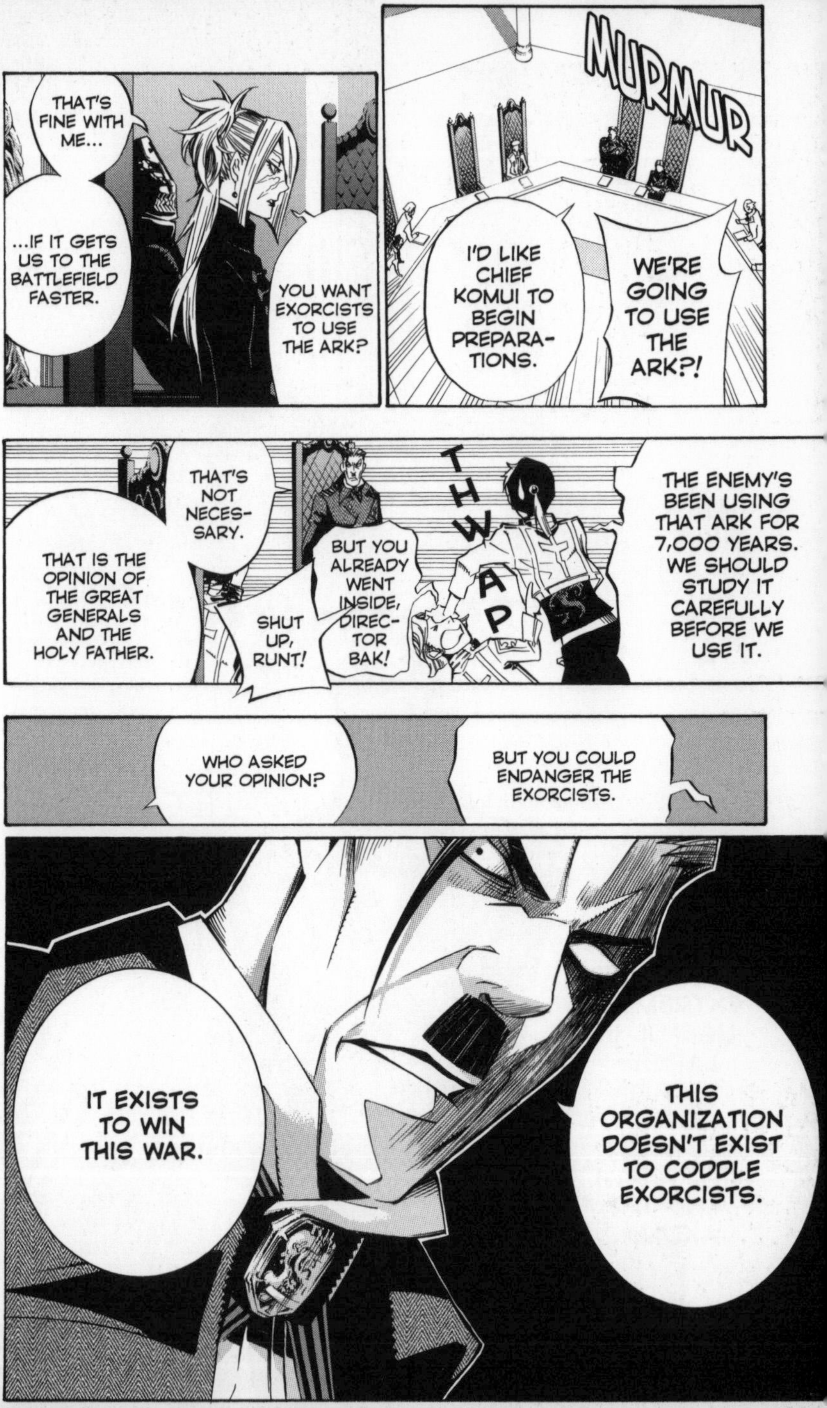
MURMUR
WE'RE GOING TO USE THE ARK?!
I'D LIKE CHIEF KOMUI TO BEGIN PREPARA-TIONS.
YOU WANT EXORCISTS TO USE THE ARK?
THAT'S FINE WITH ME...
...IF IT GETS US TO THE BATTLEFIELD FASTER.
THE ENEMY'S BEEN USING THAT ARK FOR 7,000 YEARS. WE SHOULD STUDY IT CAREFULLY BEFORE WE USE IT.
THWAP
BUT YOU ALREADY WENT INSIDE, DIREC-TOR BAK!
SHUT UP, RUNT!
THAT'S NOT NECES-SARY.
THAT IS THE OPINION OF THE GREAT GENERALS AND THE HOLY FATHER.
BUT YOU COULD ENDANGER THE EXORCISTS.
WHO ASKED YOUR OPINION?
THIS ORGANIZATION DOESN'T EXIST TO CODDLE EXORCISTS.
IT EXISTS TO WIN THIS WAR.

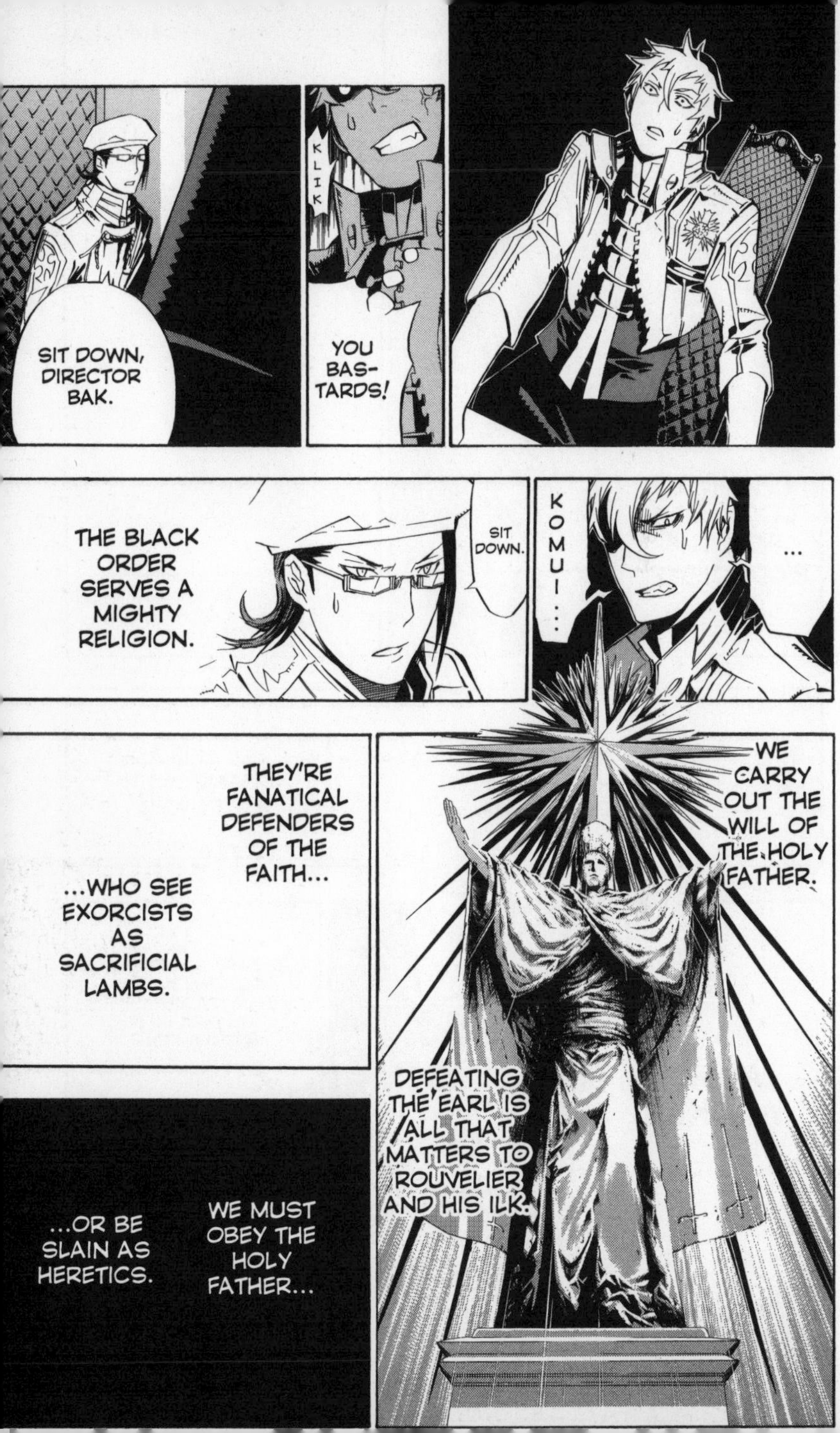
KLIK
YOU BASTARDS!
SIT DOWN, DIRECTOR BAK.
...
KOMUI...
SIT DOWN.
THE BLACK ORDER SERVES A MIGHTY RELIGION.
WE CARRY OUT THE WILL OF THE HOLY FATHER.
DEFEATING THE EARL IS ALL THAT MATTERS TO ROUVELIER AND HIS ILK.
THEY'RE FANATICAL DEFENDERS OF THE FAITH...
...WHO SEE EXORCISTS AS SACRIFICIAL LAMBS.
WE MUST OBEY THE HOLY FATHER...
...OR BE SLAIN AS HERETICS.

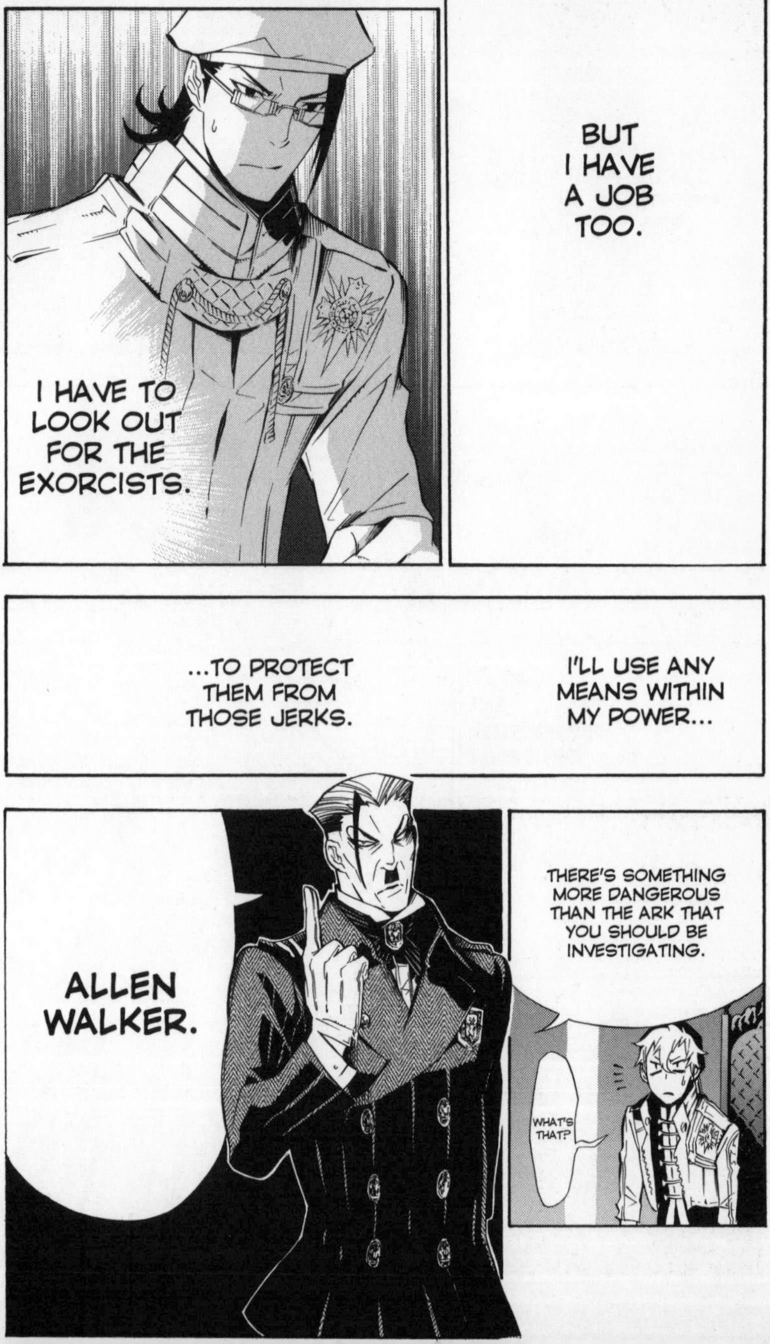
BUT I HAVE A JOB TOO.
I HAVE TO LOOK OUT FOR THE EXORCISTS.
I'LL USE ANY MEANS WITHIN MY POWER...
...TO PROTECT THEM FROM THOSE JERKS.
THERE'S SOMETHING MORE DANGEROUS THAN THE ARK THAT YOU SHOULD BE INVESTIGATING.
WHAT'S THAT?
ALLEN WALKER.

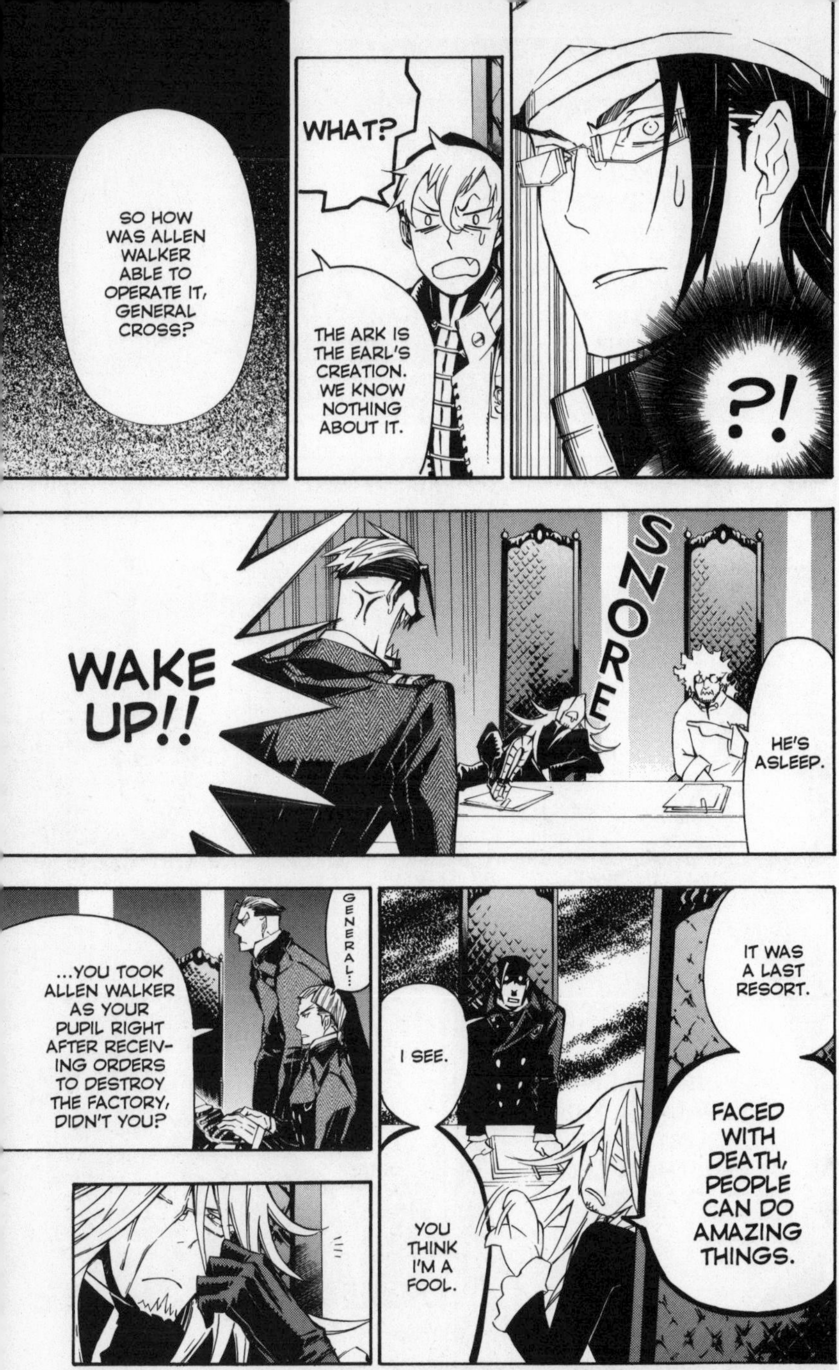
?!
WHAT?
THE ARK IS THE EARL'S CREATION. WE KNOW NOTHING ABOUT IT.
SO HOW WAS ALLEN WALKER ABLE TO OPERATE IT, GENERAL CROSS?
HE'S ASLEEP.
SNORE
WAKE UP!!
IT WAS A LAST RESORT.
FACED WITH DEATH, PEOPLE CAN DO AMAZING THINGS.
I SEE.
YOU THINK I'M A FOOL.
GENERAL...
...YOU TOOK ALLEN WALKER AS YOUR PUPIL RIGHT AFTER RECEIV-ING ORDERS TO DESTROY THE FACTORY, DIDN'T YOU?

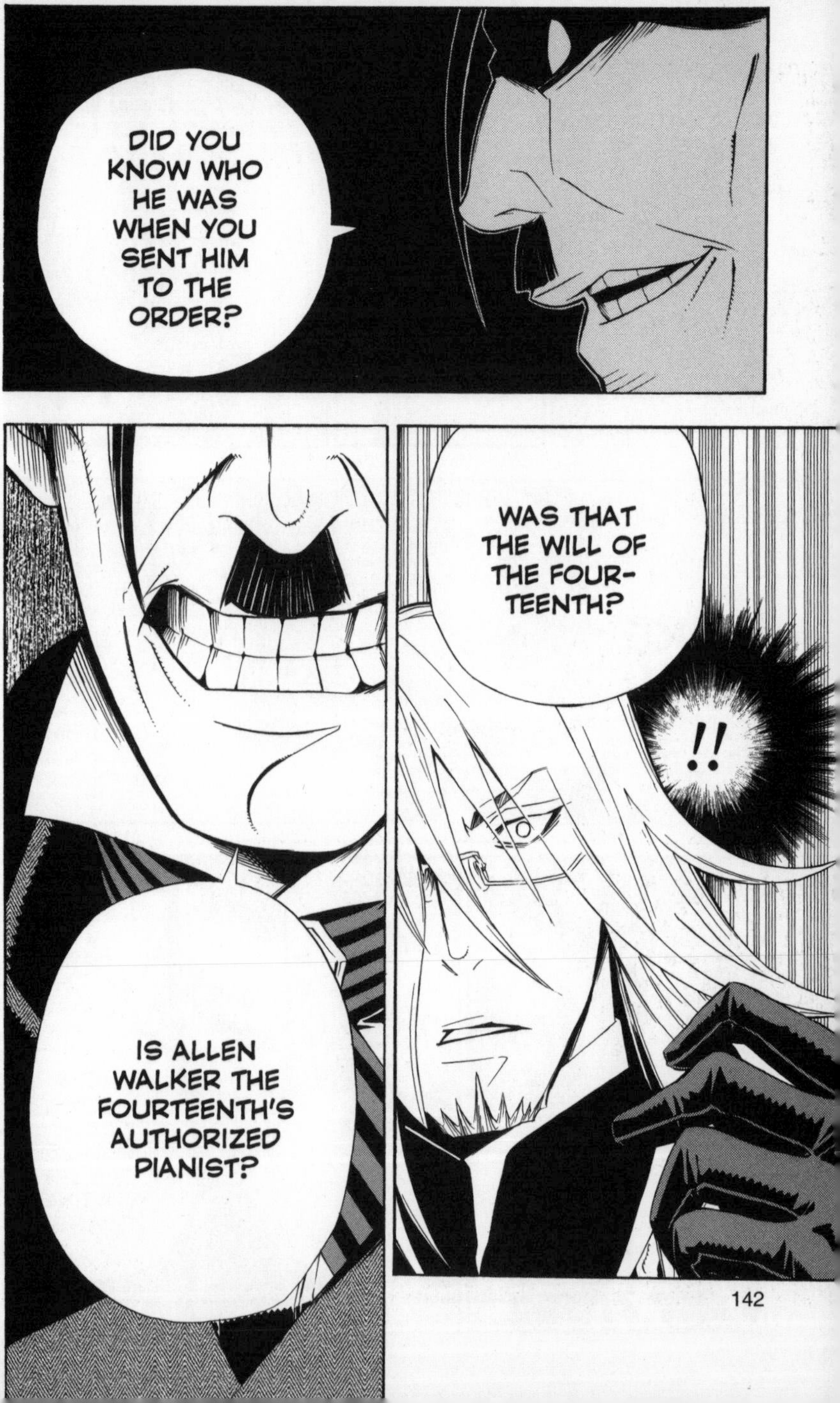
DID YOU KNOW WHO HE WAS WHEN YOU SENT HIM TO THE ORDER?
WAS THAT THE WILL OF THE FOUR-TEENTH?
!!
IS ALLEN WALKER THE FOURTEENTH'S AUTHORIZED PIANIST?

READ THIS WAY

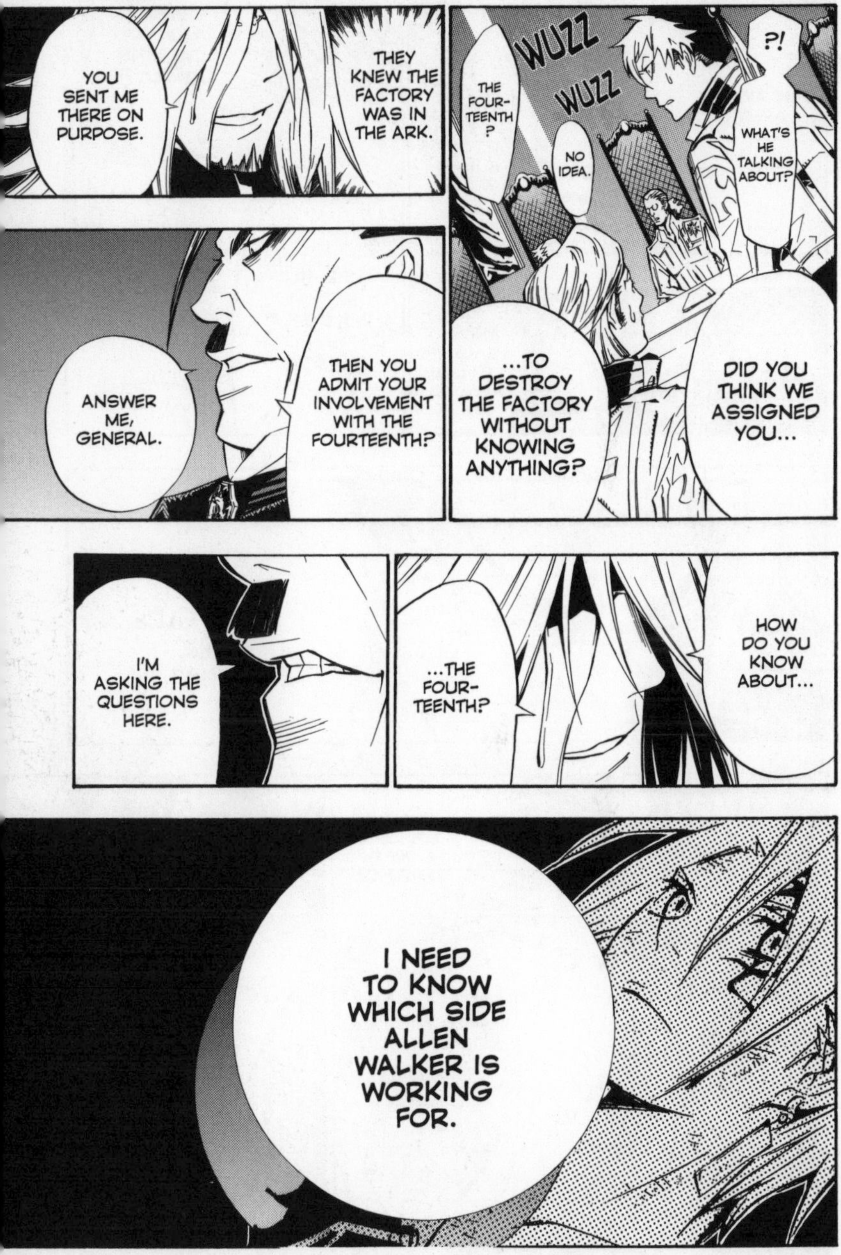
?!
WHAT'S HE TALKING ABOUT?
WUZZ WUZZ
THE FOUR-TEENTH?
NO IDEA.
DID YOU THINK WE ASSIGNED YOU...
...TO DESTROY THE FACTORY WITHOUT KNOWING ANYTHING?
THEY KNEW THE FACTORY WAS IN THE ARK.
YOU SENT ME THERE ON PURPOSE.
THEN YOU ADMIT YOUR INVOLVEMENT WITH THE FOURTEENTH?
ANSWER ME, GENERAL.
HOW DO YOU KNOW ABOUT...
...THE FOUR-TEENTH?
I'M ASKING THE QUESTIONS HERE.
I NEED TO KNOW WHICH SIDE ALLEN WALKER IS WORKING FOR.

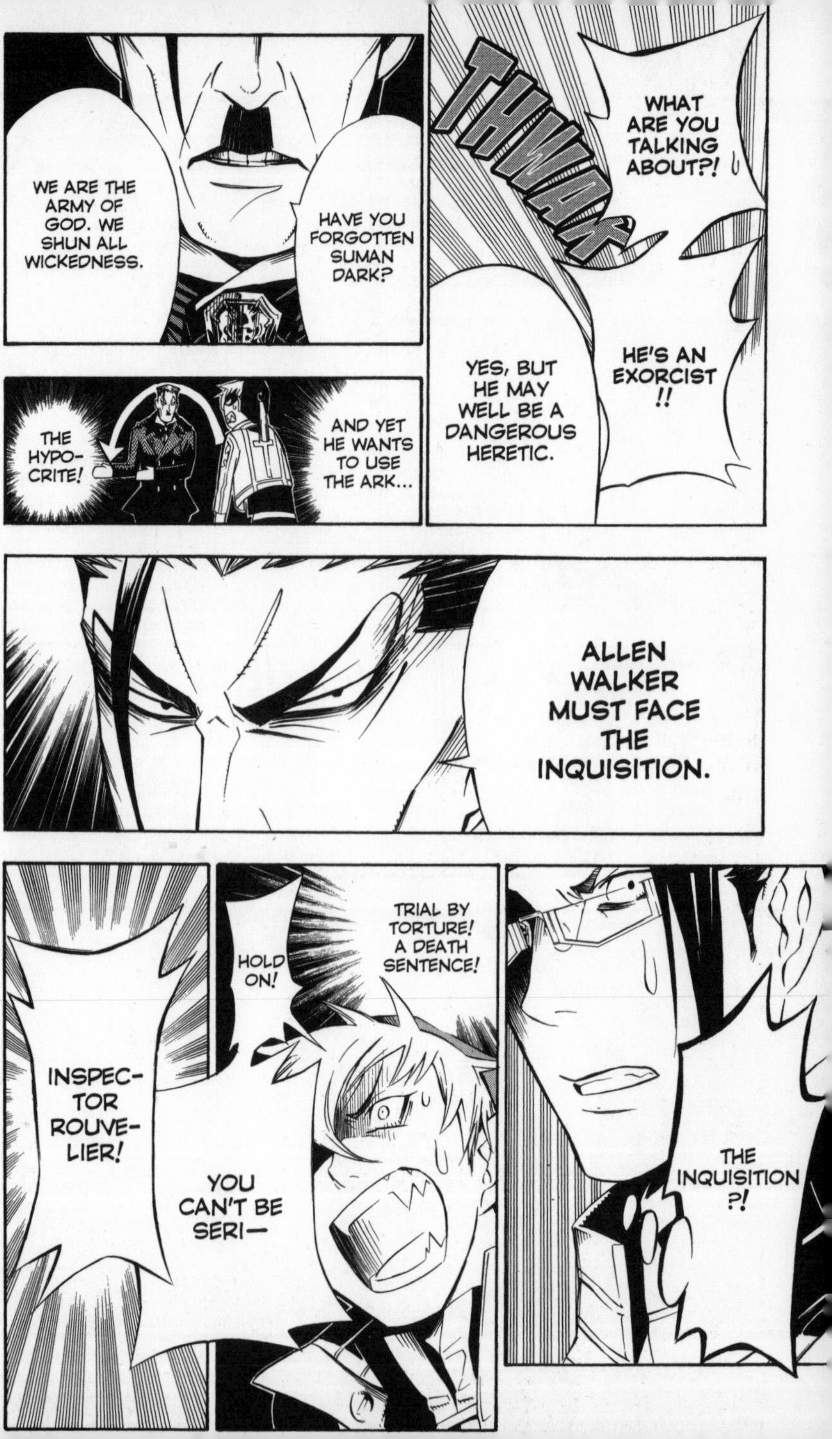
THWAK
WHAT ARE YOU TALKING ABOUT?!
HE'S AN EXORCIST!!
YES, BUT HE MAY WELL BE A DANGEROUS HERETIC.
HAVE YOU FORGOTTEN SUMAN DARK?
WE ARE THE ARMY OF GOD. WE SHUN ALL WICKEDNESS.
AND YET HE WANTS TO USE THE ARK...
THE HYPOCRITE!
ALLEN WALKER MUST FACE THE INQUISITION.
THE INQUISITION?!
TRIAL BY TORTURE! A DEATH SENTENCE!
HOLD ON!
INSPECTOR ROUVELIER!
YOU CAN'T BE SERI—

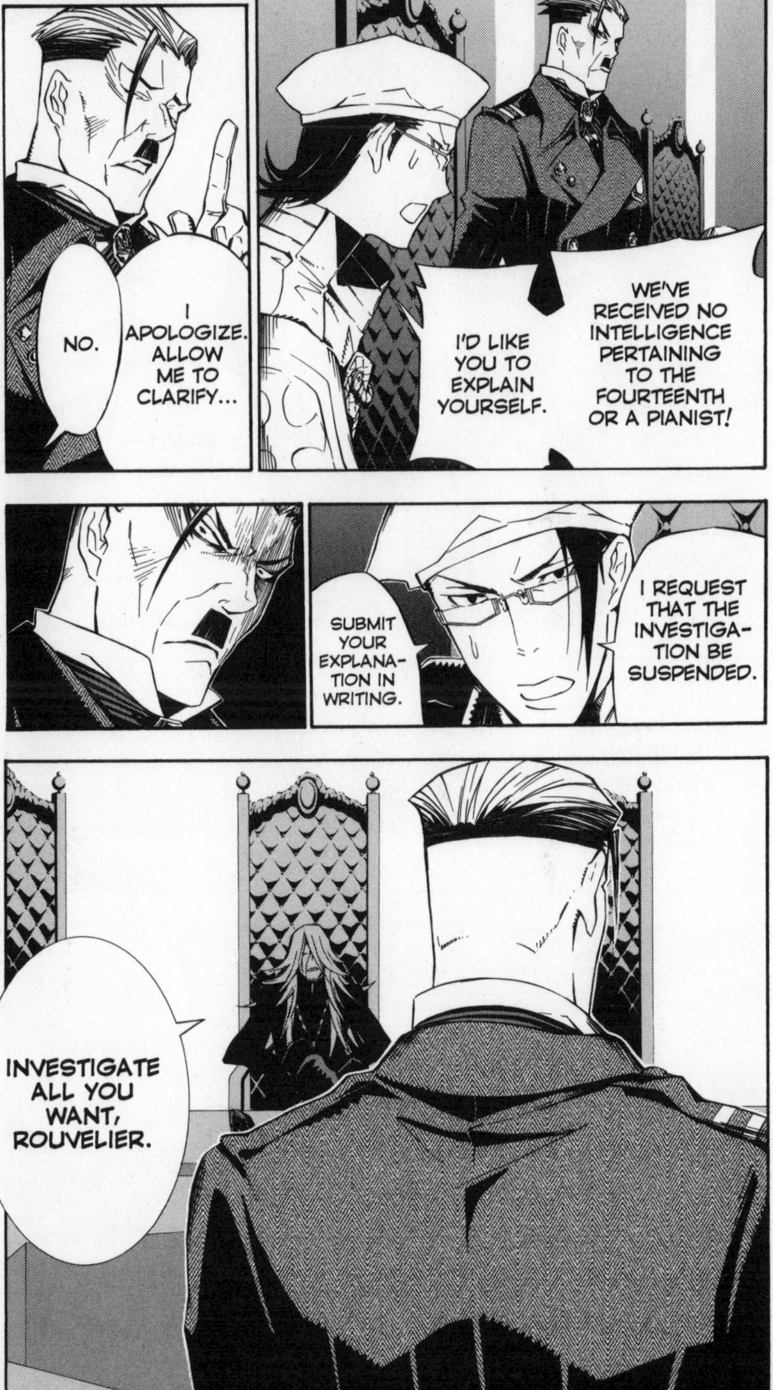
WE'VE RECEIVED NO INTELLIGENCE PERTAINING TO THE FOURTEENTH OR A PIANIST!
I'D LIKE YOU TO EXPLAIN YOURSELF.
I APOLOGIZE. ALLOW ME TO CLARIFY...
NO.
I REQUEST THAT THE INVESTIGATION BE SUSPENDED.
SUBMIT YOUR EXPLANATION IN WRITING.
INVESTIGATE ALL YOU WANT, ROUVELIER.

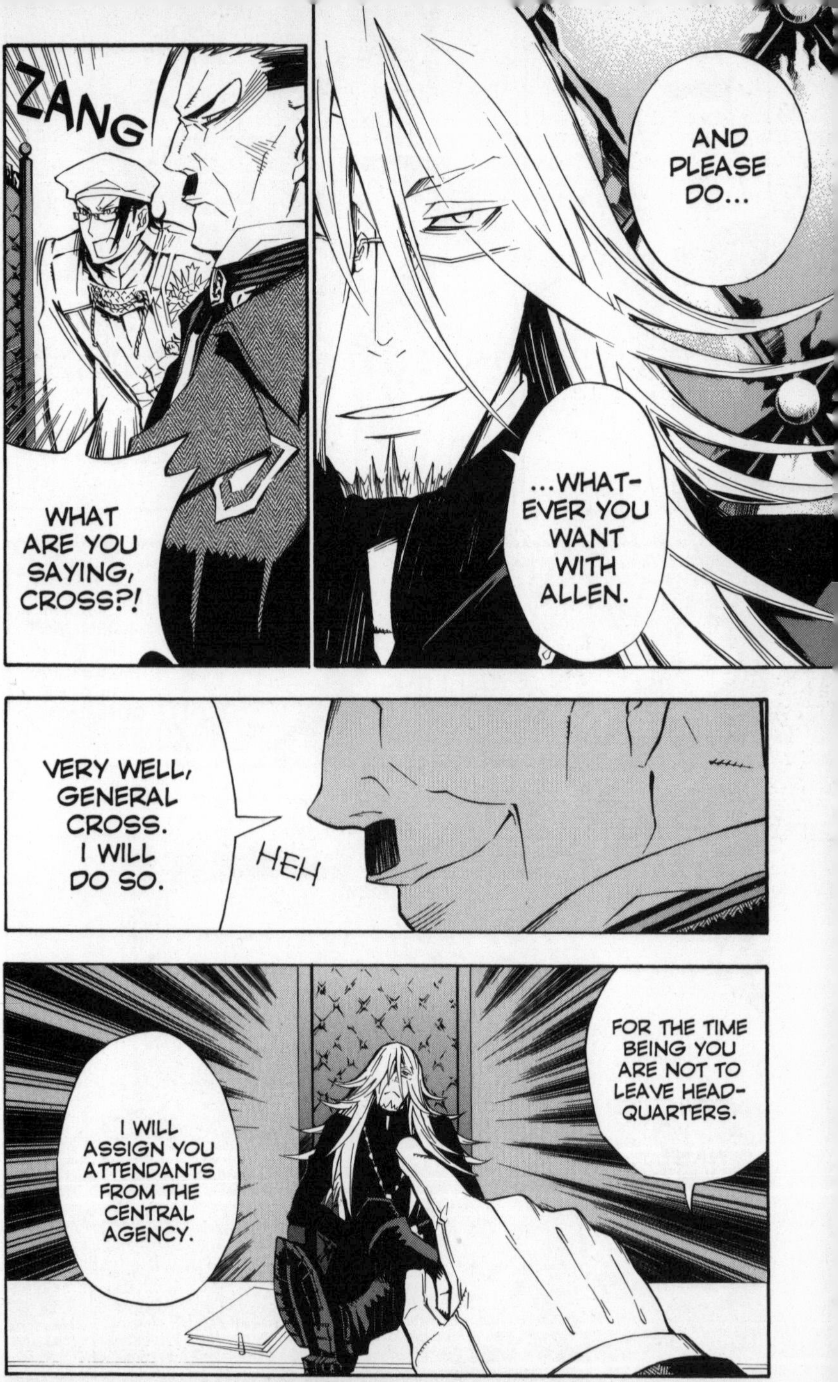
AND PLEASE DO...
...WHATEVER YOU WANT WITH ALLEN.
ZANG
WHAT ARE YOU SAYING, CROSS?!
HEH
VERY WELL, GENERAL CROSS. I WILL DO SO.
FOR THE TIME BEING YOU ARE NOT TO LEAVE HEADQUARTERS.
I WILL ASSIGN YOU ATTENDANTS FROM THE CENTRAL AGENCY.

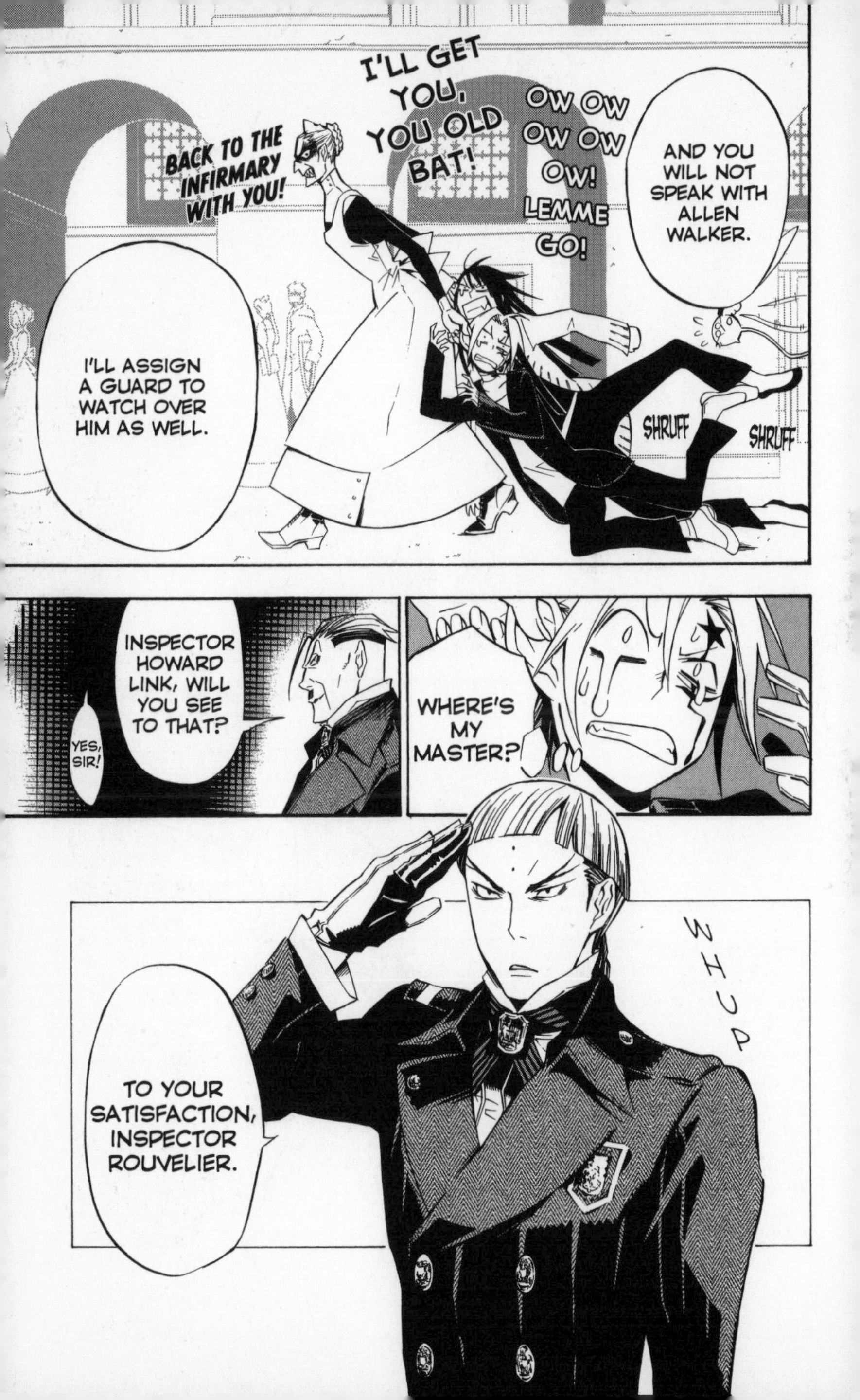
AND YOU WILL NOT SPEAK WITH ALLEN WALKER.
OW OW OW OW OW! LEMME GO!
I'LL GET YOU, YOU OLD BAT!
BACK TO THE INFIRMARY WITH YOU!
SHRUFF
SHRUFF
I'LL ASSIGN A GUARD TO WATCH OVER HIM AS WELL.
WHERE'S MY MASTER?
INSPECTOR HOWARD LINK, WILL YOU SEE TO THAT?
YES, SIR!
WHUP
TO YOUR SATISFACTION, INSPECTOR ROUVELIER.

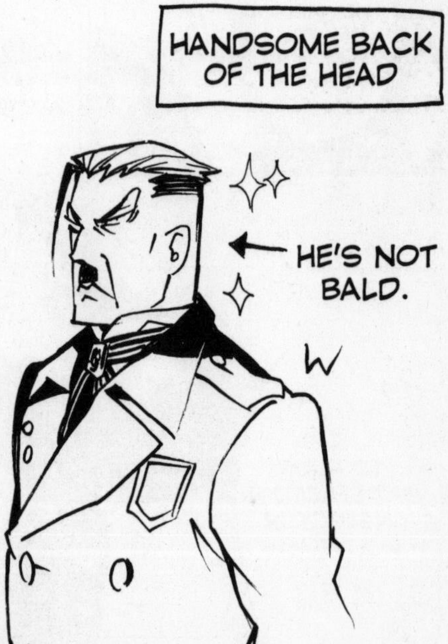
HANDSOME BACK OF THE HEAD
HE'S NOT BALD.

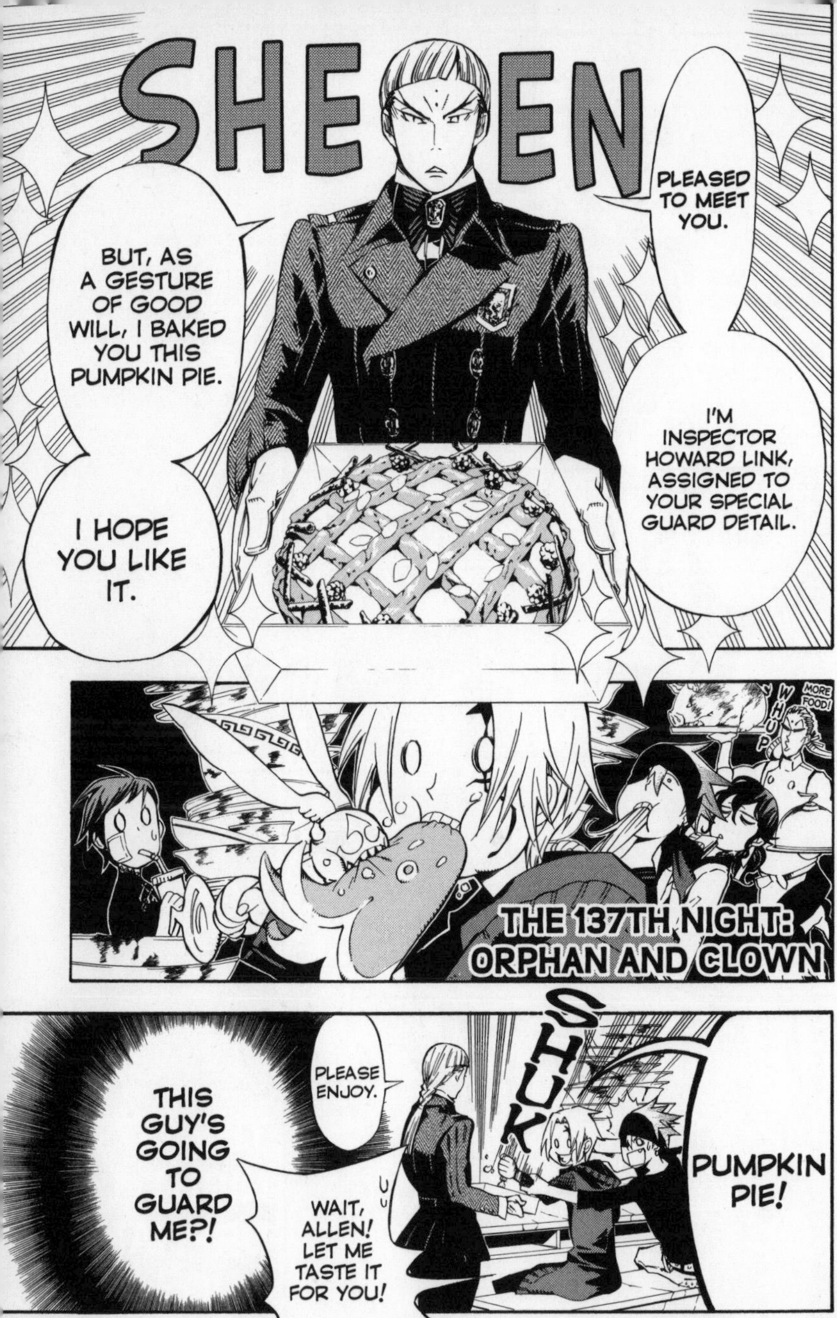
SHEEN
PLEASED TO MEET YOU.
I'M INSPECTOR HOWARD LINK, ASSIGNED TO YOUR SPECIAL GUARD DETAIL.
BUT, AS A GESTURE OF GOOD WILL, I BAKED YOU THIS PUMPKIN PIE.
I HOPE YOU LIKE IT.
MORE FOOD!
WHUP
THE 137TH NIGHT: ORPHAN AND CLOWN
PUMPKIN PIE!
SHUK
PLEASE ENJOY.
WAIT, ALLEN! LET ME TASTE IT FOR YOU!
THIS GUY'S GOING TO GUARD ME?!

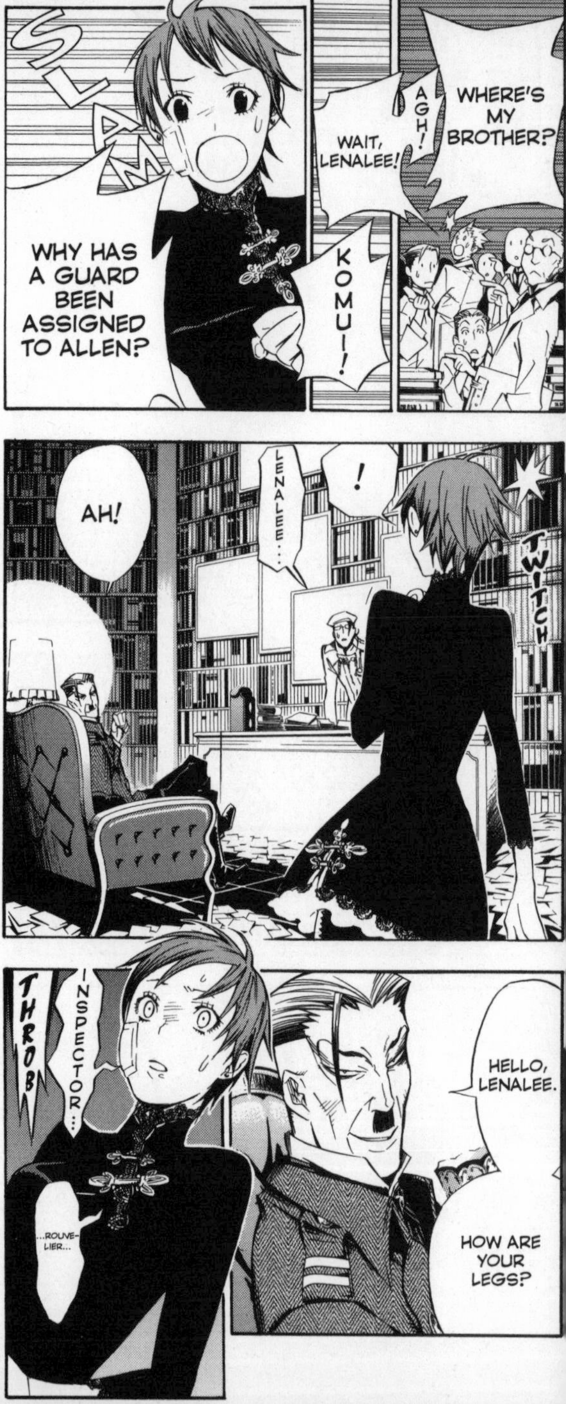
WHERE'S MY BROTHER?
AGH!
WAIT, LENALEE!
KOMUI!
SLAM
WHY HAS A GUARD BEEN ASSIGNED TO ALLEN?
TWITCH
!
LENALEE...
AH!
HELLO, LENALEE.
HOW ARE YOUR LEGS?
INSPECTOR...
THROB
...ROUVELIER...

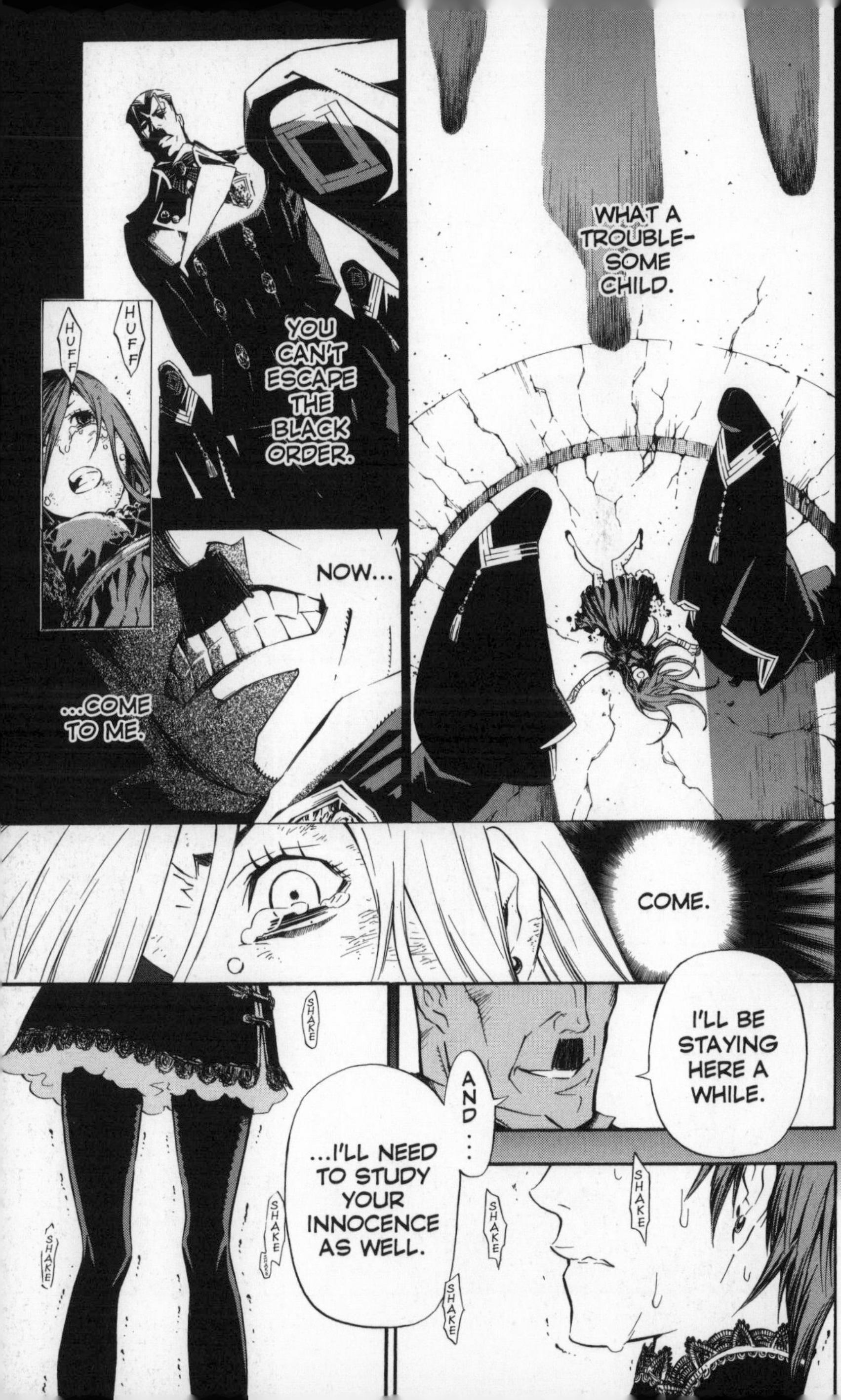
WHAT A TROUBLE-SOME CHILD.
YOU CAN'T ESCAPE THE BLACK ORDER.
HUFF
HUFF
NOW...
...COME TO ME.
COME.
I'LL BE STAYING HERE A WHILE.
AND...
...I'LL NEED TO STUDY YOUR INNOCENCE AS WELL.
SHAKE
SHAKE
SHAKE
SHAKE
SHAKE
SHAKE
SHAKE

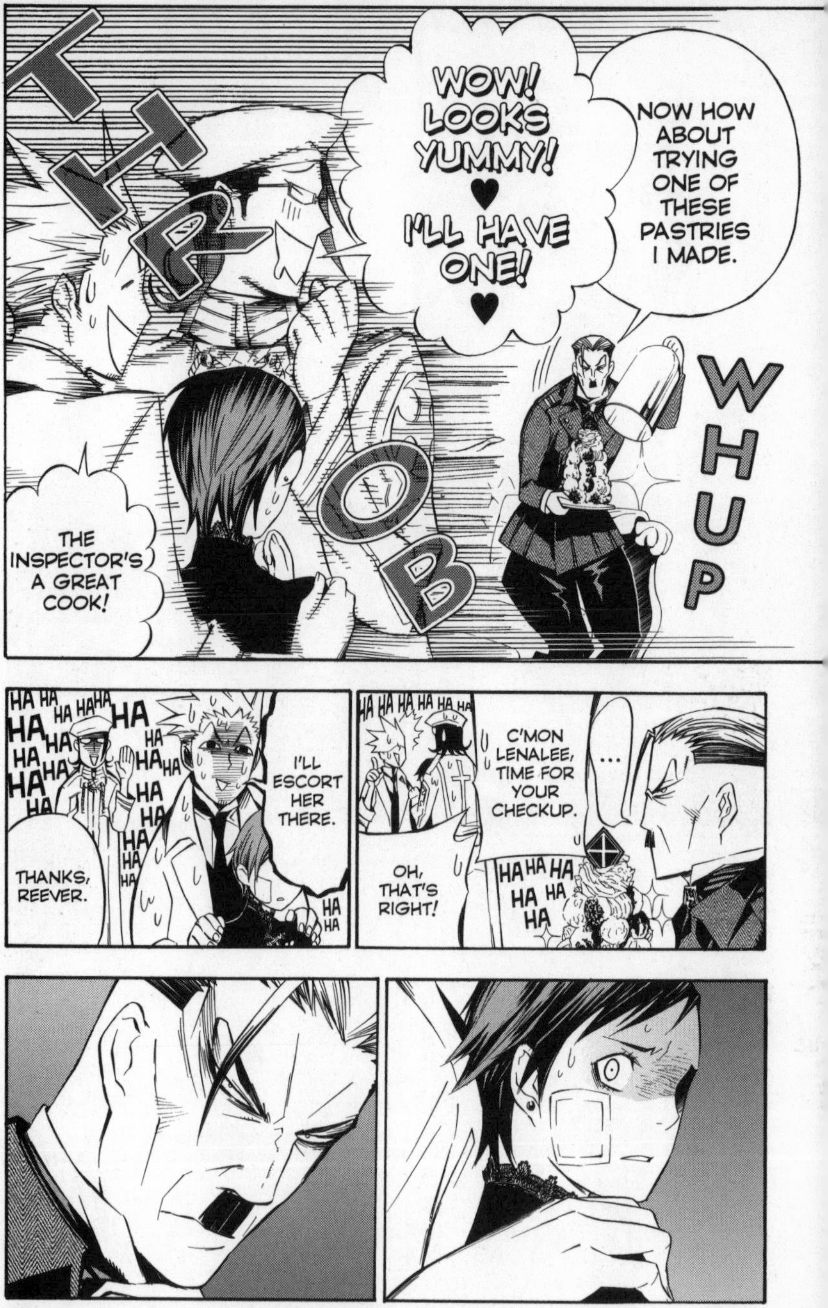
NOW HOW ABOUT TRYING ONE OF THESE PASTRIES I MADE.
WHUP
WOW! LOOKS YUMMY! ♥ I'LL HAVE ONE! ♥
THROB
THE INSPECTOR'S A GREAT COOK!
...
HA HA HA HA HA HA
C'MON LENALEE, TIME FOR YOUR CHECKUP.
OH, THAT'S RIGHT!
HA HA HA HA HA HA
I'LL ESCORT HER THERE.
HA HA HA HA HA HA HA HA HA HA HA HA HA HA HA HA HA HA
THANKS, REEVER.
HA HA

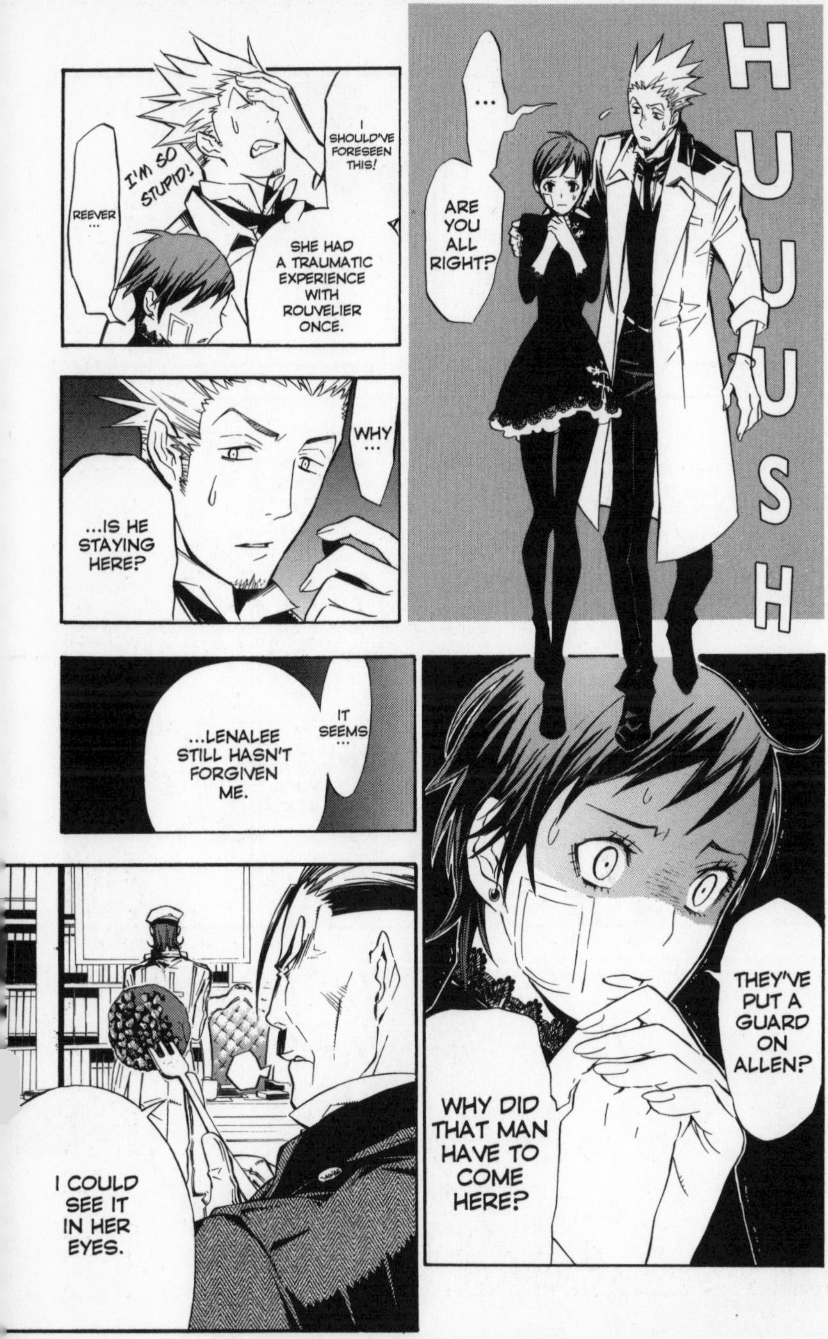
HUUUUSH
...
ARE YOU ALL RIGHT?
I SHOULD'VE FORESEEN THIS!
I'M SO STUPID!
SHE HAD A TRAUMATIC EXPERIENCE WITH ROUVELIER ONCE.
REEVER...
WHY...
...IS HE STAYING HERE?
THEY'VE PUT A GUARD ON ALLEN?
WHY DID THAT MAN HAVE TO COME HERE?
IT SEEMS...
...LENALEE STILL HASN'T FORGIVEN ME.
I COULD SEE IT IN HER EYES.

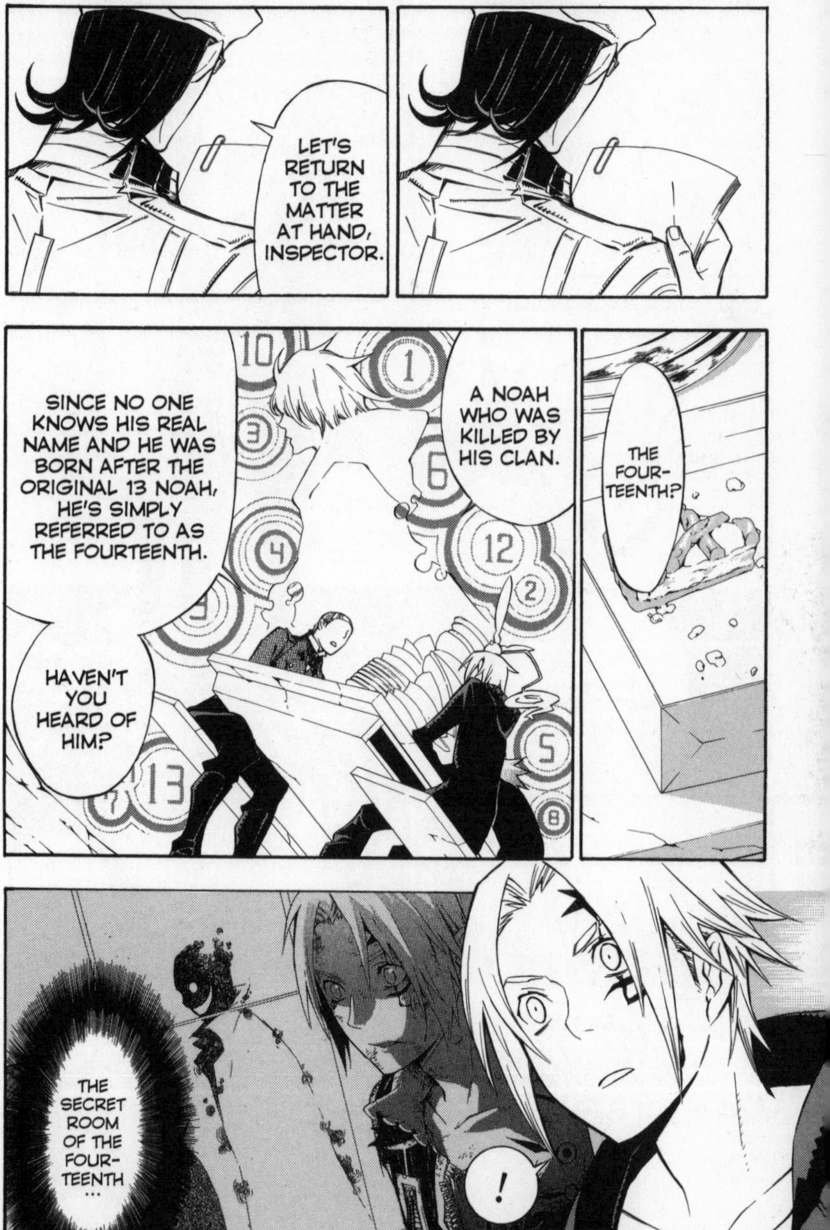
LET'S RETURN TO THE MATTER AT HAND, INSPECTOR.
THE FOURTEENTH?
A NOAH WHO WAS KILLED BY HIS CLAN.
SINCE NO ONE KNOWS HIS REAL NAME AND HE WAS BORN AFTER THE ORIGINAL 13 NOAH, HE'S SIMPLY REFERRED TO AS THE FOURTEENTH.
HAVEN'T YOU HEARD OF HIM?
!
THE SECRET ROOM OF THE FOURTEENTH...

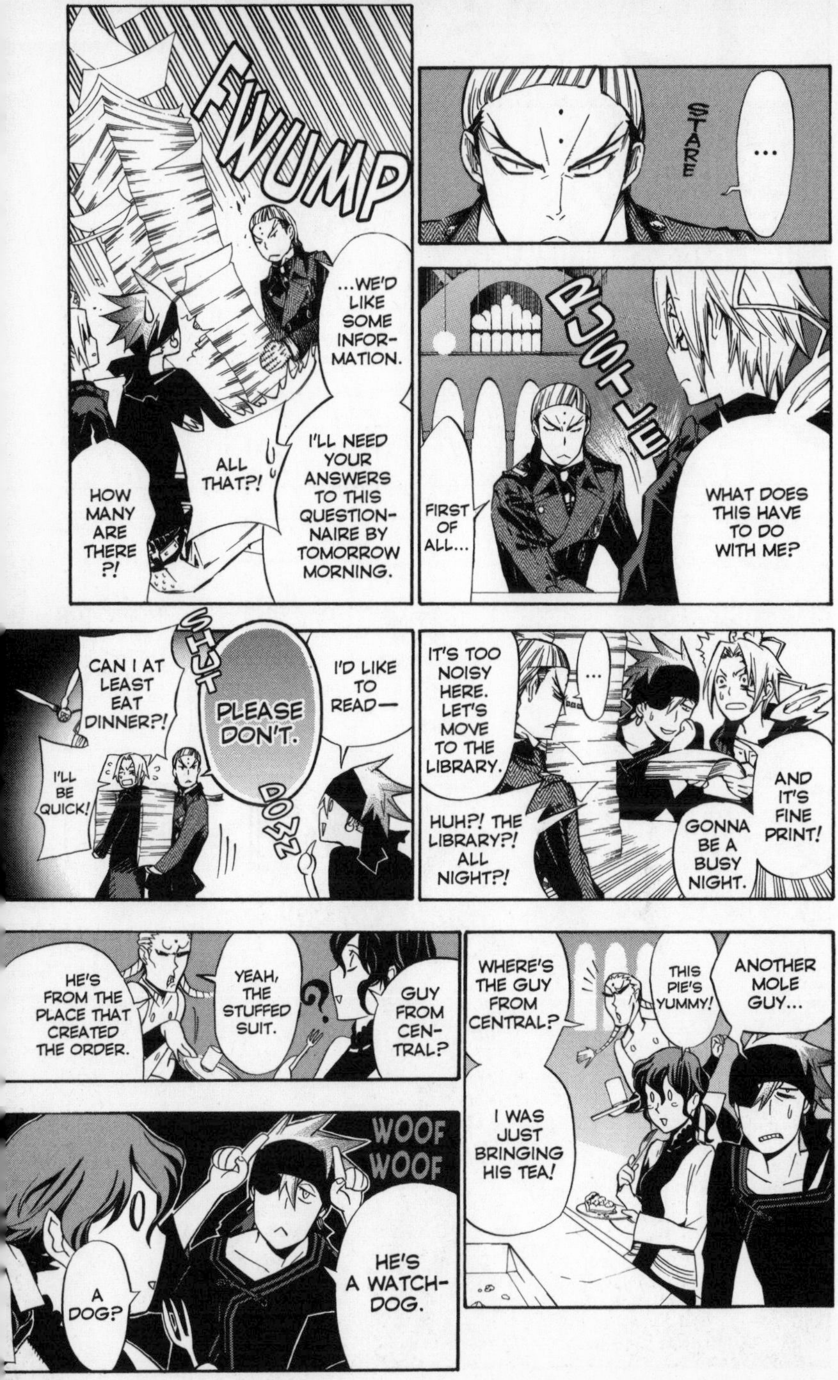
...
STARE
RUSTLE
WHAT DOES THIS HAVE TO DO WITH ME?
FIRST OF ALL...
FWUMP
...WE'D LIKE SOME INFORMATION.
I'LL NEED YOUR ANSWERS TO THIS QUESTIONNAIRE BY TOMORROW MORNING.
ALL THAT?!
HOW MANY ARE THERE?!
AND IT'S FINE PRINT!
...
IT'S TOO NOISY HERE. LET'S MOVE TO THE LIBRARY.
GONNA BE A BUSY NIGHT.
HUH?! THE LIBRARY?! ALL NIGHT?!
I'D LIKE TO READ—
PLEASE DON'T.
SHUT
DOWN
CAN I AT LEAST EAT DINNER?!
I'LL BE QUICK!
ANOTHER MOLE GUY...
THIS PIE'S YUMMY!
WHERE'S THE GUY FROM CENTRAL?
I WAS JUST BRINGING HIS TEA!
GUY FROM CENTRAL?
YEAH, THE STUFFED SUIT.
HE'S FROM THE PLACE THAT CREATED THE ORDER.
WOOF WOOF
HE'S A WATCHDOG.
A DOG?

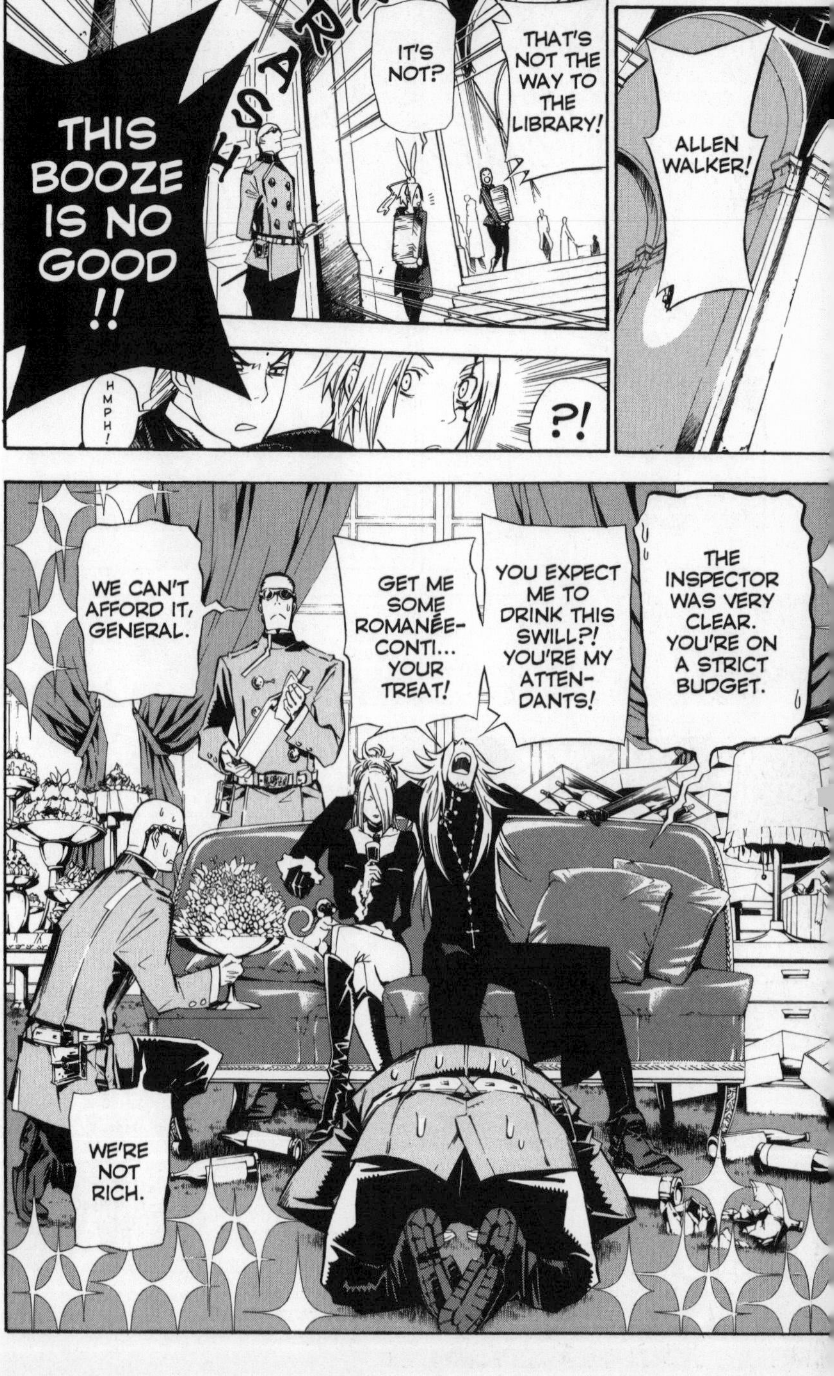
ALLEN WALKER!
THAT'S NOT THE WAY TO THE LIBRARY!
IT'S NOT?
THIS BOOZE IS NO GOOD!!
?!
HMPH!
THE INSPECTOR WAS VERY CLEAR. YOU'RE ON A STRICT BUDGET.
YOU EXPECT ME TO DRINK THIS SWILL?! YOU'RE MY ATTENDANTS!
GET ME SOME ROMANÉE-CONTI... YOUR TREAT!
WE CAN'T AFFORD IT, GENERAL.
WE'RE NOT RICH.

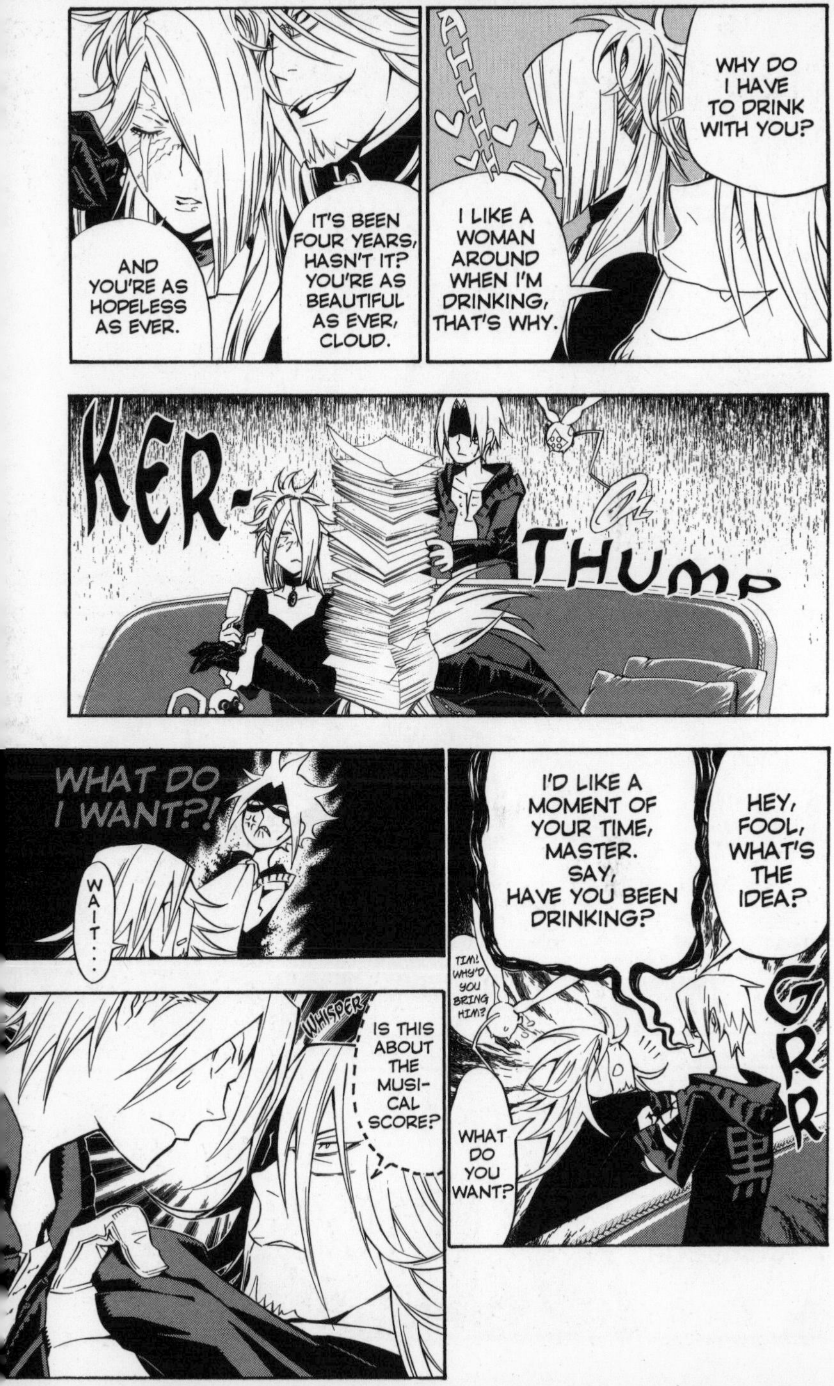
WHY DO I HAVE TO DRINK WITH YOU?
AHHHHH
I LIKE A WOMAN AROUND WHEN I'M DRINKING, THAT'S WHY.
IT'S BEEN FOUR YEARS, HASN'T IT? YOU'RE AS BEAUTIFUL AS EVER, CLOUD.
AND YOU'RE AS HOPELESS AS EVER.
KER-
THUMP
HEY, FOOL, WHAT'S THE IDEA?
I'D LIKE A MOMENT OF YOUR TIME, MASTER. SAY, HAVE YOU BEEN DRINKING?
GRRR
TIM! WHY'D YOU BRING HIM?
WHAT DO YOU WANT?
WHAT DO I WANT?!
WAIT...
WHISPER
IS THIS ABOUT THE MUSICAL SCORE?

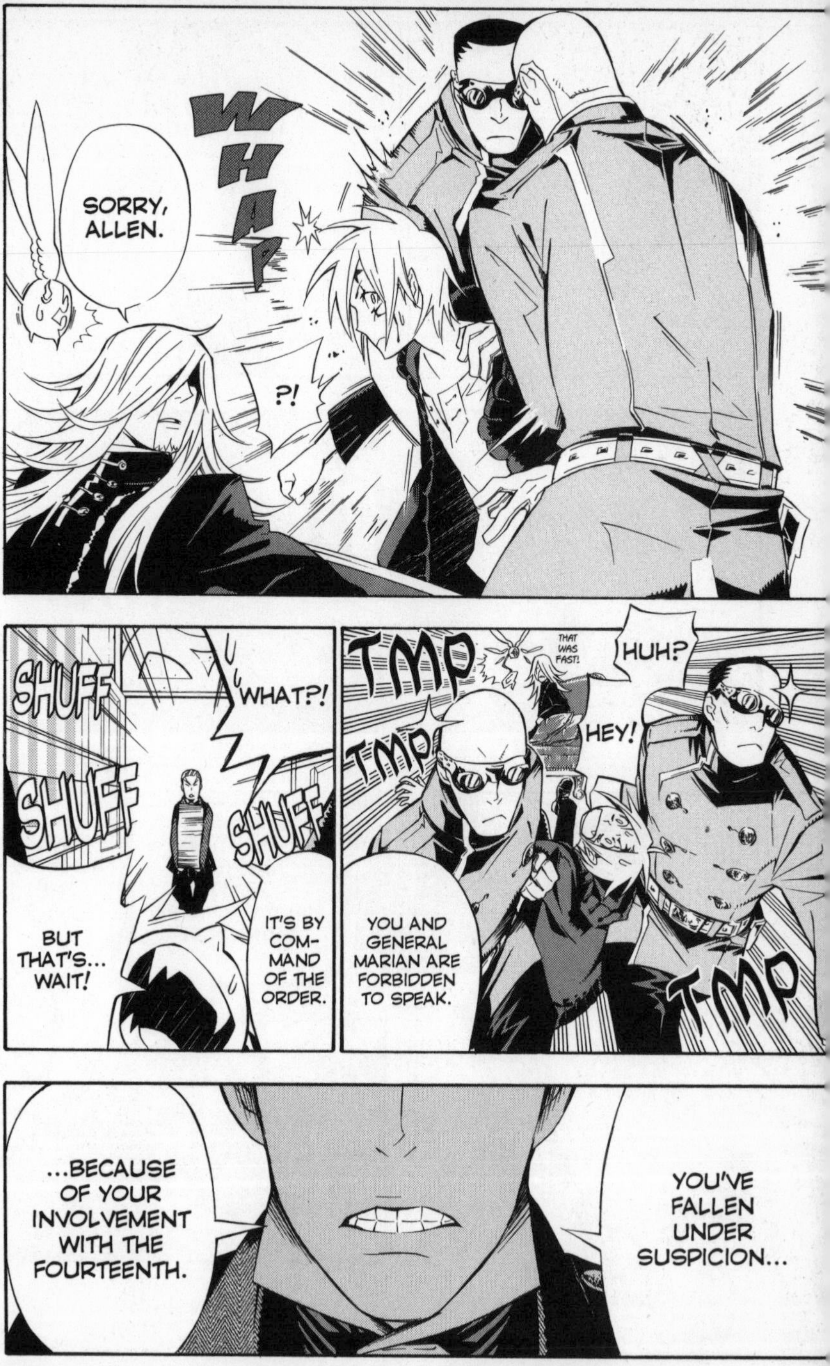
WHAP
SORRY, ALLEN.
?!
HUH?
THAT WAS FAST!
HEY!
TMP
TMP
TMP
YOU AND GENERAL MARIAN ARE FORBIDDEN TO SPEAK.
WHAT?!
SHUFF
SHUFF
SHUFF
IT'S BY COMMAND OF THE ORDER.
BUT THAT'S... WAIT!
YOU'VE FALLEN UNDER SUSPICION...
...BECAUSE OF YOUR INVOLVEMENT WITH THE FOURTEENTH.

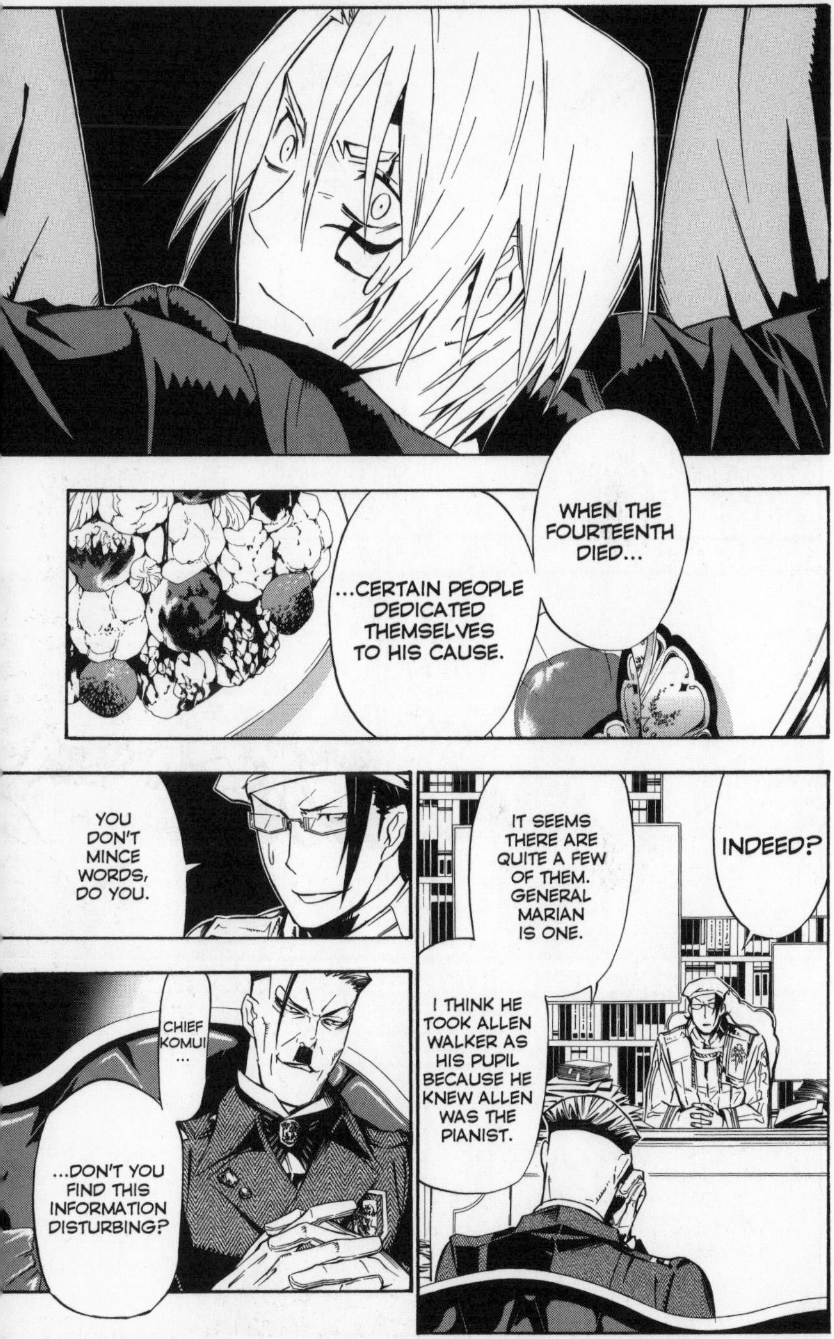
WHEN THE FOURTEENTH DIED...
...CERTAIN PEOPLE DEDICATED THEMSELVES TO HIS CAUSE.
INDEED?
IT SEEMS THERE ARE QUITE A FEW OF THEM. GENERAL MARIAN IS ONE.
I THINK HE TOOK ALLEN WALKER AS HIS PUPIL BECAUSE HE KNEW ALLEN WAS THE PIANIST.
YOU DON'T MINCE WORDS, DO YOU.
CHIEF KOMUI ...
...DON'T YOU FIND THIS INFORMATION DISTURBING?

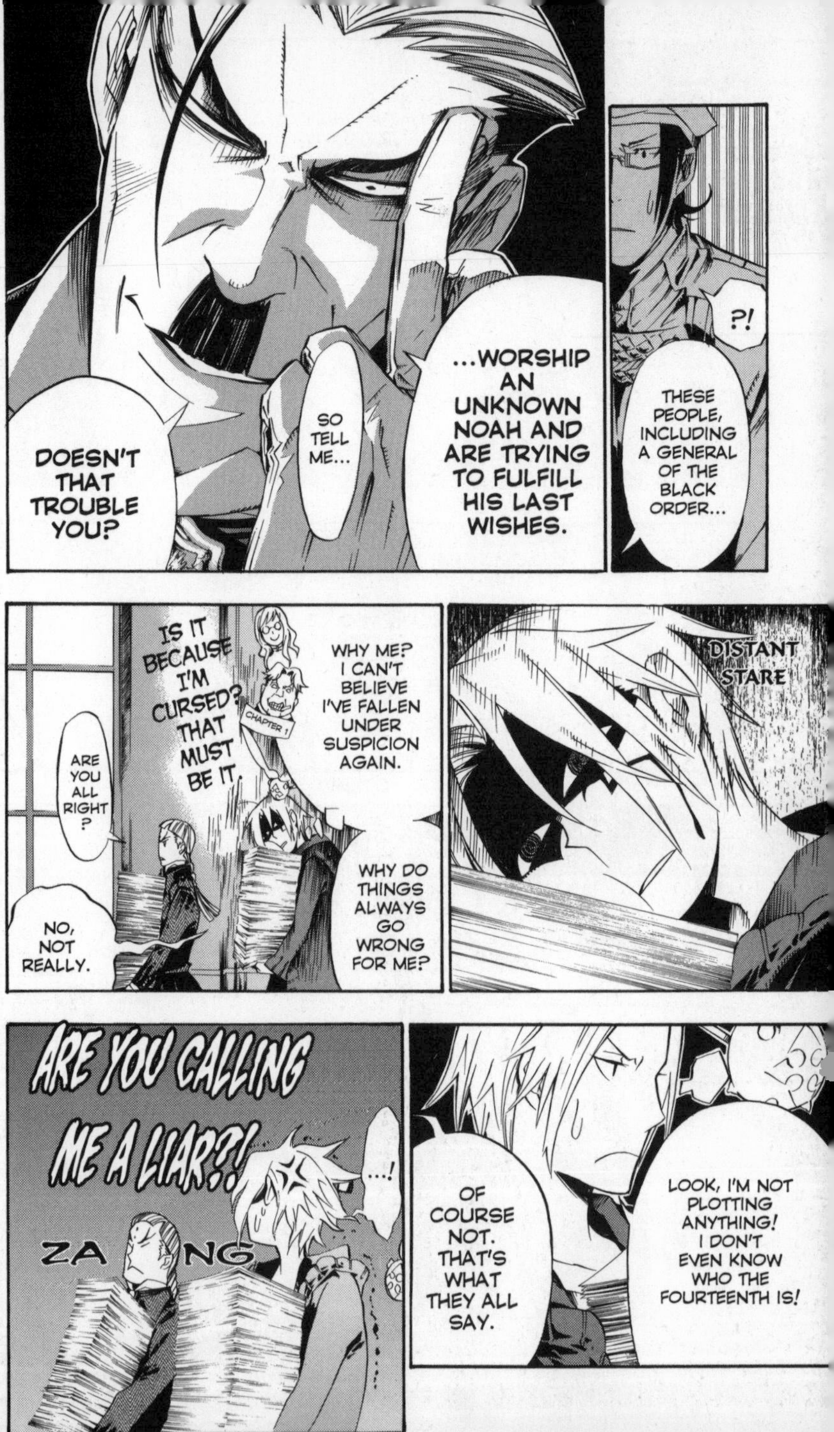
?!
THESE PEOPLE, INCLUDING A GENERAL OF THE BLACK ORDER...
...WORSHIP AN UNKNOWN NOAH AND ARE TRYING TO FULFILL HIS LAST WISHES.
SO TELL ME...
DOESN'T THAT TROUBLE YOU?
DISTANT STARE
WHY ME? I CAN'T BELIEVE I'VE FALLEN UNDER SUSPICION AGAIN.
IS IT BECAUSE I'M CURSED? THAT MUST BE IT.
CHAPTER 1
WHY DO THINGS ALWAYS GO WRONG FOR ME?
ARE YOU ALL RIGHT?
NO, NOT REALLY.
LOOK, I'M NOT PLOTTING ANYTHING! I DON'T EVEN KNOW WHO THE FOURTEENTH IS!
OF COURSE NOT. THAT'S WHAT THEY ALL SAY.
...!
ARE YOU CALLING ME A LIAR?!
ZANG

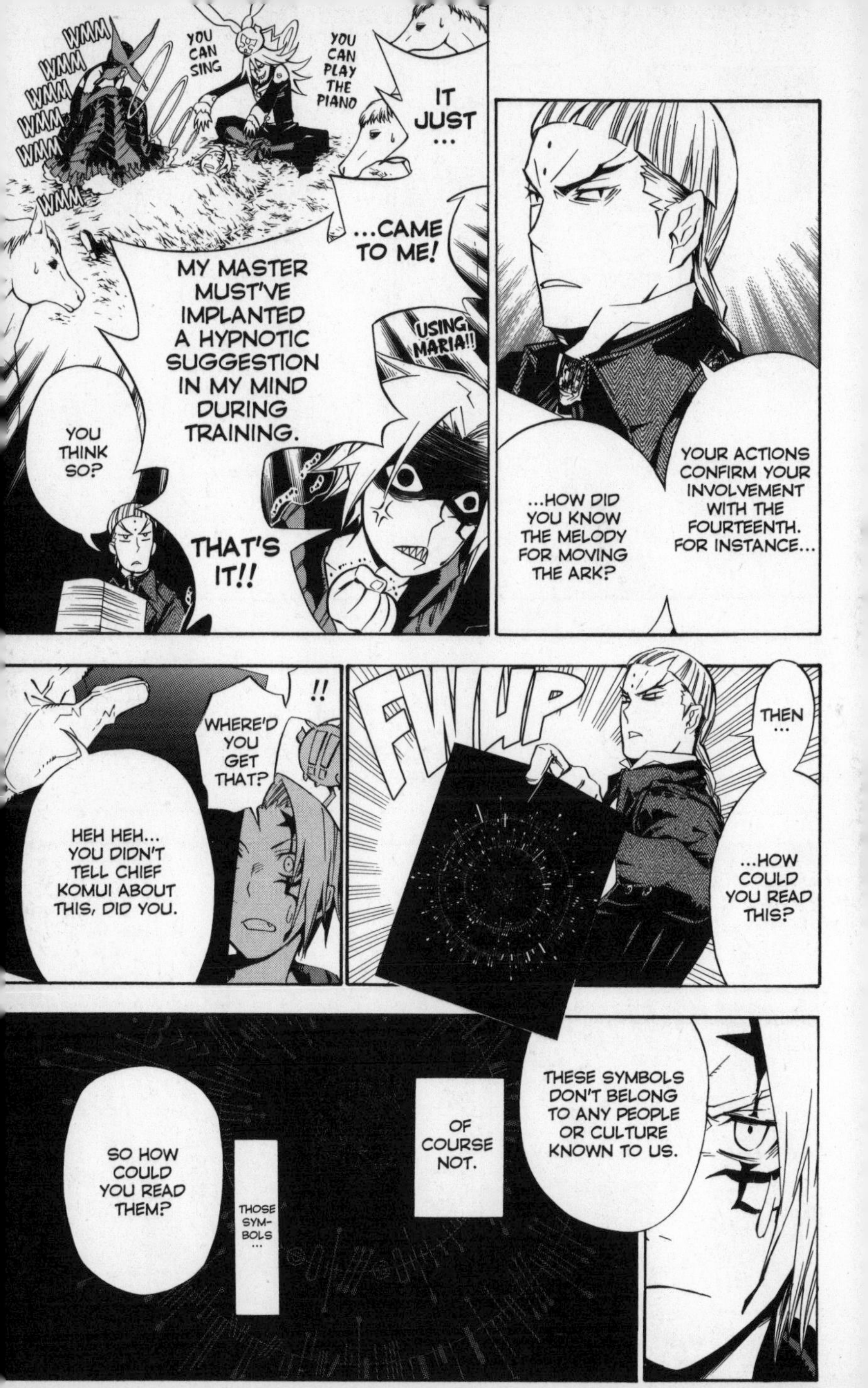
YOUR ACTIONS CONFIRM YOUR INVOLVEMENT WITH THE FOURTEENTH. FOR INSTANCE...
...HOW DID YOU KNOW THE MELODY FOR MOVING THE ARK?
IT JUST ...
...CAME TO ME!
YOU CAN PLAY THE PIANO
YOU CAN SING
WMM WMM WMM WMM WMM WMM
USING MARIA!!
MY MASTER MUST'VE IMPLANTED A HYPNOTIC SUGGESTION IN MY MIND DURING TRAINING.
THAT'S IT!!
YOU THINK SO?
THEN ...
FWUP
...HOW COULD YOU READ THIS?
!!
WHERE'D YOU GET THAT?
HEH HEH... YOU DIDN'T TELL CHIEF KOMUI ABOUT THIS, DID YOU.
THESE SYMBOLS DON'T BELONG TO ANY PEOPLE OR CULTURE KNOWN TO US.
OF COURSE NOT.
THOSE SYM-BOLS ...
SO HOW COULD YOU READ THEM?

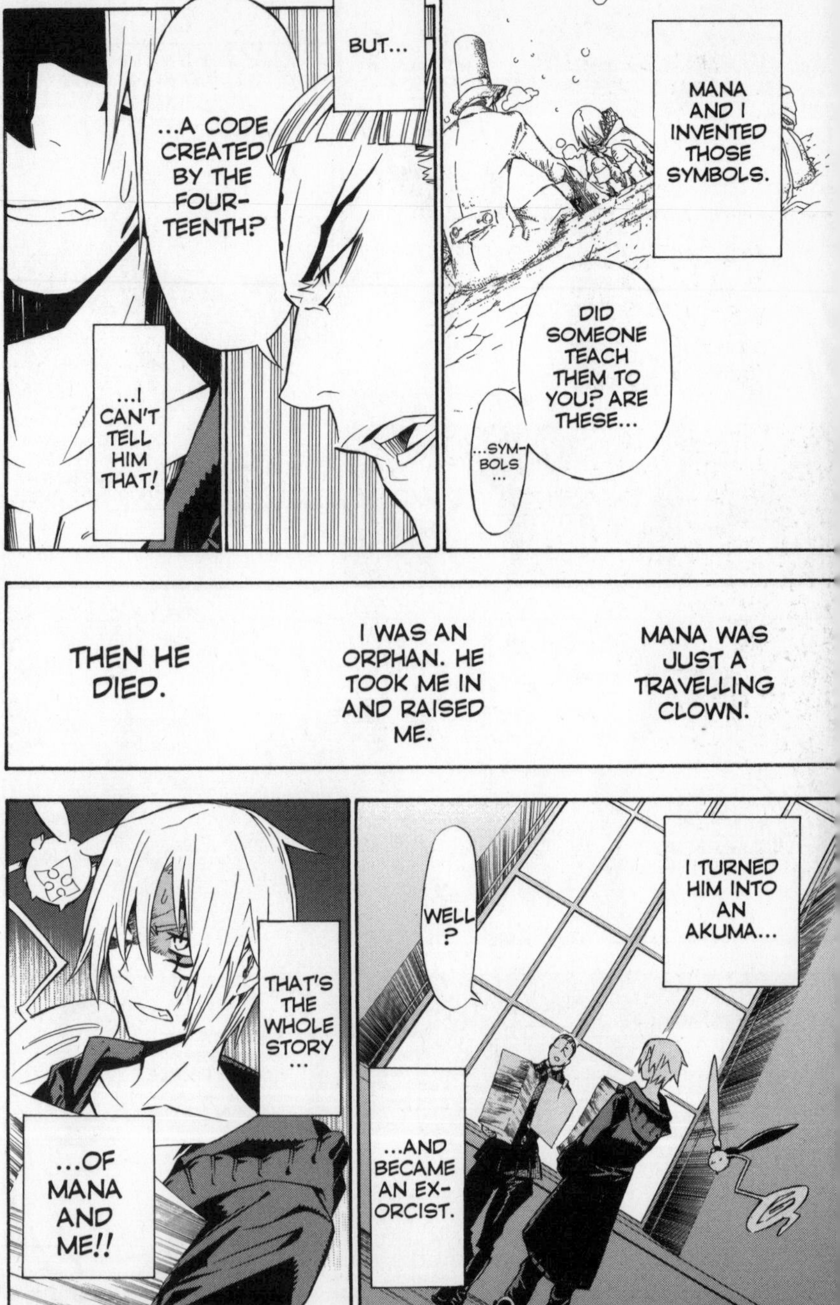
MANA AND I INVENTED THOSE SYMBOLS.
DID SOMEONE TEACH THEM TO YOU? ARE THESE...
...SYMBOLS...
BUT...
...A CODE CREATED BY THE FOURTEENTH?
...I CAN'T TELL HIM THAT!
MANA WAS JUST A TRAVELLING CLOWN.
I WAS AN ORPHAN. HE TOOK ME IN AND RAISED ME.
THEN HE DIED.
I TURNED HIM INTO AN AKUMA...
WELL?
...AND BECAME AN EXORCIST.
THAT'S THE WHOLE STORY...
...OF MANA AND ME!!

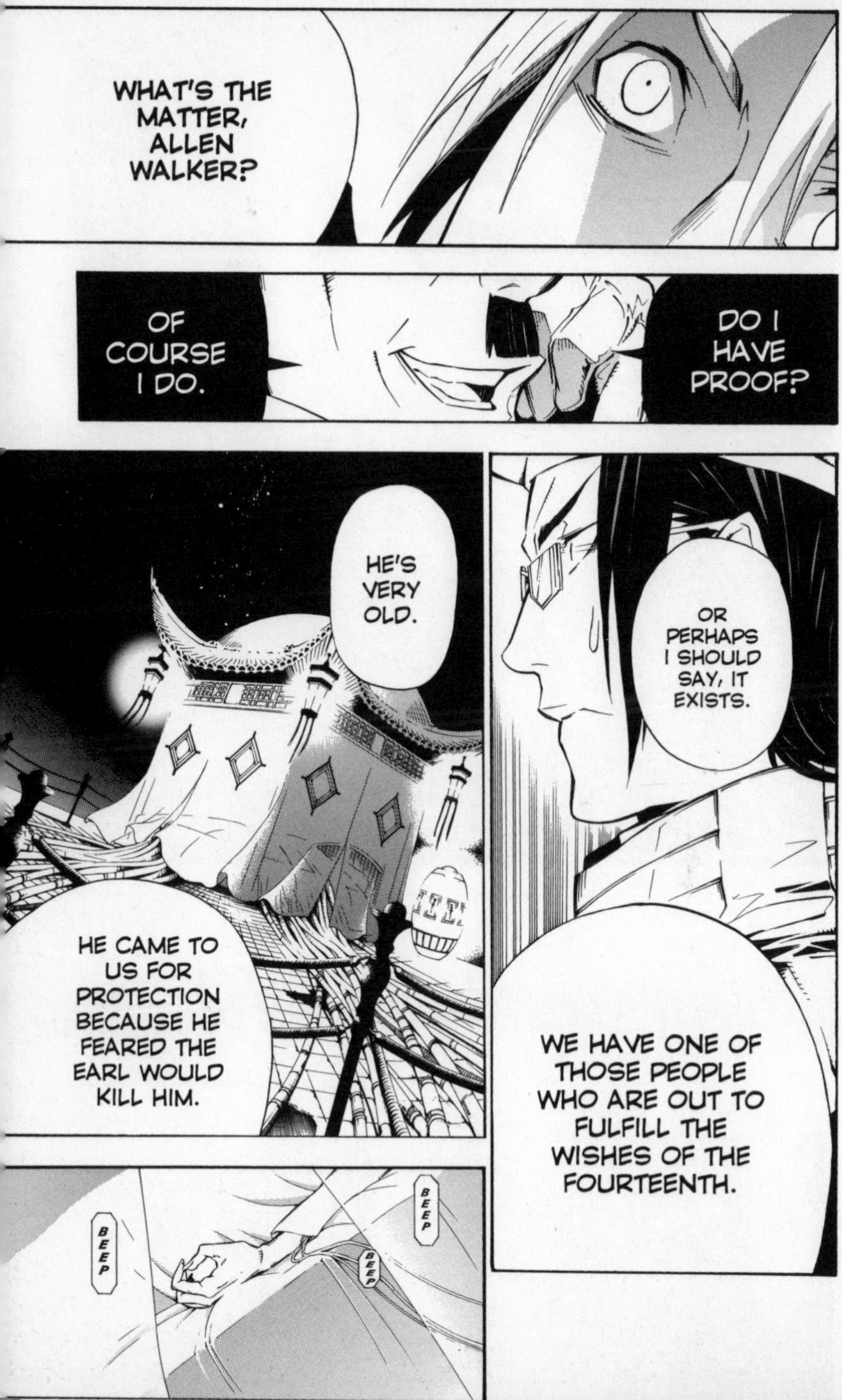
WHAT'S THE MATTER, ALLEN WALKER?
DO I HAVE PROOF?
OF COURSE I DO.
OR PERHAPS I SHOULD SAY, IT EXISTS.
WE HAVE ONE OF THOSE PEOPLE WHO ARE OUT TO FULFILL THE WISHES OF THE FOURTEENTH.
HE'S VERY OLD.
HE CAME TO US FOR PROTECTION BECAUSE HE FEARED THE EARL WOULD KILL HIM.
BEEP
BEEP
BEEP

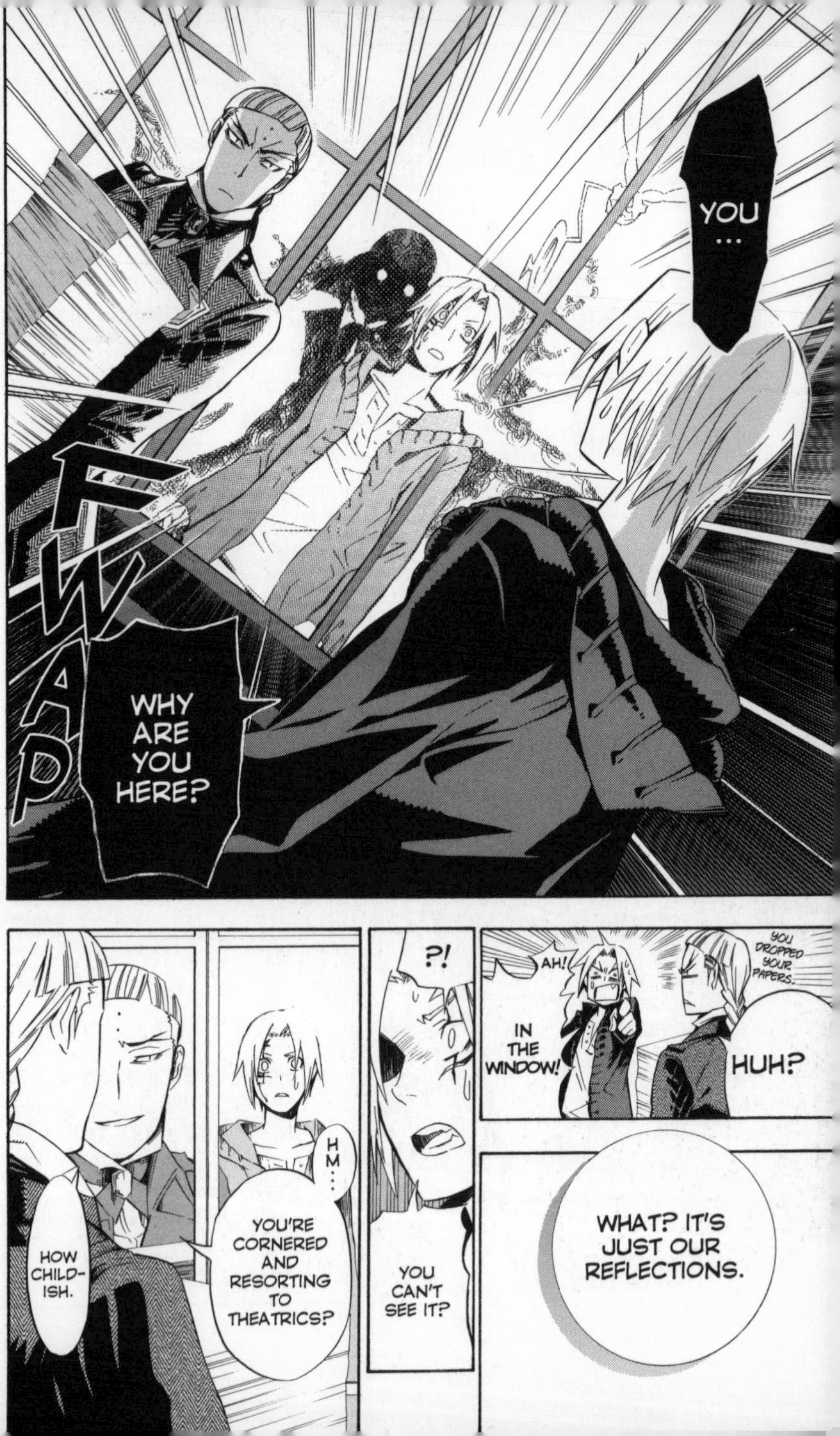
YOU...
WHY ARE YOU HERE?
FWAP
YOU DROPPED YOUR PAPERS.
HUH?
AH!
IN THE WINDOW!
WHAT? IT'S JUST OUR REFLECTIONS.
?!
YOU CAN'T SEE IT?
HM...
YOU'RE CORNERED AND RESORTING TO THEATRICS?
HOW CHILD-ISH.

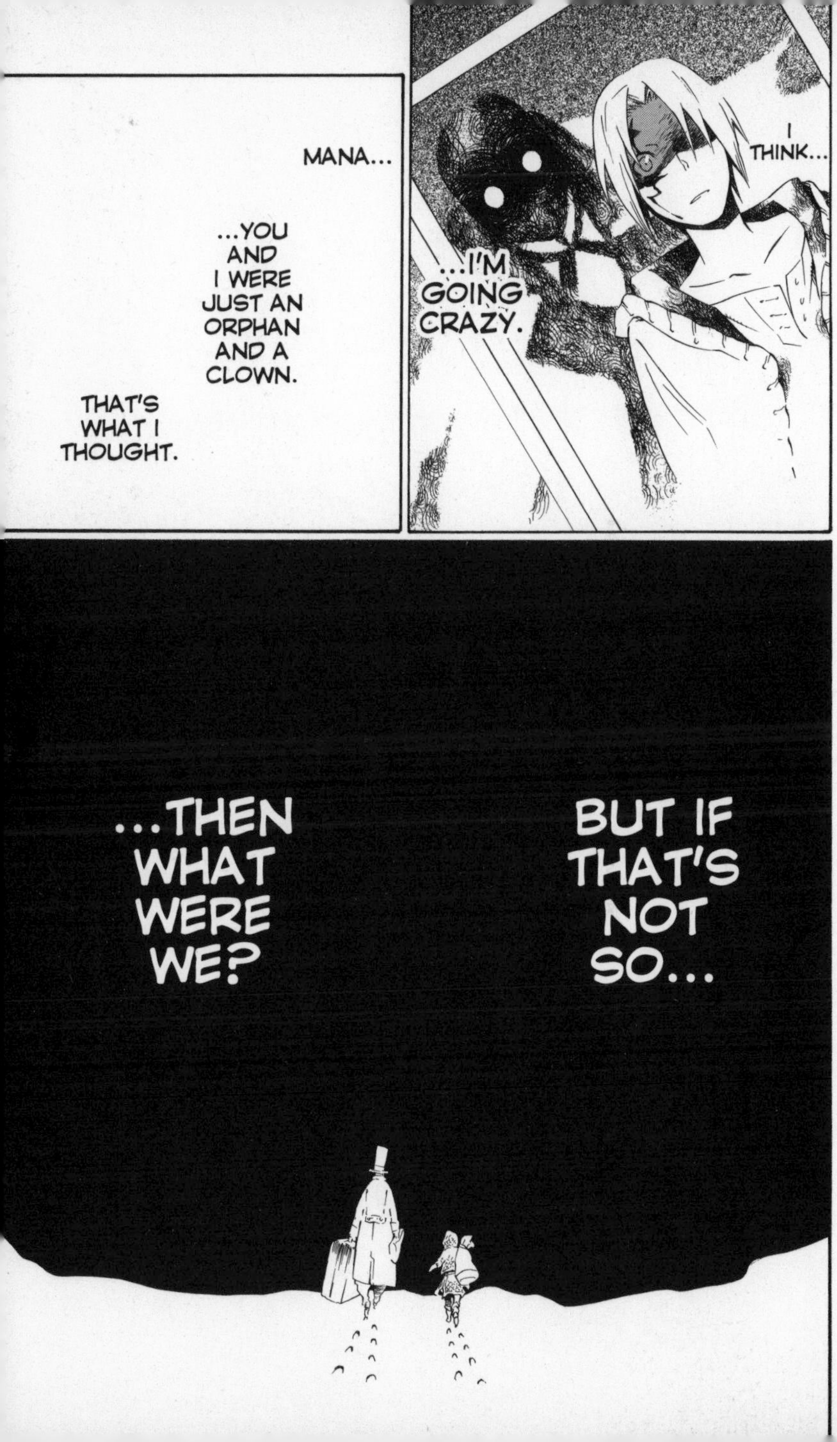
I THINK...
...I'M GOING CRAZY.
MANA...
...YOU AND I WERE JUST AN ORPHAN AND A CLOWN.
THAT'S WHAT I THOUGHT.
BUT IF THAT'S NOT SO...
...THEN WHAT WERE WE?

DISTANT
STARE

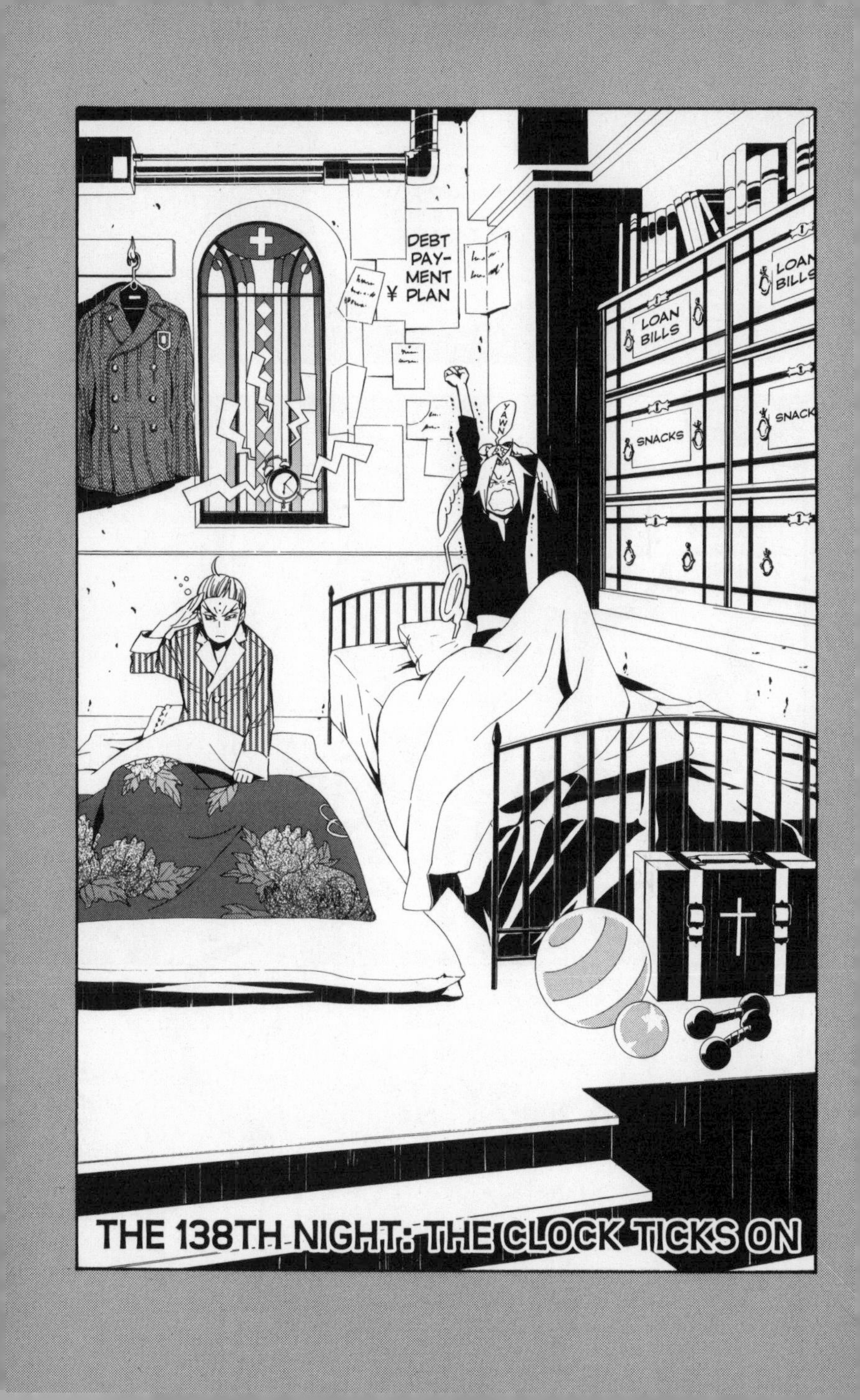
DEBT PAY-MENT PLAN
¥
LOAN BILLS
LOAN BILLS
YAWN
SNACKS
SNACKS

# THE 138TH NIGHT: THE CLOCK TICKS ON

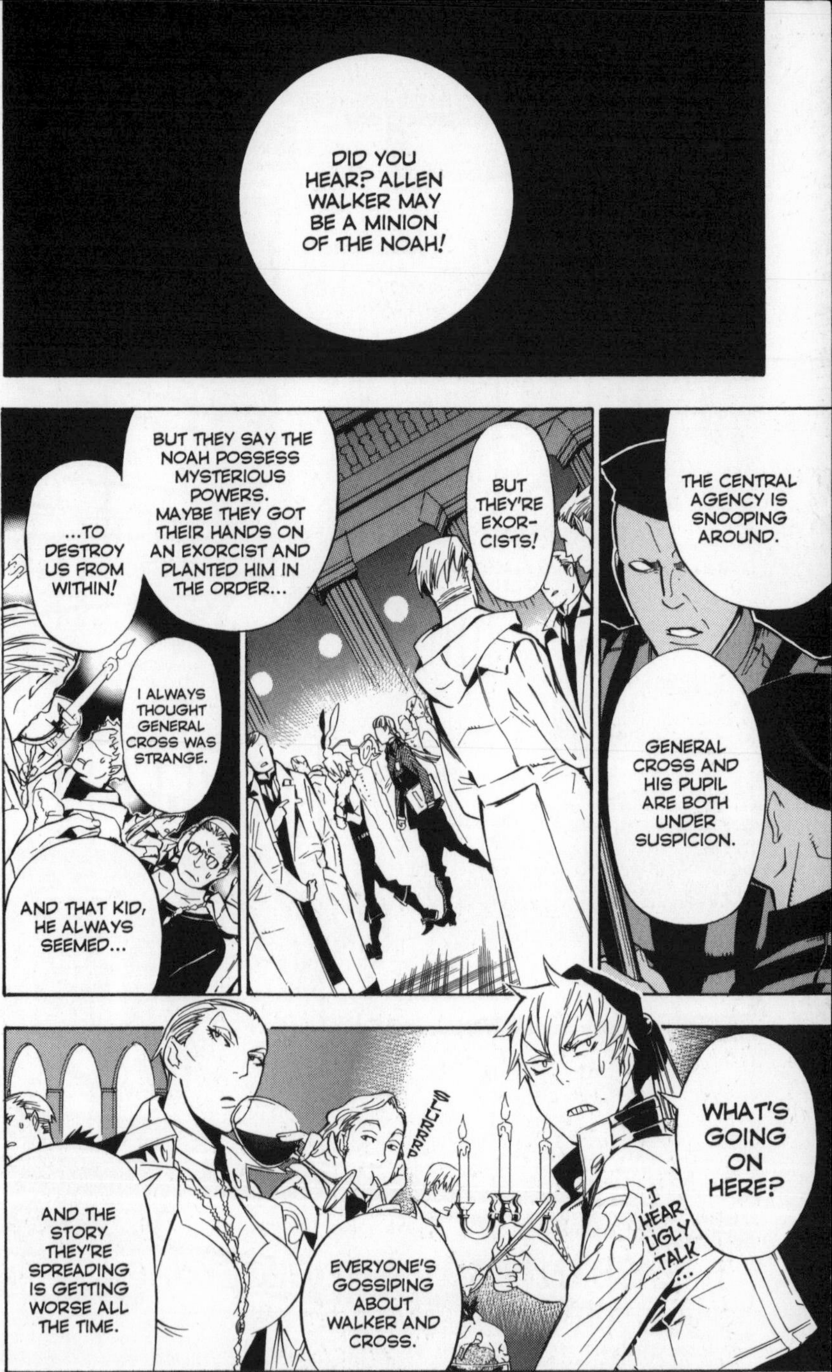
DID YOU HEAR? ALLEN WALKER MAY BE A MINION OF THE NOAH!
THE CENTRAL AGENCY IS SNOOPING AROUND.
GENERAL CROSS AND HIS PUPIL ARE BOTH UNDER SUSPICION.
BUT THEY'RE EXOR-CISTS!
BUT THEY SAY THE NOAH POSSESS MYSTERIOUS POWERS. MAYBE THEY GOT THEIR HANDS ON AN EXORCIST AND PLANTED HIM IN THE ORDER...
...TO DESTROY US FROM WITHIN!
I ALWAYS THOUGHT GENERAL CROSS WAS STRANGE.
AND THAT KID, HE ALWAYS SEEMED...
WHAT'S GOING ON HERE?
I HEAR UGLY TALK...
SLURRRP
EVERYONE'S GOSSIPING ABOUT WALKER AND CROSS.
AND THE STORY THEY'RE SPREADING IS GETTING WORSE ALL THE TIME.

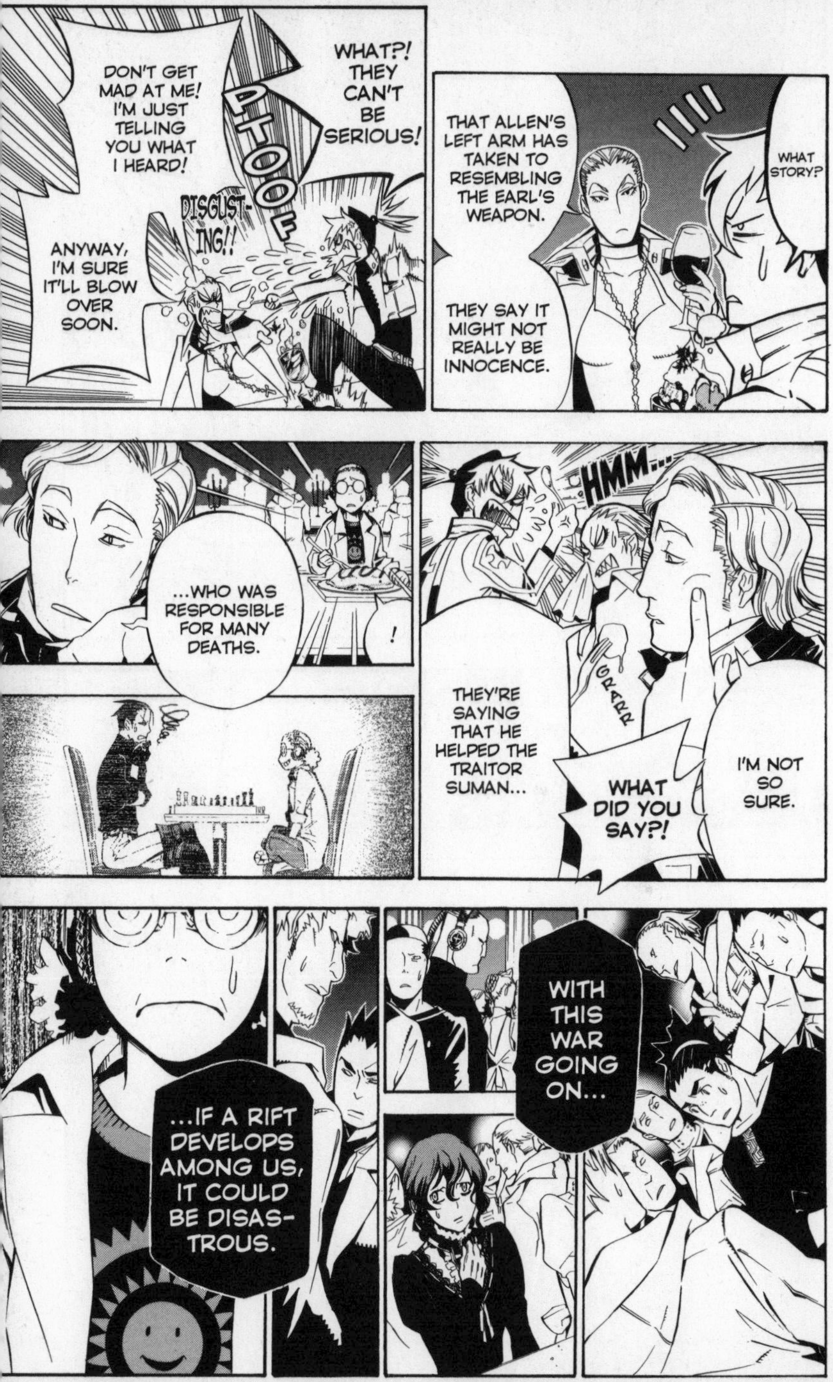
WHAT STORY?
THAT ALLEN'S LEFT ARM HAS TAKEN TO RESEMBLING THE EARL'S WEAPON.
THEY SAY IT MIGHT NOT REALLY BE INNOCENCE.
WHAT?! THEY CAN'T BE SERIOUS!
PTOOF
DON'T GET MAD AT ME! I'M JUST TELLING YOU WHAT I HEARD!
DISGUST-ING!!
ANYWAY, I'M SURE IT'LL BLOW OVER SOON.
HMM...
I'M NOT SO SURE.
THEY'RE SAYING THAT HE HELPED THE TRAITOR SUMAN...
GRARR
WHAT DID YOU SAY?!
!
...WHO WAS RESPONSIBLE FOR MANY DEATHS.
WITH THIS WAR GOING ON...
...IF A RIFT DEVELOPS AMONG US, IT COULD BE DISASTROUS.

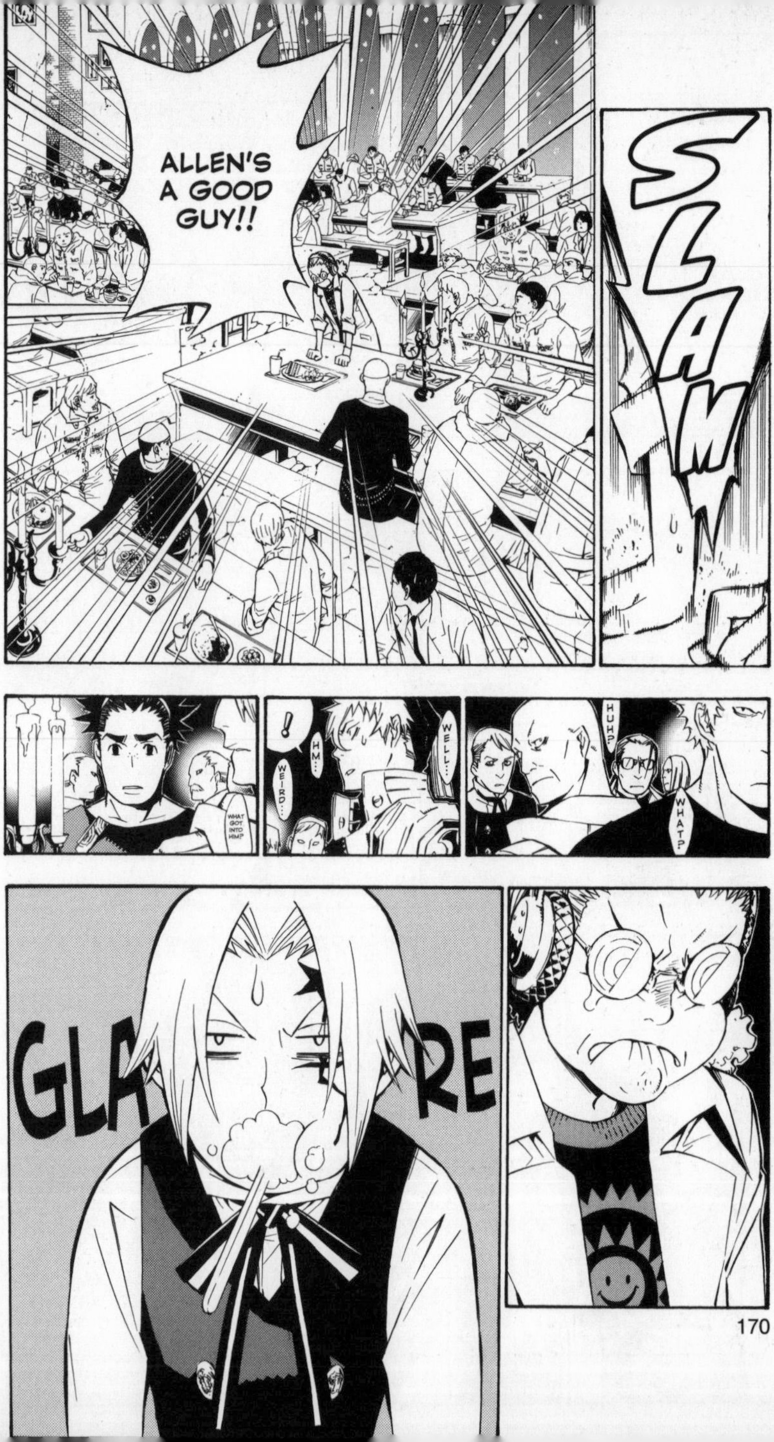
SLAM
ALLEN'S A GOOD GUY!!
HUH?
WHAT?
WELL...
HM...
WEIRD...
!
WHAT GOT INTO HIM?
GLARE

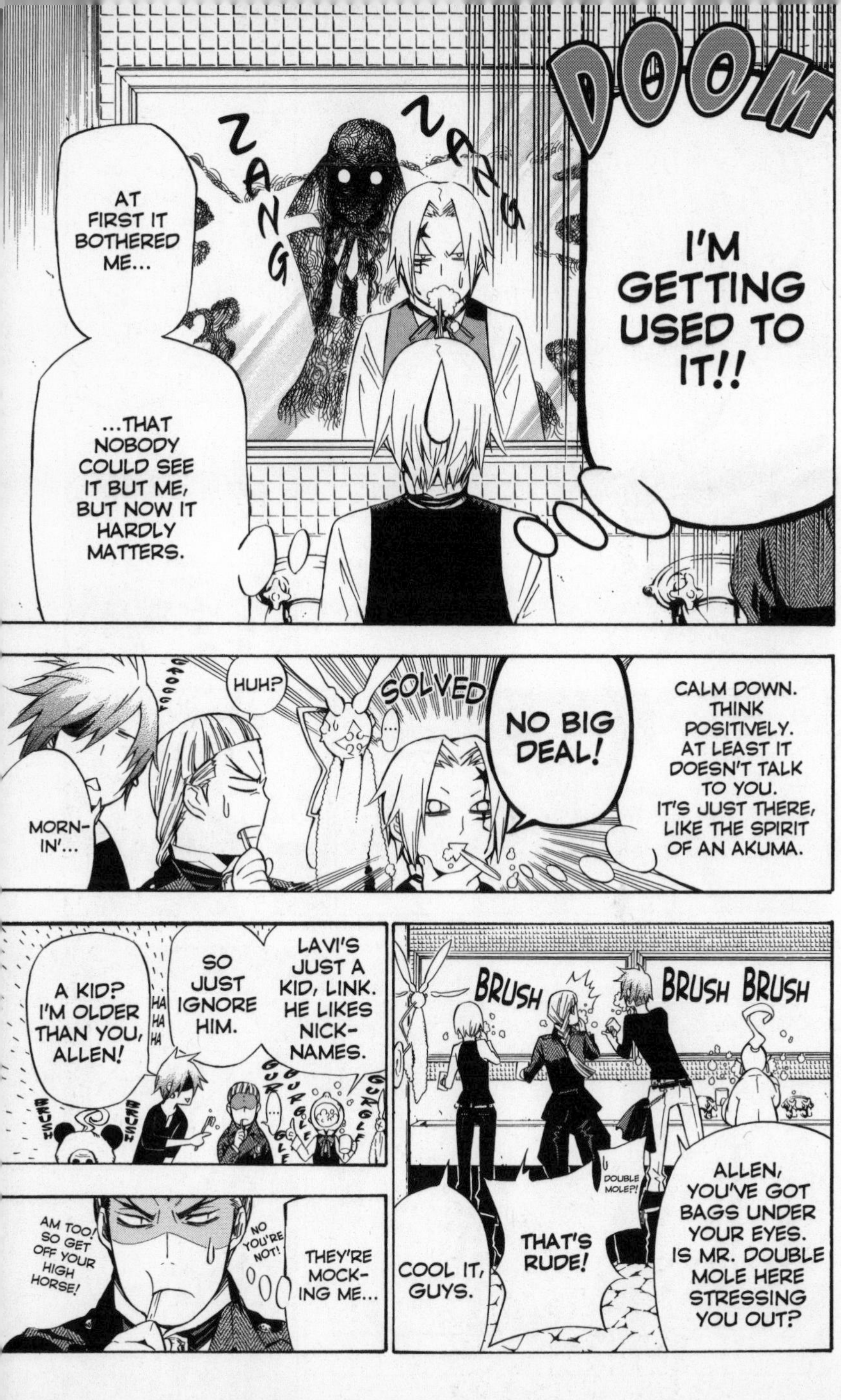
DOOM
I'M GETTING USED TO IT!!
ZANG
ZANG
AT FIRST IT BOTHERED ME...
...THAT NOBODY COULD SEE IT BUT ME, BUT NOW IT HARDLY MATTERS.
CALM DOWN. THINK POSITIVELY. AT LEAST IT DOESN'T TALK TO YOU. IT'S JUST THERE, LIKE THE SPIRIT OF AN AKUMA.
NO BIG DEAL!
SOLVED
...
HUH?
MORN-IN'...
BRUSH BRUSH
BRUSH
ALLEN, YOU'VE GOT BAGS UNDER YOUR EYES. IS MR. DOUBLE MOLE HERE STRESSING YOU OUT?
DOUBLE MOLE?!
THAT'S RUDE!
COOL IT, GUYS.
LAVI'S JUST A KID, LINK. HE LIKES NICK-NAMES.
SO JUST IGNORE HIM.
HA HA HA
A KID? I'M OLDER THAN YOU, ALLEN!
GURGLE
GURGLE
...
GURGLE
BRUSH
BRUSH
THEY'RE MOCK-ING ME...
NO YOU'RE NOT!
AM TOO! SO GET OFF YOUR HIGH HORSE!

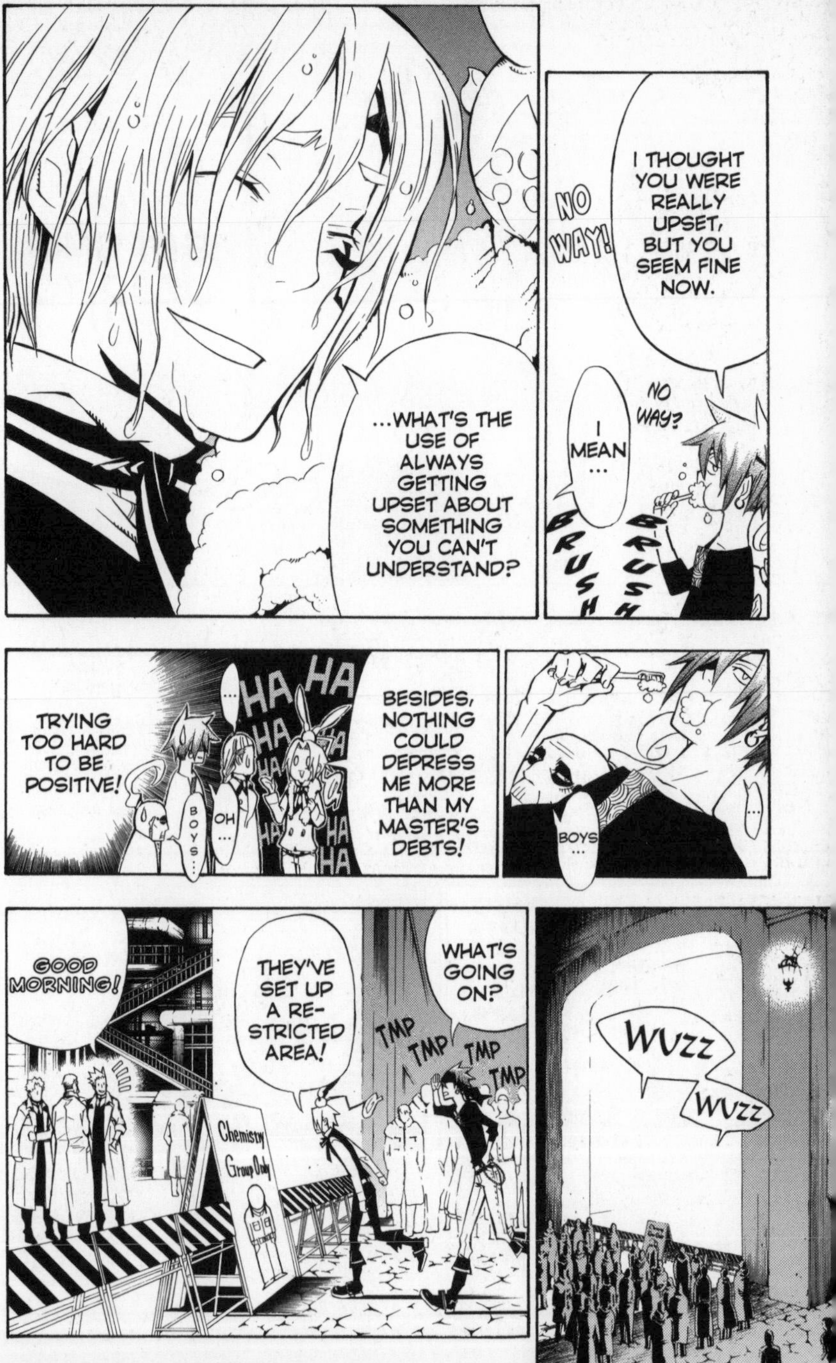
I THOUGHT YOU WERE REALLY UPSET, BUT YOU SEEM FINE NOW.
NO WAY!
NO WAY?
I MEAN...
BRUSH BRUSH
...WHAT'S THE USE OF ALWAYS GETTING UPSET ABOUT SOMETHING YOU CAN'T UNDERSTAND?
...
BOYS...
BESIDES, NOTHING COULD DEPRESS ME MORE THAN MY MASTER'S DEBTS!
HA HA HA HA HA HA HA
...
TRYING TOO HARD TO BE POSITIVE!
OH...
BOYS...
WVZZ
WVZZ
WHAT'S GOING ON?
TMP TMP TMP TMP
THEY'VE SET UP A RE-STRICTED AREA!
GOOD MORNING!
Chemistry Group Only

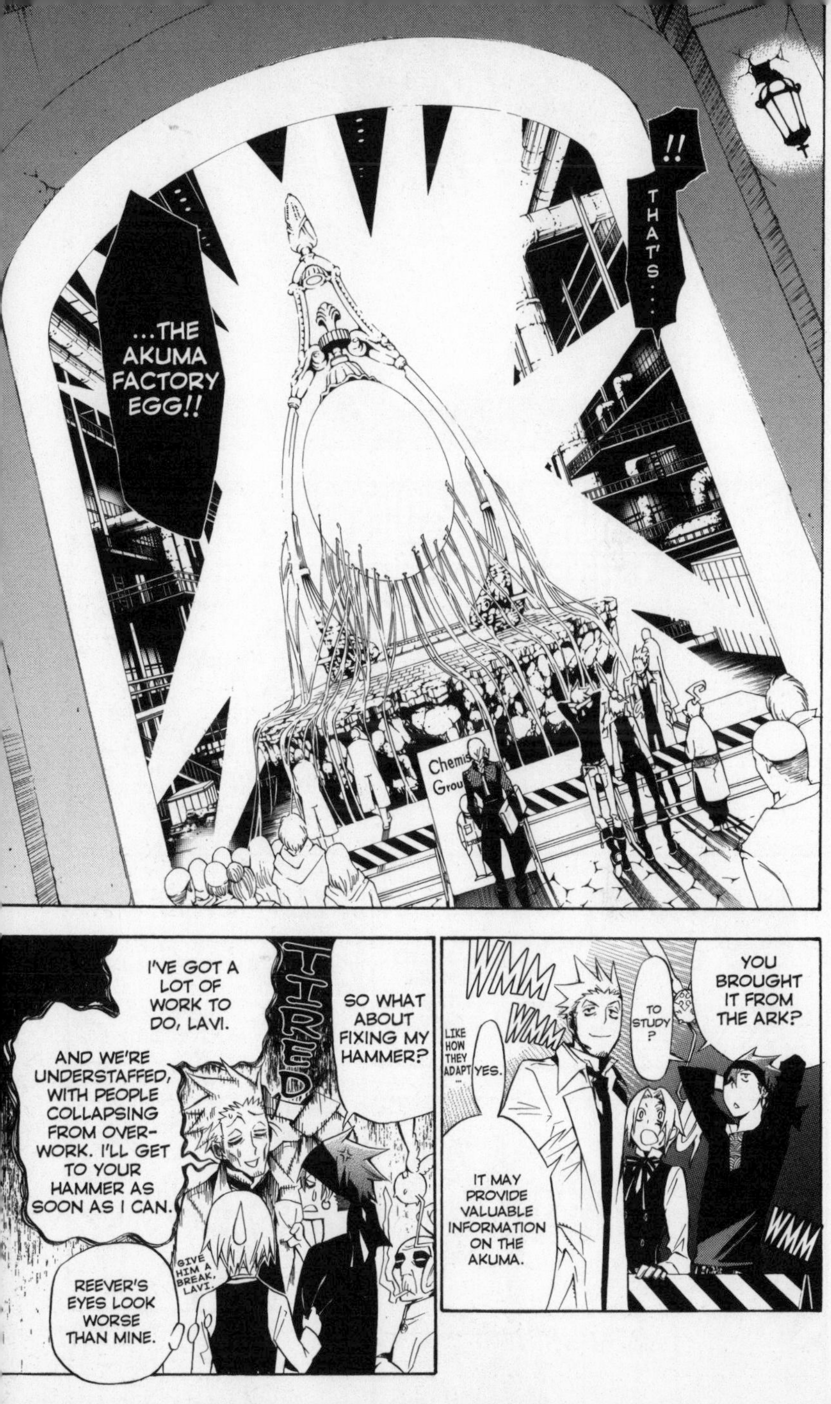
!!
THAT'S...
...THE AKUMA FACTORY EGG!!
Chemis
Grou
WMM
WMM
YOU BROUGHT IT FROM THE ARK?
TO STUDY?
YES.
LIKE HOW THEY ADAPT...
IT MAY PROVIDE VALUABLE INFORMATION ON THE AKUMA.
WMM
SO WHAT ABOUT FIXING MY HAMMER?
TIRED
I'VE GOT A LOT OF WORK TO DO, LAVI.
AND WE'RE UNDERSTAFFED, WITH PEOPLE COLLAPSING FROM OVER-WORK. I'LL GET TO YOUR HAMMER AS SOON AS I CAN.
GIVE HIM A BREAK, LAVI.
REEVER'S EYES LOOK WORSE THAN MINE.

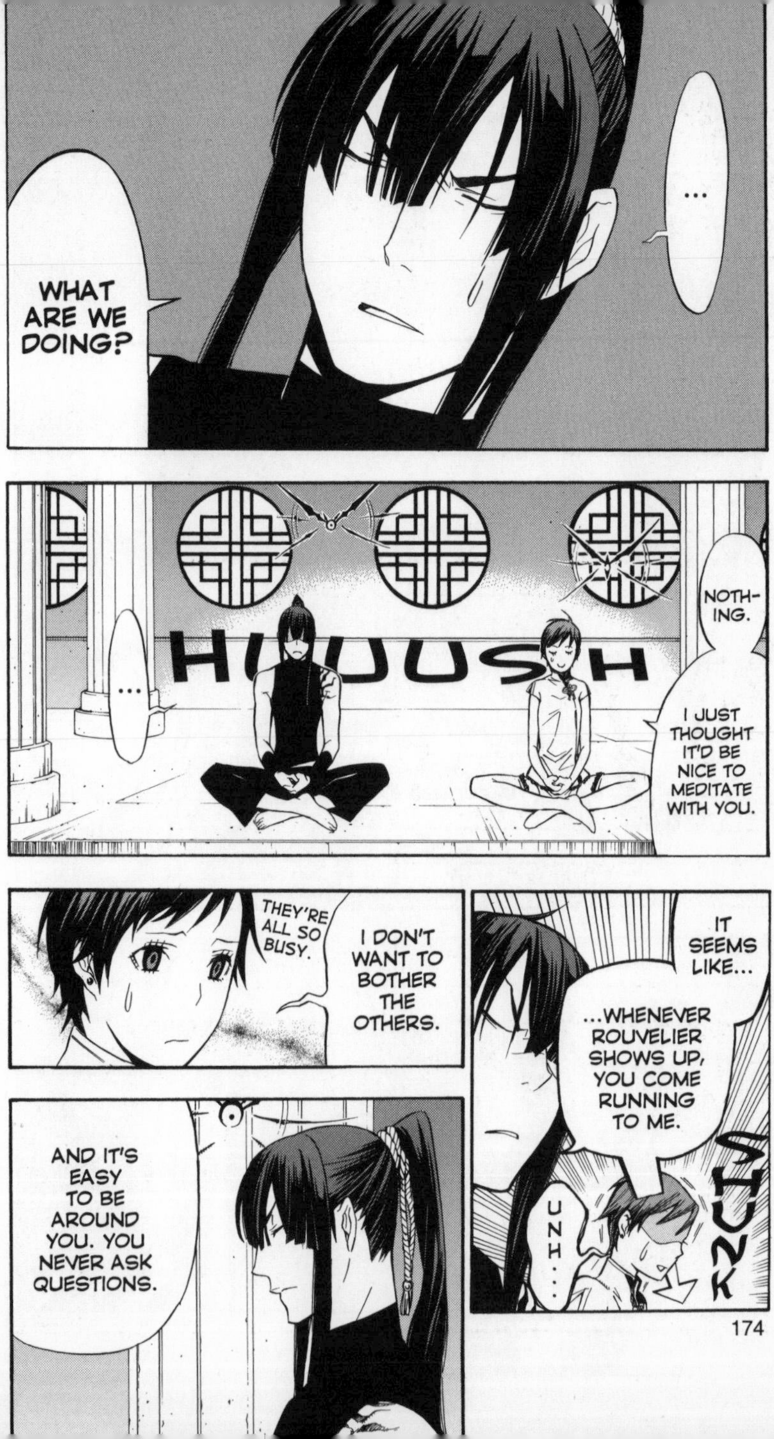
...
WHAT ARE WE DOING?
NOTH-ING.
I JUST THOUGHT IT'D BE NICE TO MEDITATE WITH YOU.
...
IT SEEMS LIKE...
...WHENEVER ROUVELIER SHOWS UP, YOU COME RUNNING TO ME.
UNH...
SHUNK
THEY'RE ALL SO BUSY.
I DON'T WANT TO BOTHER THE OTHERS.
AND IT'S EASY TO BE AROUND YOU. YOU NEVER ASK QUESTIONS.

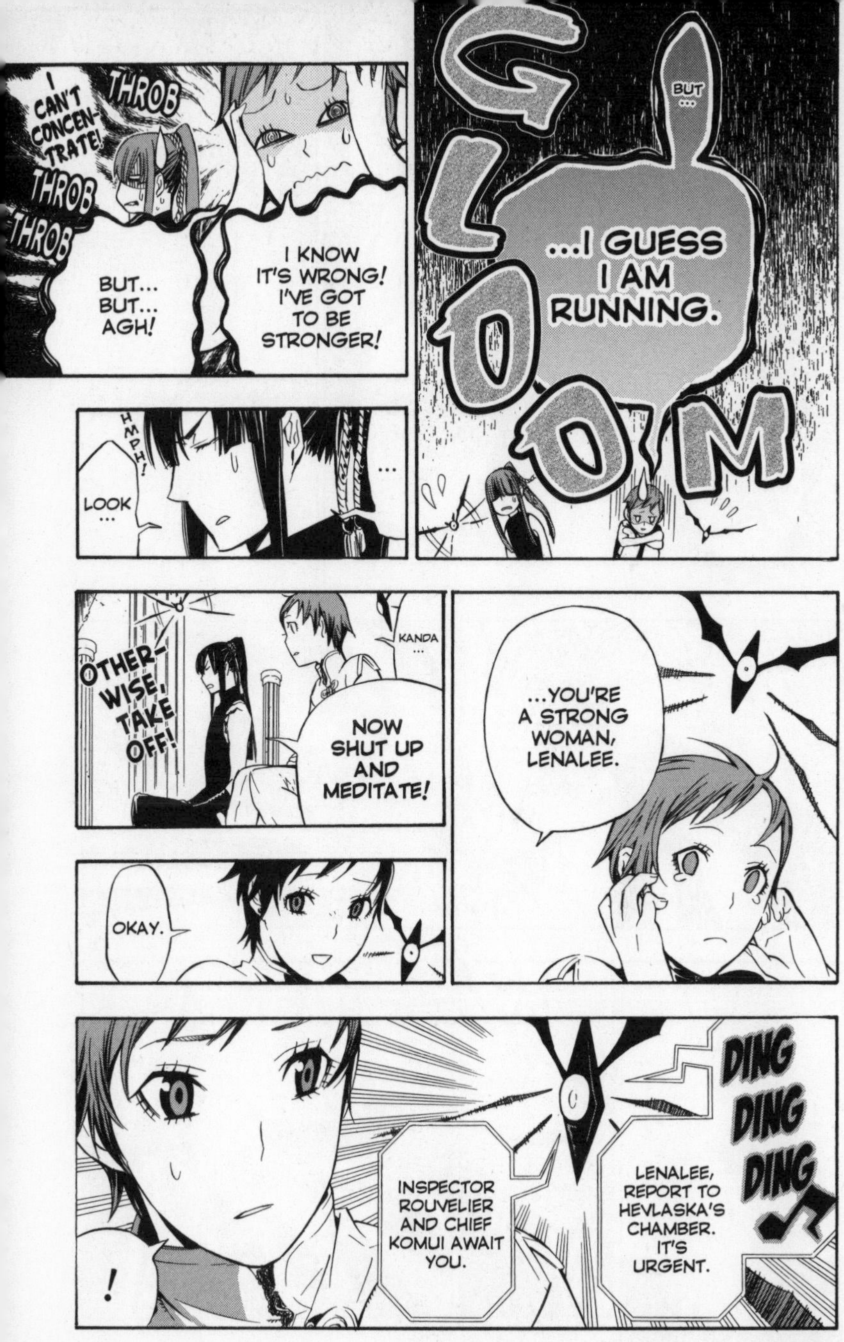
GLOOM
BUT...
...I GUESS I AM RUNNING.
THROB
I CAN'T CONCENTRATE!
I KNOW IT'S WRONG! I'VE GOT TO BE STRONGER!
THROB THROB
BUT... BUT... AGH!
...
HMPH!
LOOK...
...YOU'RE A STRONG WOMAN, LENALEE.
KANDA...
NOW SHUT UP AND MEDITATE!
OTHERWISE, TAKE OFF!
OKAY.
DING DING DING
LENALEE, REPORT TO HEVLASKA'S CHAMBER. IT'S URGENT.
INSPECTOR ROUVELIER AND CHIEF KOMUI AWAIT YOU.
!

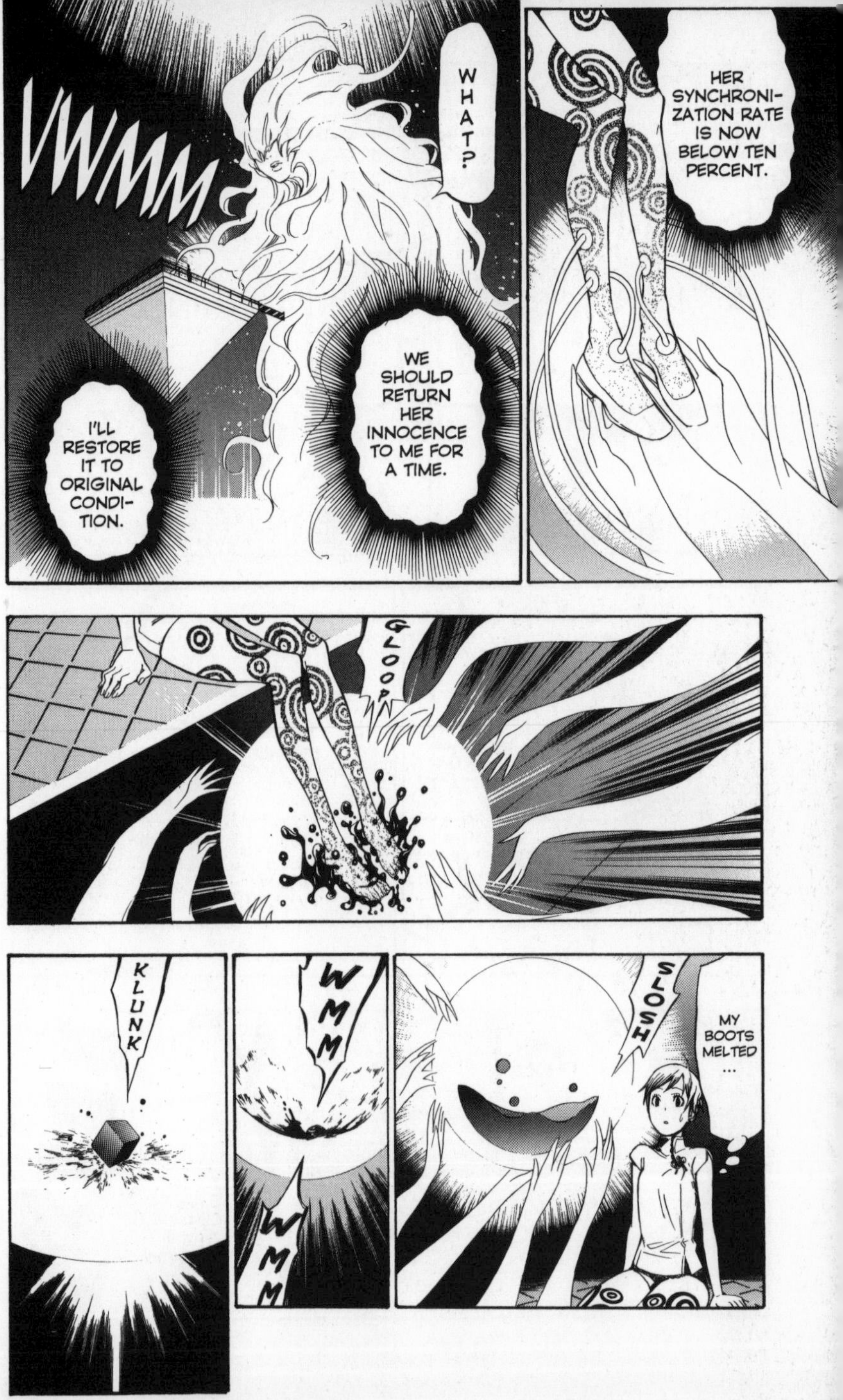
HER SYNCHRONI-ZATION RATE IS NOW BELOW TEN PERCENT.
WHAT?
VWMM
WE SHOULD RETURN HER INNOCENCE TO ME FOR A TIME.
I'LL RESTORE IT TO ORIGINAL CONDI-TION.
GLOOP
SLOSH
MY BOOTS MELTED...
WMM
WMM
KLUNK

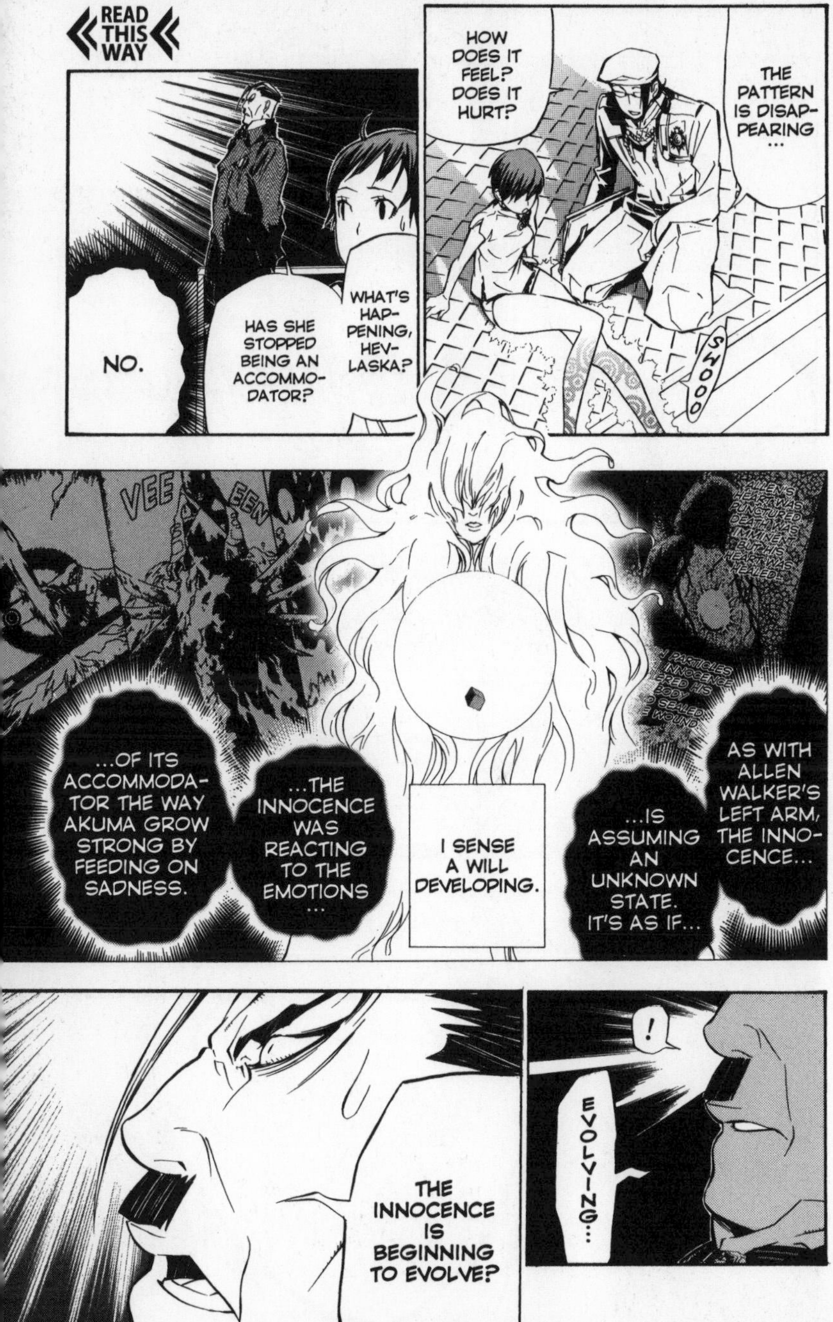
READ THIS WAY
THE PATTERN IS DISAP-PEARING...
HOW DOES IT FEEL? DOES IT HURT?
SWOOO
WHAT'S HAP-PENING, HEV-LASKA?
HAS SHE STOPPED BEING AN ACCOMMODATOR?
NO.
ALLEN'S HEART WAS PUNCTURED. DEATH WAS IMMINENT, BUT HIS HEART WAS HEALED...
EEN
VEE
AS WITH ALLEN WALKER'S LEFT ARM, THE INNOCENCE...
...IS ASSUMING AN UNKNOWN STATE. IT'S AS IF...
I SENSE A WILL DEVELOPING.
...THE INNOCENCE WAS REACTING TO THE EMOTIONS...
...OF ITS ACCOMMODATOR THE WAY AKUMA GROW STRONG BY FEEDING ON SADNESS.
!
EVOLVING...
THE INNOCENCE IS BEGINNING TO EVOLVE?

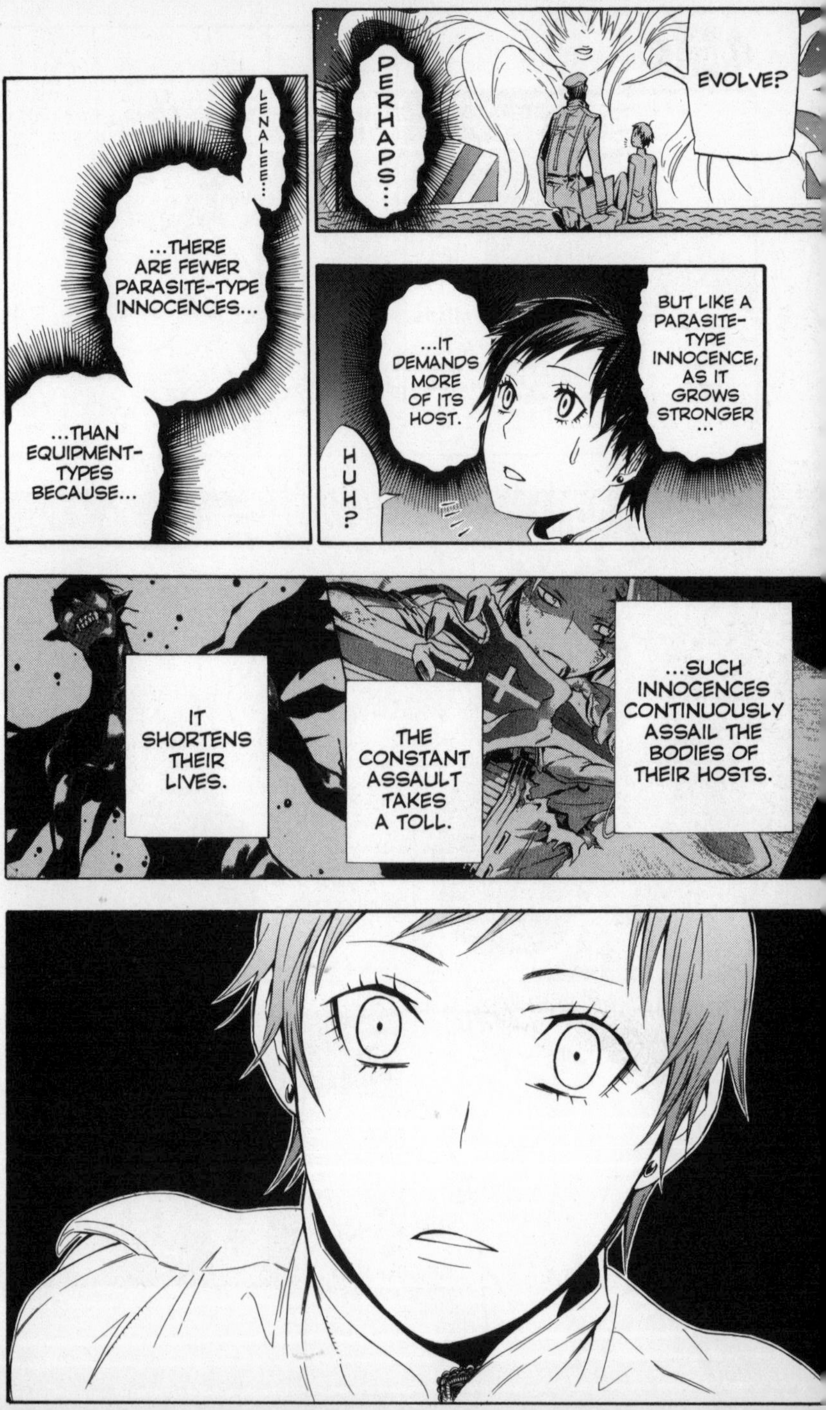
EVOLVE?
PERHAPS...
BUT LIKE A PARASITE-TYPE INNOCENCE, AS IT GROWS STRONGER ...
...IT DEMANDS MORE OF ITS HOST.
HUH?
LENALEE...
...THERE ARE FEWER PARASITE-TYPE INNOCENCES...
...THAN EQUIPMENT-TYPES BECAUSE...
...SUCH INNOCENCES CONTINUOUSLY ASSAIL THE BODIES OF THEIR HOSTS.
THE CONSTANT ASSAULT TAKES A TOLL.
IT SHORTENS THEIR LIVES.

READ THIS WAY

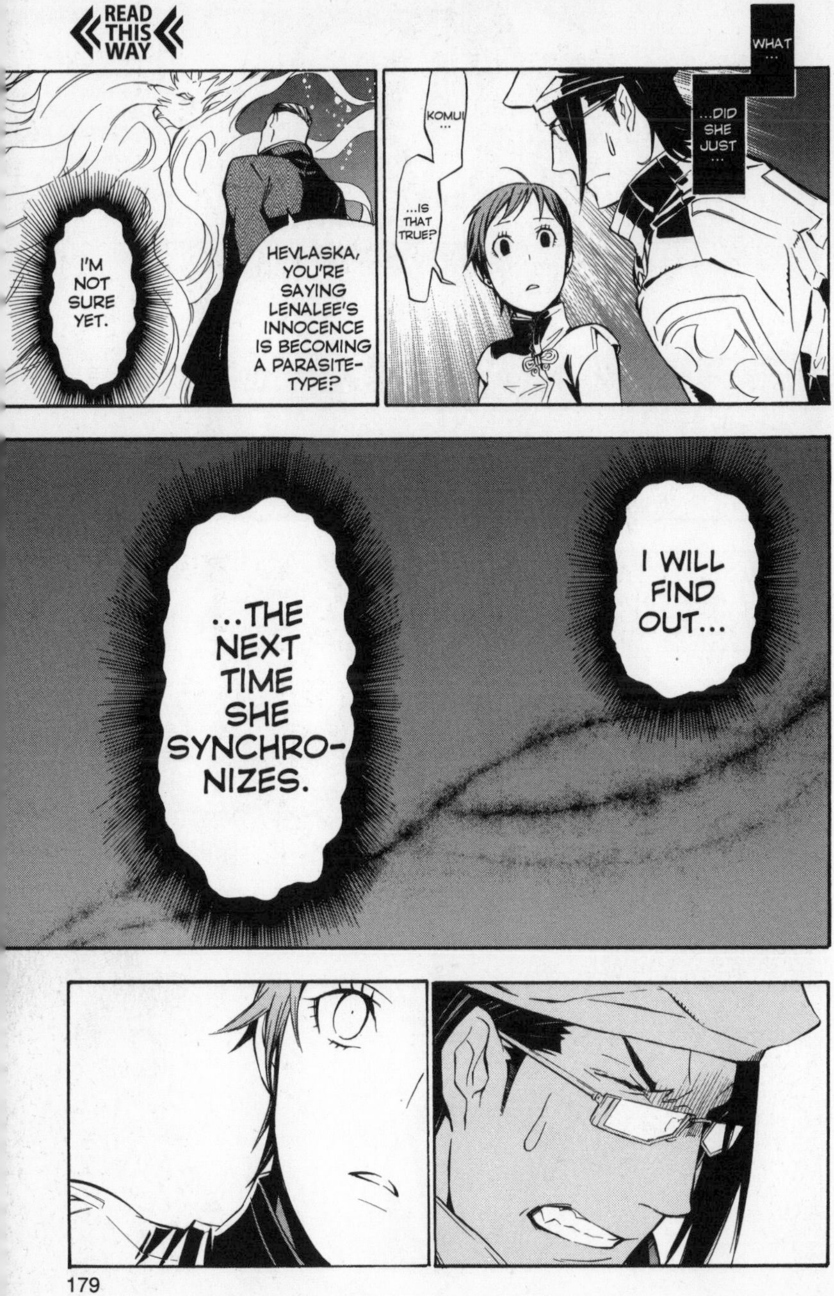
WHAT ...
...DID SHE JUST ...
KOMUI ...
...IS THAT TRUE?
HEVLASKA, YOU'RE SAYING LENALEE'S INNOCENCE IS BECOMING A PARASITE-TYPE?
I'M NOT SURE YET.
I WILL FIND OUT...
...THE NEXT TIME SHE SYNCHRO-NIZES.

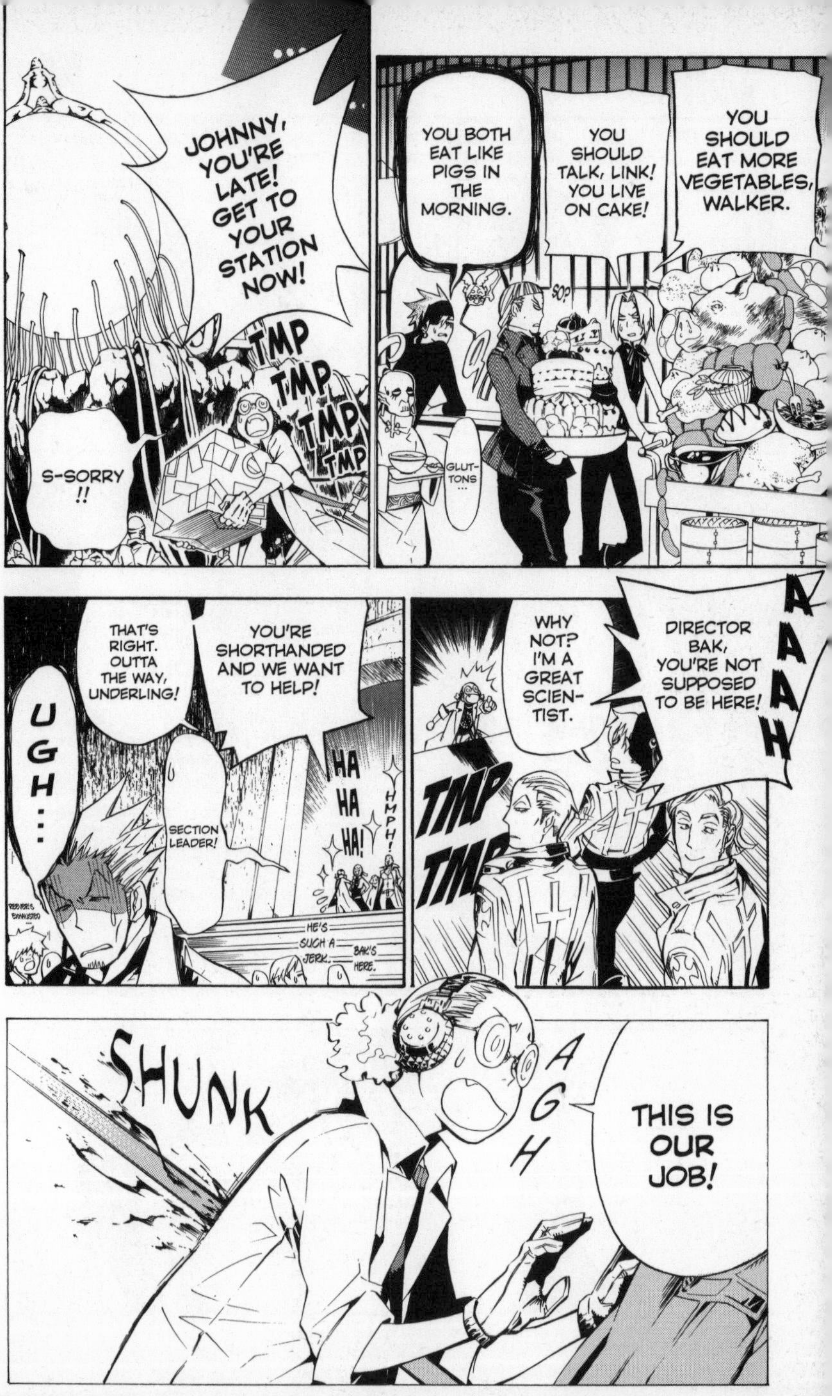
YOU SHOULD EAT MORE VEGETABLES, WALKER.
YOU SHOULD TALK, LINK! YOU LIVE ON CAKE!
YOU BOTH EAT LIKE PIGS IN THE MORNING.
SOP
GLUT-TONS...
JOHNNY, YOU'RE LATE! GET TO YOUR STATION NOW!
TMP TMP TMP TMP
S-SORRY!!
AAAH
DIRECTOR BAK, YOU'RE NOT SUPPOSED TO BE HERE!
WHY NOT? I'M A GREAT SCIEN-TIST.
TMP TMP
YOU'RE SHORTHANDED AND WE WANT TO HELP!
THAT'S RIGHT. OUTTA THE WAY, UNDERLING!
HA HA HA!
HMPH!
SECTION LEADER!
UGH...
BAK'S HERE.
HE'S SUCH A JERK.
REEVER'S EXHAUSTED...
THIS IS OUR JOB!
AGH
SHUNK

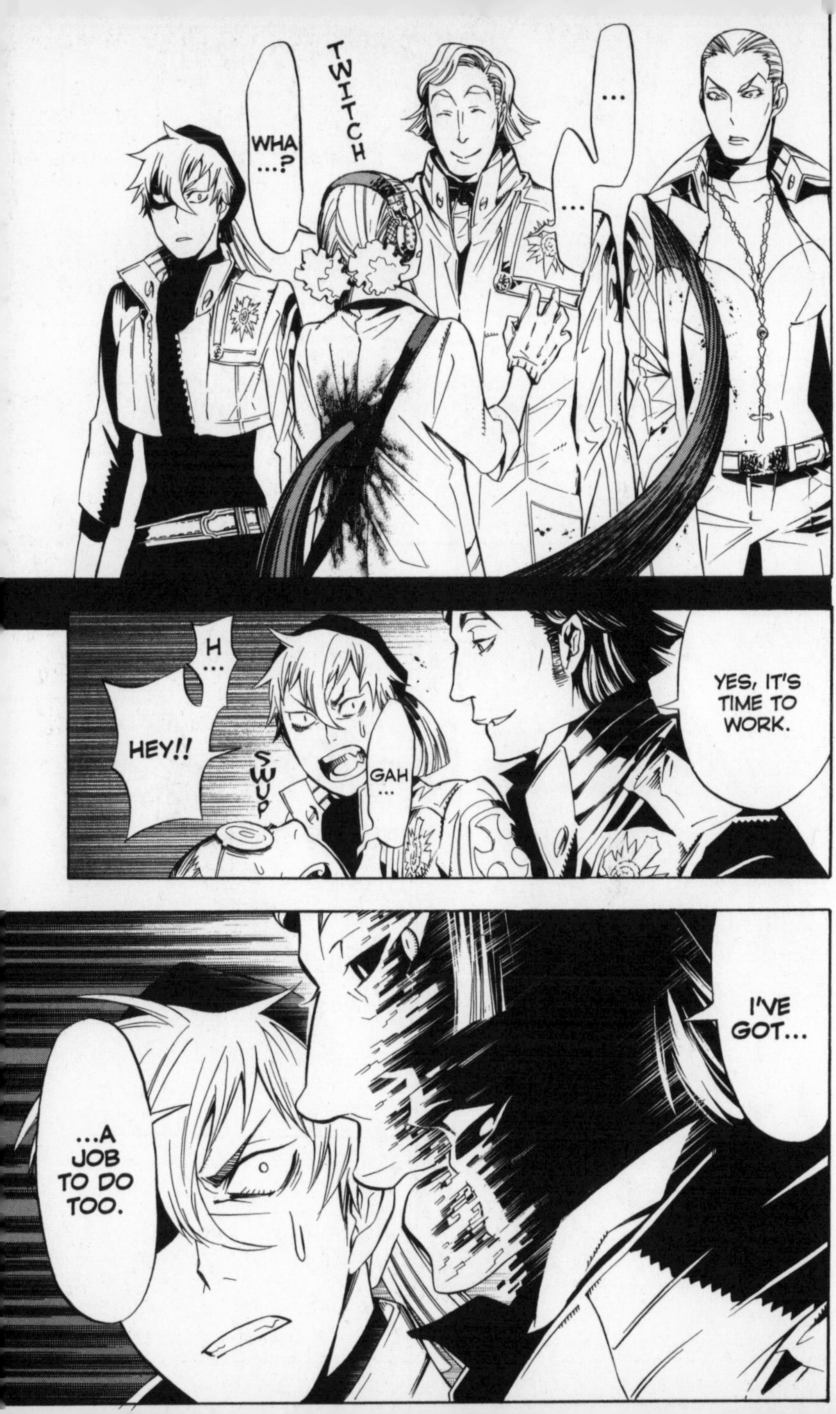
...
...
TWITCH
WHA ...?
YES, IT'S TIME TO WORK.
GAH ...
SWUP
H ...
HEY!!
I'VE GOT...
...A JOB TO DO TOO.

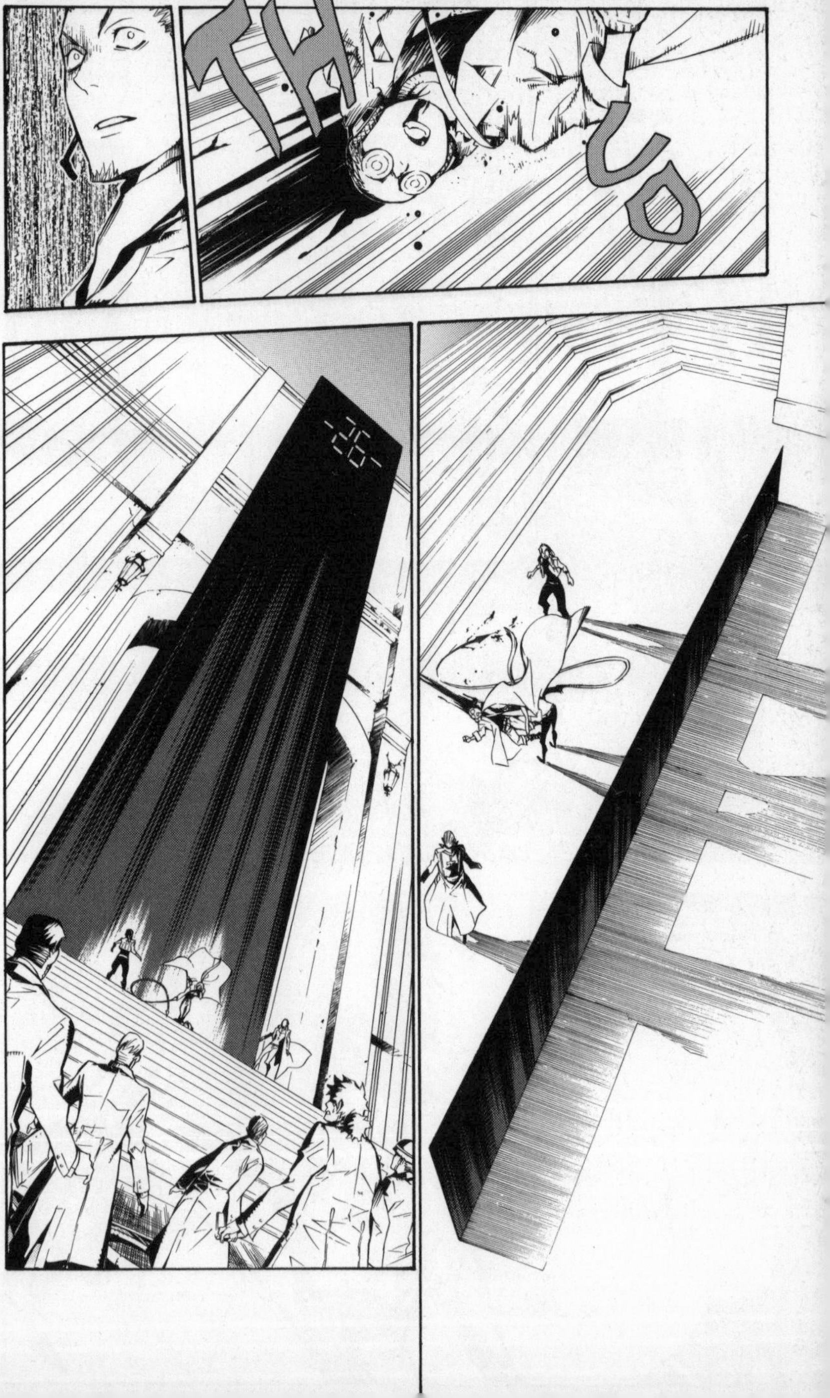
THUD
-26-

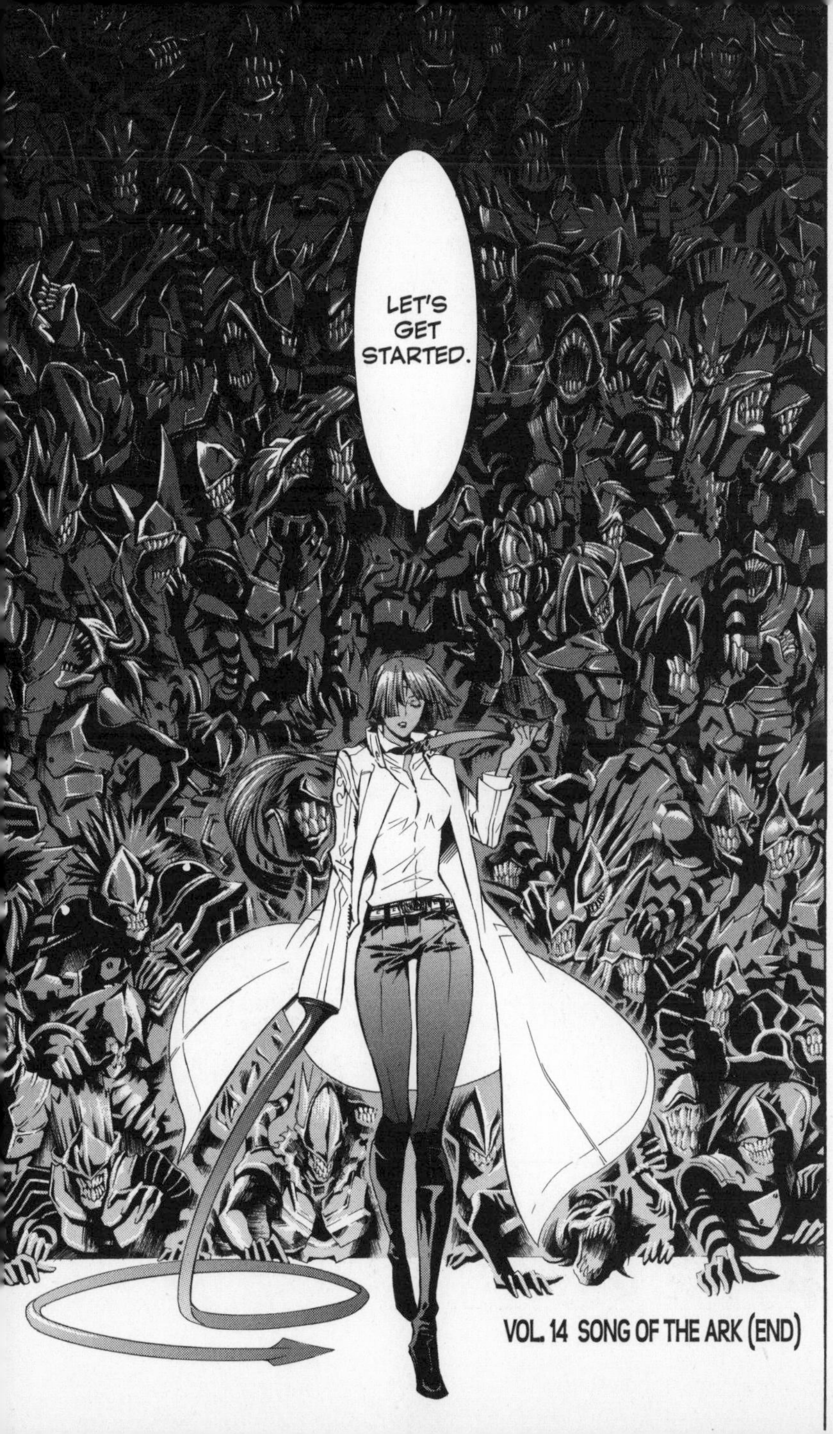
LET'S GET STARTED.

VOL. 14 SONG OF THE ARK (END)

ディー・グレイマン
D.Gray-man

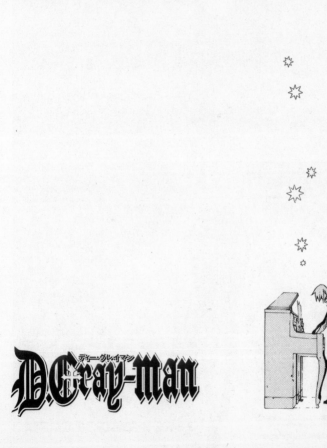

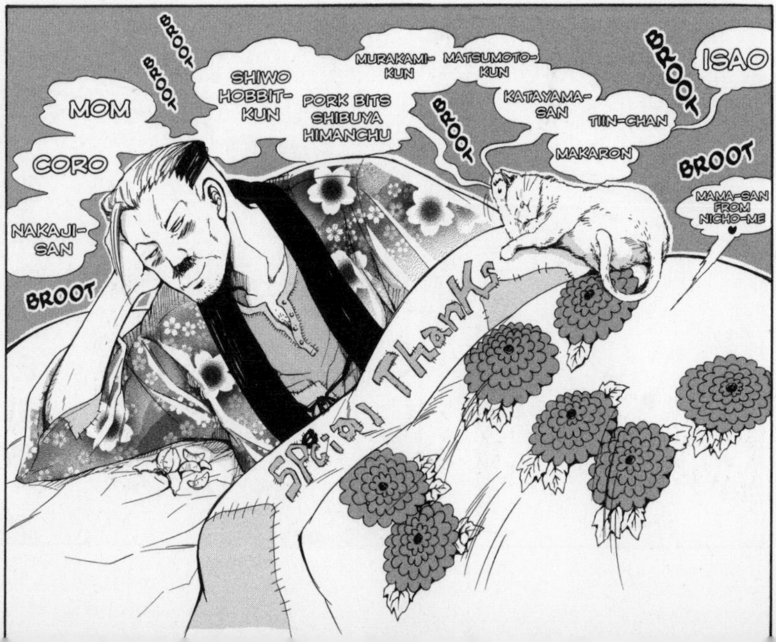
ISAO
BROOT
MATSUMOTO-KUN
MURAKAMI-KUN
KATAYAMA-SAN
TIIN-CHAN
BROOT
MAKARON
BROOT
MAMA-SAN FROM NICHO-ME ♥
PORK BITS SHIBUYA HIMANCHU
SHIWO HOBBIT-KUN
BROOT
BROOT
MOM
CORO
NAKAJI-SAN
BROOT
Special Thanks

# D.GRAY THEATER

BY MAMA-SAN FROM NICHO-ME

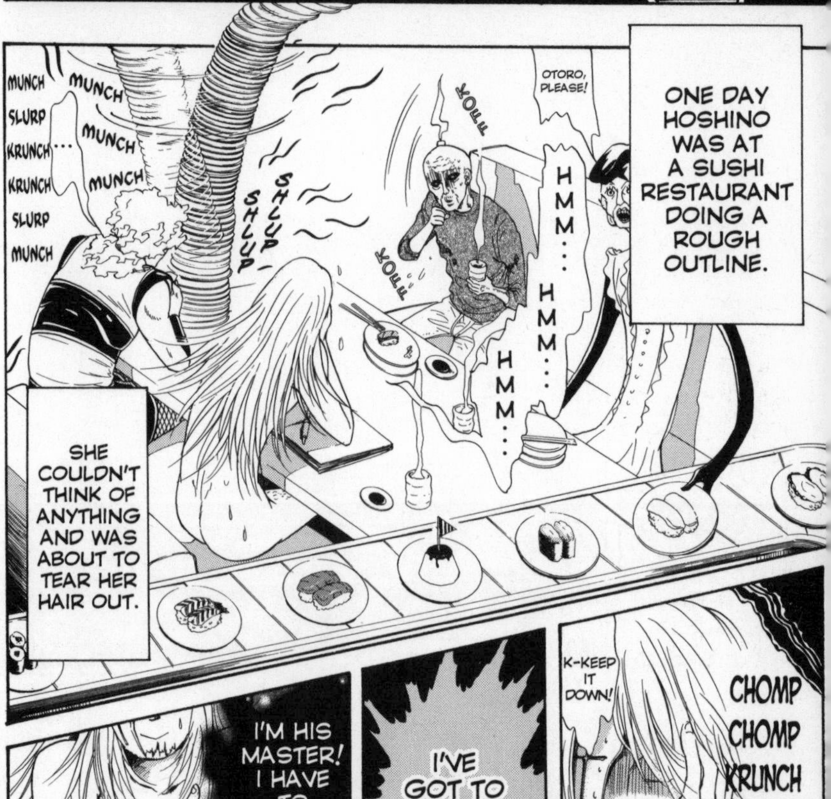
ONE DAY HOSHINO WAS AT A SUSHI RESTAURANT DOING A ROUGH OUTLINE.
OTORO, PLEASE!
KOFF
KOFF
HMM... HMM... HMM...
SHLUP SHLUP
MUNCH
MUNCH
...
MUNCH
SLURP
KRUNCH
KRUNCH
SLURP
MUNCH
SHE COULDN'T THINK OF ANYTHING AND WAS ABOUT TO TEAR HER HAIR OUT.
K-KEEP IT DOWN!
CHOMP CHOMP KRUNCH KRUNCH GULP GULP MUNCH
I'VE GOT TO CONCEN-TRATE!!
NOT DONE YET?
I'M HIS MASTER! I HAVE TO WARN HIM!
AHH

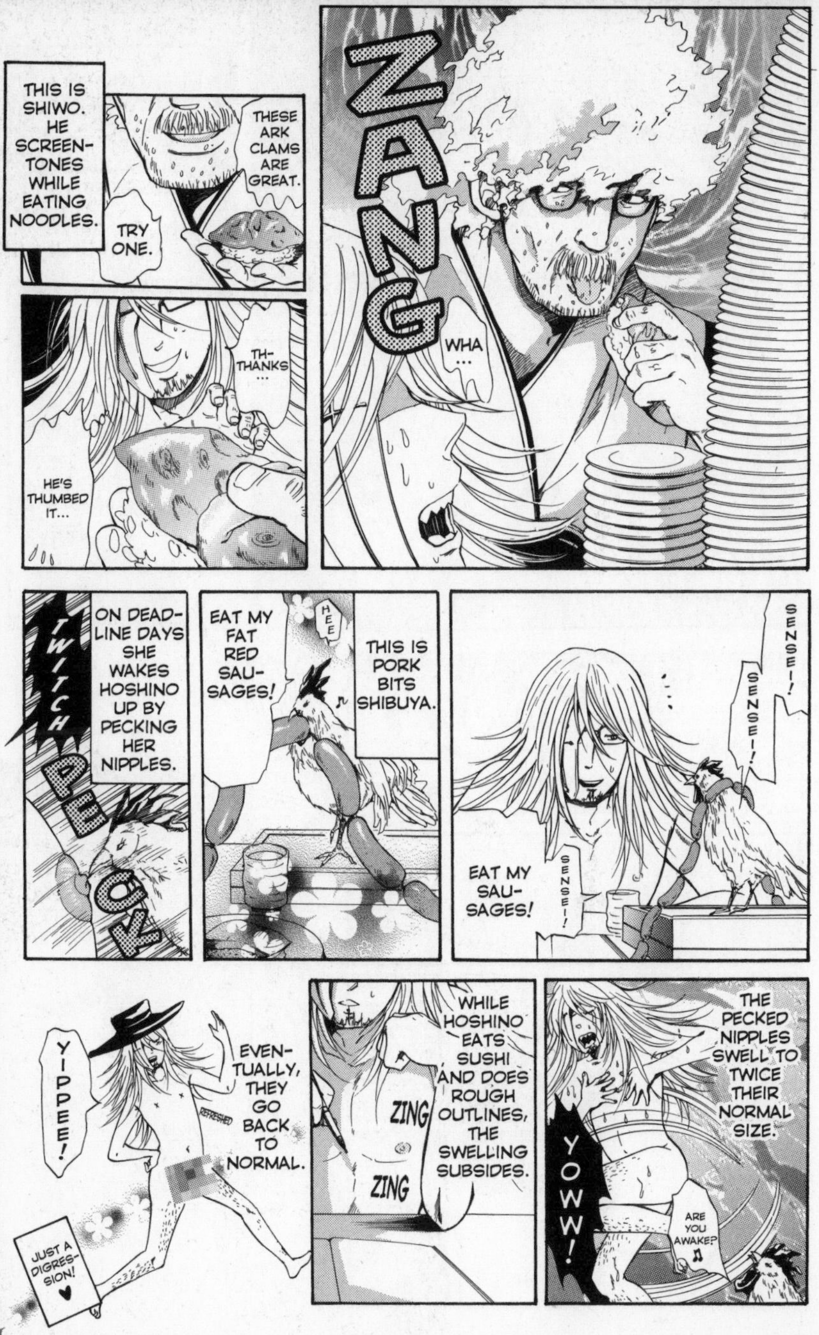
ZANG
WHA...
THESE ARK CLAMS ARE GREAT.
THIS IS SHIWO. HE SCREEN-TONES WHILE EATING NOODLES.
TRY ONE.
TH-THANKS...
HE'S THUMBED IT...
SENSEI!
SENSEI!
...
EAT MY SAUSAGES!
SENSEI!
THIS IS PORK BITS SHIBUYA.
HEE
EAT MY FAT RED SAU-SAGES!
ON DEAD-LINE DAYS SHE WAKES HOSHINO UP BY PECKING HER NIPPLES.
TWITCH
PECK
THE PECKED NIPPLES SWELL TO TWICE THEIR NORMAL SIZE.
YOWW!
ARE YOU AWAKE? ♫
WHILE HOSHINO EATS SUSHI AND DOES ROUGH OUTLINES, THE SWELLING SUBSIDES.
ZING
ZING
EVEN-TUALLY, THEY GO BACK TO NORMAL.
YIPPEE!
REFRESHED
JUST A DIGRES-SION! ♥

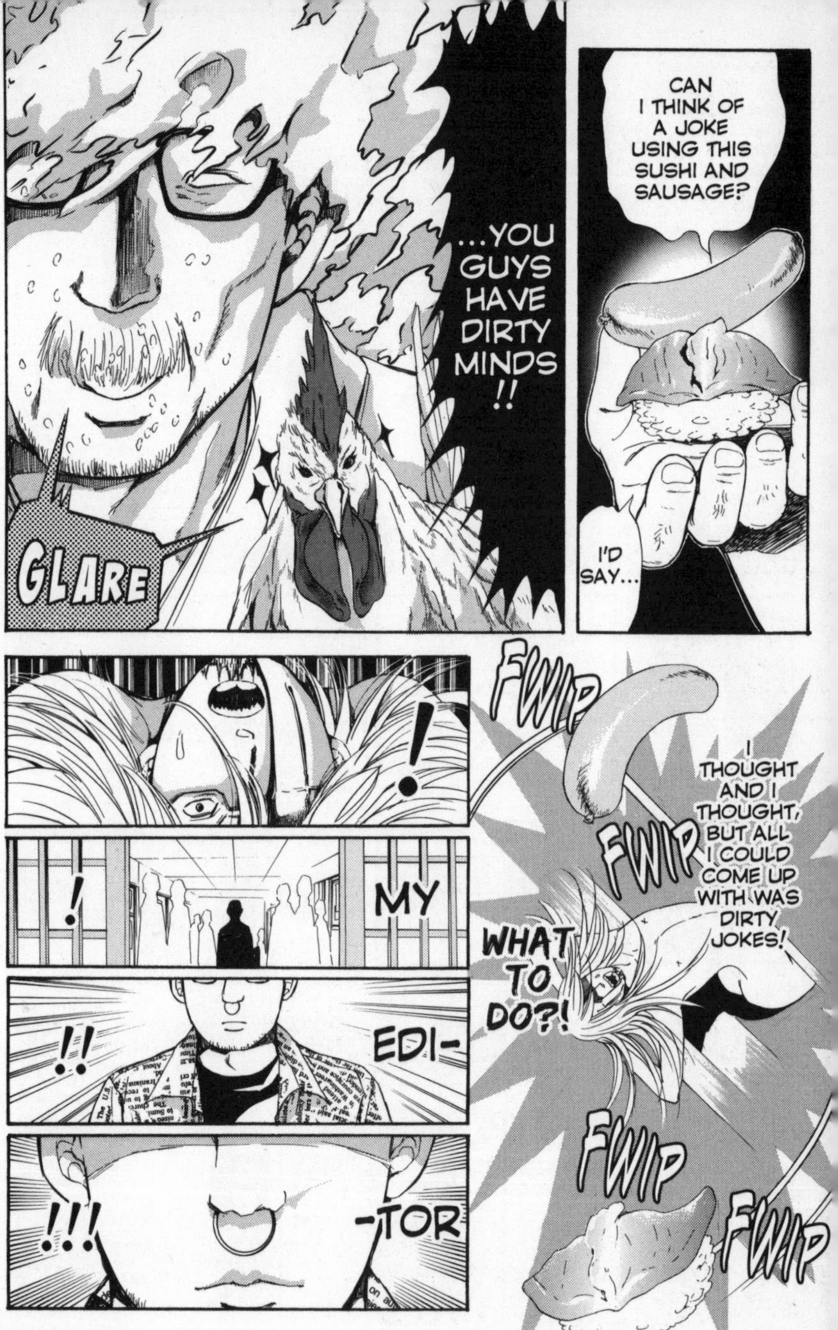
CAN I THINK OF A JOKE USING THIS SUSHI AND SAUSAGE?
I'D SAY...
...YOU GUYS HAVE DIRTY MINDS!!
GLARE
FWIP
FWIP
I THOUGHT AND I THOUGHT, BUT ALL I COULD COME UP WITH WAS DIRTY JOKES!
WHAT TO DO?!
FWIP
FWIP
!
!
MY
!!
EDI-
!!!
-TOR

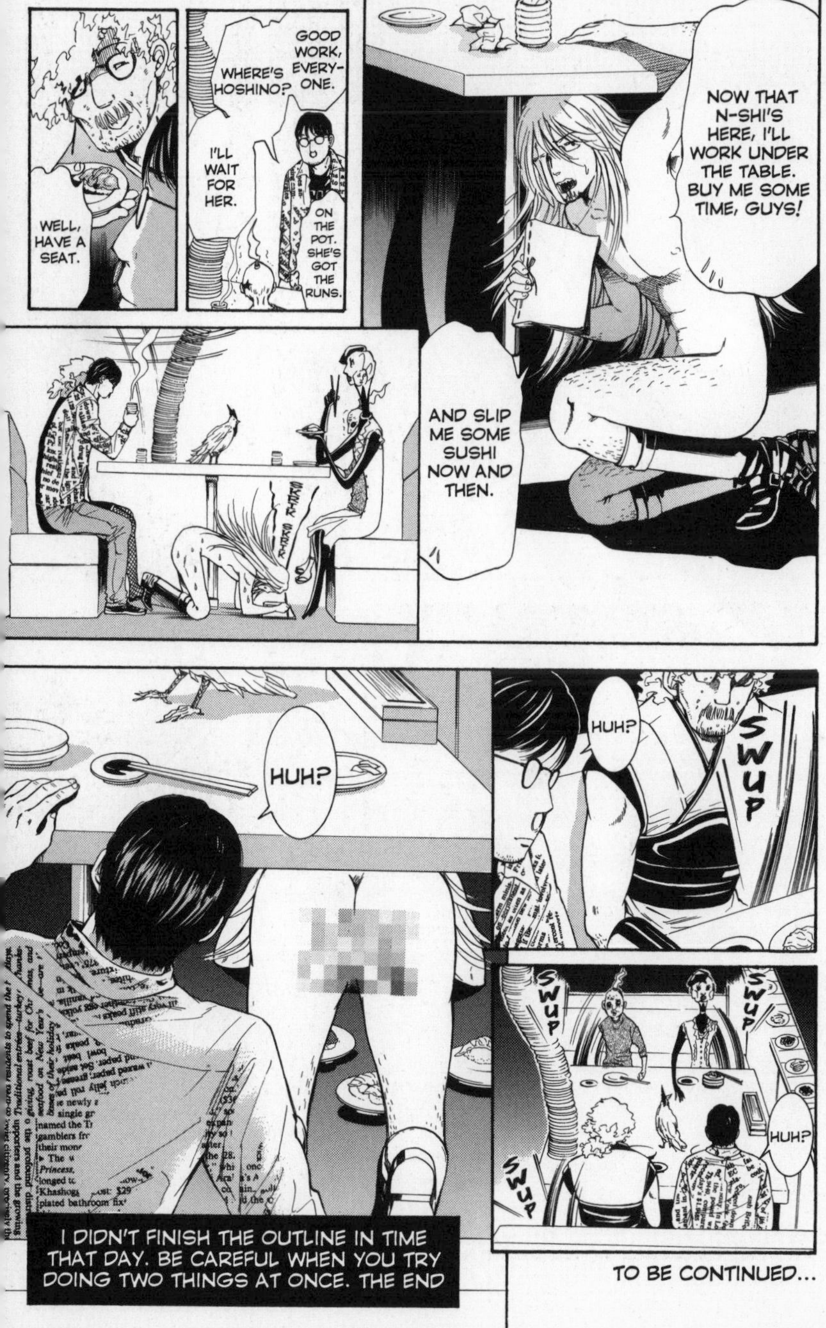
NOW THAT N-SHI'S HERE, I'LL WORK UNDER THE TABLE. BUY ME SOME TIME, GUYS!
AND SLIP ME SOME SUSHI NOW AND THEN.
GOOD WORK, EVERYONE.
WHERE'S HOSHINO?
I'LL WAIT FOR HER.
ON THE POT. SHE'S GOT THE RUNS.
WELL, HAVE A SEAT.
SKRTK SKRTK
HUH?
SWUP
SWUP
SWUP
SWUP
HUH?
HUH?
I DIDN'T FINISH THE OUTLINE IN TIME THAT DAY. BE CAREFUL WHEN YOU TRY DOING TWO THINGS AT ONCE. THE END
TO BE CONTINUED...

# N THE NEXT VOLUME...

A mysterious woman leads an invasion of Akuma into Black Order HQ. She's come to acquire the Egg for the Earl after the Earl was unable to transfer it from the disintegrating Ark. Komui desperately tries to protect his incapacitated exorcists, but the situation only goes from bad to worse with the arrival of a squad of Skulls out to find brains worthy of adding to their ranks!

Available Now!

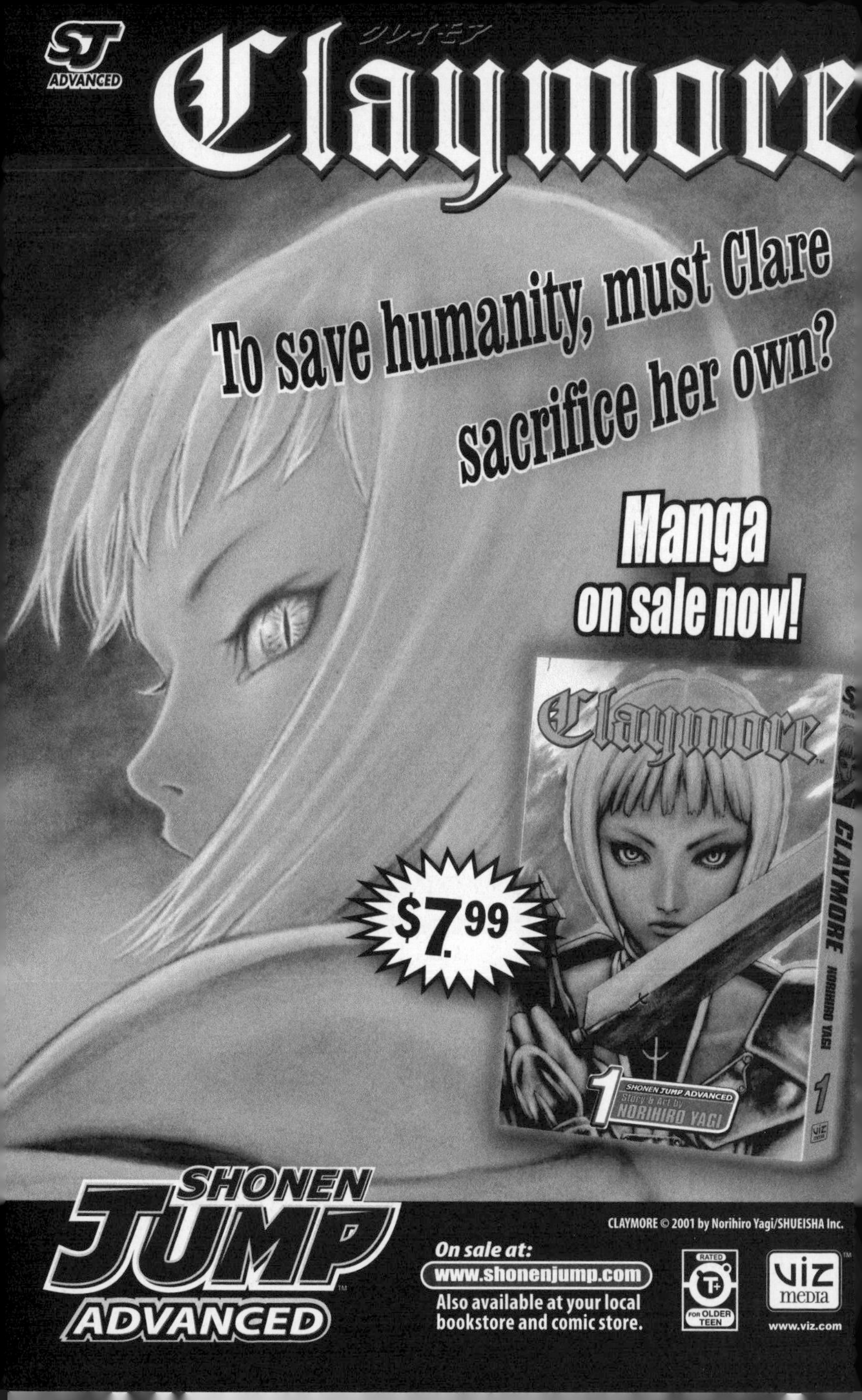
SJ ADVANCED
クレイモア
Claymore
To save humanity, must Clare sacrifice her own?
Manga on sale now!
$7.99
Claymore
CLAYMORE
NORIHIRO YAGI
1
SHONEN JUMP ADVANCED
Story & Art by
NORIHIRO YAGI
SHONEN JUMP ADVANCED
CLAYMORE © 2001 by Norihiro Yagi/SHUEISHA Inc.
On sale at:
www.shonenjump.com
Also available at your local bookstore and comic store.
RATED T+ FOR OLDER TEEN
VIZ media
www.viz.com

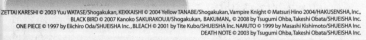